SECOND EDITION

Programming Pig

Alan Gates and Daniel Dai

Beijing · Boston · Farnham · Sebastopol · Tokyo

Programming Pig, Second Edition

by Alan Gates and Daniel Dai

Copyright © 2017 Alan Gates, Daniel Dai. All rights reserved.

Printed in the United States of America.

Published by O'Reilly Media, Inc., 1005 Gravenstein Highway North, Sebastopol, CA 95472.

O'Reilly books may be purchased for educational, business, or sales promotional use. Online editions are also available for most titles (*http://oreilly.com/safari*). For more information, contact our corporate/institutional sales department: 800-998-9938 or *corporate@oreilly.com*.

Editor: Marie Beaugureau

Production Editor: Nicholas Adams

Copyeditor: Rachel Head

Proofreader: Kim Cofer

Indexer: Lucie Haskins

Interior Designer: David Futato

Cover Designer: Randy Comer

Illustrator: Rebecca Demarest

November 2016:   Second Edition

Revision History for the Second Edition

2016-11-08:   First Release

See *http://oreilly.com/catalog/errata.csp?isbn=9781491937099* for release details.

978-1-491-93709-9

[LSI]

To my wife, Barbara, and our boys, Adam and Joel. Their support, encouragement, and sacrificed Saturdays have made this book possible.

—Alan

To my wife Jenny, my older son Ethan, and my younger son Charlie who was delivered during the writing of the book.

—Daniel

Table of Contents

Preface

Data is addictive. Our ability to collect and store it has grown massively in the last several decades, yet our appetite for ever more data shows no sign of being satiated. Scientists want to be able to store more data in order to build better mathematical models of the world. Marketers want better data to understand their customers' desires and buying habits. Financial analysts want to better understand the workings of their markets. And everybody wants to keep all their digital photographs, movies, emails, etc.

Before the computer and Internet revolutions, the US Library of Congress was one of the largest collections of data in the world. It is estimated that its printed collections contain approximately 10 terabytes (TB) of information (*http://bit.ly/2fvQ0yg*). Today, large Internet companies collect that much data on a daily basis. And it is not just Internet applications that are producing data at prodigious rates. For example, the Large Synoptic Survey Telescope (LSST) under construction in Chile is expected to produce 15 TB of data every day (*http://www.lsst.org*).

Part of the reason for the massive growth in available data is our ability to *collect* much more data. Every time someone clicks a website's links, the web server can record information about what page the user was on and which link he clicked. Every time a car drives over a sensor in the highway, its speed can be recorded. But much of the reason is also our ability to *store* that data. Ten years ago, telescopes took pictures of the sky every night. But they could not store the collected data at the same level of detail that will be possible when the LSST is operational. The extra data was being thrown away because there was nowhere to put it. The ability to collect and store vast quantities of data only feeds our data addiction.

One of the most commonly used tools for storing and processing data in computer systems over the last few decades has been the relational database management system (RDBMS). But as datasets have grown large, only the more sophisticated (and hence more expensive) RDBMSs have been able to reach the scale many users now desire. At the same time, many engineers and scientists involved in processing the data have realized that they do not need everything offered by an RDBMS. These systems are powerful and have many features, but many data owners who need to process terabytes or petabytes of data need only a subset of those features.

The high cost and unneeded features of RDBMSs have led to the development of many alternative data-processing systems. One such alternative system is Apache Hadoop (*http://hadoop.apache.org*). Hadoop is an open source project started by Doug Cutting. Over the past several years, Yahoo! and a number of other web companies have driven the development of Hadoop, which was based on papers published by Google describing how its engineers were dealing with the challenge of storing (*http://research.google.com/archive/gfs-sosp2003.pdf*) and processing (*http://research.google.com/archive/mapreduce-osdi04.pdf*) the massive amounts of data they were collecting. Hadoop is installed on a cluster of machines and provides a means to tie together storage and processing in that cluster. For a history of the project, see *Hadoop: The Definitive Guide*, by Tom White (O'Reilly).

The development of new data-processing systems such as Hadoop has spurred the porting of existing tools and languages and the construction of new tools, such as Apache Pig (*https://pig.apache.org/*). Tools like Pig provide a higher level of abstraction for data users, giving them access to the power and flexibility of Hadoop without requiring them to write extensive data-processing applications in low-level Java code.

Who Should Read This Book

This book is intended for Pig programmers, new and old. Those who have never used Pig will find introductory material on how to run Pig and to get them started writing Pig Latin scripts. For seasoned Pig users, this book covers almost every feature of Pig: different modes it can be run in, complete coverage of the Pig Latin language, and how to extend Pig with your own user-defined functions (UDFs). Even those who have been using Pig for a long time are likely to discover features they have not used before.

Some knowledge of Hadoop will be useful for readers and Pig users. If you're not already familiar with it or want a quick refresher, "Pig on Hadoop" on page 3 walks through a very simple example of a Hadoop job.

Small snippets of Java, Python, and SQL are used in parts of this book. Knowledge of these languages is not required to use Pig, but knowledge of Python and Java will be necessary for some of the more advanced features. Those with a SQL background may find "Comparing Query and Data Flow Languages" on page 2 to be a helpful starting point in understanding the similarities and differences between Pig Latin and SQL.

What's New in This Edition

The second edition covers Pig 0.10 through Pig 0.16, which is the latest version at the time of writing. For features introduced before 0.10, we will not call out the initial version of the feature. For newer features introduced after 0.10, we will point out the version in which the feature was introduced.

Pig runs on both Hadoop 1 and Hadoop 2 for all the versions covered in the book. To simplify our discussion, we assume Hadoop 2 is the target platform and will point out the difference for Hadoop 1 whenever applicable in this edition.

The second edition has two new chapters: "Pig on Tez" (Chapter 11) and "Use Cases and Programming Examples" (Chapter 13). Other chapters have also been updated with the latest additions to Pig and information on existing features not covered in the first edition. These include but are not limited to:

- New data types (boolean, datetime, biginteger, bigdecimal) are introduced in Chapter 3.
- New UDFs are covered in various places, including support for leveraging Hive UDFs (Chapter 4) and applying Bloom filters (Chapter 7).
- New Pig operators and constructs such as `rank`, `cube`, `assert`, nested `foreach` and nested `cross`, and casting relations to scalars are presented in Chapter 5.
- New performance optimizations—map-side aggregation, schema tuples, the shared JAR cache, auto local and direct fetch modes, etc.—are covered in Chapter 7.
- Scripting UDFs in JavaScript, JRuby, Groovy, and streaming Python are discussed in Chapter 9, and embedding Pig in scripting languages is covered in Chapter 8 and Chapter 13 ("k-Means" on page 280). We also describe the Pig progress notification listener in Chapter 8.
- We look at the new `EvalFunc` interface in Chapter 9, including the topics of compile-time evaluation, shipping dependent JARs automatically, and variable-length inputs. The new `LoadFunc`/`StoreFunc` interface is described in Chapter 10: we discuss topics such as predicate pushdown, auto-shipping JARs, and handling bad records.
- New developments in community projects such as WebHCat, Spark, Accumulo, DataFu, and Oozie are described in Chapter 12.

Conventions Used in This Book

The following typographical conventions are used in this book:

Italic
> Indicates new terms, URLs, email addresses, filenames, and file extensions.

`Constant width`
> Used for program listings, as well as within paragraphs to refer to program elements such as variable or function names, databases, data types, environment variables, statements, and keywords.

`Constant width bold`
> Shows commands or other text that should be typed literally by the user.

`Constant width italic`
> Shows text that should be replaced with user-supplied values or by values determined by context. Also used to show the output of `describe` statements in scripts.

> This icon signifies a tip, suggestion, or general note.

> This icon indicates a warning or caution.

Code Examples in This Book

Many of the example scripts, UDFs, and datasets used in this book are available for download from Alan's GitHub repository (*https://github.com/alanfgates/program mingpig/tree/2ed*). *README* files are included to help you build the UDFs and understand the contents of the datafiles. Each example script in the text that is available on GitHub has a comment at the beginning that gives the filename. Pig Latin and Python script examples are organized by chapter in the *examples* directory. UDFs, both Java and Python, are in a separate directory, *udfs*. All datasets are in the *data* directory.

For brevity, each script is written assuming that the input and output are in the local directory. Therefore, when in local mode, you should run Pig in the directory that contains the input data. When running on a cluster, you should place the data in your home directory on the cluster.

Example scripts were tested against Pig 0.15.0 and should work against Pig 0.10.0 through 0.15.0 unless otherwise indicated.

The three datasets used in the examples are real datasets, though quite small ones. The file *baseball* contains baseball player statistics. The second set contains New York Stock Exchange data in two files: *NYSE_daily* and *NYSE_dividends*. This data was trimmed to include only stock symbols starting with C from the year 2009, to make it small enough to download easily. However, the schema of the data has not changed. If you want to download the entire dataset and place it on a cluster (only a few nodes would be necessary), it would be a more realistic demonstration of Pig and Hadoop. Instructions on how to download the data are in the *README* files. The third dataset is a very brief web crawl started from Pig's home page.

Using Code Examples

This book is here to help you get your job done. In general, you may use the code in this book in your programs and documentation. You do not need to contact us for permission unless you're reproducing a significant portion of the code. For example, writing a program that uses several chunks of code from this book does not require permission. Selling or distributing a CD-ROM of examples from O'Reilly books does require permission. Answering a question by citing this book and quoting example code does not require permission. Incorporating a significant amount of example code from this book into your product's documentation does require permission.

We appreciate, but do not require, attribution. An attribution usually includes the title, authors, publisher, and ISBN. For example: "*Programming Pig* by Alan Gates and Daniel Dai (O'Reilly). Copyright 2017 Alan Gates and Daniel Dai, 978-1-491-93709-9."

If you feel your use of code examples falls outside fair use or the permission given above, feel free to contact us at *permissions@oreilly.com*.

Safari® Books Online

Safari (formerly Safari Books Online) is a membership-based training and reference platform for enterprise, government, educators, and individuals.

Members have access to thousands of books, training videos, Learning Paths, interactive tutorials, and curated playlists from over 250 publishers, including O'Reilly Media, Harvard Business Review, Prentice Hall Professional, Addison-Wesley Professional, Microsoft Press, Sams, Que, Peachpit Press, Adobe, Focal Press, Cisco Press, John Wiley & Sons, Syngress, Morgan Kaufmann, IBM Redbooks, Packt,

Adobe Press, FT Press, Apress, Manning, New Riders, McGraw-Hill, Jones & Bartlett, and Course Technology, among others.

For more information, please visit *http://oreilly.com/safari*.

How to Contact Us

Please address comments and questions concerning this book to the publisher:

O'Reilly Media, Inc.
1005 Gravenstein Highway North
Sebastopol, CA 95472
800-998-9938 (in the United States or Canada)
707-829-0515 (international or local)
707-829-0104 (fax)

We have a web page for this book, where we list errata, examples, and any additional information. You can access this page at:

http://bit.ly/programming-pig-2e

To comment or ask technical questions about this book, send email to:

bookquestions@oreilly.com

For more information about our books, conferences, Resource Centers, and the O'Reilly Network, see our website at:

http://www.oreilly.com

Acknowledgments from the First Edition (Alan Gates)

A book is like a professional football team. Much of the glory goes to the quarterback or a running back. But if the team has a bad offensive line, the quarterback never gets the chance to throw the ball. Receivers must be able to catch, and the defense must be able to prevent the other team from scoring. In short, the whole team must play well in order to win. And behind those on the field there is an array of coaches, trainers, and managers who prepare and guide the team. So it is with this book. My name goes on the cover. But without the amazing group of developers, researchers, testers, documentation writers, and users that contribute to the Pig project, there would be nothing worth writing about.

In particular, I would like to acknowledge Pig contributors and users for their contributions and feedback on this book. Chris Olston, Ben Reed, Richard Ding, Olga Natkovitch, Thejas Nair, Daniel Dai, and Dmitriy Ryaboy all provided helpful feedback on draft after draft. Julien Le Dem provided the example code for embedding Pig in Python. Jeremy Hanna wrote the section for Pig and Cassandra. Corrine Chandel deserves special mention for reviewing the entire book. Her feedback has added greatly to the book's clarity and correctness.

Thanks go to Tom White for encouraging me in my aspiration to write this book, and for the sober warnings concerning the amount of time and effort it would require. Chris Douglas of the Hadoop project provided me with very helpful feedback on the sections covering Hadoop and MapReduce.

I would also like to thank Mike Loukides and the entire team at O'Reilly. They have made writing my first book an enjoyable and exhilarating experience. Finally, thanks to Yahoo! for nurturing Pig and dedicating more than 25 engineering years (and still counting) of effort to it, and for graciously giving me the time to write this book.

Second Edition Acknowledgments (Alan Gates and Daniel Dai)

In addition to the ongoing debt we owe to those acknowledged in the first edition, we would like to thank those who have helped us with the second edition. These include Rohini Palaniswamy and Sumeet Singh for their discussion of Pig at Yahoo!, and Yahoo! for allowing them to share their experiences. Zongjun Qi, Yiping Han, and Particle News also deserve our thanks for sharing their experience with Pig at Particle News. Thanks also to Ofer Mendelevitch for his suggestions on use cases

We would like to thank Tom Hanlon, Aniket Mokashi, Koji Noguchi, Rohini Palaniswamy, and Thejas Nair, who reviewed the book and give valuable suggestions to improve it.

We would like to thank Marie Beaugureau for prompting us to write this second edition, all her support along the way, and her patience with our sadly lax adherence to the schedule.

Finally, we would like to thank Hortonworks for supporting the Pig community and us while we worked on this second edition.

## CHAPTER 1

What Is Pig?

Pig provides an engine for executing data flows in parallel on Apache Hadoop. It includes a language, Pig Latin, for expressing these data flows. Pig Latin includes operators for many of the traditional data operations (join, sort, filter, etc.), as well as providing the ability for users to develop their own functions for reading, processing, and writing data.

Pig is an Apache open source project (*http://pig.apache.org*). This means users are free to download it as source or binary, use it for themselves, contribute to it, and— under the terms of the Apache License—use it in their products and change it as they see fit.

Pig Latin, a Parallel Data Flow Language

Pig Latin is a data flow language. This means it allows users to describe how data from one or more inputs should be read, processed, and then stored to one or more outputs in parallel. These data flows can be simple linear flows, or complex workflows that include points where multiple inputs are joined and where data is split into multiple streams to be processed by different operators. To be mathematically precise, a Pig Latin script describes a *directed acyclic graph* (DAG), where the edges are data flows and the nodes are operators that process the data.

This means that Pig Latin looks different from many of the programming languages you may have seen. There are no if statements or for loops in Pig Latin. This is because traditional procedural and object-oriented programming languages describe control flow, and data flow is a side effect of the program. Pig Latin instead focuses on data flow. (For information on how to integrate the data flow described by a Pig Latin script with control flow, see Chapter 8.)

Comparing Query and Data Flow Languages

After a cursory look, people often say that Pig Latin is a procedural version of SQL. Although there are certainly similarities, there are more differences. SQL is a query language. Its focus is to allow users to form queries. It lets users describe what question they want answered, but not how they want it answered. In Pig Latin, on the other hand, the user describes exactly how to process the input data.

Another major difference is that SQL is oriented around answering one question. When users want to do several data operations together, they must either write separate queries, storing the intermediate data into temporary tables, or use subqueries inside the query to do the earlier steps of the processing. However, many SQL users find subqueries confusing and difficult to form properly. Also, using subqueries creates an inside-out design where the first step in the data pipeline is the innermost query.

Pig, however, is designed with a long series of data operations in mind, so there is no need to write the data pipeline in an inverted set of subqueries or to worry about storing data in temporary tables. This is illustrated in Examples 1-1 and 1-2.

Consider a case where a user wants to group one table on a key and then join it with a second table. Because joins happen before grouping in a SQL query, this must be expressed either as a subquery or as two queries with the results stored in a temporary table. Example 1-1 will use a temporary table, as that is more readable.

Example 1-1. Group then join in SQL

```
CREATE TEMP TABLE t1 AS
SELECT customer, sum(purchase) AS total_purchases
FROM transactions
GROUP BY customer;

SELECT customer, total_purchases, zipcode
FROM t1, customer_profile
WHERE t1.customer = customer_profile.customer;
```

In Pig Latin, on the other hand, this looks like Example 1-2.[1]

Example 1-2. Group then join in Pig Latin

```
-- Load the transactions file, group it by customer, and sum their total purchases
txns    = load 'transactions' as (customer, purchase);
grouped = group txns by customer;
total   = foreach grouped generate group, SUM(txns.purchase) as tp;
```

---

1 Lines that start with - - are comments. See "Comments" on page 46.

```
-- Load the customer_profile file
profile = load 'customer_profile' as (customer, zipcode);
-- Join the grouped and summed transactions and customer_profile data
answer  = join total by group, profile by customer;
-- Write the results to the screen
dump answer;
```

Furthermore, SQL and Pig were designed to live in different environments. SQL is designed for the RDBMS environment, where data is normalized and schemas and proper constraints are enforced (that is, there are no nulls in places they do not belong, etc.). Pig is designed for the Hadoop data-processing environment, where schemas are sometimes unknown or inconsistent. Data may not be properly constrained, and it is rarely normalized. As a result of these differences, Pig does not require data to be loaded into tables first. It can operate on data as soon as it is copied into HDFS.

An analogy with human languages and cultures might help. My wife and I (Alan) have been to France together a couple of times. I speak very little French. But because English is the language of commerce (and probably because Americans and the British like to vacation in France), there is enough English spoken in France for me to get by. My wife, on the other hand, speaks French. She has friends there to visit. She can talk to people we meet. She can explore the parts of France that are not on the common tourist itinerary. Her experience of France is much deeper than mine because she can speak the native language.

SQL is the English of data processing. It has the nice feature that everyone and every tool knows it, which means the barrier to adoption is very low. Our goal is to make Pig Latin the native language of parallel data-processing systems such as Hadoop. It may take some learning, but it will allow users to utilize the power of Hadoop much more fully.

Pig on Hadoop

Pig runs on Hadoop. It makes use of the Hadoop Distributed File System (HDFS) and Hadoop's resource management system (YARN, as of Hadoop 2). HDFS is a distributed filesystem that stores files across all of the nodes in a Hadoop cluster. It handles breaking the files into large blocks and distributing them across different machines, including making multiple copies of each block so that if any one machine fails no data is lost. It presents a POSIX-like interface to users. By default, Pig reads input files from HDFS, uses HDFS to store intermediate data between MapReduce jobs, and writes its output to HDFS. As you will see in Chapter 10, it can also read input from and write output to sources other than HDFS.

YARN stands for "Yet Another Resource Negotiator." It is the resource management layer of Hadoop 2. It consists of a per-cluster ResourceManager, a per-node Node-

Manager, and an API to write distributed applications that run on the cluster. While in Hadoop 1 the only available engine for executing operations was MapReduce, in Hadoop 2 the field has expanded. Other applications include Tez and Spark. Pig can currently run on MapReduce and Tez, with work ongoing to make it run on Spark.

MapReduce is a simple but powerful parallel data-processing paradigm. Every job in MapReduce consists of three main phases: map, shuffle, and reduce. In the map phase, the application has the opportunity to operate on each record in the input separately. Many maps are started at once, so that while the input may be gigabytes or terabytes in size, given enough machines the map phase can usually be completed in under one minute.

Part of the specification of a MapReduce job is the key on which data will be collected. For example, if you were processing web server logs for a website that required users to log in, you might choose the user ID to be your key so that you could see everything done by each user on your website. In the shuffle phase, which happens after the map phase, data is collected together by the key the user has chosen and distributed to different machines for the reduce phase. Every record for a given key will go to the same reducer.

In the reduce phase, the application is presented with each key, together with all of the records containing that key. Again this is done in parallel on many machines. After processing each group, the reducer can write its output. See the next section for a walkthrough of a simple MapReduce program.

Tez is an alternative to MapReduce for processing data on Hadoop. It executes a collection of connected tasks and moves data between those tasks. More formally, it executes directed acyclic graphs (DAGs) of tasks. Tez is more general and flexible than MapReduce. It provides better performance and lower latency, which will speed up most MapReduce applications. It has been adopted by high-level developer tools such as Pig, Hive, and Cascading as an internal execution engine. However, Tez is a low-level execution engine and is not meant to be used by end users directly. You can think of Tez as assembly language on Hadoop. You can get the best performance if you write your program in assembly language. However, how often do you actually do this? In most scenarios you write your program in a high-level language such as C++ or Java and let those tools compile your program into assembly language. The same applies to Tez and Pig. You write your script in Pig Latin, and Pig converts it into Tez tasks and executes it efficiently. The complexity of the Tez API is hidden inside Pig.

Since Tez is not user-facing, in the following discussion we will only focus on MapReduce and how it differs from Pig.

MapReduce's "Hello World"

Consider a simple MapReduce application that counts the number of times each word appears in a given text. This is the "hello world" program of MapReduce. In this example the map phase will read each line in the text, one at a time. It will then split out each word into a separate string, and, for each word, it will output the word and a 1 to indicate it has seen the word one time. The shuffle phase will use the word as the key, hashing the records to reducers. The reduce phase will then sum up the number of times each word was seen and write that together with the word as output. Let's consider the case of the nursery rhyme "Mary Had a Little Lamb." Our input will be:

```
Mary had a little lamb
its fleece was white as snow
and everywhere that Mary went
the lamb was sure to go
```

Let's assume that each line is sent to a different map task. In reality, each map is assigned much more data than this, but this simple example will be easier to follow. The data flow through MapReduce is shown in Figure 1-1.

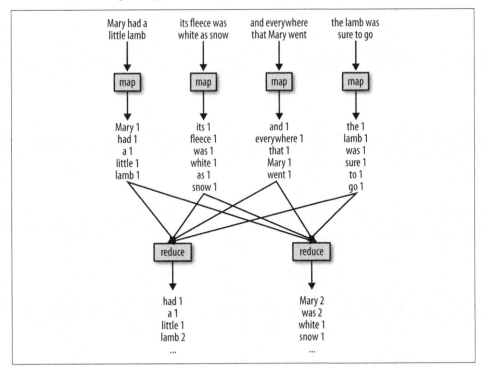

Figure 1-1. MapReduce illustration

Once the map phase is complete, the shuffle phase will collect all records with the same word onto the same reducer. For this example we assume that there are two reducers: all words that start with A–L are sent to the first reducer, and words starting with M–Z are sent to the second reducer. The reducers will then output the summed counts for each word.

When Pig is running MapReduce as the execution engine, it compiles the Pig Latin scripts that users write into a series of one or more MapReduce jobs that it then executes. See Example 1-3 for a Pig Latin script that will do a word count of "Mary Had a Little Lamb."

Example 1-3. Pig counts Mary and her lamb

```
-- Load input from the file named Mary, and call the single
-- field in the record 'line'.
input = load 'mary' as (line);

-- TOKENIZE splits the line into a field for each word.
-- flatten will take the collection of records returned by
-- TOKENIZE and produce a separate record for each one, calling the single
-- field in the record word.
words = foreach input generate flatten(TOKENIZE(line)) as word;

-- Now group them together by each word.
grpd  = group words by word;

-- Count them.
cntd  = foreach grpd generate group, COUNT(words);
-- Print out the results.
dump cntd;
```

There is no need to be concerned with map, shuffle, and reduce phases when using Pig. It will manage decomposing the operators in your script into the appropriate MapReduce phases.

How Pig Differs from MapReduce

Earlier, we made the claim that a goal of the Pig team is to make Pig Latin the native language of parallel data-processing environments such as Hadoop. But does MapReduce really not provide enough? Why is Pig necessary?

Pig offers users several advantages over using MapReduce directly. Pig Latin provides all of the standard data-processing operations, such as join, filter, group by, order by, union, etc. MapReduce provides the group by operation directly (in the shuffle and reduce phases), and it provides the order by operation indirectly through the way it implements the grouping. Filtering and projection can be implemented trivially in the map phase. But other operators—particularly join—are not provided and must instead be written by the user.

Pig furnishes some complex, nontrivial implementations of these standard data operations. For example, because the number of records per key in a dataset is rarely evenly distributed, the data sent to the reducers is often skewed. That is, one reducer may get 10 or more times the data as other reducers. Pig has join and order by operators that will handle this case and (in some cases) rebalance the reducers. But these took the Pig team months to write, and rewriting them in MapReduce would be time consuming.

In MapReduce, the data processing inside the map and reduce phases is opaque to the system. This means that MapReduce has no opportunity to optimize or check the user's code. Pig, on the other hand, can analyze a Pig Latin script and understand the data flow that the user is describing. That means it can do early error checking (did the user try to add a string field to an integer field?) and optimizations (can these two grouping operations be combined?).

MapReduce does not have a type system. This is intentional, and it gives users the flexibility to use their own data types and serialization frameworks. But the downside is that this further limits the system's ability to check users' code for errors both before and during runtime.

All of these points mean that Pig Latin is much lower-cost to write and maintain than Java code for MapReduce. Consider the following (very unscientific) experiment, where we wrote the same operation in Pig Latin and MapReduce. Given one file with user data and one with click data for a website, the Pig Latin script in Example 1-4 will find the five pages most visited by users between the ages of 18 and 25.

Example 1-4. Finding the top five URLs

```
Users = load 'users' as (name, age);
Fltrd = filter Users by age >= 18 and age <= 25;
Pages = load 'pages' as (user, url);
Jnd   = join Fltrd by name, Pages by user;
Grpd  = group Jnd by url;
Smmd  = foreach Grpd generate group, COUNT(Jnd) as clicks;
Srtd  = order Smmd by clicks desc;
Top5  = limit Srtd 5;
store Top5 into 'top5sites';
```

The first line of this program loads the file *users* and declares that this data has two fields: name and age. It assigns the name of Users to the input. The second line applies a filter to Users that passes through records with an age between 18 and 25, inclusive. All other records are discarded. Now the data has only records of users in the age range we are interested in. The results of this filter are named Fltrd.

The second load statement loads *pages* and names it Pages. It declares its schema to have two fields, user and url.

The line Jnd = join joins together Fltrd and Pages using Fltrd.name and Pages.user as the key. After this join we have found all the URLs each user has visited.

The line Grpd = group collects records together by URL, so for each value of url, such as pignews.com/frontpage, there will be one record with a collection of all records that have that value in the url field. The next line then counts how many records are collected together for each URL. So after this line we now know, for each URL, how many times it was visited by users aged 18–25.

The next thing to do is to sort this from most visits to least. The line Srtd = order sorts on the count value from the previous line and places it in desc (descending) order. Thus, the largest value will be first. Finally, we need only the top five pages, so the last line limits the sorted results to only five records. The results of this are then stored back to HDFS in the file top5sites.

In Pig Latin this comes to nine lines of code and took about 15 minutes to write and debug. The same code in MapReduce (omitted here for brevity) came out to about 170 lines of code and took four hours to get working. The Pig Latin will similarly be easier to maintain, as future developers can easily understand and modify this code.

There is, of course, a cost to all this. It is possible to develop algorithms in Map-Reduce that cannot be done easily in Pig. And the developer gives up a level of control. A good engineer can always, given enough time, write code that will outperform a generic system. So, for less common algorithms or extremely performance-sensitive ones, MapReduce is still the right choice. Basically, this is the same situation as choosing to code in Java versus a scripting language such as Python. Java has more power, but due to its lower-level nature, it requires more development time than scripting languages. Developers will need to choose the right tool for each job.

What Is Pig Useful For?

In our experience, Pig Latin use cases tend to fall into three separate categories: traditional extract-transform-load (ETL) data pipelines, research on raw data, and iterative processing.

The largest use case is data pipelines. A common example is web companies bringing in logs from their web servers, cleansing the data, and precomputing common aggregates before loading it into their data warehouses. In this case, the data is loaded onto the Hadoop cluster, and then Pig is used to clean out records from bots and records with corrupt data. It is also used to join web event data against user databases so that user cookies can be connected with known user information.

Another example of data pipelines is using Pig to build behavior prediction models. Pig is used to scan through all the user interactions with a website and split the users into various segments. Then, for each segment, a mathematical model is produced that predicts how members of that segment will respond to types of advertisements or news articles. In this way the website can show ads that are more likely to get clicked on, or offer news stories that are more likely to engage users and keep them coming back to the site.

Traditionally, ad hoc queries are done in languages such as SQL that make it easy to quickly form a question for the data to answer. However, for research on raw data, some users prefer Pig Latin. Because Pig can operate in situations where the schema is unknown, incomplete, or inconsistent, and because it can easily manage nested data, researchers who want to work on data before it has been cleaned and loaded into the warehouse often prefer Pig. Researchers who work with large datasets frequently use scripting languages such as Perl or Python to do their processing. Users with these backgrounds often prefer the data flow paradigm of Pig over the declarative query paradigm of SQL.

Users building iterative processing models are also starting to use Pig. Consider a news website that keeps a graph of all news stories on the Web that it is tracking. In this graph each news story is a node, and edges indicate relationships between the stories. For example, all stories about an upcoming election are linked together. Every five minutes a new set of stories comes in, and the data-processing engine must integrate them into the graph. Some of these stories are new, some are updates of existing stories, and some supersede existing stories. Some data-processing steps need to operate on this entire graph of stories. For example, a process that builds a behavioral targeting model needs to join user data against the entire graph of stories. Rerunning the entire join every five minutes is not feasible because it cannot be completed in five minutes with a reasonable amount of hardware. But the model builders do not want to update these models only on a daily basis, as that means an entire day of missed serving opportunities.

To cope with this problem, it is possible to first do a join against the entire graph on a regular basis—for example, daily. Then, as new data comes in every five minutes, a join can be done with just the new incoming data, and these results can be combined with the results of the join against the whole graph. This combination step takes some care, as the five-minute data contains the equivalent of inserts, updates, and deletes on the entire graph. It is possible and reasonably convenient to express this combination in Pig Latin.

One point that is implicit in everything we have said so far is that Pig (like MapReduce) is oriented around the batch processing of data. If you need to process gigabytes or terabytes of data, Pig is a good choice. But it expects to read all the records of a file and write all of its output sequentially. For workloads that require writing single or small groups of records, or looking up many different records in random order,

Pig (like MapReduce) is not a good choice. See "NoSQL Databases" on page 266 for a discussion of applications that are good for these use cases.

The Pig Philosophy

Early on, people who came to the Pig project as potential contributors did not always understand what the project was about. They were not sure how to best contribute or which contributions would be accepted and which would not. So, the Pig team produced a statement of the project's philosophy (*http://pig.apache.org/philosophy.html*) that summarizes what Pig aspires to be:

Pigs eat anything
> Pig can operate on data whether it has metadata or not. It can operate on data that is relational, nested, or unstructured. And it can easily be extended to operate on data beyond files, including key/value stores, databases, etc.

Pigs live anywhere
> Pig is intended to be a language for parallel data processing. It is not tied to one particular parallel framework. It has been implemented first on Hadoop, but we do not intend that to be only on Hadoop.

Pigs are domestic animals
> Pig is designed to be easily controlled and modified by its users.
>
> Pig allows integration of user code where ever possible, so it currently supports user defined field transformation functions, user defined aggregates, and user defined conditionals. These functions can be written in Java or in scripting languages that can compile down to Java (e.g. Jython). Pig supports user provided load and store functions. It supports external executables via its stream command and MapReduce JARs via its mapreduce command. It allows users to provide a custom partitioner for their jobs in some circumstances and to set the level of reduce parallelism for their jobs.
>
> Pig has an optimizer that rearranges some operations in Pig Latin scripts to give better performance, combines Map Reduce jobs together, etc. However, users can easily turn this optimizer off to prevent it from making changes that do not make sense in their situation.

Pigs fly
> Pig processes data quickly. We want to consistently improve performance, and not implement features in ways that weigh Pig down so it can't fly.

Pig's History

Pig started out as a research project in Yahoo! Research, where Yahoo! scientists designed it and produced an initial implementation. As explained in a paper presented at SIGMOD in 2008,[2] the researchers felt that the MapReduce paradigm presented by Hadoop "is too low-level and rigid, and leads to a great deal of custom user code that is hard to maintain and reuse." At the same time they observed that many MapReduce users were not comfortable with declarative languages such as SQL. Thus, they set out to produce "a new language called Pig Latin that we have designed to fit in a sweet spot between the declarative style of SQL, and the low-level, procedural style of MapReduce."

Yahoo! Hadoop users started to adopt Pig, so a team of development engineers was assembled to take the research prototype and build it into a production-quality product. About this same time, in fall 2007, Pig was open sourced via the Apache Incubator. The first Pig release came a year later, in September 2008. Later that same year, Pig graduated from the Incubator and became a subproject of Apache Hadoop.

Early in 2009 other companies started to use Pig for their data processing. Amazon also added Pig as part of its Elastic MapReduce service. By the end of 2009 about half of Hadoop jobs at Yahoo! were Pig jobs. In 2010, Pig adoption continued to grow, and Pig graduated from a Hadoop subproject, becoming its own top-level Apache project.

Why Is It Called Pig?

One question that is frequently asked is, "Why is it named Pig?" People also want to know whether Pig is an acronym. It is not. The story goes that the researchers working on the project initially referred to it simply as "the language." Eventually they needed to call it something. Off the top of his head, one researcher suggested Pig, and the name stuck. It is quirky yet memorable and easy to spell. While some have hinted that the name sounds coy or silly, it has provided us with an entertaining nomenclature, such as Pig Latin for a language, Grunt for a shell, and PiggyBank for a CPAN-like shared repository.

---

2 Christopher Olston et al., "Pig Latin: A Not-So-Foreign Language for Data Processing," available at *http:// portal.acm.org/citation.cfm?id=1376726.*

CHAPTER 2

Installing and Running Pig

In this chapter, we show you how to download the Pig binary and start the Pig command line.

Downloading and Installing Pig

Before you can run Pig on your machine or your Hadoop cluster, you will need to download and install it. If someone else has taken care of this, you can skip ahead to "Running Pig" on page 16.

You can download Pig as a complete package or as source code that you build. You can also get it as part of a Hadoop distribution.

Downloading the Pig Package from Apache

You can download the official version of Apache Pig, which comes packaged with all of the required JAR files, from Pig's release page (*http://pig.apache.org/releases.html*).

Pig does not need to be installed on your Hadoop cluster. It runs on the machine from which you launch Hadoop jobs. Though you can run Pig from your laptop or desktop, in practice, most cluster owners set up one or more machines that have access to their Hadoop cluster but are not part of the cluster (that is, they are not DataNodes or TaskTrackers/NodeManagers). This makes it easier for administrators to update Pig and associated tools, as well as to secure access to the clusters. These machines are called *gateway machines* or *edge machines*. In this book we use the term gateway machine.

You will need to install Pig on these gateway machines. If your Hadoop cluster is accessible from your desktop or laptop, you can install Pig there as well. Also, you can install Pig on your local machine if you plan to use Pig in local mode (see "Running Pig Locally on Your Machine" on page 17).

The core of Pig is written in Java and is thus portable across operating systems. Pig has been tested with several distributions of Linux (Red Hat, Ubuntu, Fedora, Suse, CentOS), macOS, and Windows.

 Older versions of Pig (0.11 and earlier) do not support Windows natively. They can only be run with Cygwin on Windows. This is because in earlier versions the shell script that starts Pig was a bash script. There were also bugs in how Pig handled the differences between path and directory delimiters across Windows and Linux/Unix. Starting with Pig 0.12.0, a Windows *.cmd* script has been added and Windows-specific bugs have been fixed.

Pig 0.15 and later releases require Java 1.7; older versions require Java 1.6. Pig has been tested with Oracle JDK and OpenJDK. Starting with version 0.10, Pig supports both Hadoop 2 (Hadoop 0.23.x, 2.x) and Hadoop 1 (Hadoop 0.20.x, 1.x). However, if you are using version 0.10, 0.11, or 0.12 with Hadoop 2, you need to recompile Pig with the following command:

```
ant -Dhadoopversion=23 jar-withouthadoop
```

Pig 0.16 is the last release that will support Hadoop 1; support will be dropped in 0.17.

Installation and Setup

Once you have downloaded Pig, you can place it anywhere you like on your machine, as it does not depend on being in a certain location. To install it, place the tarball in the directory of your choosing and type:

```
tar xzf filename
```

where *filename* is the TAR file you downloaded.

You will need to make sure that the environment variable JAVA_HOME is set to the directory that contains your Java distribution. Pig will fail immediately if this value is not in the environment. You can set this in your shell, or specify it on the command line when you invoke Pig. On a Linux/Unix system you can find the appropriate value for JAVA_HOME by executing which java and stripping the bin/java from the end of the result. On Windows, use where java instead.

You will also need to set the environment variable HADOOP_HOME to the directory that contains your Hadoop distribution, so that Pig can use the right Hadoop library from your local Hadoop distribution. However, if you only want to use Pig in local mode, and HADOOP_HOME is not set, Pig will use the Hadoop runtime library bundled in the Pig TAR file instead.

Downloading Pig Artifacts from Maven

In addition to the official release available from the Apache Pig site, it is possible to download Pig from Apache's Maven repository (*https://repository.apache.org/content/repositories/releases/org/apache/pig/pig*). This site includes JAR files for Pig, for the source code, and for the Javadocs, as well as the POM file that defines Pig's dependencies. Development tools that are Maven-aware can use this repository to pull down Pig's source and Javadoc. If you use mvn or ant in your build process, you can also pull the Pig JAR from this repository automatically. Note there are two Pig binary JARs. The default JAR is for Hadoop 1. If you need Pig for Hadoop 2, use the classifier h2.

Here is the POM file entry to pull Pig for Hadoop 1:

```
<dependency>
    <groupId>org.apache.pig</groupId>
    <artifactId>pig</artifactId>
</dependency>
```

And here is the POM file entry to pull Pig for Hadoop 2:

```
<dependency>
    <groupId>org.apache.pig</groupId>
    <artifactId>pig</artifactId>
    <classifier>h2</classifier>
</dependency>
```

Downloading the Source

When you download Pig from Apache, you also get the Pig source code. This enables you to debug your version of Pig or just peruse the code to see how it works. But if you want to live on the edge and try out a feature or a bug fix before it is available in a release, you can download the source from Apache's Subversion repository. You can also apply patches that have been uploaded to Pig's issue-tracking system (*http://issues.apache.org/jira/browse/PIG*) but that are not yet checked into the code repository. Information on checking out Pig using svn or cloning the repository via git is available on Pig's version control page (*http://pig.apache.org/version_control.html*).

Downloading Pig from Distributions

In addition to the official Apache version, there are companies that repackage and distribute Hadoop and associated tools. Currently Hortonworks, Cloudera, and MapR are the most popular Hadoop distributors.

The upside of using a distribution is that all of the tools are packaged and tested together. Also, if you need professional support, it is available.

The following sections give instructions on how to download Pig from these distribution providers. Note, however, that distributors frequently update their packaging and installation procedures, so you should check with the distribution of your choice to confirm the correct installation procedures.

Downloading Pig from Hortonworks

The Hortonworks Data Platform (HDP) provides options for automated installation with Apache Ambari and manual installation with RPMs, as well as sandbox images that work with VirtualBox, VMWare, or Docker (for use on your local machine only). You can download these from the Hortonworks download page (*http://horton works.com/hdp/downloads*).

HDP is free, though you can optionally purchase support from the company. You can also try Hortonworks Sandbox on Azure free for one month.

Downloading Pig from Cloudera

Cloudera's CDH distribution provides a managed installation option with Cloudera Manager and an unmanaged installation option with individual RPMs or tarballs. It also provides virtual machine images so users can download and import the images into Docker, VMWare, KVM, or VitualBox to try it locally.

For complete instructions on downloading and installing Hadoop and Pig from Cloudera, see Cloudera's download site (*http://www.cloudera.com/downloads*).

Cloudera offers CDH in a free Express edition and a paid Enterprise edition.

Downloading Pig from MapR

MapR also provides download links for its installer (*https://www.mapr.com/products/ hadoop-download*) and virtual machine images (*https://www.mapr.com/products/ mapr-sandbox-hadoop*). The Community edition of the MapR Converged Data Platform is available with an unlimited free license, and a 30-day trial license is available for the Enterprise edition.

Running Pig

You can run Pig locally on your machine or on your cluster. You can also run Pig in the cloud or as part of a managed service such as Amazon's Elastic MapReduce or Microsoft's Azure HDInsight.

Running Pig Locally on Your Machine

Running Pig locally on your machine is referred to in Pig parlance as "local mode." Local mode is useful for prototyping and debugging your Pig Latin scripts. Some people also use it for small data when they want to apply the same processing they do to large data—so that their data pipeline is consistent across data of different sizes—but they do not want to waste cluster resources on small files and small jobs.

When running locally, Pig uses the Hadoop class LocalJobRunner, which reads from the local filesystem and executes MapReduce jobs locally. This has the nice property that Pig jobs run locally in the same way as they will on your cluster, and they all run in one process, making debugging much easier.[1]

Let's run a Pig Latin script in local mode. See "Code Examples in This Book" on page xiv for how to download the data and Pig Latin for this example. The simple script in Example 2-1 loads the file *NYSE_dividends*, groups the file's rows by stock ticker symbol, and then calculates the average dividend for each symbol.

Example 2-1. Running Pig in local mode

```
--average_dividend.pig
-- load data from NYSE_dividends, declaring the schema to have 4 fields
dividends = load 'NYSE_dividends' as (exchange, symbol, date, dividend);
-- group rows together by stock ticker symbol
grouped   = group dividends by symbol;
-- calculate the average dividend per symbol
avg       = foreach grouped generate group, AVG(dividends.dividend);
-- store the results to average_dividend
store avg into 'average_dividend';
```

If you use head -5 to look at the *NYSE_dividends* file, you will see:

```
NYSE    CPO 2009-12-30  0.14
NYSE    CPO 2009-09-28  0.14
NYSE    CPO 2009-06-26  0.14
NYSE    CPO 2009-03-27  0.14
NYSE    CPO 2009-01-06  0.14
```

This matches the schema we declared in our Pig Latin script. The first field is the exchange this stock is traded on, the second field is the stock ticker symbol, the third is the date the dividend was paid, and the fourth is the amount of the dividend.

---

1 Older versions of Pig executed scripts in Pig's own local mode execution engine rather than LocalJobRunner. However, as Pig added features that took advantage of more advanced MapReduce features, it became difficult or impossible to replicate those features in local mode. Thus, in 0.7, Pig dropped support for its own local mode and switched to LocalJobRunner.

Switch to the directory where *NYSE_dividends* is located. You can then run this example on your local machine by entering:

```
pig_path/bin/pig -x local average_dividend.pig
```

where *pig_path* is the path to the Pig installation on your local machine.

The result should be a lot of output on your screen. Much of this is MapReduce's LocalJobRunner generating logs. But some of it is Pig telling you how it will execute the script, giving you the status as it executes, etc. Near the bottom of the output you should see the simple message Success!. This means all went well. The script stores its output to *average_dividend*, so you might expect to find a file by that name in your local directory. Instead, you will find a directory named *average_dividend* that contains a file named *part-r-00000*.[2] Because Hadoop is a distributed system, the output will be a collection of files in a directory. For similar reasons, the input path will often be a directory and all files in that directory will be read. We can look in that part file for the results by entering:

```
cat average_dividend/part-r-00000 | head -5
```

which returns:

```
CA      0.04
CB      0.35
CE      0.04
CF      0.1
CI      0.04
```

Starting with Pig 0.14, you can also run Pig locally with Tez local mode. To do this, you just need to make one change—instead of using -x local on the command line, use -x tez_local:

```
pig_path/bin/pig -x tez_local average_dividend.pig
```

When you specify Tez, internally Pig uses the Tez execution engine instead of Map-Reduce to run the Pig script locally. This allows you to test your scripts with Tez locally before running them on the cluster.

There is also a Spark local mode currently under development. You may run Pig with Spark local mode using the following command line:

```
pig_path/bin/pig -x spark_local average_dividend.pig
```

However, you will need to check out the Spark branch and build Pig by yourself. See "PIG-4059" (*https://issues.apache.org/jira/browse/PIG-4059*) for instructions.

---

2 Part file naming is different in Tez. It takes the form *part-vvertexnumberv-ooutputnumber-r-tasknumber*. For example, *part-v001-o000-r-00000*.

Running Pig on Your Hadoop Cluster

Most of the time you will be running Pig on your Hadoop cluster. As was covered in "Downloading and Installing Pig" on page 13, Pig runs locally on your local or your gateway machine. All of the parsing, checking, and planning is done locally. Pig then executes jobs in your cluster.

 When we say "your gateway machine," we mean the machine from which you are launching Pig jobs. Usually this will be one or more machines that have access to your Hadoop cluster. However, depending on your configuration, it could be your local machine as well.

Pig needs to know the configuration of your cluster. For Hadoop 2, it needs the location of your cluster's NameNode and ResourceManager. For Hadoop 1, it needs the location of the NameNode and JobTracker. These locations can be found in *core-site.xml*, *hdfs-site.xml*, *yarn-site.xml* (Hadoop 2 only), and *mapred-site.xml*. It is also possible you will find all those entries in *hadoop-site.xml* if your Hadoop administrator is still using the old-style config files. If you are using Pig on Tez, you don't need *mapred-site.xml*, but you need to include *tez-site.xml*.

If you are already running Hadoop jobs from your gateway machine you most likely have these files present. If not, you should work with your cluster administrator to get the files installed and the proper values set.

In most cases, Pig will find the Hadoop configuration files in the standard location (`$HADOOP_CONF_DIR` if defined; otherwise, `$HADOOP_HOME/conf` for Hadoop 1 or `$HADOOP_HOME/etc/hadoop` for Hadoop 2). If not, you will need to tell Pig which directory they are in by setting the `PIG_CLASSPATH` environment variable to that directory. Note that this must point to the *directory* that the XML file is in, not the file itself. Pig will read all XML and properties files in that directory.

Let's run the same script on your cluster that we ran in the local mode example (Example 2-1). If you are running on a Hadoop cluster you have never used before, you will need to create a home directory. You can do this with the Hadoop `hdfs` command:

```
pig_pathhdfs -mkdir /user/username
```

Or you can do the same thing with Pig itself:

```
pig_path/bin/pig -e fs -mkdir /user/username
```

where `pig_path` is the path to Pig on your gateway machine, and `username` is your username on the gateway machine.

Remember, you need to set JAVA_HOME before executing any Pig commands. See "Downloading the Pig Package from Apache" on page 13 for details. You also need to set HADOOP_HOME to where your Hadoop client is installed or PIG_CLASSPATH to the directory containing your Hadoop configuration files before running these Pig commands.

In order to run this example on your cluster, you first need to copy the data to your cluster:

```
hdfs -copyFromLocal NYSE_dividends NYSE_dividends
```

Or, if you would like to do it in Pig:

```
pig_path/bin/pig -e fs -copyFromLocal NYSE_dividends NYSE_dividends
```

Now you are ready to run the Pig Latin script itself:

```
pig_path/bin/pig average_dividend.pig
```

The first few lines of output will tell you how Pig is connecting to your cluster. After that it will describe its progress in executing your script.

Near the end of the output there should be a line saying Success!. This means that your execution succeeded. You can see the results by entering:

```
pig_path/bin/pig -e cat average_dividend
```

which should give you the same connection information and then dump all of the stock ticker symbols and their average dividends.

Earlier, we made the point that *average_dividend* is a directory, and thus you had to cat the part file contained in that directory to get the results. However, in this example we ran cat directly on *average_dividend*. If you list *average_dividend*, you will see that it is still a directory in this example, but in Pig, cat can operate on directories. See "Grunt" on page 26 for a discussion of this.

We can run this same example using Tez as the execution engine. (You must have Pig 0.14 or later for this.) To do this, simply add -x tez in the command line:

```
pig_path/bin/pig -x tez average_dividend.pig
```

Pig will then use the Tez execution engine instead of MapReduce to run the Pig Latin script. In most cases Tez provides much better performance than MapReduce, so if you are using Pig 0.14 or later, we recommended using it. For more information about Tez mode and installation of Tez, see Chapter 11.

It is also possible to run the example using the Spark execution engine, which is still under development:

```
pig_path/bin/pig -x spark average_dividend.pig
```

However, Spark execution engine code has not been merged into the main codebase at this time. You will need to check out the code from the Spark branch and build Pig yourself (*https://issues.apache.org/jira/browse/PIG-4059*) before using it.

Running Pig in the Cloud

Cloud computing[3] and the Software as a Service (SaaS) model have taken off in recent years. This has been fortuitous for hardware-intensive applications such as Hadoop. Setting up and maintaining a Hadoop cluster is an expensive proposition in terms of hardware acquisition, facility costs, and maintenance and administration. Many users find that it is cheaper to rent the hardware they need instead.

There are two ways to use Hadoop and Pig in the cloud. The first option is to rent virtual machines from a cloud service provider, and then install Hadoop and Pig yourself. Options for this include Amazon's EC2, Microsoft's Azure, Google's Compute Engine, Rackspace, and others. The instructions for running Pig on your cluster are the same; see "Running Pig on Your Hadoop Cluster" on page 19.

Some cloud providers also offer Hadoop and Pig as a service. They handle building and deploying virtual machines with Hadoop software installed. On top of this, they provide features such as the ability to add/remove nodes dynamically and graphical user interfaces (GUIs) for managing your cluster and jobs. Here we introduce three popular services: Amazon's Elastic MapReduce (EMR), Microsoft's HDInsight, and the Google Cloud Platform.

Amazon Elastic MapReduce

EMR users can run Pig jobs either from the AWS console (*https://console.aws.amazon.com/elasticmapreduce*) or using the AWS Command Line Interface (CLI). The AWS console provides a GUI where users can create a Pig job with several clicks. After that, users can access their rented Pig cluster via a web browser, SSH, or a web services API. For information about EMR, visit *http://aws.amazon.com/elasticmapreduce*. We suggest beginning with this nice tutorial (*https://www.youtube.com/watch?v=iMOzC835H4I*), which will introduce you to the service.

To automate the process, users can use the AWS Command Line Interface. You can find information about how to install and use this tool at *http://aws.amazon.com/cli/*. A typical AWS CLI command to run a Pig script looks like:

```
aws emr create-cluster --steps Type=PIG,Name='Get hosts',ActionOnFailure=CONTINUE
,Args=[-f,s3://programming-pig-2e/gethosts_from_log.pig,-p,INPUT=
```

---

3 Cloud computing can refer to public clouds such as Amazon's EC2 where anyone can rent compute time or private clouds maintained within an organization. In this section we are discussing public clouds.

```
s3://programming-pig-2e/tomcatlog.tar.gz,-p,OUTPUT=s3://programming-pig-
2e/output] --applications Name=Pig --ami-version 3.8.0 --instance-groups
InstanceGroupType=MASTER,InstanceCount=1,InstanceType=m3.xlarge,BidPrice=0.10
InstanceGroupType=CORE,InstanceCount=2,InstanceType=m3.xlarge,BidPrice=0.10
```

In this example, the Pig script *gethosts_from_log.pig* is stored in an S3 bucket called *programming-pig-2e*. The Pig script requires two parameters: INPUT and OUTPUT. The command line will launch three Amazon m3.xlarg instances. One is the master and the other two are slaves. The master instance will run Hadoop's NameNode and ResourceManager. The slave instances will each run a Hadoop DataNode and Node-Manager. Once the command line is issued, you can find the newly created cluster ID on your AWS console.

Microsoft HDInsight

On Microsoft's Azure cloud, you can create an HDInsight Hadoop cluster using the Azure management GUI (*https://manage.windowsazure.com*). Once created, you can access your cluster via Windows Azure PowerShell or HDInsight Tools for Visual Studio. However, the easiest way is to connect to the cluster head node using Microsoft's remote desktop functionality. To do that, you first need to enable "remote access" in the Microsoft Azure management console. Next, download the *.rdp* file from the management console. Once you open the *.rdp* file using Microsoft Remote Desktop Connection you will be able to access the head node. On the head node you can open a CMD window and issue Pig commands the same way you would if Pig was installed on a local Windows machine.

As with Amazon EMR, you have the ability to change the size of your cluster even after the cluster has been created.

Google Cloud Platform

Google Cloud Platform provides a hosted Hadoop service along with tools to deploy Hadoop on virtual machines.

The hosted Hadoop service is called Cloud Dataproc. You can create a Hadoop cluster in the Google Cloud Platform Console (*https://console.cloud.google.com*). In the "Big Data" section of the menu at the top left, you will find a "Dataproc" option. This is the entry point to create Hadoop clusters and submit Hadoop jobs. Click the "Create a project" button, and you'll see a web page where you can specify the configuration of the cluster. Once the provision of the cluster is finished, you can submit Pig jobs to run on the cluster. On the job submission page, you can either type in the Pig statements you want to run or provide the location of Pig script in Google Cloud Storage.

If you prefer the command line, you can create a Hadoop cluster and submit Pig jobs with the gcloud command-line tool (*https://cloud.google.com/dataproc/docs/quick*

starts/quickstart-gcloud). Here is an example of how to submit a Pig job to an existing Hadoop cluster:

```
gcloud beta dataproc jobs submit pig --cluster mycluster --file test.pig
```

The "Click to Deploy" tool does not deploy Pig, but fortunately Google provides a command-line tool, bdutil (*https://cloud.google.com/hadoop/bdutil*), that will do so. You can create a Hadoop cluster including Pig with all three major Hadoop distributions: Hortonworks, Cloudera, or MapR. Here is a sample command line to create a Hortonworks HDP cluster with bdutil:

```
bdutil deploy -p programming-pig-2e --zone=us-central1-f
--bucket programming-pig-2e -e platforms/hdp/ambari_env.sh
```

The console message will show you the command line to connect to the master node:

```
To log in to the master: gcloud --project=programming-pig-2e compute ssh
--zone=us-central1-f hadoop-m
```

After you log in to the master node, you can run Pig from the command line since it is installed on the master.

 The services described here are provided by cloud infrastructure providers as add-ons. Other companies, such as Altiscale (*https://www.altiscale.com/*) and Qubole (*http://www.qubole.com/*), focus on providing Hadoop and related tools like Pig as a service. They usually hide virtual machine provision details from the user so that you can focus on the high-level services without worrying about the low-level details.

Command-Line and Configuration Options

You've already seen how to invoke Pig from the command line. In this section, we want to discuss more options in the Pig command line.

There are a number of command-line options that you can use with Pig. You can see the full list by entering pig -h. Most of these options will be discussed later, in the sections that cover the features these options control. In this section we'll discuss the remaining miscellaneous options:

-e *or* -execute

Execute a single command in Pig. For example, pig -e fs -ls will list your home directory.

-h *or* -help

List the available command-line options.

`-h properties`
> List the properties that Pig will use if they are set by the user.

`-P` *or* `-propertyFile`
> Specify a properties file that Pig should read.

`-version`
> Print the version of Pig.

Pig also uses a number of Java properties. The entire list can be printed out with `pig -h properties`. Specific properties are discussed later in the sections that cover the features they control.

Hadoop also has a number of Java properties it uses to determine its behavior. For example, you can pass options to use a higher heap size to the JVM that runs your map and reduce tasks by setting `mapreduce.map.java.opts` and `mapreduce.reduce.java.opts`. You should also set the task container's maximum physical memory usage limit (`mapreduce.map.memory.mb` and `mapreduce.reduce.memory.mb`) to a higher value if you increase the heap size.

Properties can be passed to Pig in several ways:

1. You can add them to the *conf/pig.properties* file that is part of your Pig distribution.

2. You can specify a separate properties file by using `-P` on the command line.

3. You can set the environment variable `PIG_OPTS`, as in:

   ```
   export PIG_OPTS="
   -Dmapreduce.map.java.opts=-Xmx1024m
   -Dmapreduce.reduce.java.opts=-Xmx1024m
   -Dmapreduce.map.memory.mb=1536
   -Dmapreduce.reduce.memory.mb=1536"
   ```

4. You can use `-D` on the command line in the same way as any Java property. For example:

   ```
   bin/pig -D mapreduce.map.java.opts=-Xmx1024m
   -D mapreduce.reduce.java.opts=-Xmx1024m
   -D mapreduce.map.memory.mb=1536
   -D mapreduce.reduce.memory.mb=1536
   ```

   When placed on the command line, these property definitions must come before any Pig-specific command-line options (such as `-x local`).

5. You can use the `set` command in the Pig script:

   ```
   set mapreduce.map.java.opts '-Xmx1024m'
   set mapreduce.reduce.java.opts '-Xmx1024m'
   ```

```
set mapreduce.map.memory.mb '1536'
set mapreduce.reduce.memory.mb '1536'
```

See "set" on page 106 for details.

The options here are given in order of increasing precedence. Thus, if you define a property in multiple places, the last definition in the preceding list will be used. For example, if you added `mapreduce.reduce.java.opts=-Xmx256m` to your *pig.properties* file but then added `-Dmapreduce.reduce.java.opts=-Xmx512m` to your command line, the reducers would be started with a heap size of 512 MB rather than 256 MB.

You can verify the current values of all properties by including `set` with no arguments in your Pig Latin script or typing it in the Grunt shell. All currently defined properties and their values will be printed out:

```
grunt> set
...
system: mapreduce.map.java.opts=-Xmx1024m
system: mapreduce.reduce.java.opts=-Xmx1024m
...
```

Return Codes

In bash or Windows shell programming, the return code is used to determine whether or not the last command was successful and, if not, the reason for the failure.

Pig commands use the return codes described in Table 2-1 to communicate success or failure.

Table 2-1. Pig return codes

Value	Meaning	Comments
0	Success	
1	Retriable failure	
2	Failure	
3	Partial failure	Used with the multiquery optimization; see "split and Nonlinear Data Flows" on page 102
4	Illegal arguments passed to Pig	
5	IOException thrown	Would usually be thrown by a UDF
6	PigException thrown	Usually means a Python UDF raised an exception
7	ParseException thrown (can happen after parsing if variable substitution is being done)	
8	Throwable thrown (an unexpected exception)	

Grunt

Grunt[4] is Pig's interactive shell. It enables you to enter Pig Latin interactively and provides a shell for you to interact with HDFS.

To enter Grunt, invoke Pig with no script or command to run. Typing:

```
pig -x local
```

will result in the prompt:

```
grunt>
```

This gives you a Grunt shell to interact with your local filesystem. If you omit the `-x local` and have a cluster configuration set via `HADOOP_HOME` or `PIG_CLASSPATH`, this will put you in a Grunt shell that will interact with HDFS on your cluster.

As you would expect with a shell, Grunt provides command-line history and editing, as well as tab completion. It does not provide filename completion via the Tab key. That is, if you type `kil` and then press the Tab key, it will complete the command as `kill`. But if you have a file *foo* in your local directory and you type `ls fo` and then hit Tab, it will not complete it as `ls foo`. This is because the response time from HDFS to connect and find whether the file exists is too slow to be useful.

Although Grunt is a useful shell, it is not a full-featured shell. It does not provide a number of commands found in standard Unix shells, such as pipes, redirection, and background execution.

To exit Grunt you can type `quit` or enter Ctrl-D.

If you are in the middle of executing a Pig script, you can use Ctrl-C to terminate the execution. Pig will automatically kill the YARN applications (or MapReduce jobs in Hadoop 1) in progress.

Entering Pig Latin Scripts in Grunt

One of the main uses of Grunt is to enter Pig Latin in an interactive session. This can be particularly useful for quickly sampling your data and for prototyping new Pig Latin scripts.

You can enter Pig Latin directly into Grunt. Pig will not start executing the Pig Latin you enter until it sees either a `store` or `dump`. However, it will do basic syntax and semantic checking to help you catch errors quickly. If you do make a mistake while

---

4 According to Ben Reed, one of the researchers at Yahoo! who helped start Pig, they named the shell "Grunt" because they felt the initial implementation was so limited that it was not worthy even of the name "oink."

entering a line of Pig Latin in Grunt, you can reenter the line using the same alias, and Pig will take the last instance of the line you enter. For example:

```
$ pig -x local
grunt> dividends = load 'NYSE_dividends' as (exchange, symbol, date, dividend);
grunt> symbols = foreach dividends generate symbl;
...Error during parsing. Invalid alias: symbl ...
grunt> symbols = foreach dividends generate symbol;
...
```

HDFS Commands in Grunt

Besides entering Pig Latin interactively, Grunt's other major use is to act as a shell for HDFS. All `hadoop fs` shell commands are available in Pig. They are accessed using the keyword `fs`. The dash (`-`) used in the `hadoop fs` is also required:

```
grunt> fs -ls
```

You can see a complete guide to the available commands in Hadoop's documentation (*http://bit.ly/GruntCommands*). A number of the commands come directly from Unix shells and will operate in ways that are familiar: these include `chgrp`, `cat`, `chmod`, `chown`, `cp`, `du`, `ls`, `mkdir`, `mv`, `rm`, and `stat`. A few of them will either look like Unix commands you are used to but behave slightly differently or be unfamiliar, including:

copyFromLocal *localfile hdfsfile*
> Copy a file from your local disk to HDFS. This is done serially, not in parallel.

copyToLocal *hdfsfile localfile*
> Copy a file from HDFS to your local disk. This is done serially, not in parallel.

rmr *filename*
> Remove files recursively. This is equivalent to `rm -r` in Unix. Use this with caution.

Besides `hadoop fs` commands, Grunt also has its own implementation of some of these commands: `cat`,[5] `cd`, `copyFromLocal`, `copyToLocal`, `cp`, `ls`, `mkdir`, `mv`, `pwd`, `rm`,[6] and `rmf`. However, with the exception of `cd` and `pwd`, most of these commands are deprecated in favor of using `hadoop fs`. They might be removed in the future.

---

5 Pig's version of `cat` can operate on directories while the HDFS version cannot. When passed a directory, Pig's version of `cat` will concatenate all files in the directory. So, doing `cat dir` is equivalent to doing `fs -cat dir/*`.

6 This removes directories recursively, like Hadoop's `rmr` or Unix's `rm -r`.

Often you want to remove a file or directory recursively if it exists. The recommended way to do that is to use the command `fs -rm -r -f`. However, the `-f` option was introduced in Hadoop 2.6. If you are using an earlier version of Hadoop the command `fs -rm -r` will throw an exception and quit the Pig script if the target file or directory does not exist. In that case, you will need to use Grunt's `rmf` command instead.

Controlling Pig from Grunt

Grunt also provides commands for controlling Pig and YARN:

`kill` *applicationid*
> Kill the YARN application (or MapReduce job in Hadoop 1) associated with *applicationid*. The output of the `pig` command that spawned the application will list the application's ID. You can also find the application's ID by looking at Hadoop's ResourceManager GUI (or JobTracker GUI in Hadoop 1), which lists all applications currently running on the cluster. The *applicationid* starts with "job_" in MapReduce and "application_" in Tez.[7] You may need to replace the prefix if your ID is different from what Pig is expecting. Note that this command kills a particular YARN application. If your Pig job contains other YARN applications that do not depend on the killed YARN application, these applications will still continue. If you want to kill all of the YARN applications associated with a particular Pig job, it is best to terminate the process running Pig, and then use this command to kill any YARN applications that are still running. Make sure to terminate the Pig process with a Ctrl-C or a Unix `kill`, not a Unix `kill -9`. The latter does not give Pig the chance to terminate the launched Pig jobs and clean up temporary files it is using, which can waste resources and leave garbage in your cluster.

`exec [-param` *param_name* `=` *param_value*`] [-param_file` *filename*`] [`*script*`]`
> Execute the Pig Latin script *script*. Aliases defined in *script* are not imported into Grunt. This command is useful for testing your Pig Latin scripts while inside a Grunt session. For information on the `-param` and `-param_file` options, see "Parameter Substitution" on page 108. You can also run `exec` without parameters to only run the Pig statements before `exec`. Pig will not combine Pig statements before `exec` with the rest of the script in execution. We typically use `exec` to avoid multiquery optimization (see "split and Nonlinear Data Flows" on page 102), which may combine too many statements in a single job.

---

7 In fact, `kill` does not work in Tez mode due to a bug (PIG-5030 (*https://issues.apache.org/jira/browse/PIG-5030*)). You can kill Tez applications in MapReduce mode using `kill job_xxxxxx`.

```
run [-param param_name = param_value] [-param_file filename] script
```
Execute the Pig Latin script *script* in the current Grunt shell. All aliases referenced in *script* will be available to Grunt, and the commands in *script* will be accessible via the shell history. This is another option for testing Pig Latin scripts while inside a Grunt session. For information on the `-param` and `-param_file` options, see "Parameter Substitution" on page 108.

Running External Commands

You can also run non-Pig commands within Grunt:

```
sh shell commands
```
`sh` gives you access to the local shell. You can execute any shell commands, including those involve pipes or redirects. It is better to work with absolute paths, as `sh` does not always properly track the current working directory.

```
sql HCatalog commands
```
The `sql` command gives you access to Apache Hive's HCatalog (*https://cwiki.apache.org/confluence/display/Hive/HCatalog*). You can issue HCatalog DDL commands with it, which allows you to create, alter, and drop tables, partitions, etc. in Pig. This is useful when you are accessing Hive data in Pig via HCatalog. A prerequisite to use the `sql` command is to configure the `hcat.bin` entry in your *conf/pig.properties* file. Set it to the absolute path of the `hcat` script so Pig knows where to find HCatalog.

Others

Other useful commands include:

```
set [key value]
```
`set` without parameters shows all properties in Pig. This includes all Java properties, Pig properties, and Hadoop properties. You can set the value of a property with the two-parameter version of `set`. The first parameter is the key and the second parameter is the value. If the value is string, it is recommended to enclose it with single quotes.

```
clear
```
Clear the screen and position the cursor at the top of the screen.

```
history [-n]
```
Show the command history of the Grunt shell. Without the `-n` parameter, `history` will show line numbers along with the command history. The `-n` parameter suppresses the line numbers.

## CHAPTER 3

Pig's Data Model

Before we take a look at the operators that Pig Latin provides, we first need to understand Pig's data model. This includes Pig's data types, how it handles concepts such as missing data, and how you can describe your data to Pig.

Types

Pig's data types can be divided into two categories: scalar types, which contain a single value, and complex types, which contain other types.

Scalar Types

Pig's scalar types are simple types that appear in most programming languages. With the exception of bytearrays, they are all represented in Pig interfaces by `java.lang` classes, making them easy to work with in UDFs:

Int

> An integer. Ints are represented in interfaces by `java.lang.Integer`. They store four-byte signed integers. Constant integers are expressed as integer numbers: for example, 42.

Long

> A long integer. Longs are represented in interfaces by `java.lang.Long`. They store eight-byte signed integers. Constant longs are expressed as integer numbers with an L appended: for example, `5000000000L`.

Biginteger (since Pig 0.12)

> An integer of effectively infinite size (it is bounded only by available memory). Bigintegers are represented in interfaces by `java.math.BigInteger`. There are no

biginteger constants.[1] Chararray and numeric types can be cast to biginteger to produce a constant value in the script. An important note: performance of biginteger is significantly worse than ints or longs. Whenever your value will fit into one of those types you should use it rather than biginteger.

Float

A floating-point number. Floats are represented in interfaces by `java.lang.Float` and use four bytes to store their value. You can find the range of values representable by Java's `float` type at *http://docs.oracle.com/javase/ specs/jls/se8/html/jls-4.html#jls-4.2.3*. Note that because this is a floating-point number, in some calculations it will lose precision. For calculations that require no loss of precision, you should use bigdecimal instead. Constant floats are expressed as a floating-point number with an `f` appended. Floating-point numbers can be expressed in simple format, as in `3.14f`, or in exponent format, as in `6.022e23f`.

Double

A double-precision floating-point number. Doubles are represented in interfaces by `java.lang.Double` and use eight bytes to store their value. You can find the range of values representable by Java's `double` type at *http://docs.oracle.com/ javase/specs/jls/se8/html/jls-4.html#jls-4.2.3*. Note that because this is a floating-point number, in some calculations it will lose precision. For calculations that require no loss of precision, you should use bigdecimal instead. Constant doubles are expressed as floating-point numbers in either simple format (e.g., `2.71828`) or exponent format (e.g., `6.626e-34`).

Bigdecimal (since Pig 0.12)

A fixed-point number. Unlike floating-point numbers (floats and doubles), bigdecimals can be used in calculations where exact decimal operations are required (e.g., accounting). In interfaces, bigdecimals are represented by `java.math.Big Decimal`. Bigdecimals are not limited in size, except by the memory available to store them. This type comes with several caveats. First, Pig does not give you a way to declare the precision of a bigdecimal. Instead, it assumes all precision to be infinite. When dividing two bigdecimals, the result can therefore be infinite (e.g., 1 divided by 3), leading to an out of memory error.[2] Second, the performance of bigdecimal is significantly slower than the floating-point types. Bigdec-

---

1 This is fixed in PIG-4798 (*https://issues.apache.org/jira/browse/PIG-4798*) and you will able to create a biginteger constant with "BI" suffix.

2 This is fixed in PIG-4973 (*https://issues.apache.org/jira/browse/PIG-4973*) and will be available in a future release.

imal constants are not supported. Instead, you must use a floating-point constant or chararray and a cast to generate a bigdecimal.[3]

Chararray

A string or character array. Chararrays are represented in interfaces by `java.lang.String`. Constant chararrays are expressed as string literals with single quotes: for example, `'fred'`. In addition to standard alphanumeric and symbolic characters, you can express certain characters in chararrays by using backslash codes, such as `\t` for Tab and `\n` for Return. Unicode characters can be expressed as `\u` followed by their four-digit hexadecimal Unicode value. For example, the value for Ctrl-A is expressed as `\u0001`.

Boolean

A Boolean logical value. Booleans are represented in interfaces by `java.lang.Boolean`. Boolean constants are `true` and `false`. Boolean constants are not case-sensitive.

datetime (since Pig 0.11)

An object representing a particular point on the timeline. Datetimes are represented in interfaces by `org.joda.time.DateTime`. The precision of a datetime is milliseconds. There are no datetime constants in Pig Latin. To provide a datetime constant in your script you can use the `ToDate` function. For example:

```
ToDate('20150823 19:20:30', 'yyyyMMdd HH:mm:ss', 'America/Los_Angeles')
```

As can be seen in this example, datetimes include time zone information. If you do not specify the time zone of a datetime, then Pig will use the default time zone on the machine that creates the datetime. Keep in mind that which machine creates the object can vary depending on its position in the Pig Latin script. Constants in the script will be evaluated on the gateway machine you are running Pig on, but if you invoke `ToDate` or other datetime UDFs on data values read from your inputs, those will be evaluated on task nodes inside the cluster. You can override the use of the default time zone of the machine you are on by setting the `pig.datetime.default.tz` property to the time zone you wish datetimes to default to.

bytearray

A blob or array of bytes. Bytearrays are represented in interfaces by a Java class `DataByteArray` that wraps a Java `byte[]`. There is no way to specify a constant bytearray.

---

3 This is fixed in PIG-4798 (*https://issues.apache.org/jira/browse/PIG-4798*) and you will able to create a bigdecimal constant with "BD" suffix.

Complex Types

Pig has three complex data types: maps, tuples, and bags. All of these types can contain data of any type, including other complex types. So, it is possible to have a map where the value field is a bag, which contains a tuple where one of the fields is a map.

Map

A map in Pig is a chararray-to–data element mapping, where that element can be any Pig type, including a complex type. The chararray is called a *key* and is used as an index to find the element, referred to as the *value*.

There are two types of map: typed or untyped. For a typed map, the value of the map must be the declared data type.

For an untyped map, Pig does not know the type of the value, and it will assume it is a bytearray. However, the actual value might be something different. If you know what the actual type is (or what you want it to be), you can cast it; see "Casts" on page 39. If you do not cast the value, Pig will make a best guess based on how you use the value in your script. If the value is of a type other than bytearray, Pig will figure that out at runtime and handle it. (See "Schemas" on page 36 for more information on how Pig handles unknown types.) There is no requirement that all values in an untyped map must be of the same type. It is legitimate to have a map with two keys name and age, for example, where the value for name is a chararray and the value for age is an int.

It is recommended to use typed maps as it allows you to avoid the casting.

Map constants are formed using brackets to delimit the map, a hash between keys and values, and a comma between key/value pairs. For example, ['name'#'bob', 'age'#55] will create a map with two keys, name and age. The first value is a chararray, and the second is an integer.

Tuple

A tuple is a fixed-length, ordered collection of Pig data elements. Tuples are divided into fields, with each field containing one data element. These elements can be of any type—they do not all need to be the same type. A tuple is analogous to a row in SQL, with the fields being SQL columns. Because tuples are ordered, it is possible to refer to the fields by position; see "Expressions in foreach" on page 49 for details. A tuple can, but is not required to, have a schema associated with it that describes each field's type and provides a name for each field. This allows Pig to check that the data in the tuple is what the user expects, and it allows the user to reference the fields of the tuple by name.

Tuple constants use parentheses to indicate the tuple and commas to delimit fields in the tuple. For example, ('bob', 55) describes a tuple constant with two fields.

Bag

A bag is an unordered collection of tuples. Because it has no order, it is not possible to reference tuples in a bag by position. Like tuples, a bag can, but is not required to, have a schema associated with it. In the case of a bag, the schema describes all tuples within the bag.

Bag constants are constructed using braces, with tuples in the bag separated by commas. For example, {('bob', 55), ('sally', 52), ('john', 25)} constructs a bag with three tuples, each with two fields.

Pig users often notice that Pig does not provide a list or set type that can store items of any type. It is possible to mimic a set type using the bag, by wrapping the desired type in a tuple of one field. For instance, if you want to store a set of integers, you can create a bag with a tuple with one field, which is an int. This is a bit cumbersome, but it works.

Bag is the one type in Pig that is not required to fit into memory. As you will see later, because they are used to store collections when grouping, bags can become quite large. Pig has the ability to spill bags to disk when necessary, keeping only partial sections of the bag in memory. The size of the bag is limited to the amount of local disk available for spilling the bag.

Memory Requirements of Pig Data Types

In the previous sections we often referenced the size of the value stored for each type (four bytes for ints, eight bytes for longs, etc.). This tells you how large (or small) a value those types can hold. However, this does not tell you how much memory is actually used by objects of those types. Because Pig uses Java objects to represent these values internally, there is an additional overhead. This overhead depends on your JVM, but it is usually eight bytes per object. It is even worse for chararrays because Java's String uses two bytes per character rather than one.

So, if you are trying to figure out how much memory you need in Pig to hold all of your data (e.g., if you are going to do a join that needs to hold a hash table in memory), do not count the bytes on disk and assume that is how much memory you need. The multiplication factor between disk and memory is dependent on your data, whether your data is compressed on disk, your disk storage format, etc. As a rule of thumb, it takes about four times as much memory as it does disk to represent the uncompressed data.

Nulls

Pig includes the concept of a data element being null. Data of any type can be null. It is important to understand that the concept of null in Pig is the same as in SQL, which is completely different from the concept of null in C, Java, Python, etc. In Pig a null data element means the value is unknown. This might be because the data is missing, an error occurred in processing it, etc. In most procedural languages, a data value is said to be null when it is unset or does not point to a valid address or object. This difference in the meaning of null is important and affects the way Pig treats null data, especially when operating on it. See "foreach" on page 49, "group" on page 57, "join" on page 62, and "COUNT and COUNT_STAR" on page 57 for details of how nulls are handled in expressions and relations in Pig.

Unlike SQL, Pig does not have a notion of constraints on the data. In the context of nulls, this means that any data element can always be null. As you write Pig Latin scripts and UDFs, you will need to keep this in mind.

Schemas

Pig has a very lax attitude when it comes to schemas. This is a consequence of Pig's philosophy of eating anything (see "The Pig Philosophy" on page 10). If a schema for the data is available, Pig will make use of it, both for up-front error checking and for optimization. But if no schema is available, Pig will still process the data, making the best guesses it can based on how the script treats the data. First, we will look at ways that you can communicate the schema to Pig; then, we will examine how Pig handles the case where you do not provide it with a schema.

The easiest way to communicate the schema of your data to Pig is to explicitly tell Pig what it is when you load the data:

```
dividends = load 'NYSE_dividends' as
    (exchange:chararray, symbol:chararray, date:chararray, dividend:float);
```

Pig now expects your data to have four fields. If it has more, it will truncate the extra ones. If it has less, it will pad the ends of the records with nulls.

It is also possible to specify the schema without giving explicit data types. In this case, the data type is assumed to be bytearray:

```
dividends = load 'NYSE_dividends' as (exchange, symbol, date, dividend);
```

Also, when you declare a schema, you do not have to declare the inner schemas of complex types, but you can if you want to. For example, if your data has a tuple in it, you can declare that field to be a tuple without specifying the fields it contains. You can also declare that field to be a tuple that has three columns, all of which are integers. Table 3-1 gives the details of how to specify each data type inside a schema declaration.

Table 3-1. Schema syntax

Data type	Syntax	Example
Int	`int`	`as (a:int)`
Long	`long`	`as (a:long)`
Biginteger	`biginteger`	`as (a:biginteger)`
Float	`float`	`as (a:float)`
Double	`double`	`as (a:double)`
Bigdecimal	`bigdecimal`	`as (a:bigdecimal)`
Chararray	`chararray`	`as (a:chararray)`
Boolean	`boolean`	`as (a:boolean)`
Datetime	`datetime`	`as (a:datetime)`
Bytearray	`bytearray`	`as (a:bytearray)`
Map	`map[]` or `map[`*type*`]`, where *type* is any valid type. This declares all values in the map to be of this type.	`as (a:map[], b:map[int])`
Tuple	`tuple()` or `tuple(`*list_of_fields*`)`, where *list_of_fields* is a comma-separated list of field declarations.	`as (a:tuple(),` `b:tuple(x:int, y:int))`
Bag	`bag{}` or `bag{t:(`*list_of_fields*`)}`, where *list_of_fields* is a comma-separated list of field declarations. Note that, oddly enough, the tuple inside the bag must have a name, here specified as t, even though you will never be able to access that tuple t directly.	`(a:bag{}, b:bag{t:` `(x:int, y:int)})`

The runtime declaration of schemas is very nice. It makes it easy for users to operate on data without having to first load it into a metadata system. It also means that if you are interested in only the first few fields, you only have to declare those fields.

But for production systems that run over the same data every hour or every day, it has a couple of significant drawbacks. One, whenever your data changes, you have to change your Pig Latin. Two, although this works fine on data with 5 columns, it is painful when your data has 100 columns. To address these issues, there is another way to load schemas in Pig.

If the load function you are using already knows the schema of the data, the function can communicate that to Pig. (Load functions are how Pig reads data; see "load" on page 46 for details.) The load function might already know the schema because it is stored in a metadata repository such as HCatalog, or it might be stored in the data itself (if, for example, the data is stored in Avro, ORC, or Parquet format). In this case, you do not have to declare the schema as part of the load statement. And you can still refer to fields by name because Pig will fetch the schema from the load function before doing error checking on your script:

```
mdata = load 'mydata' using HCatLoader();
cleansed = filter mdata by name is not null;
...
```

But what happens when you cross the streams? What if you specify a schema and the loader returns one? If they are identical, all is well. If they are not identical, Pig will determine whether it can adapt the one returned by the loader to match the one you gave. For example, if you specified a field as a long and the loader said it was an int, Pig can and will do that cast. However, if it cannot determine a way to make the loader's schema fit the one you gave, it will give an error. See "Casts" on page 39 for a list of casts Pig can and cannot do to make the schemas work together.

Now let's look at the case where neither you nor the load function tells Pig what the data's schema is. In addition to being referenced by name, fields can be referenced by position, starting from zero. The syntax is a dollar sign, then the position: $0 refers to the first field. So, it's easy to tell Pig which field you want to work with. But how does Pig know the data type? It doesn't, so it starts by assuming everything is a bytearray. Then it looks at how you use those fields in your script, drawing conclusions about what you think those fields are and how you want to use them. Consider the following:

```
--no_schema.pig
daily = load 'NYSE_daily';
calcs = foreach daily generate $7 / 1000,
    $3 * 100.0, SUBSTRING($0, 0, 1), $6 - $3;
```

In the expression $7 / 1000, 1000 is an integer, so it is a safe guess that the eighth field of *NYSE_daily* is an integer or something that can be cast to an integer. In the same way, $3 * 100.0 indicates $3 is a double, and the use of $0 in a function that takes a chararray as an argument indicates the type of $0. But what about the last expression, $6 - $3? The - operator is used only with numeric types in Pig, so Pig can safely guess that $3 and $6 are numeric. But should it treat them as integers or floating-point numbers? Here Pig plays it safe and guesses that they are floating points, casting them to doubles. This is the safer bet because if they actually are integers, those can be represented as floating-point numbers, but the reverse is not true. However, because floating-point arithmetic is much slower and subject to loss of precision, if these values really are integers, you should cast them so that Pig uses integer types in this case.

There are also cases where Pig cannot make any intelligent guess:

```
--no_schema_filter
daily = load 'NYSE_daily';
fltrd = filter daily by $6 > $3;
```

> is a valid operator on numeric, chararray, and bytearray types in Pig Latin. So, Pig has no way to make a guess. In this case, it treats these fields as if they were bytearrays, which means it will do a byte-to-byte comparison of the data in these fields.

Pig also has to handle the case where it guesses wrong and must adapt on the fly. Consider the following:

```
--unintended_walks.pig
player     = load 'baseball' as (name:chararray, team:chararray,
               pos:bag{t:(p:chararray)}, bat:map[]);
unintended = foreach player generate bat#'base_on_balls' - bat#'ibbs';
```

Because the values in untyped maps can be of any type, Pig has no idea what type
bat#'base_on_balls' and bat#'ibbs' are. By the rules laid out previously, Pig will
assume they are doubles. But let's say they actually turn out to be represented internally as integers.[4] In that case, Pig will need to adapt at runtime and convert what it
thought was a cast from bytearray to double into a cast from int to double. Note that
it will still produce a double output and not an int output. This might seem nonintui-
tive; see "How Strongly Typed Is Pig?" on page 42 for details on why this is.

Finally, Pig's knowledge of the schema can change at different points in the Pig Latin
script. In all of the previous examples where we loaded data without a schema and
then passed it to a foreach statement, the data started out without a schema. But
after the foreach, the schema is known. Similarly, Pig can start out knowing the
schema, but if the data is mingled with other data without a schema, the schema can
be lost. That is, lack of schema is contagious:

```
--no_schema_join.pig
divs  = load 'NYSE_dividends' as (exchange, stock_symbol, date, dividends);
daily = load 'NYSE_daily';
jnd   = join divs by stock_symbol, daily by $1;
```

In this example, because Pig does not know the schema of daily, it cannot know the
schema of the join of divs and daily.

To view the schema of a relation, use describe (see "describe" on page 114).

Casts

The previous sections have referenced casts in Pig without defining how casts work.
The syntax for casts in Pig is the same as in Java—the type name in parentheses
before the value:

```
--unintended_walks_cast.pig
player     = load 'baseball' as (name:chararray, team:chararray,
               pos:bag{t:(p:chararray)}, bat:map[]);
unintended = foreach player generate (int)bat#'base_on_balls' - (int)bat#'ibbs';
```

The syntax for specifying types in casts is exactly the same as specifying them in schemas, as shown previously in Table 3-1.

---

4 That is not the case in the example data. For that to be the case, you would need to use a loader that did load
the bat map with these values as integers.

Not all conceivable casts are allowed in Pig. Table 3-2 describes which casts are allowed between scalar types. Casting to or from datetime is not allowed. Casts to bytearrays are never allowed because Pig does not know how to represent the various data types in binary format. Casts from bytearrays to any type are allowed. Casts to and and from complex types currently are not allowed, except from bytearray, although conceptually in some cases they could be.

Table 3-2. Supported casts

	To int	To long	To biginteger	To float	To double	To bigdecimal	To chararray	To boolean
From int	No.	Yes.	Yes.	Yes.	Yes.	Yes.	Yes.	Yes. 0 values will result in false, nonzero values in true.
From long	Yes. Any values greater than 2^{31} or less than -2^{31} will be truncated.	No.	Yes.	Yes.	Yes.	Yes.	Yes.	Yes. 0 values will result in false, nonzero values in true.
From biginteger	Yes. Values will be truncated to int values.	Yes. Values will be truncated to long values.	No.	Yes. Values will be truncated to float values.	Yes. Values will be truncated to double values.	Yes.	Yes.	Yes. 0 values will result in false, nonzero values in true.
From float	Yes. Values will be truncated to int values.	Yes. Values will be truncated to long values.	Yes. Values will be truncated to integer values.	No.	Yes.	Yes.	Yes.	Yes. 0 values will result in false, nonzero values in true.

	To int	To long	To biginteger	To float	To double	To bigdecimal	To chararray	To boolean
From double	Yes. Values will be truncated to int values.	Yes. Values will be truncated to long values.	Yes. Values will be truncated to integer values.	Yes. Values with precision beyond what float can represent will be truncated.	No.	Yes.	Yes.	Yes. 0 values will result in false, nonzero values in true.
From bigdecimal	Yes. Values will be truncated to int values.	Yes. Values will be truncated to long values.	Yes. Values will be truncated to integer values.	Yes. Values will be truncated to float values.	Yes. Values will be truncated to double values.	No.	Yes.	Yes. 0 values will result in false, nonzero values in true.
From chararray	Yes. Chararrays with nonnumeric characters result in null.	Yes. Chararrays with nonnumeric characters result in true null.	Yes. Chararrays with nonnumeric characters result in an error.	Yes. Chararrays with nonnumeric characters result in null.	Yes. Chararrays with nonnumeric characters result in null.	Yes. Chararrays with nonnumeric characters result in an error.	No.	Yes. The chararray 'true' (case-insensitive) results in true, 'false' in false. Any other chararray results in null.
From boolean	Yes. Boolean true results in 1, false in 0.	Yes. Boolean true results in 1, false in 0.	Yes. Boolean true results in 1, false in 0.	Yes. Boolean true results in 1, false in 0.	Yes. Boolean true results in 1, false in 0.	Yes. Boolean true results in 1, false in 0.	Yes. Boolean true results in chararray 'true', false in chararray 'false'.	No.

One type of casting that requires special treatment is casting from bytearray to other types. Because bytearray indicates a string of bytes, Pig does not know how to convert its contents to any other type. Continuing the previous example, both bat#'base_on_balls' and bat#'ibbs' were loaded as bytearrays. The casts in the script indicate that you want them treated as ints.

Pig does not know whether integer values in *baseball* are stored as ASCII strings, Java serialized values, binary-coded decimal, or some other format. So it asks the load function, because it is that function's responsibility to cast bytearrays to other types. In general this works nicely, but it does lead to a few corner cases where Pig does not know how to cast a bytearray. In particular, if a UDF returns a bytearray, Pig will not know how to perform casts on it because that bytearray is not generated by a load function.

Before leaving the topic of casts, we need to consider cases where Pig inserts casts for the user. These casts are implicit, compared to explicit casts where the user indicates the cast. Consider the following:

```
--total_trade_estimate.pig
daily = load 'NYSE_daily' as (exchange:chararray, symbol:chararray,
        date:chararray, open:float, high:float, low:float, close:float,
        volume:int, adj_close:float);
rough = foreach daily generate volume * close;
```

In this case, Pig will change the second line to `(float)volume * close` to do the operation without losing precision. In general, Pig will always widen types to fit when it needs to insert these implicit casts. So, int and long together will result in a long; int or long and float will result in a float; and int, long, or float and double will result in a double. There are no implicit casts between numeric types and chararrays or other types.

How Strongly Typed Is Pig?

In a strongly typed computer language (e.g., Java), the user must declare up front the types for all variables. In weakly typed languages (e.g., Perl), variables can take on values of different types and adapt as the occasion demands. So which is Pig? For the most part it is strongly typed. If you describe the schema of your data, Pig expects your data to be what you said. But when Pig does not know the schema, it will adapt to the actual types at runtime. (Perhaps we should say Pig is "gently typed." It is strong but willing to work with data that does not live up to its expectations.) To see the differences between these two cases, look again at this example:

```
--unintended_walks.pig
player     = load 'baseball' as (name:chararray, team:chararray,
                pos:bag{t:(p:chararray)}, bat:map[]);
unintended = foreach player generate bat#'base_on_balls' - bat#'ibbs';
```

In this example, remember we are pretending that the values for base_on_balls and ibbs turn out to be represented as integers internally (that is, the load function constructed them as integers). If Pig were weakly typed, the output of unintended would be records with one field typed as an integer. As it is, Pig will output records with one field typed as a double. Pig will make a guess and then do its best to massage the data into the types it guessed.

The downside here is that users coming from weakly typed languages are surprised, and perhaps frustrated, when their data comes out as a type they did not anticipate. However, on the upside, by looking at a Pig Latin script it is possible to know what the output data type will be in these cases without knowing the input data.

CHAPTER 4

Introduction to Pig Latin

It is time to dig into Pig Latin. This chapter provides you with the basics of Pig Latin, enough to write your first useful scripts. More advanced features of Pig Latin are covered in Chapter 5.

Preliminary Matters

Pig Latin is a data flow language. Each processing step results in a new dataset, or relation. In `input = load 'data'`, `input` is the name of the relation that results from loading the dataset `data`. A relation name is referred to as an *alias*. Relation names look like variables, but they are not. Once made, an assignment is permanent. It is possible to reuse relation names; for example, this is legitimate:

```
A = load 'NYSE_dividends' (exchange, symbol, date, dividends);
A = filter A by dividends > 0;
A = foreach A generate UPPER(symbol);
```

However, it is not recommended. It looks here as if you are reassigning A, but really you are creating new relations called A, and losing track of the old relations called A. Pig is smart enough to keep up, but it still is not a good practice. It leads to confusion when trying to read your programs (which A am I referring to?) and when reading error messages.

In addition to relation names, Pig Latin also has field names. They name a field (or column) in a relation. In the previous snippet of Pig Latin, `dividends` and `symbol` are examples of field names. These are somewhat like variables in that they will contain a different value for each record as it passes through the pipeline, but you cannot assign values to them.

Both relation and field names must start with an alphabetic character, and then they can have zero or more alphabetic, numeric, or _ (underscore) characters. All characters in the name must be ASCII.

Case Sensitivity

Keywords in Pig Latin are not case-sensitive; for example, LOAD is equivalent to load. But relation and field names are, so A = load 'foo'; is not equivalent to a = load 'foo';. UDF names are also case-sensitive; thus, COUNT is not the same UDF as count.

Comments

Pig Latin has two types of comment operators: SQL-style single-line comments (--) and Java-style multiline comments (/* */). For example:

```
A = load 'foo'; --this is a single-line comment
/*
 * This is a multiline comment.
 */
B = load /* a comment in the middle */'bar';
```

Input and Output

Before you can do anything interesting, you need to be able to add inputs and outputs to your data flows.

load

The first step in any data flow is to specify your input. In Pig Latin this is done with the load statement. By default, load looks for your data on HDFS in a tab-delimited file using the default load function PigStorage. divs = load '/data/examples/NYSE_dividends'; will look for a file called *NYSE_dividends* in the directory */data/examples*. You can also specify relative pathnames. By default, your Pig jobs will run in your home directory on HDFS, */users/yourlogin*. Unless you change directories, all relative paths will be evaluated from there. You can also specify a full URL for the path: for example, 'hdfs://nn.acme.com/data/examples/NYSE_dividends' to read the file from the HDFS instance that has nn.acme.com as a NameNode.

In practice, most of your data will not be in tab-separated text files. You also might be loading data from storage systems other than HDFS. Pig allows you to specify the function for loading your data with the using clause. For example, if you wanted to load your data from HBase, you would use the loader for HBase:

```
divs = load 'NYSE_dividends' using HBaseStorage();
```

If you do not specify a load function, the built-in function PigStorage will be used. You can also pass arguments to your load function via the using clause. For example, if you are reading comma-separated text data, PigStorage takes an argument to indicate which character to use as a separator:

```
divs = load 'NYSE_dividends' using PigStorage(',');
```

The load statement also can have an as clause, which allows you to specify the schema of the data you are loading (the syntax and semantics of declaring schemas in Pig Latin is discussed in "Schemas" on page 36):

```
divs = load 'NYSE_dividends' as (exchange, symbol, date, dividends);
```

When specifying a "file" to read from HDFS, you can specify a directory. In this case, Pig will find all files under the directory you specify and use them as input for that load statement. So, if you had a directory *input* with two datafiles *today* and *yesterday* under it, and you specified *input* as your file to load, Pig would read both *today* and *yesterday* as input. If the directory you specify contains other directories, files in those directories will be included as well.

PigStorage and TextLoader, the two built-in Pig load functions that operate on HDFS files, support globs.[1] With globs, you can read multiple files that are not under the same directory or read some but not all files under a directory. Table 4-1 describes globs that are valid in Hadoop 0.20. Be aware that glob meaning is determined by HDFS, not Pig, so the globs that will work for you depend on your version of HDFS. Also, if you are issuing Pig Latin commands from a Unix shell command line, you will need to escape many of the glob characters to prevent your shell from expanding them.

Table 4-1. Globs in Hadoop 0.20

Glob	Meaning
?	Matches any single character.
*	Matches zero or more characters.
[abc]	Matches a single character from the character set (a,b,c).
[a-z]	Matches a single character from the character range (a..z), inclusive. The first character must be lexicographically less than or equal to the second character.
[^abc]	Matches a single character that is not in the character set (a,b,c). The ^ character must appear immediately to the right of the opening bracket.
[^a-z]	Matches a single character that is not from the character range (a..z), inclusive. The ^ character must appear immediately to the right of the opening bracket.

---

1 Any loader that uses FileInputFormat as its InputFormat will support globs. Most loaders that load data from HDFS use this InputFormat.

Glob	Meaning
\c	Removes (escapes) any special meaning of the character c.
{ab,cd}	Matches a string from the string set {ab,cd}.

store

After you have finished processing your data, you will want to write it out somewhere. Pig provides the `store` statement for this purpose. In many ways it is the mirror image of the `load` statement. By default, Pig stores your data on HDFS in a tab-
delimited file using `PigStorage`:[2]

```
store processed into '/data/examples/processed';
```

Pig will write the results of your processing into a directory *processed* in the directory */data/examples*. You can specify relative pathnames as well as a full URL for the
path, such as `'hdfs://nn.acme.com/data/examples/processed'`.

If you do not specify a store function, `PigStorage` will be used. You can specify a different store function with a `using` clause:

```
store processed into 'processed' using
    HBaseStorage();
```

You can also pass arguments to your store function. For example, if you want to store
your data as comma-separated text data, `PigStorage` takes an argument to indicate
which character to use as a separator:

```
store processed into 'processed' using PigStorage(',');
```

As noted in "Running Pig" on page 16, when writing to a filesystem, *processed* will be
a directory with part files rather than a single file. But how many part files will be
created? That depends on the parallelism of the last job before the `store`. If it has
reduces, it will be determined by the `parallel` level set for that job. See "parallel" on
page 65 for information on how this is determined. If it is a map-only job, it will be
determined by the number of maps. See "Map Parallelism" on page 67.

dump

In most cases you will want to store your data somewhere when you are done processing it. But occasionally you will want to see it on the screen. This is particularly
useful during debugging and prototyping sessions. It can also be useful for quick ad
hoc jobs. `dump` directs the output of your script to your screen:

```
dump processed;
```

---

2 A single function can be both a load and a store function, as `PigStorage` is.

Unlike store, whose execution is deferred until the whole Pig script has been parsed, Pig will run the dump command immediately, without considering the Pig statements after it. It is possible that dump will generate a less optimal plan for the whole Pig script. Unless you are debugging, you should use store rather than dump.

dump outputs each record on a separate line, and fields are separated by commas. Nulls are indicated by missing values. If the output contains complex data, Pig will surround it with special marks. Maps are surrounded by [] (brackets), tuples by () (parentheses), and bags by {} (braces). Because each record in the output is a tuple, it is surrounded by ().

Be careful; you might be inundated with the outputs of dump if your dataset is large.

Relational Operations

Relational operators are the main tools Pig Latin provides to operate on your data. They allow you to transform it by sorting, grouping, joining, projecting, and filtering. This section covers the basic relational operators. More advanced features of these operators, as well as advanced relational operators, are covered in "Advanced Relational Operations" on page 77. What is covered here will be enough to get you started on programming in Pig Latin.

foreach

foreach takes a set of expressions and applies them to every record in the data pipeline—hence the name foreach. From these expressions it generates new records to send down the pipeline to the next operator. For those familiar with database terminology, it is Pig's projection operator. For example, the following code loads an entire record, but then removes all but the user and id fields from the record:

```
A = load 'input' as (user:chararray, id:long, address:chararray, phone:chararray,
        preferences:map[]);
B = foreach A generate user, id;
```

Expressions in foreach

foreach supports a list of expressions. The simplest are constants and field references. The syntax for constants has already been discussed in "Types" on page 31. Field references can be by name (as shown in the preceding example) or by position. Positional references are preceded by a $ (dollar sign) and start from zero:

```
prices = load 'NYSE_daily' as (exchange, symbol, date, open, high, low, close,
            volume, adj_close);
gain   = foreach prices generate close - open;
gain2  = foreach prices generate $6 - $3;
```

Here, the relations gain and gain2 will contain the same values. Positional-style references are useful in situations where the schema is unknown or undeclared.

In addition to using names and positions, you can refer to all fields using * (an asterisk), which produces a tuple that contains all the fields. You can also refer to ranges of fields using .. (two periods). This is particularly useful when you have many fields and do not want to repeat them all in your foreach command:

```
prices    = load 'NYSE_daily' as (exchange, symbol, date, open,
                high, low, close, volume, adj_close);
beginning = foreach prices generate ..open; -- produces exchange, symbol,
                                            -- date, open
middle    = foreach prices generate open..close; -- produces open, high,
                                                 -- low, close
end       = foreach prices generate volume..; -- produces volume, adj_close
```

Standard arithmetic operators for integers and floating-point numbers are supported: + for addition, - for subtraction, * for multiplication, and / for division. These operators return values of their own type, so 5/2 is 2, whereas 5.0/2.0 is 2.5. In addition, for integers the modulo operator % is supported. The unary negative operator (-) is also supported for both integers and floating-point numbers. Pig Latin obeys the standard mathematical precedence rules. For information on what happens when arithmetic operators are applied across different types (for example, 5/2.0), see "Casts" on page 39.

Null values are viral for all arithmetic operators. That is, x + null = null for all values of x.

Pig also provides a binary condition operator, often referred to as *bincond*. It begins with a Boolean test, followed by a ?, then the value to return if the test is true, then a :, and finally the value to return if the test is false. If the test returns null, bincond returns null. Both value arguments of the bincond must return the same type:

```
2 == 2 ? 1 : 4 --returns 1
2 == 3 ? 1 : 4 --returns 4
null == 2 ? 1 : 4 -- returns null
2 == 2 ? 1 : 'fred' -- type error; both values must be of the same type
```

Note that when you use the bincond operator, you will need to put the entire bincond expression inside parentheses:

```
daily = load 'NYSE_daily' as (exchange:chararray, symbol:chararray,
                date:chararray, open:float, high:float, low:float, close:float,
                volume:int, adj_close:float);
updown = foreach daily generate (close>open?'up':'down');
```

Pig will return a syntax error if you omit the parentheses.

To extract data from complex types, use the projection operators. For maps this is # (the pound sign or hash), followed by the name of the key as a string:

```
bball = load 'baseball' as (name:chararray, team:chararray,
        position:bag{t:(p:chararray)}, bat:map[]);
avg = foreach bball generate bat#'batting_average';
```

Keep in mind that the value associated with a key may be of any type. If you reference a key that does not exist in the map, the result is a null. Tuple projection is done with ., the dot operator. As with top-level records, the field can be referenced by name (if you have a schema for the tuple) or by position:

```
A = load 'input' as (t:tuple(x:int, y:int));
B = foreach A generate t.x, t.$1;
```

Referencing a field name that does not exist in the tuple will produce an error. Referencing a nonexistent positional field in the tuple will return null. Bag projection is not as straightforward as map and tuple projection. Bags do not guarantee that their tuples are stored in any order, so allowing a projection of the tuple inside the bag would not be meaningful. Instead, when you project fields in a bag, you are creating a new bag with only those fields:

```
A = load 'input' as (b:bag{t:(x:int, y:int)});
B = foreach A generate b.x;
```

This will produce a new bag whose tuples have only the field x in them. You can project multiple fields in a bag by surrounding the fields with parentheses and separating them by commas:

```
A = load 'input' as (b:bag{t:(x:int, y:int)});
B = foreach A generate b.(x, y);
```

This seemingly pedantic distinction that b.x is a bag and not a scalar value has consequences. Consider the following Pig Latin, which will not work:

```
A = load 'foo' as (x:chararray, y:int, z:int);
B = group A by x; -- produces bag A containing all records for a given value of x
C = foreach B generate SUM(A.y + A.z);
```

It is clear what the programmer is trying to do here. But because A.y and A.z are bags and the addition operator is not defined on bags, this will produce an error.[3] The correct way to do this calculation in Pig Latin is:

```
A = load 'foo' as (x:chararray, y:int, z:int);
A1 = foreach A generate x, y + z as yz;
```

---

3 You might object and say that Pig could figure out what is intended here and do it, since SUM(A.y + A.z) could be decomposed to "foreach record in A, add y and z and then take the sum." This is true. But when we change the group to a cogroup so that there are two bags A and B involved (see "cogroup" on page 88) and change the sum to SUM(A.y + B.z), because neither A nor B guarantees any ordering, this is not a well-defined operation. The rationale in designing the language was that it was better to be consistent and always say that bags could not be added rather than allowing it in some instances and not others.

```
B = group A1 by x;
C = foreach B generate SUM(A1.yz);
```

UDFs in foreach

User-defined functions (UDFs) can be invoked in `foreach` statements. These are called *evaluation functions,* or *eval funcs.* Because they are part of a `foreach` statement, these UDFs take one record at a time and produce one output. Keep in mind that either the input or the output can be a bag, so this one record can contain a bag of records:

```
-- udf_in_foreach.pig
divs  = load 'NYSE_dividends' as (exchange, symbol, date, dividends);
--make sure all strings are uppercase
upped = foreach divs generate UPPER(symbol) as symbol, dividends;
grpd  = group upped by symbol;   --output a bag upped for each value of symbol
--take a bag of integers, and produce one result for each group
sums  = foreach grpd generate group, SUM(upped.dividends);
```

In addition, eval funcs can take * as an argument, which passes the entire record to the function. They can also be invoked with no arguments at all.

For a complete list of UDFs that are provided with Pig, see Appendix A. For a discussion of how to invoke UDFs not distributed as part of Pig, see "User-Defined Functions" on page 68.

Generating complex data

It is sometimes useful in a `foreach` statement to build a complex field from simple fields. For example, you might want to combine two simple types together into a tuple. The same notation used for complex constants (see "Complex Types" on page 34) can be used to build complex types from scalar fields: [ ] for maps, ( ) for tuples, and { } for bags. There are some differences though:

- Instead of using # to separate the map key and value, use a comma:

```
divs  = load 'NYSE_dividends' as
    (exchange:chararray, symbol, date, dividends:double);
maps = foreach divs generate [exchange, dividends];
describe maps;
```

  maps: {map[double]}

The reason for using the comma as a delimiter is because # is also used in map projection. There could be ambiguity if it were used as the key/value delimiter. Consider the expression [a#b#c]. Pig has no idea if this means a map of key a#b and value c, or a map of key a and value b#c. With the comma delimiter, [a#b, c] creates a map of the key a#b and the value c. We don't have such a problem in map constant.

- You cannot create a single-field tuple—Pig will treat parentheses as an arithmetic operator:

```
divs  = load 'NYSE_dividends' as
    (exchange:chararray, symbol, date, dividends:double);
tuples = foreach divs generate (exchange), (exchange, dividends) as t;
describe tuples;
```

tuples: {exchange: chararray, t: (exchange: chararray, dividends: double)}

(exchange) will not create a tuple in this example.

- If the bag consists of single-item tuples, the parentheses around the item can be omitted:

```
divs  = load 'NYSE_dividends' as
    (exchange:chararray, symbol:chararray, date, dividends);
bags = foreach divs generate {exchange, symbol};
describe bags;
```

bags:

You can also use the built-in UDFs TOMAP, TOTUPLE, and TOBAG to generate complex fields from simple fields.

Naming fields in foreach

The result of each foreach statement is a new tuple, usually with a different schema than the tuple that was input to foreach. Pig can almost always infer the data types of the fields in this schema from the foreach statement. But it cannot always infer the names of those fields. For fields that are simple projections with no other operators applied, Pig keeps the same names as before:

```
divs = load 'NYSE_dividends' as (exchange:chararray, symbol:chararray,
        date:chararray, dividends:float);
sym  = foreach divs generate symbol;
describe sym;
```

sym: {symbol: chararray}

Once any expression beyond simple projection is applied, however, Pig does not assign a name to the field. If you do not explicitly assign a name, the field will be nameless and will be addressable only via a positional parameter; for example, $0. You can assign a name with the as clause:

```
divs    = load 'NYSE_dividends' as (exchange:chararray, symbol:chararray,
            date:chararray, dividends:float);
in_cents = foreach divs generate dividends * 100.0 as dividend,
            dividends * 100.0;
describe in_cents;
```

```
in_cents: {dividend: double,double}
```

The second field is unnamed since we didn't assign a name to it.

After a `flatten`, which can produce multiple values, you can assign a name to each value:

```
crawl = load 'webcrawl' as (url, pageid);
extracted = foreach crawl generate flatten(REGEX_EXTRACT_ALL(url,
    '(http|https)://(.*?)/(.*)')) as (protocol,
    host, path);
```

Notice that in a `foreach` the `as` is attached to each expression. This is different from in `load`, where it is attached to the entire statement. The reason for this will become clear when we discuss `flatten`.[4]

In a few cases Pig cannot infer the data type of an expression in a `foreach` statement. Consider the following example:

```
extracted = foreach crawl generate flatten(REGEX_EXTRACT_ALL(url,
    '(http|https)://(.*?)/(.*)')) as (protocol:chararray, host:chararray,
    path:chararray);
```

The UDF `REGEX_EXTRACT_ALL` only declares its return type as a tuple; it does not declare the types of the fields of that tuple. However, we know it will return a chararray. In this case you have the option to declare a type along with the name, as shown in this example. The syntax is the same as for declaring names and types in `load`. Note that until version 0.16, Pig does not insert a cast operator. It assumes you are correct in declaring the type. If you are not, this could result in an error.[5]

The following script will result in a compilation error:

```
in_cents = foreach divs generate (symbol, dividends)
    as (symbol:chararray, dividends:double);
```

On the left side, (`symbol`, `dividends`) will create a tuple. On the right side, (`symbol:chararray`, `dividends:double`) in the `as` statement declares two individual fields. They don't match. We need to change it to:

```
in_cents = foreach divs generate (symbol, dividends)
    as (t:(symbol:chararray, dividends:double));
```

This produces a tuple schema:

---

4 We will discuss the details of `flatten` in "flatten" on page 77. Here all you need to know is that, in this example `flatten` generates three fields: protocol, host, and path.

5 This will change in the future: Pig will insert a real cast operator to cast the field to the declared type. More detail can be found in PIG-2315 (*https://issues.apache.org/jira/browse/PIG-2315*).

```
in_cents: {t: (symbol: chararray,dividends: double)}
```

CASE expressions

Starting with Pig 0.12, you can use `CASE` for multicondition branches. (If you are using Pig 0.11 or earlier, a semantically equivalent chain of bincond operators can be constructed. `CASE` was added because it is much simpler.) Here's an example:

```
processed = FOREACH loaded GENERATE (
  CASE i
    WHEN 0 THEN 'one'
    WHEN 1 THEN 'two'
    ELSE 'three'
  END
);
```

Depending on the value of i, foreach will generate a chararray value of 'one', 'two', or 'three'.

Both the conditions (in this example 0 and 1) and the condition values (in this example 'one', etc.) can be expressions. If no value matches the condition and `ELSE` is missing, the result will be `null`. This syntax cannot be used to test for null values, since `null == null` is `null`, not `true`. In the following example, if gender is 'M' the result is 1, if gender is 'F' the result is 2, and if gender is something else, such as 'other', the result is `null`:

```
processed = FOREACH loaded GENERATE (
  CASE UPPER(gender)
    WHEN UPPER('m') THEN 1
    WHEN UPPER('f') THEN 2
  END
) as gendercode;
```

filter

The `filter` statement allows you to select which records will be retained in your data pipeline. A `filter` contains a predicate. If that predicate evaluates to true for a given record, that record will be passed down the pipeline. Otherwise, it will not.

Predicates can contain the equality operators you expect, including == to test equality and !=, >, >=, <, and <=. These comparators can be used on any scalar data type. == and != can be applied to maps and tuples. To use these with two tuples, both tuples must have either the same schema or no schema. None of the equality operators can be applied to bags.

Starting with Pig 0.12, you can test whether the value of a scalar field is within a set of values using the IN operator:

```
divs = load 'NYSE_dividends' as (exchange:chararray, symbol:chararray,
    date:chararray, dividends:float);
cme_ctb_cht = filter divs by symbol in ('CME', 'CTB', 'CHT');
```

Pig Latin follows the operator precedence rules that are standard in most programming languages, where arithmetic operators have precedence over equality operators. So, x + y == a + b is equivalent to (x + y) == (a + b).

For chararrays, users can test to see whether the chararray matches a regular expression:

```
-- filter_matches.pig
divs         = load 'NYSE_dividends' as (exchange:chararray, symbol:chararray,
                    date:chararray, dividends:float);
startswithcm = filter divs by symbol matches 'CM.*';
```

 Pig uses Java's regular expression format (*http://bit.ly/regexpat tern*). This format requires the entire chararray to match, not just a portion as in Perl-style regular expressions. For example, if you are looking for all fields that contain the string "fred", you must say '.*fred.*' and not 'fred'. The latter will match only the chararray fred.

You can find chararrays that do not match a regular expression by preceding the test with not:

```
-- filter_not_matches.pig
divs            = load 'NYSE_dividends' as (exchange:chararray, symbol:chararray,
                    date:chararray, dividends:float);
notstartswithcm = filter divs by not symbol matches 'CM.*';
```

You can combine multiple predicates into one by using the Boolean operators and and or, and you can reverse the outcome of any predicate by using the Boolean not operator. As is standard, the precedence of Boolean operators, from highest to lowest, is not, and, or. Thus, a and b or not c is equivalent to (a and b) or (not c).

Pig will short-circuit Boolean operations when possible. If the first (left) predicate of an and is false, the second (right) predicate will not be evaluated. So, in 1 == 2 and udf(x), the UDF will never be invoked. Similarly, if the first predicate of an or is true, the second predicate will not be evaluated. 1 == 1 or udf(x) will never invoke the UDF.

For Boolean operators, nulls follow the SQL ternary logic. Thus, x == null results in a value of null, not true (*even when x is null also*) or false. Filters pass through only those values that are true. Consider the following example:

```
A = load 'input.txt' as (x:int, y:int);
B1 = filter A by x == 2;
C1 = store B1 into 'output1';
```

```
B2 = filter A by x != 2;
C2 = store B2 into 'output2';
```

If the input file had three rows, (2,1), (null,1), (4,1), C1 would store (2,1), C2 would store (4,1), and (null,1) would appear in neither C1 nor C2. The way to look for null values is to use the is null operator, which returns true whenever the value is null. To find values that are not null, use is not null.

Likewise, null neither matches nor fails to match any regular expression value.

Just as there are UDFs to be used in evaluation expressions, there are UDFs specifically for filtering records, called *filter funcs*. These are eval funcs that return a Boolean value and can be invoked in the filter statement. Filter funcs can also be used in foreach statements.

group

The group statement collects together records with the same key. It is the first operator we have looked at that shares its syntax with SQL, but it is important to understand that the grouping operator in Pig Latin is fundamentally different from the one in SQL. In SQL the group by clause creates a group that must feed directly into one or more aggregate functions. In Pig Latin there is no direct connection between group and aggregate functions. Instead, group does exactly what it says: collects all records with the same value for the provided key together into a bag. You can then pass this to an aggregate function if you want, or do other things with it:

```
-- count.pig
daily = load 'NYSE_daily' as (exchange, stock);
grpd  = group daily by stock;
cnt   = foreach grpd generate group, COUNT(daily);
```

COUNT and COUNT_STAR

Both COUNT and COUNT_STAR count the tuples inside a bag. However, COUNT does not count a tuple if the first item is null. For example:

```
COUNT({(1),(2),(null)})=2
COUNT_STAR({(1),(2),(null)})=3
```

In the previous Pig script, if exchange contains null, you can use the following foreach statement to only count the stock with exchange:

```
cnt = foreach grpd generate group, COUNT(daily.exchange);
```

That example groups records by the key stock and then counts them. It is just as legitimate to group them and then store them for processing at a later time:

```
-- group.pig
daily = load 'NYSE_daily' as (exchange, stock);
grpd  = group daily by stock;
store grpd into 'by_group';
```

The records coming out of the group by statement have two fields: the key and the bag of collected records. The key field is named group.[6] The bag is named for the alias that was grouped, so in the previous examples it will be named daily and have the same schema as the relation daily. If the relation daily has no schema, the bag daily will have no schema. For each record in the group, the entire record (including the key) is in the bag. Changing the last line of the previous script from store grpd... to describe grpd; will produce:

```
grpd: {group: bytearray,daily: {exchange: bytearray,stock: bytearray}}
```

You can also group on multiple keys, but the keys must be surrounded by parentheses. The resulting records still have two fields. In this case, the group field is a tuple with a field for each key:

```
--twokey.pig
daily = load 'NYSE_daily' as (exchange, stock, date, dividends);
grpd  = group daily by (exchange, stock);
avg   = foreach grpd generate group, AVG(daily.dividends);
describe grpd;

grpd: {group: (exchange: bytearray,stock: bytearray),daily: {exchange: bytearray,
stock: bytearray,date: bytearray,dividends: bytearray}}
```

You can also use all to group together all of the records in your pipeline:

```
--countall.pig
daily = load 'NYSE_daily' as (exchange, stock);
grpd  = group daily all;
cnt   = foreach grpd generate COUNT(daily);
```

The record coming out of group all has the chararray literal all as a key. Usually this does not matter because you will pass the bag directly to an aggregate function such as COUNT. But if you plan to store the record or use it for another purpose, you might want to project out the artificial key first.

group is the first operator we have looked at that usually will force a reduce phase.[7] Grouping means collecting all records where the key has the same value. If the pipeline is in a map phase, this will force it to shuffle and then reduce. If the pipeline is

---

6 Thus, the keyword group is overloaded in Pig Latin. This is unfortunate and confusing, but would be hard to change now.

7 As explained previously, we are using MapReduce as the backend throughout the book for examples, unless otherwise noted. The same notion applies to Tez or Spark, although it may not be called a "reduce phase."

already in a reduce phase, this will force it to pass through the map, shuffle, and reduce phases.

Because grouping collects *all* records with the same value for the key, you often get skewed results. That is, just because you have specified that your job will have 100 reducers, there is no reason to expect that the number of values per key will be distributed evenly. The values might have a Gaussian or power law distribution.[8] For example, suppose you have an index of web pages and you group by the base URL. Certain values, such as yahoo.com, are going to have far more entries than most, which means that some reducers will get far more data than others. Because your MapReduce job is not finished (and any subsequent ones cannot start) until all your reducers have finished, this skew will significantly slow your processing. In some cases it will also be impossible for one reducer to manage that much data.

Pig has a number of ways that it tries to manage this skew to balance out the load across your reducers. The one that applies to grouping is Hadoop's *combiner*. This does not remove all skew, but it places a bound on it. And because for most jobs the number of mappers will be at most in the tens of thousands, even if the reducers get a skewed number of records, the absolute number of records per reducer will be small enough that the reducers can handle them quickly.

Unfortunately, not all calculations can be done using the combiner. Calculations that can be decomposed into any number of steps, such as sum, are called *distributive*. These fit nicely into the combiner. Calculations that can be decomposed into an initial step, any number of intermediate steps, and a final step are referred to as *algebraic*. Count is an example of such a function, where the initial step is a count and the intermediate and final steps are sums. Distributive is a special case of algebraic, where the initial, intermediate, and final steps are all the same. Session analysis, where you want to track a user's actions on a website, is an example of a calculation that is not algebraic. You must have all the records sorted by timestamp before you can start analyzing the user's interaction with the site.

Pig's operators and built-in UDFs use the combiner whenever possible, because of its skew-reducing features and because early aggregation greatly reduces the amount of data shipped over the network and written to disk, thus speeding performance significantly. UDFs can indicate when they can work with the combiner by implementing the Algebraic interface. For information on how to make your UDFs use the combiner, see "The Algebraic Interface" on page 186.

For information on how to determine the level of parallelism when executing your group operation, see "parallel" on page 65. Also, keep in mind that when using group all, you are necessarily serializing your pipeline. That is, this step and any steps after

---

8 In our experience, the vast majority of data tracking human activity follows a power law distribution.

it until you split out the single bag now containing all of your records will not be done in parallel.

Finally, group handles nulls in the same way that SQL handles them: by collecting all records with a null key into the same group. Note that this is in direct contradiction to the way expressions handle nulls (remember that neither null == null nor null != null is true) and to the way join (see "join" on page 62) handles nulls.

order by

The order statement sorts your data for you, producing a total order for your output data. Total order means that not only is the data sorted in each partition of your data, but it is also guaranteed that all records in partition *n* are less than all records in partition *n - 1* for all *n*. When your data is stored on HDFS, where each partition is a part file, this means that cat will output your data in order.

The syntax of order is similar to group. You indicate a key or set of keys by which you wish to order your data. One glaring difference is that there are no parentheses around the keys when multiple keys are indicated in order:

```
--order.pig
daily   = load 'NYSE_daily' as (exchange:chararray, symbol:chararray,
            date:chararray, open:float, high:float, low:float, close:float,
            volume:int, adj_close:float);
bydate = order daily by date;

--order2key.pig
daily          = load 'NYSE_daily' as (exchange:chararray, symbol:chararray,
                    date:chararray, open:float, high:float, low:float,
                    close:float, volume:int, adj_close:float);
bydatensymbol  = order daily by date, symbol;
```

It is also possible to reverse the order of the sort by appending desc to a key in the sort. In order statements with multiple keys, desc applies only to the key it immediately follows. Other keys will still be sorted in ascending order:

```
--orderdesc.pig
daily   = load 'NYSE_daily' as (exchange:chararray, symbol:chararray,
            date:chararray, open:float, high:float, low:float, close:float,
            volume:int, adj_close:float);
byclose = order daily by close desc, open;
dump byclose; -- open still sorted in ascending order
```

Data is sorted based on the types of the indicated fields: numeric values are sorted numerically; chararray fields are sorted lexically; and bytearray fields are sorted lexically, using byte values rather than character values. Sorting by map, tuple, or bag fields produces errors. For all data types, nulls are taken to be smaller than all possible values for that type, and thus will always appear first (or last when desc is used).

As discussed in the previous section, skew of the values in data is very common. This affects order just as it does group, causing some reducers to take significantly longer than others. To address this, Pig balances the output across reducers. It does this by first sampling the input of the order statement to get an estimate of the key distribution. Based on this sample, it then builds a partitioner that produces a balanced total order. For example, suppose you are ordering on a chararray field with the values a, b, e, e, e, e, e, m, q, r, z, and you have three reducers. The partitioner in this case would decide to partition your data such that values a–e go to reducer 1, e goes to reducer 2, and m–z go to reducer 3. Notice that the value e can be sent to either reducer 1 or 2. Some records with key e will be sent to reducer 1 and some to 2. This allows the partitioner to distribute the data evenly. In practice, we rarely see variance in reducer time exceed 10% when using this algorithm.

An important side effect of the way Pig distributes records to minimize skew is that it breaks the MapReduce convention that all instances of a given key are sent to the same partition. If you have other processing that depends on this convention, do not use Pig's order statement to sort data for it.

order always causes your data pipeline to go through a reduce phase. This is necessary to collect all equal records together. Also, Pig adds an additional MapReduce job to your pipeline to do the sampling. Because this sampling is very lightweight (it reads only the first record of every block[9]), it generally takes less than 5% of the total job time.

distinct

The distinct statement is very simple. It removes duplicate records. It works only on entire records, not on individual fields:

```
--distinct.pig
-- Find a distinct list of ticker symbols for each exchange.
-- This load will truncate the records, picking up just the first two fields.
daily   = load 'NYSE_daily' as (exchange:chararray, symbol:chararray);
uniq    = distinct daily;
```

Because it needs to collect like records together in order to determine whether they are duplicates, distinct forces a reduce phase. It does make use of the combiner to remove any duplicate records it can delete in the map phase.

The use of distinct shown here is equivalent to select distinct x in SQL. To learn how to do the equivalent of select count(distinct x), see "Nested foreach" on page 79.

---

9 Actually, it reads all records but skips all but the first.

join

`join` is one of the workhorses of data processing, and it is likely to be in many of your Pig Latin scripts. `join` selects records from one input to put together with records from another input. This is done by indicating keys for each input. When those keys are equal,[10] the two rows are joined. Records for which no match is found are dropped:

```
--join.pig
daily = load 'NYSE_daily' as (exchange, symbol, date, open, high, low, close,
            volume, adj_close);
divs  = load 'NYSE_dividends' as (exchange, symbol, date, dividends);
jnd   = join daily by symbol, divs by symbol;
```

You can also join on multiple keys. In all cases you must have the same number of keys, and they must be of the same or compatible types (where compatible means that an implicit cast can be inserted; see "Casts" on page 39):

```
-- join2key.pig
daily = load 'NYSE_daily' as (exchange, symbol, date, open, high, low, close,
            volume, adj_close);
divs  = load 'NYSE_dividends' as (exchange, symbol, date, dividends);
jnd   = join daily by (symbol, date), divs by (symbol, date);
```

Like `foreach`, `join` preserves the names of the fields of the inputs passed to it. It also prepends the name of the relation the field came from, followed by `::`. Adding `describe jnd;` to the end of the previous example produces:

```
jnd: {daily::exchange: bytearray,daily::symbol: bytearray,daily::date: bytearray,
daily::open: bytearray,daily::high: bytearray,daily::low: bytearray,
daily::close: bytearray,daily::volume: bytearray,daily::adj_close: bytearray,
divs::exchange: bytearray,divs::symbol: bytearray,divs::date: bytearray,
divs::dividends: bytearray}
```

The `daily::` prefix needs to be used only when the field name is no longer unique in the record. In this example, you will need to use `daily::date` or `divs::date` if you wish to refer to one of the `date` fields after the join, but fields such as `open` and `divs` do not need a prefix because there is no ambiguity.

Pig also supports outer joins. In outer joins, records that do not have a match on the other side are included, with null values being filled in for the missing fields. Outer joins can be `left`, `right`, or `full`. A left outer join means records from the left side will be included even when they do not have a match on the right side. Likewise, a right outer join means records from the right side will be included even when they do

---

10 Actually, joins can be on any condition, not just equality, but Pig only supports joins on equality (called equi-joins). See "cross" on page 90 for information on how to do non-equi-joins in Pig.

not have a match on the left side. A full outer join means records from both sides are taken even when they do not have matches. Here's an example of a left outer join:

```
--leftjoin.pig
daily = load 'NYSE_daily' as (exchange, symbol, date, open, high, low, close,
            volume, adj_close);
divs  = load 'NYSE_dividends' as (exchange, symbol, date, dividends);
jnd   = join daily by (symbol, date) left outer, divs by (symbol, date);
```

outer is optional and can be omitted. Unlike in some SQL implementations, however, full is not optional. C = join A by x outer, B by u; will generate a syntax error, not a full outer join.

Outer joins are supported only when Pig knows the schema of the data on the side(s) for which it might need to fill in nulls. Thus, for left outer joins, it must know the schema of the right side; for right outer joins, it must know the schema of the left side; and for full outer joins, it must know both. This is because, without the schema, Pig will not know how many null values to fill in.[11]

As in SQL, null values for keys do not match anything—*even null values from the other input.* So, for inner joins, all records with null key values are dropped. For outer joins, they will be retained but will not match any records from the other input.

Pig can also do multiple joins in a single operation, as long as they are all being joined on the same key(s). This can be done only for inner joins:

```
A = load 'input1' as (x, y);
B = load 'input2' as (u, v);
C = load 'input3' as (e, f);
alpha = join A by x, B by u, C by e;
```

Self joins are supported, though the data must be loaded twice:

```
--selfjoin.pig
-- For each stock, find all dividends that increased between two dates
divs1     = load 'NYSE_dividends' as (exchange:chararray, symbol:chararray,
              date:chararray, dividends);
divs2     = load 'NYSE_dividends' as (exchange:chararray, symbol:chararray,
              date:chararray, dividends);
jnd       = join divs1 by symbol, divs2 by symbol;
increased = filter jnd by divs1::date < divs2::date and
              divs1::dividends < divs2::dividends;
```

---

11 You may object that Pig could determine this by looking at other records in the join and inferring the correct number of fields. However, this does not work, for two reasons. First, when no schema is present, Pig does not enforce a semantic that every record has the same schema. So, assuming Pig can infer one record from another is not valid. Second, there might be no records in the join that match, and thus Pig might have no record to infer from.

If the preceding code were changed to the following, it would fail:

```
--selfjoin.pig
-- For each stock, find all dividends that increased between two dates
divs1     = load 'NYSE_dividends' as (exchange:chararray, symbol:chararray,
                date:chararray, dividends);
jnd       = join divs1 by symbol, divs1 by symbol;
increased = filter jnd by divs1::date < divs2::date and
                divs1::dividends < divs2::dividends;
```

It seems like this ought to work, since Pig could split the `divs1` dataset and send it to `join` twice. But the problem is that field names would be ambiguous after the join, so the `load` statement must be written twice. The next best thing would be for Pig to figure out that these two `load` statements are loading the same input and then run the load only once, but it does not do that currently.

Pig does these joins in MapReduce by using the map phase to annotate each record with which input it came from. It then uses the join key as the shuffle key. Thus, `join` forces a new reduce phase. Once all of the records with the same value for the key are collected together, Pig does a cross product between the records from both inputs. To minimize memory usage, it has MapReduce order the records coming into the reducer using the input annotation it added in the map phase. So, all of the records for the left input arrive first, and Pig caches these in memory. All of the records for the right input then arrive. As each of these records arrives, it is crossed with each record from the left side to produce an output record. In a multiway join, the left $n - 1$ inputs are held in memory, and the nth is streamed through. It is important to keep this in mind when writing joins in your Pig queries. If you know that one of your inputs has more records per value of the chosen key, placing that larger input on the right side of your join will lower memory usage and possibly increase your script's performance.

limit

Sometimes you want to see only a limited number of results. `limit` allows you do this:

```
--limit.pig
divs    = load 'NYSE_dividends';
first10 = limit divs 10;
```

The example here will return at most 10 lines (if your input has less than 10 lines total, it will return them all). Note that for all operators except `order`, Pig does not guarantee the order in which records are produced. Thus, because *NYSE_dividends* has more than 10 records, the example script could return different results every time it's run. Putting an `order` *immediately* before the `limit` will guarantee that the same results are returned every time.

limit causes an additional reduce phase, since it needs to collect the records together to count how many it is returning. It does optimize this phase by limiting the output of each map and then applying the limit again in the reducer. In the case where limit is combined with order, the two are done together on the map and the reduce. That is, on the map side, the records are sorted by MapReduce and the limit is applied in the combiner. They are then sorted again by MapReduce as part of the shuffle, and Pig applies the limit again in the reducer.

Whenever possible, Pig terminates reading of the input early once it has reached the number of records specified by limit. This can significantly reduce the time it takes to run the script.

sample

sample offers a simple way to get a sample of your data. It reads through all of your data but returns only a percentage of rows. What percentage it returns is expressed as a double value, between 0 and 1. So, in the following example, 0.1 indicates 10%:

```
--sample.pig
divs = load 'NYSE_dividends';
some = sample divs 0.1;
```

Currently the sampling algorithm is very simple. The sample A 0.1 is rewritten to filter A by random() <= 0.1. Obviously this is nondeterministic, so results of a script with sample will vary with every run. Also, the percentage will not be an exact match, but close. There has been discussion about adding more sophisticated sampling techniques, but it has not been done yet.

parallel

One of Pig's core claims is that it provides a language for parallel data processing. One of the tenets of Pig's philosophy is that Pigs are domestic animals (see "The Pig Philosophy" on page 10), so Pig prefers that you tell it how parallel to be. To this end, it provides the parallel clause.

The parallel clause can be attached to any relational operator in Pig Latin. However, it controls only reduce-side parallelism, so it makes sense only for operators that force a reduce phase. These are: group*, order, distinct, join*, limit, cogroup*, cross, and union. Operators marked with an asterisk have multiple implementations, some of which force a reduce and some of which do not. union forces a reduce only in Tez. For details on this and on operators not covered in this chapter, see Chapter 5. `parallel` also works in local modes, though it does not make Pig scripts run faster than a single reduce as reduces run serially.[12]

Let's take a look at an example:

```
--parallel.pig
daily   = load 'NYSE_daily' as (exchange, symbol, date, open, high, low, close,
              volume, adj_close);
bysymbl = group daily by symbol parallel 10;
```

In this example, `parallel` will cause the MapReduce job spawned by Pig to have 10 reducers. If you list the files inside *output*, you will see 10 part files.

However, the `group all` statement aggregates all inputs, and it is impossible to use more than one reducer. No matter how many reduce tasks you specify in the `paral lel` clause, Pig will only use one:

```
daily   = load 'NYSE_daily' as (exchange, symbol, date, open, high, low, close,
              volume, adj_close);
bysymbl = group daily all parallel 10;
```

You can also see this by listing the files in *output*.

`parallel` clauses apply only to the statements to which they are attached; they do not carry through the script. So, if this `group` were followed by an `order`, `parallel` would need to be set for that `order` separately. Most likely the `group` will reduce your data size significantly and you will want to change the parallelism:

```
--parallel.pig
daily   = load 'NYSE_daily' as (exchange, symbol, date, open, high, low, close,
              volume, adj_close);
bysymbl = group daily by symbol parallel 10;
average = foreach bysymbl generate group, AVG(daily.close) as avg;
sorted  = order average by avg desc parallel 2;
```

If, however, you do not want to set `parallel` separately for every reduce-invoking operator in your script, you can set a script-wide value using the `set` command. In this script, all MapReduce jobs will be done with 10 reducers:

```
--defaultparallel.pig
set default_parallel 10;
daily   = load 'NYSE_daily' as (exchange, symbol, date, open, high, low, close,
              volume, adj_close);
bysymbl = group daily by symbol;
average = foreach bysymbl generate group, AVG(daily.close) as avg;
sorted  = order average by avg desc;
```

---

12 Older versions of Pig ignore `parallel` in local mode due to a Hadoop bug. This bug was fixed in Pig 0.14. Note that parallel tasks are run serially in local mode.

When you set a `default_parallel` level, you can still add a `parallel` clause to any statement to override the default value. Thus, you can set a default value as a base to use in most cases and specifically add a `parallel` clause only when you have an operator that needs a different value.

All of this is rather static, however. What happens if you run the same script across different inputs that have different characteristics? Or what if your input data varies significantly sometimes? You do not want to have to edit your script each time. Using parameter substitution, you can write your `parallel` clauses with variables, providing values for those variables at runtime. See "Parameter Substitution" on page 108 for details.

So far, we have assumed that you know what your `parallel` value should be. See "Select the Right Level of Parallelism" on page 139 for information on how to determine that.

Finally, what happens if you do not specify a `parallel` level? Pig will do a gross estimate of what the parallelism should be set to. It looks at the initial input size, assumes there will be no data size changes, and then allocates a reducer for every 1 GB of data by default. This can be customized by setting `pig.exec.reduc ers.bytes.per.reducer`. The maximum number of reducers to be used in the estimation is defined in `pig.exec.reducers.max`, which defaults to `999`. It must be emphasized that this is not a good algorithm. It is provided only to prevent mistakes that result in scripts running very slowly and, in some extreme cases, mistakes that cause MapReduce itself to have problems. This is a safety net, not an optimizer.

Map Parallelism

`parallel` only lets you set reduce parallelism. What about map parallelism? We see users try setting `mapred.map.tasks` in Pig, but that doesn't work. MapReduce only allows users to set reduce parallelism: it controls map parallelism itself. In Map-Reduce, data is read using a class that extends `InputFormat`. Part of an `InputFormat`'s purpose is to tell MapReduce how many map tasks to run. It also suggests where they should be run.

Because Pig cannot control map parallelism, it cannot expose that to its users either. However, you can influence how MapReduce decides to split your data. If you are using `PigStorage` to load your data, the `InputFormat` it uses, `TextInputFormat`, takes a configuration value `mapreduce.input.fileinputformat.split.maxsize`. This controls the size of the splits. Thus, if you know your input size you can divide it by the desired number of splits and set this value accordingly.

For complete control, Pig allows you to build and run your own `InputFormat` as part of building your own load function. See Chapter 10 for details on how to do this.

Pig's split combination behavior also impacts the number of map tasks. For efficiency, Pig combines small splits together and processes them in a single map. This is especially useful if you have lots of small input files. After your load function's `Input Format` returns input splits, Pig will combine splits that are smaller than `pig.maxCombinedSplitSize`. By default this is set to the block size of the cluster.

User-Defined Functions

Much of the power of Pig lies in its ability to let users combine its operators with their own or others' code via UDFs. Pig UDFs can be written in many programming languages, including Java, Jython, JavaScript, Ruby, Groovy (since Pig 0.11), and Python[13] (since Pig 0.12).

Pig itself comes packaged with a large number of built-in UDFs. For a complete list and descriptions of the built-in UDFs, see "Built-in UDFs" on page 301.

PiggyBank (*https://cwiki.apache.org/confluence/display/PIG/PiggyBank*) is a collection of user-contributed UDFs that is packaged and released along with Pig. PiggyBank UDFs are not included in the Pig JAR, and thus you have to register them manually in your scripts. See "PiggyBank" on page 332 for more information.

There are also third-party Pig UDF libraries, notably DataFu (*https://datafu.incuba tor.apache.org/*) from LinkedIn and Elephant Bird (*https://github.com/twitter/ elephant-bird/*) from Twitter.

Of course, you can also write your own UDFs or use those written by other users. For details of how to write your own, see Chapter 9. Finally, you can use some static Java functions as UDFs as well.

Registering Java UDFs

When you use a UDF that is not already built into Pig, Pig needs to be able to find the Java JAR that contains the UDF. If the JAR is in your Java classpath, then Pig will automatically locate and load the JAR. If not, you have to tell Pig where to look for that UDF. This is done via the `register` command. For example, let's say you want to use the `Reverse` UDF provided in PiggyBank (for information on where to find the PiggyBank JAR, see "PiggyBank" on page 332):

---

13 The difference between Jython UDFs and Python UDFs is that the former use Jython and the latter use CPython as the engine. In fact, Python is the only non-JVM language in the list. Python UDFs are usually slower since they run in a separate process and thus need to serialize the parameters in and deserialize the result out. However, since Jython does not support all Python features and libraries, Python provides an alternative.

```
--register.pig
register 'your_path_to_piggybank/piggybank.jar';
divs      = load 'NYSE_dividends' as (exchange:chararray, symbol:chararray,
               date:chararray, dividends:float);
backwards = foreach divs generate
               org.apache.pig.piggybank.evaluation.string.Reverse(symbol);
```

This example tells Pig that it needs to include code from *your_path_to_piggybank/piggybank.jar*.

If your UDF requires additional JARs beyond the one it is contained in (e.g., third-party libraries), Pig may ship those automatically if the UDF supports "auto-shipping" (see "Shipping JARs Automatically" on page 185 and "Shipping JARs Automatically" on page 228). With auto-shipping, the UDF will tell Pig about the dependent JARs it requires. However, if your UDF implementation is old or does not support the new auto-shipping features, you will have to register those JARs manually even if they are present in your Java classpath. Pig cannot do the dependency analysis to determine what additional JARs a UDF requires.

In this example, we have to give Pig the full package and class name of the UDF. This verbosity can be alleviated in two ways. The first option is to use the `define` command (see "define and UDFs" on page 71). The second option is to include a set of packages on the command line for Pig to search when looking for UDFs. So, if instead of invoking Pig with `pig register.pig` we change our invocation to this:

```
pig -Dudf.import.list=org.apache.pig.piggybank.evaluation.string register.pig
```

We can change our script to:

```
register 'your_path_to_piggybank/piggybank.jar';
divs      = load 'NYSE_dividends' as (exchange:chararray, symbol:chararray,
               date:chararray, dividends:float);
backwards = foreach divs generate Reverse(symbol);
```

Using yet another property, we can get rid of the `register` command as well. If we add `-Dpig.additional.jars=/usr/local/pig/piggybank/piggybank.jar` to our command line, this command is no longer necessary.[14]

You may wonder if you should add your JARs to the classpath as well. The quick answer is no. When you register the JARs, Pig also changes its own class loader to include them, so it will find the JARs in the frontend even though the classpath does

---

14 The delimiter in `pig.additional.jars` is a colon. On Windows, the colon is also used in drive partitions. To resolve this conflict, Pig 0.14 introduced `pig.additional.jars.comma`, which uses a comma as the delimiter instead.

not include them. However, if you do not register your JARs and you are expecting Pig to ship JARs automatically (using the auto-shipping feature discussed in the previous note), you need to add them in your classpath. Otherwise, Pig won't know how to find them.

In many cases it is better to deal with registration and definition issues explicitly in the script via the `register` and `define` commands than to use these properties. Otherwise, everyone who runs your script has to know how to configure the command line. However, in some situations your scripts will always use the same set of JARs and always look in the same places for them. For instance, you might have a set of JARs used by everyone in your company. In this case, placing these properties in a shared properties file and using that with your Pig Latin scripts will make sharing those UDFs easier and ensure that everyone is using the correct versions of them.

The `register` command can also take an HDFS path as well as other protocols that Hadoop understands, such as S3. You could say `register 'hdfs:///user/jar/acme.jar';` or `register 's3://mybucket/jar/acme.jar';` if your JARs are stored in HDFS or S3.

`register` accepts globs too, so if all of the JARs you need were stored in one directory, you could include them all with `register '/usr/local/share/pig/udfs/*.jar'`.

Registering UDFs in Scripting Languages

`register` is also used to locate resources for scripting UDFs that you use in your Pig Latin scripts. In this case you do not register a JAR, but rather a script that contains your UDF. The script must be referenced from your current directory. Using the examples provided in the example code, copying *udfs/python/production.py* to the *data* directory looks like this:

```
--batting_production.pig
register 'production.py' using jython as bballudfs;
players  = load 'baseball' as (name:chararray, team:chararray,
            pos:bag{t:(p:chararray)}, bat:map[]);
nonnull  = filter players by bat#'slugging_percentage' is not null and
            bat#'on_base_percentage' is not null;
calcprod = foreach nonnull generate name, bballudfs.production(
            (float)bat#'slugging_percentage',
            (float)bat#'on_base_percentage');
```

The important differences here are the `using jython` and `as bballudfs` portions of the `register` statement. `using jython` tells Pig that this UDF is written in Jython, not Java, and it should use Jython to compile the UDF.

`as bballudfs` defines a namespace that UDFs from this file are placed in. All UDFs from this file must now be invoked as `bballudfs.`*udfname*. Each script file you load should be given a separate namespace. This avoids naming collisions when you register two scripts with duplicate function names.

You can register UDFs written in JavaScript, JRuby, Groovy, and Python using similar syntax:

JavaScript
```
register 'production.js' using javascript as bballudfs;
```

JRuby
```
register 'production.rb' using jruby as bballudfs;
```

Groovy
```
register 'production.groovy' using groovy as bballudfs;
```

Python
```
register 'production.py' using streaming_python as bballudfs;
```

define and UDFs

As was alluded to earlier, `define` can be used to provide an alias so that you do not have to use full package names for your Java UDFs. It can also be used to provide constructor arguments to your UDFs. `define` is used in defining streaming commands too, but this section covers only its UDF-related features. For information on using `define` with streaming, see "stream" on page 99.

The following provides an example of using `define` to provide an alias for `org.apache.pig.piggybank.evaluation.string.Reverse`:

```
--define.pig
register 'your_path_to_piggybank/piggybank.jar';
define reverse org.apache.pig.piggybank.evaluation.string.Reverse();
divs     = load 'NYSE_dividends' as (exchange:chararray, symbol:chararray,
                date:chararray, dividends:float);
backwards = foreach divs generate reverse(symbol);
```

Eval and filter functions can also take one or more strings as constructor arguments. If you are using a UDF that takes constructor arguments, `define` is the place to provide those arguments. For example, consider a method `CurrencyConverter` that takes two constructor arguments, the first indicating which currency you are converting from and the second which currency you are converting to:

```
--define_constructor_args.pig
register 'acme.jar';
define convert com.acme.financial.CurrencyConverter('dollar', 'euro');
divs     = load 'NYSE_dividends' as (exchange:chararray, symbol:chararray,
                date:chararray, dividends:float);
backwards = foreach divs generate convert(dividends);
```

Calling Static Java Functions

Java has a rich collection of utilities and libraries. Because Pig is implemented in Java, some of these functions can be exposed to Pig users. Starting in version 0.8, Pig offers invoker methods that allow you to treat certain static Java functions as if they were Pig UDFs.

Any public static Java function that takes either no arguments or some combination of `int`, `long`, `float`, `double`, `String`, or arrays thereof[15] and returns an `int`, `long`, `float`, `double`, or `String` value can be invoked in this way.

Because Pig Latin does not support overloading on return types, there is an invoker for each return type: `InvokeForInt`, `InvokeForLong`, `InvokeForFloat`, `InvokeForDouble`, and `InvokeForString`. You must pick the appropriate invoker for the type you wish to return. These methods take two constructor arguments. The first is the full package, class name, and method name. The second is a space-separated list of parameters the Java function expects. Only the types of the parameters are given. If the parameter is an array, `[]` (square brackets) are appended to the type name. If the method takes no parameters, the second constructor argument is omitted.

For example, if you wanted to use Java's `Integer` class to translate decimal values to hexadecimal values, you could do:

```
--invoker.pig
define hex InvokeForString('java.lang.Integer.toHexString', 'int');
divs  = load 'NYSE_daily' as (exchange, symbol, date, open, high, low,
            close, volume, adj_close);
nonnull = filter divs by volume is not null;
inhex = foreach nonnull generate symbol, hex((int)volume);
```

If your method takes an array of types, Pig will expect to pass it a bag where each tuple has a single field of that type. So, if you had a Java method called `com.yourcompany.Stats.stdev` that took an array of doubles, you could use it like this:

```
define stdev InvokeForDouble('com.acme.Stats.stdev', 'double[]');
A = load 'input' as (id: int, dp:double);
B = group A by id;
C = foreach B generate group, stdev(A.dp);
```

---

15 For `int`, `long`, `float`, and `double`, invoker methods can call Java functions that take the scalar types but not the associated Java classes (so `int` but not `Integer`, etc.).

Invokers do not use the `Accumulator` or `Algebraic` interfaces, and are thus likely to be much slower and to use much more memory than UDFs written specifically for Pig. This means that before you pass an array argument to an invoker method, you should think carefully about whether those inefficiencies are acceptable. For more information on these interfaces, see "The Accumulator Interface" on page 190 and "The Algebraic Interface" on page 186.

Invoking Java functions in this way does have a small cost because reflection is used to find and invoke the methods.

Invoker functions throw a Java `IllegalArgumentException` when they are passed null input. You should place a filter before the invocation to prevent this.

Calling Hive UDFs

Pig 0.15 added support for calling Apache Hive UDFs inside Pig.

There are three types of UDFs in Hive: standard UDFs, UDTFs (user-defined table-generating functions), and UDAFs (user-defined aggregate functions). Hive's standard UDFs are similar to Pig's standard UDFs, which take one input and produce one output at a time.

A Hive standard UDF extends either `org.apache.hadoop.hive.ql.exec.UDF` or `org.apache.hadoop.hive.ql.udf.generic.GenericUDF`. Hive's UDTFs, on the other hand, are able to produce any number of outputs per input. Hive UDTFs extend `org.apache.hadoop.hive.ql.udf.generic.GenericUDTF`. Hive's UDAFs are similar to Pig's algebraic UDFs in the sense that both aggregate the inputs and produce one output. Hive UDAFs extend either `org.apache.hadoop.hive.ql.udf.generic.AbstractGenericUDAFResolver` or `org.apache.hadoop.hive.ql.exec.UDAF` . For more information about Hive UDFs, please refer to the Hive UDF documentation (*http://bit.ly/languagemanualudf*).

Hive UDFs are accessed via corresponding built-in Pig UDFs. For a standard Hive UDF, invoke `HiveUDF`, for a Hive UDTF invoke `HiveUDTF`, and for a Hive UDAF invoke `HiveUDAF`.

All three types of UDF share the same syntax. Here is one example of invoking a standard Hive UDF:

```
define lower HiveUDF('org.apache.hadoop.hive.ql.udf.generic.StringLower');
divs = load 'NYSE_dividends' as (exchange:chararray, symbol:chararray,
                date:chararray, dividends:float);
lowersymbol = foreach divs generate exchange, lower(symbol), date, dividends;
```

You need to pass the name of the Hive UDF as a constructor argument to `HiveUDF`. The name you pass can be the fully qualified class name, or the abbreviation defined in the Hive `FunctionRegistry` for built-in Hive UDFs. In the preceding example, `org.apache.hadoop.hive.ql.udf.generic.StringLower` is a Hive built-in UDF and has the abbreviation `lower`, so we can rewrite the `define` statement as follows:

```
define lower HiveUDF('lower');
```

Here is an example using a Hive UDTF:

```
define posexplode HiveUDTF('posexplode');
divs = load 'NYSE_dividends' as (exchange:chararray, symbol:chararray,
                    date:chararray, dividends:float);
grouped = group divs by symbol;
exploded = foreach grouped generate flatten(posexplode(divs));
```

For every input, `HiveUDTF` creates a bag of the outputs. There is also one additional output that includes the outputs generated in the `close` method of the Hive UDTF. This is because the Hive UDTF may choose to generate an additional output when it is informed that it has seen all its input.[16] You will need to flatten the bag to get the same flattened outputs as Hive.

Here is an example with `HiveUDAF`:

```
define variance HiveUDAF('variance');
divs = load 'NYSE_dividends' as (exchange:chararray, symbol:chararray,
                    date:chararray, dividends:double);
grouped = group divs by symbol;
aggregated = foreach grouped generate variance(divs.dividends);
```

`HiveUDAF` is implemented as an algebraic UDF. Algebraic Pig UDFs aggregate their input both in the combiner and in the reducer. However, the way Hive aggregates inputs is very different from how Pig does it. Hive does not use the combiner; rather, it handles aggregation itself in the map task. `HiveUDAF` fills the gap by simulation. In the combiner, `HiveUDAF` invokes the `iterate` and `terminatePartial` methods of the Hive UDAF. In the reducer, `HiveUDAF` invokes the Hive UDAF's `merge` and `termi nate` methods.

The other difference between Hive UDFs and Pig UDFs is in the initialization stage. Hive uses the class `ObjectInspector` to communicate the input schema to a UDF on the frontend, while Pig uses its `Schema` class. Hive's `ObjectInspector` carries a little more information: whether an input field is a constant or not. Pig UDFs have no way to tell and thus cannot pass this information to Hive UDFs. To fill the gap, `HiveUDF` provides an optional second constructor argument carrying constant inputs. Here is one example:

---

16 You may wonder what values other fields in the `foreach` will have for this additional output. Pig attaches an artificial all null input to the `foreach` before generating the outputs. Thus, fields besides the `HiveUDTF` field will be null (unless they have a constant or a UDF that produces a nonnull result).

```
define in_file HiveUDF('in_file', '(null, \'symbol.txt\')');
divs = load 'NYSE_dividends' as (exchange:chararray, symbol:chararray,
                    date:chararray, dividends:float);
infile = foreach divs generate symbol, in_file(symbol, 'symbol.txt');
```

The second construct or argument, (null, 'symbol.txt'), tells Pig the second argument for in_file is a string constant, 'symbol.txt'. For the first field, which is not a constant, we simply put null. Note that the single quotes need to be escaped. HiveUDF understands double quotes as well, so you can use double quotes instead of escaping:

```
define in_file HiveUDF('in_file', '(null, "symbol.txt")');
```

In the foreach statement, you need to put the 'symbol.txt' string in the position of the second input field as well. This is because some Hive UDFs use the constant inferred from ObjectInspector while other Hive UDFs use the actual input data. It is assumed both are the same value.

Pig also simulates the runtime environment for Hive UDFs. The configuration object and counters inside Hive UDFs function properly within Pig.

Not surprisingly, there is some overhead when using Hive UDFs in Pig. This is caused by converting input and output objects between Pig data types and Hive data types, simulations, extra method calls, runtime environment preparations, etc. You should expect approximately a 10–20% slowdown compared to implementing the same functionality in a Pig UDF. But the convenience of invoking existing functionality rather than reimplementing it in many cases outweighs the performance losses. Finally, it is worth mentioning that as a result of this feature, an interesting third-party library now available in Pig is Hivemall (*https://github.com/daijyc/hivemall/wiki/PigHome*), which is a large set of Hive UDFs for machine learning.[17] With it, you can use many popular machine learning algorithms in Pig.

---

17 At the time of writing, Hivemall had just been accepted as an Apache incubator project (*http://incubator.apache.org/projects/hivemall.html*).

## CHAPTER 5

Advanced Pig Latin

In the previous chapter we worked through the basics of Pig Latin. In this chapter we will plumb its depths, and we will also discuss how Pig handles more complex data flows. Finally, we will look at how to use macros and modules to modularize your scripts.

Advanced Relational Operations

We will now discuss the more advanced Pig Latin operators, as well as additional options for operators that were introduced in the previous chapter.

Advanced Features of foreach

In our introduction to foreach (see "foreach" on page 49), we discussed how it could take a list of expressions to output for every record in your data pipeline. Now we will look at ways it can explode the number of records in your pipeline, and also how it can be used to apply a set of operations to each record.

flatten

Sometimes you have data in a bag or a tuple and you want to remove that level of nesting. The *baseball* data available on GitHub (see "Code Examples in This Book" on page xiv) can be used as an example. Because a player can play more than one position, position is stored in a bag. This allows us to still have one entry per player in the *baseball* file.[1] But when you want to switch around your data on the fly and group by a particular position, you need a way to pull those entries out of the bag. To do this, Pig provides the flatten modifier in foreach:

```
--flatten.pig
players = load 'baseball' as (name:chararray, team:chararray,
            position:bag{t:(p:chararray)}, bat:map[]);
pos     = foreach players generate name, flatten(position) as position;
bypos   = group pos by position;
```

A foreach with a flatten produces a cross product of every record in the bag with all of the other expressions in the generate statement. Looking at the first record in *baseball*, we see it is the following (replacing tabs with commas for clarity):

```
Jorge Posada,New York Yankees,{(Catcher),(Designated_hitter)},...
```

Once this has passed through the flatten statement, it will be two records:

```
Jorge Posada,Catcher
Jorge Posada,Designated_hitter
```

If there is more than one bag and both are flattened, this cross product will be done with members of each bag as well as other expressions in the generate statement. So, rather than getting *n* rows (where *n* is the number of records in one bag), you will get *n * m* rows.

One side effect that surprises many users is that if the bag is empty, no records are produced. So, if there had been an entry in *baseball* with no position, either because the bag was null or empty, that record would not be contained in the output of *flatten.pig*. The record with the empty bag would be swallowed by foreach. There are a couple of reasons for this behavior. One, since Pig may or may not have the schema of the data in the bag, it might have no idea how to fill in nulls for the missing fields. Two, from a mathematical perspective, this is what you would expect. Crossing a set S with the empty set results in the empty set. If you wish to avoid this, use a bincond to replace empty bags with a constant bag:

```
--flatten_noempty.pig
players = load 'baseball' as (name:chararray, team:chararray,
            position:bag{t:(p:chararray)}, bat:map[]);
noempty = foreach players generate name,
            ((position is null or IsEmpty(position)) ? {('unknown')} : position)
```

---

[1] Those with database experience will notice that this is a violation of the first normal form as defined by E. F. Codd. This intentional denormalization of data is very common in online analytical processing systems in general, and in large data-processing systems such as Hadoop in particular. RDBMS tend to make joins common and then work to optimize them. In systems such as Hadoop, where storage is cheap and joins are expensive, it is generally better to use nested data structures to avoid the joins.

```
           as position;
pos      = foreach noempty generate name, flatten(position) as position;
bypos    = group pos by position;
```

`flatten` can also be applied to a tuple. In this case, it does not produce a cross product; instead, it elevates each field in the tuple to a top-level field. Again, empty tuples will remove the entire record.

If the fields in a bag or tuple that is being flattened have names, Pig will carry those names along. As with `join`, to avoid ambiguity, each field name will have the bag's name and `::` prepended to it. As long as the field name is not ambiguous, you are not required to use the *bagname*`::` prefix.

If you wish to change the names of the fields, or if the fields initially did not have names, you can attach an `as` clause to your `flatten`, as in the preceding example. If there is more than one field in the bag or tuple that you are assigning names to, you must surround the set of field names with parentheses.

Finally, if you flatten a bag or tuple without a schema and do not provide an `as` clause, the resulting records coming out of your `foreach` will have a null schema. This is because Pig will not know how many fields the `flatten` will result in.

Nested foreach

So far, all of the examples of `foreach` that we have seen immediately generate one or more lines of output. But `foreach` is more powerful than this. It can also apply a set of relational operations to each record in your pipeline. This is referred to as a nested `foreach`, or inner `foreach`. One example of how this can be used is to find the number of unique entries in a group. For example, to find the number of unique stock symbols for each exchange in the *NYSE_daily* data:

```
--distinct_symbols.pig
daily    = load 'NYSE_daily' as (exchange, symbol); -- not interested in
                                                    -- other fields
grpd     = group daily by exchange;
uniqcnt  = foreach grpd {
           sym      = daily.symbol;
           uniq_sym = distinct sym;
           generate group, COUNT(uniq_sym);
};
```

There are several new things here to unpack; we will walk through each. In this example, rather than `generate` immediately following `foreach`, a `{` (open brace) signals that we will be nesting operators inside this `foreach`. In this nested code, each record passed to `foreach` is handled one at a time.

In the first line we see a syntax that we have not seen outside of `foreach`. In fact, `sym = daily.symbol` would not be legal outside of `foreach`. It is roughly equivalent to the

```
```

top-level statement `sym = foreach grpd generate daily.symbol`, but it is not stated that way inside the `foreach` because it is not really another `foreach`. There is no
relation for it to be associated with (that is, `grpd` is not defined here). This line takes
the bag `daily` and produces a new relation `sym`, which is a bag with tuples that have
only the field `symbol`.

The second line applies the `distinct` operator to the relation, `sym`. You can also combine the first two lines into a single line:

```
uniq_sym = distinct daily.symbol;
```

Note that, in general, relational operators can be applied only to relations; they cannot be applied to expressions. `distinct` inside `foreach` is the only exception. It can
take a list of fields of a relation. Internally, Pig will translate this into a nested `dis
tinct` followed by a nested `foreach`. Other expressions are not accepted. The reason
for such a restriction is to make Pig Latin have a coherent definition as a language.
Without this, strange statements such as `C = distinct 1 + 2` would be legal. The
assignment operator inside `foreach` can be used to take an expression and create a
relation, as happens in this example.

The last line in a nested `foreach` must always be `generate`. This tells Pig how to take
the results of the nested operations and produce a record to be put in the outer relation (in this case, `uniqcnt`). So, `generate` is the operator that takes the inner relations
and turns them back into expressions for inclusion in the outer relation. That is, if
the script read `generate group, uniq_sym`, `uniq_sym` would be treated as a bag for
the purpose of the `generate` statement.

Currently, `distinct`, `filter`, `limit`, `order`, `foreach`, and `cross` are supported inside
`foreach`.

Let's look at a few more examples of how this feature can be useful, such as to sort the
contents of a bag before the bag is passed to a UDF. This is convenient for UDFs that
require all of their input to come in a certain order. Consider a stock-analysis UDF
that wants to track information about a particular stock over time. The UDF will
want input sorted by timestamp:

```
--analyze_stock.pig
register 'acme.jar';
define analyze com.acme.financial.AnalyzeStock();
daily    = load 'NYSE_daily' as (exchange:chararray, symbol:chararray,
               date:chararray, open:float, high:float, low:float,
               close:float, volume:int, adj_close:float);
grpd     = group daily by symbol;
analyzed = foreach grpd {
               sorted = order daily by date;
               generate group, analyze(sorted);
};
```

Doing the sorting in Pig Latin, rather than in your UDF, is important for a couple of reasons. One, it means Pig can offload the sorting to MapReduce. MapReduce has the ability to sort data by a secondary key while grouping it, so the order statement in this case does not require a separate sorting operation. Two, it means that your UDF does not need to wait for all data to be available before it starts processing. Instead, it can use the Accumulator interface (see "The Accumulator Interface" on page 190), which is much more memory efficient.

This feature can be used to find the top *k* elements in a group. The following example will find the top three dividends payed for each stock:

```
--hightest_dividend.pig
divs = load 'NYSE_dividends' as (exchange:chararray, symbol:chararray,
        date:chararray, dividends:float);
grpd = group divs by symbol;
top3 = foreach grpd {
        sorted = order divs by dividends desc;
        top    = limit sorted 3;
        generate group, flatten(top);
};
```

A nested foreach can also be used to manipulate the result of a cogroup, which involves two or more relations. We will discuss this use in "More on Nested foreach" on page 92, after we introduce cogroup and cross.

Currently, these nested portions of code are always run serially for each record handed to them. Of course, the foreach itself will be running in multiple map or reduce tasks, but each instance of the foreach will not spawn subtasks to do the nested operations in parallel. So, if we added a parallel 10 clause to the grpd = group divs by symbol statement in the previous example, this ordering and limiting would take place in 10 reducers, but each group of stocks would be sorted and the top 3 records taken serially within one of those 10 reducers.

There is, of course, no requirement that the pipeline inside the foreach be a simple linear pipeline. For example, if you wanted to calculate two distinct counts together, you could do the following:

```
--double_distinct.pig
divs = load 'NYSE_dividends' as (exchange:chararray, symbol:chararray);
grpd = group divs all;
uniq = foreach grpd {
        exchanges     = divs.exchange;
        uniq_exchanges = distinct exchanges;
        symbols       = divs.symbol;
        uniq_symbols  = distinct symbols;
        generate COUNT(uniq_exchanges), COUNT(uniq_symbols);
};
```

For simplicity, Pig actually runs this pipeline once for each expression in generate. Here this has no side effects because the two data flows are completely disjointed. However, if you constructed a pipeline where there was a split in the flow, and you put a UDF in the shared portion, you would find that it was invoked more often than you expected.

Casting a Relation to a Scalar

Sometimes a relation contains a single value that you would like to use in an expression with other scalars. To support this, Pig allows you to cast relations to scalars. For example, if you wanted to find the volume of each stock compared to the maximum volume in terms of percentage, you could first find the maximum volume of the whole input. Then you could use that max volume as a scalar in a foreach statement to get the final result:

```
daily = load 'NYSE_daily' as (exchange:chararray, symbol:chararray,
        date:chararray, open:float, high:float, low:float,
        close:float, volume:int, adj_close:float);
grouped = group daily all;
scalar_relation = foreach grouped generate MAX(daily.volume) as max_volume;
volumn_percent = foreach daily generate symbol,
        (double)volume/scalar_relation.max_volume;
```

Typically a relation such as scalar_relation is used as the input of a statement. However, in this example, we used scalar_relation as an expression in a foreach statement. Pig will cast the relation into a scalar in this scenario. For this to work, the relation must contain only one row. Otherwise, Pig will throw an exception with the message Scalar has more than one row in the output. The relation will be treated as a tuple, and you will need to project a column from it to be used in an expression. The scalar relation may contain multiple columns. The following example calculates both the percentage of the max volume and the fraction of the total volume:

```
daily = load 'NYSE_daily' as (exchange:chararray, symbol:chararray,
        date:chararray, open:float, high:float, low:float,
        close:float, volume:int, adj_close:float);
grouped = group daily all;
scalar_relation = foreach grouped generate MAX(daily.volume) as max_volume,
        SUM(daily.volume) as total_volume;
calculated = foreach daily generate symbol,
        (double)volume/scalar_relation.max_volume,
        (double)volume/scalar_relation.total_volume;
```

In most cases, you will use group all to generate the scalar, since group all generates only one row. However, this is not required. The following script without group also works:

```
daily = load 'NYSE_daily' as (exchange:chararray, symbol:chararray,
        date:chararray, open:float, high:float, low:float,
        close:float, volume:int, adj_close:float);
sorted = order daily by volume desc;
max_volume_relation = limit sorted 1;
volumn_percent = foreach daily generate symbol,
        (double)volume/max_volume_relation.volume;
```

You can also use the scalar in statements other than `foreach`, such as `filter`:

```
daily = load 'NYSE_daily' as (exchange:chararray, symbol:chararray,
        date:chararray, open:float, high:float, low:float,
        close:float, volume:int, adj_close:float);
grouped = group daily all;
scalar_relation = foreach grouped generate AVG(daily.volume) as avg_volume;
filtered = filter daily by volume > scalar_relation.avg_volume;
```

`scalar` is implemented in two steps in MapReduce mode. First, the scalar relation is stored into an HDFS file. Second, the scalar in the expression is replaced with a UDF that reads the single-row HDFS file. The following script illustrates how the first example script is implemented in Pig:[2]

```
daily = load 'NYSE_daily' as (exchange:chararray, symbol:chararray,
        date:chararray, open:float, high:float, low:float,
        close:float, volume:int, adj_close:float);
grouped = group daily all;
scalar_relation = foreach grouped generate MAX(daily.volume) as max_volume;
store scalar_relation into 'scalar_relation_file';
volumn_percent = foreach daily generate symbol,
        (double)volume/ReadScalars(0,'scalar_relation_file');
```

The parameters of `ReadScalars` instruct `ReadScalars` to read the first field of the HDFS file *scalar_relation_file*.

Using Different Join Implementations

When we covered `join` in the previous chapter (see "join" on page 62), we discussed only the default join behavior. However, Pig offers multiple join implementations, which we will discuss here.

In RDBMS, traditionally the SQL optimizer chooses a join implementation for the user. This is nice as long as the optimizer chooses well, which it does in most cases—but Pig has taken a different approach. Pig is docile; its optimizer is located between the user's chair and keyboard. Pig empowers the user to make these choices rather than having Pig make them. So, for operators such as `join` where there are multiple

---

2 Note the actual scalar implementation also takes care of the return type of `ReadScalars`. The script is only for demonstration purposes; it will not run as is.

implementations, Pig lets the user indicate her choice via a using clause. Pig does not have cost-based join optimization to make such choices automatically.

This approach fits well with the philosophy that Pigs are domestic animals (i.e., Pig does what you tell it; see "The Pig Philosophy" on page 10). Also, as a relatively new product, Pig has a lot of functionality to add. It makes more sense to focus on adding implementation choices and letting the user choose which ones to use, rather than focusing on building an optimizer capable of choosing well.

Joining small to large data

A common type of join is doing a lookup in a smaller input. For example, suppose you were processing data where you needed to translate a US zip code (postal code) to the state and city it referred to. As there are at most 100,000 zip codes in the US, this translation table should easily fit in memory. Rather than forcing a reduce phase that will sort your big file plus this tiny zip code translation file, it makes sense instead to send the zip code file to every machine, load it into memory, and then do the join by streaming through the large file and looking up each record in the zip code file. This is called a *fragment-replicate join* (because you fragment one file and replicate the other):

```
--repljoin.pig
daily = load 'NYSE_daily' as (exchange:chararray, symbol:chararray,
            date:chararray, open:float, high:float, low:float,
            close:float, volume:int, adj_close:float);
divs  = load 'NYSE_dividends' as (exchange:chararray, symbol:chararray,
            date:chararray, dividends:float);
jnd   = join daily by (exchange, symbol), divs by (exchange, symbol)
            using 'replicated';
```

The using 'replicated' tells Pig to use the fragment-replicate algorithm to execute this join. Because no reduce phase is necessary, all of this can be done in the map task.

The second input listed in the join (in this case, divs) is always the input that is loaded into memory. Pig does not check beforehand that the specified input will fit into memory. If Pig cannot fit the replicated input into memory, it will hit an out of memory error or GC overhead limit exceeded error and fail.

 Due to the way Java stores objects in memory, the size of the data on disk will not be the size of the data in memory. See "Memory Requirements of Pig Data Types" on page 35 for a discussion of how data expands in memory in Pig. You will need more memory for a replicated join than you need space on disk to store the replicated input. It is possible to save some space by turning on the schema tuple optimization, however. See "Schema Tuple Optimization" on page 149 for more information.

Fragment-replicate joins support only inner and left outer joins. A right outer join is not possible, because when a given map task sees a record in the replicated input that does not match any record in the fragmented input, it has no idea whether it would match a record in a different fragment. So, it does not know whether to emit a record. If you want a right or full outer join, you will need to use the default join operation.

Fragment-replicate joins can be used with more than two tables. In this case, all but the first (leftmost) table are read into memory.

Pig implements the fragment-replicate join by loading the replicated input into Hadoop's distributed cache. The distributed cache is a tool provided by Hadoop that preloads a file onto the local disk of nodes that will be executing the maps or reduces for that job. This has two important benefits. First, if you have a fragment-replicate join that is going to run on 1,000 maps, opening one file in HDFS from 1,000 different machines all at once puts a serious strain on the NameNode and the three DataNodes that contain the block for that file. The distributed cache is built specifically to manage these kinds of issues without straining HDFS. Second, if multiple map tasks are located on the same physical machine, the files in the distributed cache are shared between those instances, thus reducing the number of times the file has to be copied.

Pig runs a map-only MapReduce job to preprocess the file and get it ready for loading into the distributed cache. If there is a `filter` or `foreach` between the `load` and `join`, these will be done as part of this initial job so that the file to be stored in the distributed cache is as small as possible. The join itself will be done in a second map-only job.

Joining skewed data

As we have seen elsewhere, much of the data you will be processing with Pig has significant skew in the number of records per key. For example, if you were building a map of the Web and joining by the domain of the URL (your key), you would expect to see significant skew for values such as yahoo.com. Pig's default join algorithm is very sensitive to skew, because it collects all of the records for a given key together on a single reducer. In many datasets, there are a few keys that have three or more orders of magnitude more records than other keys. This results in one or two reducers that will take much longer than the rest. To deal with this, Pig provides the *skew join*.

A skew join works by first sampling one input for the join. In that input it identifies any keys that have so many records that it estimates it will not be able to fit them all into memory. Then, in a second MapReduce job, it does the join. For all records except those identified in the sample, it does a standard join, collecting records with the same key onto the same reducer. Those keys identified as too large are treated differently. Based on how many records were seen for a given key, those records are split across the appropriate number of reducers. The number of reducers is chosen based on Pig's estimate of how the data must be split such that each reducer can fit its split into memory. For the input to the join that is not split, those keys that were split are then replicated to each reducer that contains that key.[3]

For example, let's look at how the following Pig Latin script would work:

```
users = load 'users' as (name:chararray, city:chararray);
cinfo = load 'cityinfo' as (city:chararray, population:int);
jnd   = join cinfo by city, users by city using 'skewed';
```

Assume that the cities in *users* are distributed such that 20 users live in Barcelona, 100,000 in New York, and 350 in Portland. Let's further assume that Pig determined that it could fit 75,000 records into memory on each reducer. When this data was joined, New York would be identified as a key that needed to be split across reducers. During the join phase, all records with keys other than New York would be treated as in a default join. Records from *users* with New York as the key would be split between two separate reducers. Records from *cityinfo* with New York as a key would be duplicated and sent to both of those reducers.

The second input in the join, in this case *users*, is the one that will be sampled and have its keys with a large number of values split across reducers. The first input will have records with those values replicated across reducers.

This algorithm addresses skew in only one input. If both inputs have skew, this algorithm will still work, but it will be slow. Much of the motivation behind this approach was that it guarantees the join will still finish, given time. Before Pig introduced skew joins in version 0.4, data that was skewed on both sides could not be joined in Pig because it was not possible to fit all the records for the high-cardinality key values in memory for either side.

Skew joins can be inner or outer joins. However, they can take only two join inputs. Multiway joins must be broken into a series of joins if they need to use this option.

Since data often has skew, why not use skew joins all of the time? There is a small performance penalty, because one of the inputs must be sampled first to find any key values with a large number of records. This usually adds about 5% to the time it takes to calculate the join. If your data frequently has skew, though, it might be worth it to always use skew joins and pay the 5% tax in order to avoid failing or running very slowly with the default join and then needing to rerun with a skew join.

As stated earlier, Pig estimates how much data it can fit into memory when deciding which key values to split and how wide to split them. For the purposes of this calculation, Pig looks at the record sizes in the sample and assumes it can use 30% of the

---

3 This algorithm was proposed in the paper "Practical Skew Handling in Parallel Joins," presented by David J. DeWitt, Jeffrey F. Naughton, Donovan A. Schneider, and S. Seshadri at the 18th International Conference on Very Large Databases.

JVM's heap to materialize records that will be joined. In your particular case, you might find you need to increase or decrease this size. You should decrease the value if your join is still failing with out of memory errors even when using 'skewed'. This indicates that Pig is estimating memory usage improperly, so you should tell it to use less. If profiling indicates that Pig is not utilizing all of your heap, you might want to increase the value in order to do the join more efficiently; the fewer ways the key values are split, the more efficient the join will be. You can do that by setting the property pig.skewedjoin.reduce.memusage to a value between 0 and 1. For example, if you wanted it to use 25% instead of 30% of the heap, you could add -Dpig.skewed join.reduce.memusage=0.25 to your Pig command line or define the value in your properties file.

> Like order, skew joins break the MapReduce convention that all records with the same key will be processed by the same reducer. This means records with the same key might be placed in separate part files. If you plan to process the data in a way that depends on all records with the same key being in the same part file, you cannot use skew joins.

Joining sorted data

A common database join strategy is to first sort both inputs on the join key and then walk through both inputs together, doing the join. This is referred to as a sort-merge join. In MapReduce, because a sort requires a full MapReduce job, as does Pig's default join, this technique is not more efficient than the default. However, if your inputs are already sorted on the join key, this approach makes sense. The join can be done in the map phase by opening both files and walking through them. Pig refers to this as a merge join because it is a sort-merge join, but the sort has already been done:

```
--mergejoin.pig
-- use sort_for_mergejoin.pig to build NYSE_daily_sorted and
-- NYSE_dividends_sorted
daily = load 'NYSE_daily_sorted' as (exchange:chararray, symbol:chararray,
            date:chararray, open:float, high:float, low:float,
            close:float, volume:int, adj_close:float);
divs  = load 'NYSE_dividends_sorted' as (exchange:chararray, symbol:chararray,
            date:chararray, dividends:float);
jnd   = join daily by symbol, divs by symbol using 'merge';
```

To execute this join, Pig will first run a MapReduce job that samples the second input, *NYSE_dividends_sorted*. This sample builds an index that tells Pig the value of the join key, symbol, in the first record in every input split (usually each HDFS block). Because this sample reads only one record per split, it runs very quickly. Pig will then run a second MapReduce job that takes the first input, *NYSE_daily_sorted*, as its input. When each map reads the first record in its split of *NYSE_daily_sorted*, it takes the value of symbol and looks it up in the index built by the previous job. It looks for the last entry that is less than its value of symbol. It then opens *NYSE_dividends_sorted* at the corresponding block for that entry. For example, if the index contained entries (CA, 1), (CHY, 2), (CP, 3), and the first symbol in a given map's input split of *NYSE_daily_sorted* was CJA, that map would open block 2 of *NYSE_dividends_sorted*. (Even if CP was the first user ID in *NYSE_daily_sorted*'s split, block 2 of *NYSE_dividends_sorted* would be opened, as there could be records with a key of CP in that block.) Once *NYSE_dividends_sorted* is opened, Pig throws away records until it reaches a record with a symbol of CJA. Once it finds a match, it collects all the records with that value into memory and then does the join. It then advances the first input, *NYSE_daily_sorted*. If the key is the same, it again does the join. If not, it advances the second input, *NYSE_dividends_sorted*, again until it finds a value greater than or equal to the next value in the first input, *NYSE_daily_sorted*. If the value is greater, it advances the first input and continues. Because both inputs are sorted, it never needs to look in the index after the initial lookup.

All of this can be done without a reduce phase, and so it is more efficient than a default join. Currently, this algorithm supports only two-way inner joins.

cogroup

cogroup is a generalization of group. Instead of collecting records of one input based on a key, it collects records of *n* inputs based on a key. The result is a record with a key and one bag for each input. Each bag contains all records from that input that have the given value for the key:

```
A = load 'input1' as (id:int, val:float);
B = load 'input2' as (id:int, val2:int);
C = cogroup A by id, B by id;
describe C;

C: {group: int,A: {id: int,val: float},B: {id: int,val2: int}}
```

Another way to think of cogroup is as the first half of a join. The keys are collected together, but the cross product is not done. In fact, cogroup plus foreach, where each bag is flattened, is equivalent to a join—as long as there are no null values in the keys.

cogroup handles null values in the keys similarly to group and unlike join. That is, all records with a null value in the key will be collected together.

cogroup is useful when you want to do join-like things but not a full join. For example, Pig Latin does not have a semi-join operator, but you can do a semi-join with cogroup:

```
--semijoin.pig
daily = load 'NYSE_daily' as (exchange:chararray, symbol:chararray,
            date:chararray, open:float, high:float, low:float,
```

```
                  close:float, volume:int, adj_close:float);
divs  = load 'NYSE_dividends' as (exchange:chararray, symbol:chararray,
            date:chararray, dividends:float);
grpd  = cogroup daily by (exchange, symbol), divs by (exchange, symbol);
sjnd  = filter grpd by not IsEmpty(divs);
final = foreach sjnd generate flatten(daily);
```

Because cogroup needs to collect records with like keys together, it requires a reduce phase.

union

Sometimes you want to put two datasets together by concatenating them instead of joining them. Pig Latin provides union for this purpose. If you had two files you wanted to use for input and there was no glob that could describe them, you could do the following:

```
A = load '/user/me/data/files/input1';
B = load '/user/someoneelse/info/input2';
C = union A, B;
A = load 'input1' as (x:int, y:float);
B = load 'input2' as (x:int, y:float);
C = union A, B;
describe C;

C: {x: int,y: float}

A = load 'input1' as (x:int, y:float);
B = load 'input2' as (x:int, y:double);
C = union A, B;
describe C;

C: {x: int,y: double}

A = load 'input1' as (x:int, y:float);
B = load 'input2' as (x:int, y:chararray);
C = union A, B;
describe C;

Schema for C unknown.
```

Unlike union in SQL, Pig does not require that both inputs share the same schema. If both do share the same schema, the output of the union will have that schema. If one schema can be produced from another by a set of implicit casts, the union will have that resulting schema. If neither of these conditions holds, the output will have no schema (that is, different records will have different fields). This schema comparison includes names, so even different field names will result in the output having no schema. You can get around this by placing a foreach before the union that renames fields.

union does not perform a mathematical set union. That is, duplicate records are not eliminated. In this manner it is like SQL's union all. Also, union does not require a separate reduce phase.

union onschema

Sometimes your data changes over time. If you have data you collect every month, you might add a new column this month. Now you are prevented from using union because your schemas do not match. If you want to union this data and force your data into a common schema, you can add the keyword onschema to your union statement:

```
A = load 'input1' as (w:chararray, x:int, y:float);
B = load 'input2' as (x:int, y:double, z:chararray);
C = union onschema A, B;
describe C;

C: {w: chararray,x: int,y: double,z: chararray}
```

union onschema requires that all inputs have schemas. It also requires that a shared schema for all inputs can be produced by adding fields and implicit casts. Matching of fields is done by name, not position. So, in the preceding example, w:chararray is added from *input1* and z:chararray is added from *input2*. Also, a cast from float to double is added for *input1* so that field y is a double. If a shared schema cannot be produced by this method, an error is returned. When the data is read, nulls are inserted for fields not present in a given input.

cross

cross matches the mathematical set operation of the same name. In the following Pig Latin, cross takes every record in *NYSE_daily* and combines it with every record in *NYSE_dividends*:

```
--cross.pig
-- you may want to run this in a cluster; it produces about 3G of data
daily     = load 'NYSE_daily' as (exchange:chararray, symbol:chararray,
```

```
                    date:chararray, open:float, high:float, low:float,
                    close:float, volume:int, adj_close:float);
divs      = load 'NYSE_dividends' as (exchange:chararray, symbol:chararray,
                    date:chararray, dividends:float);
tonsodata = cross daily, divs parallel 10;
```

cross tends to produce a lot of data. Given inputs with *n* and *m* records, respectively, cross will produce output with *n* * *m* records.

Pig does implement cross in a parallel fashion. It does this by generating a synthetic join key, replicating rows, and then doing the cross as a join. The previous script is rewritten to:

```
daily     = load 'NYSE_daily' as (exchange:chararray, symbol:chararray,
                    date:chararray, open:float, high:float, low:float,
                    close:float, volume:int, adj_close:float);
divs      = load 'NYSE_dividends' as (exchange:chararray, symbol:chararray,
                    date:chararray, dividends:float);
A         = foreach daily generate flatten(GFCross(0, 2)), flatten(*);
B         = foreach divs generate flatten(GFCross(1, 2)), flatten(*);
C         = cogroup A by ($0, $1), B by ($0, $1) parallel 10;
tonsodata = foreach C generate flatten(A), flatten(B);
```

GFCross is an internal UDF. The first argument is the input number, and the second argument is the total number of inputs. In this example, the output is a bag that contains four records. These records have a schema of (int, int). The field that is the same number as the first argument to GFCross contains a random number between 0 and 3. The other field counts from 0 to 3. So, if we assume for a given two records, one in each input, that the random number for the first input is 3 and for the second it is 2, then the outputs of GFCross would look like:

```
A {(3, 0), (3, 1), (3, 2), (3, 3)}
B {(0, 2), (1, 2), (2, 2), (3, 2)}
```

When these records are flattened, four copies of each input record will be created in the map. They will then be joined on the artificial keys. For every record in each input, it is guaranteed that there is one and only one instance of the artificial keys that will match and produce a record. Because the random numbers are chosen differently for each record, the resulting joins are done on an even distribution of the reducers.

This algorithm does enable crossing of data in parallel. However, it creates a burden on the shuffle phase by increasing the number of records in each input being shuffled. Also, no matter what you do, cross outputs a lot of data. Writing all of this data to disk is expensive, even when done in parallel.

This is not to say you should not use cross. There are instances when it is indispensable. Pig's join operator supports only equi-joins—that is, joins on an equality condition. Because general join implementations in MapReduce (ones that do not depend on the data being sorted or small enough to fit in memory) depend on collecting records with the same join key values onto the same reducer, non-equi-joins (also called *theta joins*) are difficult to do. They can be done in Pig using `cross` followed by `filter`:

```
--thetajoin.pig
--we recommend running this one on a cluster too
daily   = load 'NYSE_daily' as (exchange:chararray, symbol:chararray,
            date:chararray, open:float, high:float, low:float,
            close:float, volume:int, adj_close:float);
divs    = load 'NYSE_dividends' as (exchange:chararray, symbol:chararray,
            date:chararray, dividends:float);
crossed = cross daily, divs;
tjnd    = filter crossed by daily::date < divs::date;
```

Fuzzy joins could also be done in this manner, where the fuzzy comparison is done after the cross. However, whenever possible, it is better to use a UDF to conform fuzzy values to a standard value and then do a regular join. For example, if you wanted to join two inputs on `city` but wanted to join any time two cities were in the same metropolitan area (e.g., you wanted "Los Angeles" and "Pasadena" to be viewed as equal), you could first run your records through a UDF that generated a single join key for all cities in a metropolitan area and then do the join.

More on Nested foreach

As mentioned previously, `cross` and `cogroup` can be used in a nested `foreach`. Let's put all of these together and look at an example of how they can be used in a single pass over the data. Using the NYSE data, we want to find the average closing price after the last dividend date for each stock. We can use the following Pig Latin script:

```
divs  = load 'NYSE_dividends' as (exchange:chararray, symbol:chararray,
            date:chararray, dividends:float);
divs_dividends = foreach divs generate date, symbol, dividends;
daily = load 'NYSE_daily' as (exchange:chararray, symbol:chararray,
            date:chararray, open:float, high:float, low:float,
            close:float, volume:int, adj_close:float);
daily_price = foreach daily generate date, symbol, close;
cogrouped  = cogroup divs_dividends by symbol, daily_price by symbol;
aggregated = foreach cogrouped {
    sort_dividend = order divs_dividends by date desc;
    top_dividend  = limit sort_dividend 1;
    crossproduct  = cross daily_price, top_dividend;
    postdividend  = filter crossproduct by daily_price::date >
        top_dividend::date;
    generate group, AVG(postdividend.close) as avg_price;
}
avgprice = filter aggregated by avg_price is not null;
```

In the nested foreach, we first do a limited sort to get the latest dividend date of the stock. Then we do a non-equi-join using cross and filter to get all daily prices after the latest dividend, then finally we do an aggregation. Without the nested foreach, there is no way we could get this result in a single pass over the data.

rank

Introduced in Pig 0.11, rank is used to add a global ranking column to the input data-set. There are three modes in rank: regular, dense, and row count. Regular and dense modes can produce a rank on one or multiple fields,[4] each in ascending (the default) or descending order. Here is an example of a regular rank:

```
daily = load 'NYSE_daily' as (exchange:chararray, symbol:chararray,
        date:chararray, open:float, high:float, low:float,
        close:float, volume:int, adj_close:float);
ranked = rank daily by exchange, symbol desc;
```

If you do a describe, you will find there is one additional field added in the front of the schema. The name of the field is prefixed by rank_ followed by the input relation name. The data type of the field is long:

```
describe ranked:
```

ranked: {rank_daily: long,exchange: chararray,symbol: chararray,date: chararray, open: float,high: float,low: float,close: float,volume: int,adj_close: float}

Ranking starts with 1. If there is a tie, all the ties are assigned the same rank. Here are a few lines from the result of the script:

```
...
(1,NYSE,CZZ,2009-01-05,3.55,3.63,3.18,3.28,761900,3.28)
(1,NYSE,CZZ,2009-01-06,3.36,3.71,3.35,3.71,674500,3.71)
(1,NYSE,CZZ,2009-01-07,3.55,3.72,3.5,3.61,1148900,3.61)
(253,NYSE,CYT,2009-12-31,36.9,37.06,36.33,36.42,220300,36.41)
(253,NYSE,CYT,2009-12-30,36.65,37.04,36.41,36.81,101500,36.8)
...
```

Since there are 252 rows of symbol CZZ, all are assigned a rank of 1. The next symbol, CYT, is given the rank 253.

You can also rank a relation in dense mode. To do this, put the keyword dense at the end of the rank statement:

```
ranked = rank daily by exchange, symbol desc dense;
```

---

4 Ranking on expressions is not supported. If you want to rank on an expression, you will need to generate it first using foreach and then rank on the generated field.

Dense mode means multiple records with the same rank do not cause subsequent rank values to be skipped, thus there is no gap in the rankings. Here is the corresponding section of output in dense mode:

```
...
(1,NYSE,CZZ,2009-01-05,3.55,3.63,3.18,3.28,761900,3.28)
(1,NYSE,CZZ,2009-01-06,3.36,3.71,3.35,3.71,674500,3.71)
(1,NYSE,CZZ,2009-01-07,3.55,3.72,3.5,3.61,1148900,3.61)
(2,NYSE,CYT,2009-12-31,36.9,37.06,36.33,36.42,220300,36.41)
(2,NYSE,CYT,2009-12-30,36.65,37.04,36.41,36.81,101500,36.8)
...
```

Note in both regular and dense modes, the output is sorted as part of generating the rank. However, row count mode will rank the input without sorting it. In row count mode, every rank value is different even if there is a tie. This can be used to generate a row IDs for the input. You do not specify any field to rank on, and there is no descending order in row count mode. You might expect the rankings to be continuously assigned to the input as stored in the source (e.g., your HDFS file), but that is not always true. With split combination (see "Data Layout Optimization" on page 143), nonconsecutive input splits can be combined together and assigned ranks sequentially, which is different from the order from the input. Here is the syntax for row count rank:

```
ranked = rank daily;
```

Here is how Pig implements rank. For row counting mode, Pig will first run a counting-only job to count the number of records for every map task. After aggregating the counts, Pig can then assign a starting rank for each map. The follow-up job will use these starting ranks within each map as a starting point for assigning local ranks to every record. Note that this algorithm assumes the input splits are exactly the same for the two jobs. In most cases this holds, but we have seen a few rare cases where a custom InputFormat is nondeterministic in its split generation. When this happens the algorithm fails and ranks are incorrectly assigned (you will see some duplicate ranks as well as gaps in the rank values).

In regular mode or dense mode, Pig first groups by the ranking keys because the same ranking will be assigned to all records within the group. Then Pig sorts on the ranking keys using an algorithm similar to order by. That is, a first job will sample the data and a second job will do the actual sorting. In addition to what order by does, rank will also add two fields, task id and task offset, to each record. task id captures the reduce task ID of the second job processing the record, and task off set is the record offset within the task. At the same time the operator aggregates counts for each group in each task. So, at the end of the job, we know the global offset for the start ranking of every task ID. Currently Pig uses Hadoop counters to perform global aggregation. If there are too many reducers for the second job, Hadoop might complain "too many counters."[5] If this happens, set the parallelism lower so that you have less reducers in the second job. The third job makes use of the global starting offset for each task ID and the information piggybacked in every record (including the task ID and task inner offset) to assign a ranking to every record.

cube

Also introduced in Pig 0.11, cube computes multilevel aggregations in one operation. It offers the same capability as a typical data warehouse cube operator. There are two modes for cube: CUBE and ROLLUP. When using these you will need to specify a list of fields to CUBE or ROLLUP on. To illustrate how cube works, let's focus on two symbols and two dates in the input file—CLI, CSL on 2009-12-30 and 2009-12-31:

```
daily = load 'NYSE_daily' as (exchange:chararray, symbol:chararray,
            date:chararray, open:float, high:float, low:float,
            close:float, volume:int, adj_close:float);
selected_daily = filter daily by symbol in ('CLI', 'CSL') and
        date in ('2009-12-30', '2009-12-31');
cubic = cube selected_daily by CUBE(symbol, date);
summary = foreach cubic generate flatten(group), SUM(cube.volume);
```

The schema after cube is hardcoded to be {group, cube}. group is a tuple of the cube keys, and cube is a bag containing the cube output. This is why we need to refer to group and cube in the foreach statement. Note that, unlike in SQL, the cube statement does not apply an aggregate function to the bag. You will need a foreach statement right after cube to do the aggregation. Here is what we get in the output:

```
(CLI,2009-12-30,516900)
(CLI,2009-12-31,890100)
(CSL,2009-12-30,155200)
(CSL,2009-12-31,235800)
(CLI,,1407000)
(CSL,,391000)
(,2009-12-30,672100)
(,2009-12-31,1125900)
(,,1798000)
```

The result is equivalent to unioning four levels of group results together:

- Most specific group on (symbol, date)
- Less specific group on symbol only
- Less specific group on date only
- Most general group all

---

5 The issue is solved in Tez because it uses a Tez edge to perform the aggregation instead.

You can rewrite the cube statement with a union of four groups followed by a foreach:

```
groupboth = group selected_daily by (symbol, date); -- level 1
summaryboth = foreach groupboth generate flatten(group),
    SUM(selected_daily.volume);
groupsymbol = group selected_daily by symbol; -- level 2
summarysymbol = foreach groupsymbol generate group, NULL,
    SUM(selected_daily.volume);
groupdate = group selected_daily by date; -- level 2
summarydate = foreach groupdate generate NULL, group, SUM(selected_daily.volume);
groupall = group selected_daily all; -- level 3
summaryall = foreach groupsymbol generate NULL, NULL, SUM(selected_daily.volume);
unioned = union summaryboth, summarysymbol, summarydate, summaryall;
```

The ROLLUP option generates slightly different results. While CUBE generates the entire matrix of possible groups, ROLLUP only generates the upper-left corner of that matrix. So, instead of four levels of grouping, as above, it produces only three, omitting (null, date):

```
(CLI,2009-12-30,516900)
(CLI,2009-12-31,890100)
(CSL,2009-12-30,155200)
(CSL,2009-12-31,235800)
(CLI,,1407000)
(CSL,,391000)
(,,1798000)
```

Often there is a correlation between the fields, with fields going from less to more specific. In this case ROLLUP is especially useful. An example of this is state,county,city. Aggregates on city alone do not make sense, so there is no reason to produce a cube that shows those. We can use ROLLUP instead.

CUBE and ROLLUP can be used together in one cube statement:

```
daily = load 'NYSE_daily' as (exchange:chararray, symbol:chararray,
            date:chararray, open:float, high:float, low:float,
            close:float, volume:int, adj_close:float);
projected = foreach daily generate symbol, SUBSTRING(date, 0, 4) as year,
        SUBSTRING(date, 0, 7) as month, (close-open)/open as perc;
cubic = cube projected by CUBE(symbol), ROLLUP(year, month);
avgperc = foreach cubic generate flatten(group), AVG(cube.perc);
```

This statement uses a CUBE subclause and a ROLLUP subclause. It does a CUBE on symbol and a ROLLUP on year,month. This example also demonstrates how to use an expression in cube. You can only specify field names in a cube statement. If you want to use an expression, you must generate it in a foreach statement before the cube.

The cube operator is implemented using query rewriting. The preceding query is rewritten to the following query for execution:

```
daily = load 'NYSE_daily' as (exchange:chararray, symbol:chararray,
            date:chararray, open:float, high:float, low:float,
            close:float, volume:int, adj_close:float);
projected = foreach daily generate symbol, SUBSTRING(date, 0, 4) as year,
            SUBSTRING(date, 0, 7) as month, (close-open)/open as perc;
projected_cube = foreach projected generate flatten(CubeDimensions(symbol)),
        flatten(RollupDimensions(year, month)), perc;
cubic = group projected_cube by (symbol, year, month);
avgperc = foreach cubic generate flatten(group), AVG(projected_cube.perc);
```

In this example, cube is simulated by a foreach statement with the UDFs CubeDimensions and RollupDimensions, followed by a group statement. CubeDimensions generates a bag of all combinations of the cube keys, with each key turned on and off (on means the value of the key is used; off means null is used). For example, if the input of CubeDimensions is (CLI,2009-12-30), CubeDimensions generates a bag {(CLI, 2009-12-30),(CLI,null),(null,2009-12-30),(null, null)}. By flattening the bag, we create four records for the input. They are used to generate different levels of aggregations in the group statement: (CLI,2009-12-30) is used to generate the most specific aggregation, (CLI,null) is used to generate the more general aggregation on the symbol CLI, (null,2009-12-30) is used to generate the aggregation on the date 2009-12-30, and (null,null) is used to generate the aggregation of all inputs. Similarly, RollupDimensions generates a bag consisting of leftwise combinations of the cube keys. For example, if the input of RollupDimensions is (2009,2009-12), Rollup Dimensions generates a bag {(2009,2009-12),(2009,null),(null,null)}.

If your cube statement consists of multiple CUBE or ROLLUP subclauses, you will get a cross product of the CubeDimensions or RollupDimensions output bags (see "flatten" on page 77). Note this flatten may significantly increase the number of input records for the group. In particular, CubeDimensions generates 2^n records, where n is the key size of the CUBE subclause. This might result in heavy network traffic between tasks on the backend.

One limitation of cube is that it does not handle null keys. That is, if your dimension key contains a null value, you may get the wrong result. cube treats null as an aggregation key. What if you have a null key in your input data? You will have to replace the null key before the cube operator. The other way around this issue is to not use the cube operator. Instead, you can use CubeDimensions or RollupDimensions with group as illustrated previously. CubeDimensions and RollupDimensions take a constructor argument "all" marker allowing you to use another value in the place of null. For example, we can define * as our all marker in the previous query:

```
define CUBESTAR CubeDimensions('*');
define ROLLUPSTAR RollupDimensions('*');
```

```
...
projected_cube = foreach projected generate flatten(CUBESTAR(symbol)),
        flatten(ROLLUPSTAR(year, month)), perc;
...
```

Now there is no null aggregation key in the result.

assert

assert was introduced in Pig 0.12. It is used for data validation. To use assert you provide a relation to test, followed by by and then a Boolean expression, and finally an error message. If the expression evaluates to false, Pig will terminate the job and return the error message. Here is an example:

```
daily = load 'NYSE_daily' as (exchange:chararray, symbol:chararray,
        date:chararray, open:float, high:float, low:float,
        close:float, volume:int, adj_close:float);
assert daily by exchange=='NYSE', 'exchange can only be NYSE';
otheralias = foreach daily generate symbol, date, open, close;
...
```

Notice that in the example otheralias references the relation daily. assert does not produce a new relation.

assert is implemented with a filter statement using the built-in UDF Assert. The previous example is implemented as if Pig were running the following rewritten script:

```
daily = load 'NYSE_daily' as (exchange:chararray, symbol:chararray,
        date:chararray, open:float, high:float, low:float,
        close:float, volume:int, adj_close:float);
daily = filter daily by Assert(exchange=='NYSE', 'exchange can only be NYSE');
        -- Note this will not pass the Pig parser
otheralias = foreach daily generate symbol, date, open, close;
...
```

Note that this script is just for demonstration. Pig will return a syntax error if asked to parse it, since Assert is a reserved word in Pig and will not be interpreted as a UDF.

Integrating Pig with Executables and Native Jobs

One tenet of Pig's philosophy is that Pig allows users to integrate their own code with it wherever possible (see "The Pig Philosophy" on page 10). The most obvious way Pig does that is through its UDFs. But it also allows you to directly integrate other executables and native execution engine jobs.

stream

To specify an executable that you want to insert into your data flow, use `stream`. You may want to do this when you have a legacy program that you do not want to modify or are unable to change. You can also use `stream` when you have a program you use frequently, or one you have tested on small datasets and now want to apply to a large dataset. Let's look at an example where you have a Perl program, *highdiv.pl*, that filters out all stocks with a dividend below $1.00:

```
-- streamsimple.pig
divs = load 'NYSE_dividends' as (exchange, symbol, date, dividends);
highdivs = stream divs through `highdiv.pl` as (exchange, symbol, date,
        dividends);
```

Notice the `as` clause in the `stream` command. This is not required, but Pig has no idea what the executable will return, so if you do not provide the `as` clause the relation `highdivs` will have no schema.

The executable *highdiv.pl* is invoked once on every map or reduce task. It is not invoked once per record. Pig instantiates the executable and keeps feeding data to it via *stdin*. It also keeps checking *stdout*, passing any results to the next operator in your data flow. The executable can choose whether to produce an output for every input, only every so many inputs, or only after all inputs have been received.

The preceding example assumes that you already have *highdiv.pl* installed on your cluster, and that it is runnable from the working directory on the task machines. If that is not the case, which it usually will not be, you can ship the executable to the cluster. To do this, use a `define` statement:

```
--streamship.pig
define hd `highdiv.pl` ship('highdiv.pl');
divs = load 'NYSE_dividends' as (exchange, symbol, date, dividends);
highdivs = stream divs through hd as (exchange, symbol, date, dividends);
```

This `define` does two things. First, it defines the executable that will be used. Now in `stream` we refer to *highdiv.pl* by the alias we gave it, hd, rather than referring to it directly. Second, it tells Pig to pick up the file *./highdiv.pl* and ship it to Hadoop as part of this job. This file will be picked up from the specified location on the machine where you launch the job. It will be placed in the working directory of the task on the task machines. So, the command you pass to `stream` must refer to it relative to the current working directory, not via an absolute path.

Now let's take a look at how to write the executable *highdiv.pl*. Typically, it takes *stdin* and writes to *stdout*. *stdin* is a stream of input fields written by Pig. The executable is expected to produce a stream of output fields that will be consumed by Pig. Both input and output are delimited with "\n" for lines and tabs for fields:

```
--highdiv.pl
#!/usr/bin/perl

foreach $line (<STDIN>) {
    chomp($line);
    my($exchange, $symbol, $date, $dividends) = split /\t/, $line;
    if ($dividends > 0.5) {
        print "$exchange, $symbol, $date, $dividends\n";
    }
}
```

If your executable depends on other modules or files, they can be specified as part of the ship clause as well. For example, if *highdiv.pl* depends on a Perl module called *Financial.pm*, you can send them both to the task machines:

```
define hd `highdiv.pl` ship('highdiv.pl', 'Financial.pm');
divs = load 'NYSE_dividends' as (exchange, symbol, date, dividends);
highdivs = stream divs through hd as (exchange, symbol, date, dividends);
```

Many scripting languages assume certain paths for modules based on their hierarchy. For example, Perl expects to find a module Acme::Financial in *Acme/Financial.pm*. However, the ship clause always puts files in your current working directory, and it does not take directories, so you could not ship *Acme*. One workaround for this is to create a TAR file and ship that (with the ship clause), and then have a step in your executable that unbundles the TAR file. You then need to set your module include path (for Perl, using -I or the PERLLIB environment variable) to contain . (dot). Alternatively, you can ship the TAR file by setting the mapreduce.job.cache.archives property inside your Pig script:

```
set mapreduce.job.cache.archives 'file:///absolute_path/Acme.tar.gz#Acme';
```

This command ships the local file *Acme.tar.gz* to the task nodes and unbundles it. The unbundled files will be shared by different tasks on the same node. Every task will have a symlink pointing to the shared directory containing the unbundled files in the task's current working directory. The name of the directory will be the URL fragment you provided (in this example, *Acme*). If you omit the URL fragment, the filename of the TAR will be used as the directory name (*Acme.tar.gz*). In your Perl script, you need to look up the required files inside the right directory. So, in this example, you need to look up the Perl module inside the directory *Acme*:

```
use lib 'Acme';
require Acme::Financial;
```

ship moves files into the cluster from the machine where you are launching your job. But sometimes the file you want is already on the cluster. If you have a cluster file that will be accessed by every map or reduce task in your job, the proper way to access it is via the distributed cache. The distributed cache is a mechanism Hadoop provides to share files. It reduces the load on HDFS by preloading the file to the local disk on the machine that will be executing the task. You can use the distributed cache for your executable by using the cache clause in define:

```
define hd `highdiv.pl` ship('highdiv.pl') cache('/data/shared/ignore#ignore');
divs = load 'NYSE_dividends' as (exchange, symbol, date, dividends);
highdivs = stream divs through hd as (exchange, symbol, date, dividends);
```

The new *highdiv.pl* also takes a list of ignored symbols. The list is passed to *highdiv.pl* by a text file called *ignore* in the current directory.

In the cache statement, the string before the # is the path on HDFS: in this case, */data/shared/ignore*. The string after the # is the name of the file as viewed by the executable. So, Hadoop will put a copy of */data/shared/ignore* into the task's working directory and call it *ignore*.

So far we have assumed that your executable takes data on *stdin* and writes it to *stdout*. This might not work, depending on your executable. If your executable needs a file to read from, write to, or both, you can specify that with the input and output clauses in the define command. Continuing with our previous example, let's say that *highdiv.pl* expects to read its input from a file specified by -i on its command line and write to a file specified by -o:

```
define hd `highdiv.pl` -i in -o out` input('in') output('out');
divs = load 'NYSE_dividends' as (exchange, symbol, date, dividends);
highdivs = stream divs through hd as (exchange, symbol, date, dividends);
```

Again, file locations are specified from the working directory on the task machines. In this example, Pig will write out all the input for a given task for *highdiv.pl* to *in*, then invoke the executable, and then read *out* to get the results. Again, the executable will be invoked only once per map or reduce task, so Pig will first write out all the input to the file.

native

You can also include jobs that use the underlying native execution engine, such as MapReduce, directly in your data flow with the native command.[6] This is convenient if you have processing that is better done in the native execution engine than Pig but must be integrated with the rest of your Pig data flow. It can also make it easier to incorporate legacy processing written for your native execution engine with newer processing you want to write in Pig Latin. The engine used to execute native jobs will be selected based on the engine Pig is using. For example, if you have Pig configured to use MapReduce, then native jobs will be sent to MapReduce.

---

6 Originally called mapreduce, this was renamed in Pig 0.14 and since then can also be used to launch a Tez job.

Native jobs expect to read their input from and write their output to a storage device (usually HDFS). So, to integrate them with your data flow, Pig first has to store the data, then invoke the native job, and then read the data back. This is done via `store` and `load` clauses in the `native` statement that invoke regular load and store functions. You also provide Pig with the name of the JAR that contains the code for your native job. This JAR must be runnable directly via the current native engine.

As an example, consider the blacklisting of URLs. We'll assume this is done by a native MapReduce job:

```
crawl      = load 'webcrawl' as (url, pageid);
normalized = foreach crawl generate normalize(url);
goodurls   = native 'blacklistchecker.jar'
                 store normalized into 'input'
                 load 'output' as (url, pageid);
```

`native` takes as its first argument the JAR containing the code to run a MapReduce job. It uses `load` and `store` phrases to specify how data will be moved from Pig's data pipeline to the MapReduce job. Notice that the input alias is contained in the `store` clause. As with `stream`, the output of `native` is opaque to Pig, so if we want the resulting relation, `goodurls`, to have a schema, we have to tell Pig what it is. This example also assumes that the Java code in *blacklistchecker.jar* knows which input and output files to look for and has a default class to run specified in its manifest. Often this will not be the case. Any arguments you wish to pass to the invocation of the Java command that will run the native task can be put in backquotes after the `load` clause:

```
crawl      = load 'webcrawl' as (url, pageid);
normalized = foreach crawl generate normalize(url);
goodurls   = native 'blacklistchecker.jar'
                 store normalized into 'input'
                 load 'output' as (url, pageid)
                 `com.acmeweb.security.BlackListChecker -i input -o output`;
```

The string in the backquotes will be passed directly to your native job as is, so if you want to pass Java options, etc., you can do that as well.

The `load` and `store` clauses of the `native` command have the same syntax as the `load` and `store` statements, so you can use different load and store functions, pass constructor arguments, and so on. See "load" on page 46 and "store" on page 48 for full details.

split and Nonlinear Data Flows

So far our examples have been linear data flows or trees. In a linear data flow, one input is loaded, processed, and stored. We have looked at operators that combine multiple data flows: `join`, `cogroup`, `union`, and `cross`. With these you can build tree structures where multiple inputs all flow to a single output. But in complex data-processing situations, you often also want to split your data flow. That is, one input will result in more than one output. You might also have diamonds, or places where the data flow is split and eventually joined back together. Pig supports these directed acyclic graph (DAG) data flows.

Splits in your data flow can be either implicit or explicit. In an implicit split, no specific operator or syntax is required in your script. You simply refer to a given relation multiple times. Let's consider data from our *baseball* example data. You might, for example, want to analyze players by position and by team at the same time:

```
--multiquery.pig
players   = load 'baseball' as (name:chararray, team:chararray,
              position:bag{t:(p:chararray)}, bat:map[]);
pwithba   = foreach players generate name, team, position,
              bat#'batting_average' as batavg;
byteam    = group pwithba by team;
avgbyteam = foreach byteam generate group, AVG(pwithba.batavg);
store avgbyteam into 'by_team';
flattenpos = foreach pwithba generate name, team,
              flatten(position) as position, batavg;
bypos     = group flattenpos by position;
avgbypos  = foreach bypos generate group, AVG(flattenpos.batavg);
store avgbypos into 'by_position';
```

The `pwithba` relation is referred to by the `group` operators for both the `byteam` and `bypos` relations. Pig builds a data flow that takes every record from `pwithba` and ships it to both `group` operators.

Splitting data flows can also be done explicitly via the `split` operator, which allows you to split your data flow as many ways as you like. Let's take an example where you want to split data into different files depending on the date the record was created:

```
wlogs = load 'weblogs' as (pageid, url, timestamp);
split wlogs into apr03 if timestamp < '20110404',
        apr02 if timestamp < '20110403' and timestamp > '20110401',
        apr01 if timestamp < '20110402' and timestamp > '20110331';
store apr03 into '20110403';
store apr02 into '20110402';
store apr01 into '20110401';
```

At first glance, `split` looks like a `switch` or `case` statement, *but it is not*. A single record can go to multiple legs of the split since you use different filters for each `if` clause. And a record can go to no leg. In the preceding example, if a record were found with a date of `20110331`, it would be dropped. To avoid dropping records that do not match any of the filters, you can specify a default relation using `otherwise`. Any records that return `false` for all of the other filters will be sent to the `otherwise` relation. Note, however, this will not include records that return `null` from the comparisons. This is because `otherwise` is translated into a `not` condition of all other conditions combined. For example, this:

```
wlogs = load 'weblogs' as (pageid, url, timestamp);
split wlogs into apr03 if timestamp > '20110404',
        apr02 if timestamp < '20110401',
        apr01 otherwise;
store apr03 into '20110403';
store apr02 into '20110402';
store apr01 into '20110401';
```

is equivalent to:

```
wlogs = load 'weblogs' as (pageid, url, timestamp);
split wlogs into apr03 if timestamp > '20110404',
        apr02 if timestamp < '20110401',
        apr01 if NOT(timestamp > '20110404' OR timestamp < '20110401');
store apr03 into '20110403';
store apr02 into '20110402';
store apr01 into '20110401';
```

If `timestamp` is `null`, every condition is evaluated as `null`, so it will not go to any destination.

`split` is semantically identical to an implicit split that uses filters. The previous example could be rewritten as:

```
wlogs = load 'weblogs' as (pageid, url, timestamp);
apr03 = filter wlogs by timestamp < '20110404';
apr02 = filter wlogs by timestamp < '20110403' and timestamp > '20110401';
apr01 = filter wlogs by timestamp < '20110402' and timestamp > '20110331';
store apr03 into '20110403';
store apr02 into '20110402';
store apr01 into '20110401';
```

In fact, Pig will internally rewrite the original script that has `split` in exactly this way.

Let's take a look at how Pig executes these nonlinear data flows. Whenever possible, it combines them into single MapReduce jobs. This is referred to as a *multiquery*. In cases where all operators will fit into a single map task, this is easy. Pig creates separate pipelines inside the map and sends the appropriate records to each pipeline. The example using `split` to store data by date will be executed in this way.

Pig can also combine multiple `group` operators together in many cases. In the example given at the beginning of this section, where the baseball data is grouped by both team and position, this entire Pig Latin script will be executed inside one MapReduce job. Pig accomplishes this by duplicating records on the map side and annotating each record with its pipeline number. When the data is partitioned during the shuffle, the appropriate key is used for each record. That is, records from the pipeline grouping by `team` will use `team` as their shuffle key, and records from the pipeline grouping by `position` will use `position` as their shuffle key. This is done by declaring the key type to be `tuple` and placing the correct values in the key tuple for each record. Once the data has been sent to the reducers, the pipeline number is used as part of the sort key so that records from each pipeline and group are collected together. In the reduce task, Pig instantiates multiple pipelines, one for each `group` operator. It sends each record down the appropriate pipeline based on its annotated pipeline number. In this way, input data can be scanned once but grouped many different ways. An example of how one record flows through this pipeline is shown in Figure 5-1. Although this does not provide linear speedup, we find it often approaches it.

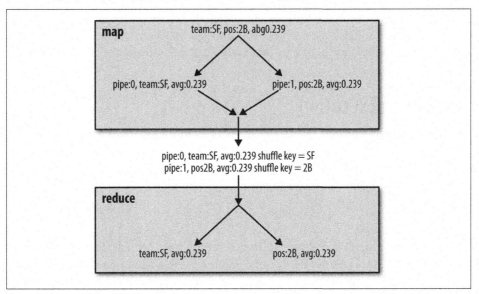

Figure 5-1. Multiquery illustration

There are cases where Pig will not combine multiple operators into a single Map-Reduce job. Pig does not use the multiquery optimization for any of the multiple-input operators—`join`, `union`, `cross`, or `cogroup`—or for `order` statements. Also, if a script has multiple `group` statements and some would use Hadoop's combiner (or "Map-Side Aggregation" on page 144) and some would not, it combines only those statements that use Hadoop's combiner into a multiquery. This is because experience has shown that combining Hadoop combiner and non–Hadoop combiner jobs together does not perform well.

Multiquery scripts tend to perform better than loading the same input multiple times, but this approach does have limits. Because it requires replicating records in the map, it does slow down the shuffle phase. Eventually the increased cost of the shuffle phase outweighs the reduced cost of rescanning the input data. Pig has no way to estimate when this will occur. Currently, the optimizer is optimistic and always combines jobs with multiquery whenever it can. If it combines too many jobs and performance becomes slower than when splitting some of the jobs, you can turn off multiquery or you can rewrite your Pig Latin into separate scripts so Pig does not attempt to combine them all. To turn off multiquery, you can pass either -M or -no_multiquery on the command line or set the property opt.multiquery to false.

We must also consider what happens when one job in a multiquery fails but others succeed. If all jobs succeed, Pig will return 0, meaning success. If all of the jobs fail, Pig will return 2. If some jobs fail and some succeed, Pig will return 3. By default, if one of the jobs fails, Pig will continue processing the other jobs. However, if you want Pig to stop as soon as one of the jobs fails, you can pass -F or -stop_on_failure. In this case, any jobs that have not yet been finished will be terminated, and any that have not started will not be started. Any jobs that are already finished will not be cleaned up.

Controlling Execution

In addition to providing many relational and data flow operators, Pig Latin provides ways for you to control how your jobs execute on MapReduce. It allows you to set values that control your environment and details of MapReduce, such as how your data is partitioned.

set

The set command is used to set up the environment in which Pig runs the MapReduce jobs. Table 5-1 shows Pig-specific parameters that can be controlled via set.

Table 5-1. Pig-specific set parameters

Parameter	Value type	Description
debug	String	Sets the logging level to DEBUG. Equivalent to passing -debug DEBUG on the command line.
default_parallel	Integer	Sets a default parallel level for all reduce operations in the script. See "parallel" on page 65 for details.
job.name	String	Assigns a name to the Hadoop job. By default the name is the filename of the script being run, or a randomly generated name for interactive sessions.
job.priority	String	If your Hadoop cluster is using the Capacity Scheduler with priorities enabled for queues, this allows you to set the priority of your Pig job. Allowed values are very_low, low, normal, high, and very_high.

For example, to set the default parallelism of your Pig Latin script and set the job name to my_job:

```
set default_parallel 10;
set job.name my_job;
users = load 'users';
```

In addition to these predefined values, set can be used to pass Java property settings to Pig and Hadoop. Both Pig and Hadoop use a number of Java properties to control their behavior. Consider an example where you want to turn multiquery optimization off for a given script, and you want to tell Hadoop to use a higher value than usual for its map-side sort buffer:

```
set opt.multiquery false;
set io.sort.mb 2048; --give it 2G
```

You can also use this mechanism to pass properties to UDFs. All of the properties are passed to the tasks on the Hadoop nodes when they are executed. They are not set as Java properties in that environment; rather, they are placed in a Hadoop object called JobConf. UDFs have access to JobConf. Thus, anything you set in the script can be seen by your UDFs. This can be a convenient way to control UDF behavior. For information on how to retrieve this information in your UDFs, see "Constructors and Passing Data from Frontend to Backend" on page 176.

Values that are set in your script are global for the whole script. If they are reset later in the script, that second value will overwrite the first and be used *throughout the whole script*.

Setting the Partitioner

Hadoop uses a class called Partitioner to partition records to reducers during the shuffle phase. Pig does not override Hadoop's default HashPartitioner, except for order operations and skew joins. The balancing operations in these require special partitioners.

Pig allows you to set the partitioner, except in the cases where it is already overriding it. To do this, you need to tell Pig which Java class to use to partition your data. This class must extend the org.apache.hadoop.mapreduce.Partitioner<KEY,VALUE> class in Hadoop. Note that this is the newer (version 0.20 and later) mapreduce API and not the older mapred:

```
register acme.jar; -- JAR containing the partitioner
users = load 'users' as (id, age, zip);
grp   = group users by id partition by com.acme.userpartitioner parallel 100;
```

Operators that reduce data can take the partition clause. These operators are cogroup, cross, distinct, group, and join (again, excluding skew joins).

Unlike with UDFs, you cannot use the DEFINE statement for the partitioner to pass constructor arguments. The only way to pass information to Partitioner is to implement the Configurable interface and override the setConf method.

A simple but useful partitioner, RoundRobinPartitioner, has been available as a built-in since Pig 0.15.

Pig Latin Preprocessor

Pig Latin has a preprocessor that runs before your Pig Latin script is parsed. This provides parameter substitution, similar to a very simple version of #define in C, and also allows inclusion of other Pig Latin scripts and function-like macro definitions, so that you can write Pig Latin in a modular way.

Parameter Substitution

Pig Latin scripts that are used frequently often have elements that need to change based on when or where they are run. For example, a script that is run every day is likely to have a date component in its input files or filters. Rather than editing the script every day, you would want to pass in the date as a parameter. Parameter substitution provides this capability with a basic string-replacement functionality. Parameter names must start with a letter or an underscore and can then contain any amount of letters, numbers, or underscores. Values for the parameters can be passed in on the command line or from a parameter file:

```
--daily.pig
daily     = load 'NYSE_daily' as (exchange:chararray, symbol:chararray,
                date:chararray, open:float, high:float, low:float, close:float,
                volume:int, adj_close:float);
yesterday = filter daily by date == '$DATE';
grpd      = group yesterday all;
minmax    = foreach grpd generate MAX(yesterday.high), MIN(yesterday.low);
```

When you run *daily.pig*, you must provide a definition for the parameter DATE; otherwise, you will get an error telling you that you have undefined parameters:

```
pig -p DATE=2009-12-17 daily.pig
```

You can repeat the -p command-line switch as many times as needed. Parameters can also be placed in a file, which is convenient if you have more than a few of them. The format of the file is *parameter=value*, one per line. Comments in the file should be preceded by a #. You then indicate the file to be used with -m or -param_file:

```
pig -param_file daily.params daily.pig
```

Parameters passed on the command line take precedence over parameters provided in files. This way, you can provide all your standard parameters in a file and override a few as needed on the command line.

Parameters can contain other parameters. So, for example, you could have the following parameter file:

```
#Param file
YEAR=2009-
MONTH=12-
```

```
DAY=17
DATE=$YEAR$MONTH$DAY
```

A parameter must be defined before it is referenced. The parameter file here would produce an error if the DAY line came after the DATE line.

If there are any additional characters following the parameter name, you must put the parameter in curly braces:

```
wlogs = load 'clicks/$YEAR${MONTH}01' as (url, pageid, timestamp);
```

Here, you need to put MONTH in curly braces. Otherwise, Pig would try to resolve a parameter MONTH01 when you meant MONTH.

When using parameter substitution, all parameters in your script must be resolved after the preprocessor is finished. If not, Pig will issue an error message and not continue. You can see the results of your parameter substitution by using the -dryrun flag on the Pig command line. Pig will write out a version of your Pig Latin script with the parameter substitution done, but it will not execute the script.

You can also define parameters inside your Pig Latin scripts using %declare and %default. %declare allows you to define a parameter in the script itself. %default is useful to provide a common default value that can be overridden when needed. Consider a case where most of the time your script is run on one Hadoop cluster, but occasionally it is run on a different cluster with different hardware:

```
%default parallel_factor 10;
wlogs = load 'clicks' as (url, pageid, timestamp);
grp   = group wlogs by pageid parallel $parallel_factor;
cntd  = foreach grp generate group, COUNT(wlogs);
```

When running your script in the usual configuration, there is no need to set the parameter parallel_factor. On the occasions it is run in a different setup, the parallel factor can be changed by passing a value on the command line.

Macros

Pig has the ability to define macros. This makes it possible to make your Pig Latin scripts modular. It also makes it possible to share segments of Pig Latin code among users. This can be particularly useful for defining standard practices and making sure all data producers and consumers use them.

Macros are declared with the define statement. A macro takes a set of input parameters, which are string values that will be substituted for the parameters when the macro is expanded. By convention, input relation names are placed first, before other parameters. The output relation name is given in a returns statement. The operators of the macro are enclosed in {} (braces). Anywhere the parameters—including the output relation name—are referenced inside the macro, they must be preceded by a $

(dollar sign). The macro is then invoked in your Pig Latin by assigning it to a relation:

```
--macro.pig
-- Given daily input and a particular year, analyze how
-- stock prices changed on days dividends were paid out.
define dividend_analysis (daily, year, daily_symbol, daily_open, daily_close)
returns analyzed {
    divs          = load 'NYSE_dividends' as (exchange:chararray,
                        symbol:chararray, date:chararray, dividends:float);
    divsthisyear  = filter divs by date matches '$year-.*';
    dailythisyear = filter $daily by date matches '$year-.*';
    jnd           = join divsthisyear by symbol, dailythisyear by $daily_symbol;
    $analyzed     = foreach jnd generate dailythisyear::$daily_symbol,
                        $daily_close - $daily_open;
};

daily   = load 'NYSE_daily' as (exchange:chararray, symbol:chararray,
            date:chararray, open:float, high:float, low:float, close:float,
            volume:int, adj_close:float);
results = dividend_analysis(daily, '2009', 'symbol', 'open', 'close');
```

It is also possible to have a macro that does not return a relation. In this case, the returns clause of the define statement is changed to returns void. This can be useful when you want to define a macro that controls how data is partitioned and sorted before being stored to a particular output, such as HBase or a database.

These macros are expanded inline. This is where an important difference between macros and functions becomes apparent. Macros cannot be invoked recursively. Macros can invoke other macros, so a macro A can invoke a macro B, but A cannot invoke itself. And once A has invoked B, B cannot invoke A. Pig will detect these loops and throw an error.

Parameter substitution (see the previous section) can be used inside macros since Pig 0.12. If the parameter is defined both in and outside a macro, Pig will take the definition inside the macro.[7] So, in this example:

```
%declare cost 10
define generate_cost() returns generated {
  %declare cost 8
  divs = load 'NYSE_dividends' as (exchange:chararray);
  $generated = foreach divs generate exchange, $cost as cost1;
}

generated = generate_cost();
regenerated = foreach generated generate exchange, cost1, $cost as cost2;
```

---

7 Before Pig 0.16, Pig will throw an exception if a parameter is declared both inside and outside a macro. See PIG-4880 (*https://issues.apache.org/jira/browse/PIG-4880*) for details.

cost1 will be 8 and cost2 will be 10.

You can use the -dryrun command-line argument to see how the macros are expanded inline. When the macros are expanded, the alias names are changed to avoid collisions with alias names in the place the macro is being expanded. If we take the previous example and use -dryrun to show us the resulting Pig Latin, we will see the following (reformatted slightly to fit on the page):

```
daily = load 'NYSE_daily' as (exchange:chararray, symbol:chararray,
        date:chararray, open:float, high:float, low:float, close:float,
        volume:int, adj_close:float);
macro_dividend_analysis_divs_0 = load 'NYSE_dividends' as (exchange:chararray,
        symbol:chararray, date:chararray, dividends:float);
macro_dividend_analysis_divsthisyear_0 =
        filter macro_dividend_analysis_divs_0 BY (date matches '2009-.*');
macro_dividend_analysis_dailythisyear_0 =
        filter daily BY (date matches '2009-.*');
macro_dividend_analysis_jnd_0 =
        join macro_dividend_analysis_divsthisyear_0 by (symbol),
        macro_dividend_analysis_dailythisyear_0 by (symbol);
results = foreach macro_dividend_analysis_jnd_0 generate
        macro_dividend_analysis_dailythisyear_0::symbol, close - open;
```

As you can see, the aliases in the macro are expanded with a combination of the macro name and the invocation number. This provides a unique key so that if other macros use the same aliases, or the same macro is used multiple times, there is still no duplication.

Including Other Pig Latin Scripts

The Pig preprocessor can be used to include one Pig Latin script in another. Together with macros, discussed in the previous section, this makes it possible to write modular Pig Latin.

import is used to include one Pig Latin script in another:

```
--main.pig
import '../examples/ch6/dividend_analysis.pig';

daily   = load 'NYSE_daily' as (exchange:chararray, symbol:chararray,
        date:chararray, open:float, high:float, low:float, close:float,
        volume:int, adj_close:float);
results = dividend_analysis(daily, '2009', 'symbol', 'open', 'close');
```

import writes the imported file directly into your Pig Latin script in place of the import statement. In the preceding example, the contents of *dividend_analysis.pig* will be placed immediately before the load statement. Note that a file cannot be imported twice. If you wish to use the same functionality multiple times, you should write it as a macro and import the file with that macro.

In the example just shown, we used a relative path for the file to be included. Fully qualified paths also can be used. By default, relative paths are taken from the current working directory of Pig when you launch the script. You can set a search path by setting the `pig.import.search.path` property. This is a comma-separated list of paths that will be searched for your files. The current working directory, . (dot), is always in the search path:

```
set pig.import.search.path '/usr/local/pig,/grid/pig';
import 'acme/macros.pig';
```

Imported files are not in separate namespaces. This means that all macros are in the same namespace, even when they have been imported from separate files. Thus, care should be taken to choose unique names for your macros.

## CHAPTER 6

Developing and Testing Pig Latin Scripts

The last few chapters focused on Pig Latin the language. Now we will turn to the practical matters of developing and testing your scripts. This chapter covers helpful debugging tools such as `describe` and `explain`. It also covers ways to test your scripts. Information on how to make your scripts perform better will be provided in the next chapter.

Development Tools

Pig provides several tools and diagnostic operators to help you develop your applications. In this section we will explore these and also look at some tools others have written to make it easier to develop Pig with standard editors and integrated development environments (IDEs).

Syntax Highlighting and Checking

Syntax highlighting often helps users write code correctly, at least syntactically, the first time around. Syntax highlighting packages exist for several popular editors. The packages listed in Table 6-1 were created and added at various times, so how their highlighting conforms with current Pig Latin syntax varies.

Table 6-1. Pig Latin syntax highlighting packages

Tool	URL
Eclipse	*https://github.com/eyala/pig-eclipse*
Emacs	*http://github.com/cloudera/piglatin-mode, http://sf.net/projects/pig-mode*
TextMate	*http://www.github.com/kevinweil/pig.tmbundle*
Vim	*http://www.vim.org/scripts/script.php?script_id=2186*

In addition to these syntax highlighting packages, Pig will also let you check the syntax of your script without running it. If you add -c or -check to the command line, Pig will just parse and run semantic checks on your script. The -dryrun command-line option will also check your syntax, expand any macros and imports, and perform parameter substitution.

describe

describe shows you the schema of a relation in your script. This can be very helpful as you are developing your scripts. It is especially useful as you are learning Pig Latin and understanding how various operators change the data. describe can be applied to any relation in your script, and you can have multiple describes in a script:

```
--describe.pig
divs    = load 'NYSE_dividends' as (exchange:chararray, symbol:chararray,
            date:chararray, dividends:float);
trimmed = foreach divs generate symbol, dividends;
grpd    = group trimmed by symbol;
avgdiv  = foreach grpd generate group, AVG(trimmed.dividends);

describe trimmed;
describe grpd;
describe avgdiv;

trimmed: {symbol: chararray,dividends: float}
grpd: {group: chararray,trimmed: {(symbol: chararray,dividends: float)}}
avgdiv: {group: chararray,double}
```

describe uses Pig's standard schema syntax (for information on this syntax, see "Schemas" on page 36). So, in this example, the relation trimmed has two fields: symbol, which is a chararray, and dividends, which is a float. grpd also has two fields: group (the name Pig always assigns to the group by key) and a bag, trimmed, which matches the name of the relation that Pig grouped to produce the bag. Tuples in trimmed have two fields: symbol and dividends. Finally, in avgdiv there are two fields, group and a double, which is the result of the AVG function and is unnamed.

You can also describe an inner relation inside foreach. The syntax is describe relation::inner_relation:

```
divs    = load 'NYSE_dividends' as (exchange:chararray, symbol:chararray,
            date:chararray, dividends:float);
grpd    = group divs by symbol;
top3    = foreach grpd {
    sorted = order divs by dividends desc;
    top    = limit sorted 3;
    generate group, flatten(top);
}
describe top3::sorted;
```

```
top3::sorted: {exchange: chararray,symbol: chararray,date: chararray,
dividends: float}
```

explain

One of Pig's goals is to allow you to think in terms of data flow instead of how the underlining execution engine, such as MapReduce, will run it. But sometimes you need to peek into the barn and see how Pig is compiling your script into jobs and tasks for the execution engine. Pig provides explain for this. explain is particularly helpful when you are trying to optimize your scripts or debug errors. It was written so that Pig developers could examine how Pig handled various scripts, and thus its output is not the most user-friendly. But with some knowledge, explain can help you write better Pig Latin. In this section, we assume the execution engine is MapReduce. We will illustrate Tez execution plans in Chapter 11.

There are two ways to use explain. You can explain any alias in your Pig Latin script, which will show the execution plan Pig would use if you stored that relation. You can also take an existing Pig Latin script and apply explain to the whole script in Grunt. This has a couple of advantages. One, you do not have to edit your script to add the explain line. Two, it will work with scripts that do not have a single store, showing how Pig will execute the entire script. So, if you have this script:

```
--explain.pig
divs   = load 'NYSE_dividends' as (exchange, symbol, date, dividends);
grpd   = group divs by symbol;
avgdiv = foreach grpd generate group, AVG(divs.dividends);
store avgdiv into 'average_dividend';
```

you can explain it as follows:

```
bin/pig -x local -e 'explain -script explain.pig'
```

Note Pig will not show the execution plan for the alias in a dump command. You need to change that to a store statement if you want Pig show the execution plan for it.

This will produce a printout of several graphs in text format; we will examine this output momentarily. When using explain on a script in Grunt, you can also have it print out the plan in graphical format. To do this, add -dot -out filename to the preceding command line. This prints out a file in DOT language containing diagrams explaining how your script will be executed. Tools that can read this language and produce graphs can then be used to view the graphs. For some tools, you might need to split the three graphs in the file into separate files.

Pig goes through several steps to transform a Pig Latin script to a set of MapReduce jobs. After doing basic parsing and semantic checking, it produces a logical plan. This plan describes the logical operators that Pig will use to execute the script. Some optimizations are done on this plan. For example, filters are pushed as far up[1] as possible in the logical plan. The logical plan for the preceding example is shown in Figure 6-1. We have trimmed a few extraneous pieces to make the output more readable (scary that this is more readable, huh?) Depending on the version of Pig you are using, the output will look slightly different, but it should be close enough that it will be recognizable.

```
avgdiv: Store 1-27 Schema: {group: bytearray,double} Type: Unknown
|
|---avgdiv: ForEach 1-26 Schema: {group: bytearray,double} Type: bag
    |     |
    |     Project 1-22 Projections: [0]
    |     FieldSchema: group: bytearray Type: bytearray
    |     Input: grpd: CoGroup 1-16
    |     |
    |     UserFunc 1-25 function: org.apache.pig.builtin.AVG
    |     FieldSchema: double Type: double
    |     |
    |     |---Project 1-23 Projections: [3]
    |         FieldSchema: dividends: bag({dividends: bytearray}) Type: bag
    |         Input: Project 1-24 Projections: [1] Overloaded: false|
    |         |---Project 1-24 Projections: [1]
    |             FieldSchema: divs: bag({exchange: bytearray,symbol: bytearray,
    |                 date: bytearray,dividends: bytearray}) Type: bag
    |             Input: grpd: CoGroup 1-16
    |
    |---grpd: CoGroup 1-16 Schema: {group: bytearray,divs: {exchange: bytearray,
        |     |   symbol: bytearray,date: bytearray,dividends: bytearray}} Type: bag
        |     |
        |     Project 1-15 Projections: [1]
        |     FieldSchema: symbol: bytearray Type: bytearray
        |     Input: divs: Load 1-14
        |
        |---divs: Load 1-14 Schema: {exchange: bytearray,symbol: bytearray,
                date: bytearray,dividends: bytearray} Type: bag
```

Figure 6-1. Logical plan

The flow of this chart is bottom to top, so the Load operator is at the very bottom. The lines between operators show the flow. Each of the four operators created by the script (Load, CoGroup, ForEach, and Store) can be seen. Each of these operators has a schema, described in standard schema syntax. The CoGroup and ForEach operators also have expressions attached to them (the lines dropping down from those operators). In the CoGroup operator, the projection indicates which field is the grouping key (in this case, field 1). The ForEach operator has a projection expression that projects field 0 (the group field) and a UDF expression, which indicates that the UDF being used is org.apache.pig.builtin.AVG. Notice how each of the Project opera-

---

1 Or down, whichever you prefer. Database textbooks usually talk of pushing filters down, closer to the scan. Because Pig Latin scripts start with a load at the top and go down, we tend to refer to it as pushing filters up toward the load.

tors has an `Input` field, indicating which operators they are drawing their input from. Figure 6-2 shows what this plan looks like when the -dot option is used instead.

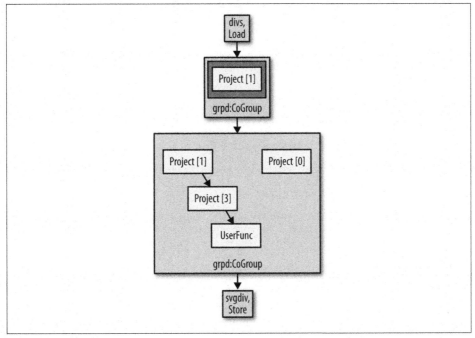

Figure 6-2. Logical plan diagram

After optimizing the logical plan, Pig produces a physical plan. This plan describes the physical operators Pig will use to execute the script, without reference to how they will be executed in MapReduce. The physical plan for our plan in Figure 6-1 is shown in Figure 6-3.

This looks like the logical plan, but there are a few notable differences. First, the load and store functions that will be used have been resolved (in this case to `org.apache.pig.builtin.PigStorage`, the default load and store function), as have the actual paths that will be used. This example was run in local mode, so the paths are to local files. If it had been run on a cluster, it would have showed paths like *hdfs://nn.machine.domain/filepath*.

```
avgdiv: Store(file:///home/gates/git/programmingpig/data/average_dividend:
        org.apache.pig.builtin.PigStorage)
|
|---avgdiv: New For Each(false,false)[bag]
    |   |
    |   Project[bytearray][0]
    |   |
    |   POUserFunc(org.apache.pig.builtin.AVG)[double]
    |   |
    |   |---Project[bag][3]
    |       |
    |       |---Project[bag][1]
    |
    |---grpd: Package[tuple]{bytearray}
        |
        |---grpd: Global Rearrange[tuple]
            |
            |---grpd: Local Rearrange[tuple]{bytearray}(false)
                |   |
                |   Project[bytearray][1]
                |
                |---divs: Load(file:///home/gates/git/programmingpig/data/
                    NYSE_dividends:org.apache.pig.builtin.PigStorage)
```

Figure 6-3. Physical plan

The other noticeable difference is that the CoGroup operator was replaced by three operators, Local Rearrange, Global Rearrange, and Package. Local Rearrange is the operator Pig uses to prepare data for the shuffle by setting up the key. Global Rearrange is a stand-in for the shuffle. Package sits in the reduce phase and directs records to the proper bags. Figure 6-4 shows a graphical representation of this plan.

Finally, Pig takes the physical plan and decides how it will place its operators into one or more MapReduce jobs. First, it walks the physical plan looking for all operators that require a new reduce. This occurs anywhere there is a Local Rearrange, Global Rearrange, or Package. After it has done this, it sees whether there are places that it can do physical optimizations. For example, it looks for places the combiner can be used, and whether sorts can be avoided by including them as part of the sorting Hadoop does in the shuffle. After all of this is done, Pig has a MapReduce plan. This plan describes the maps, combines, and reduces, along with the physical operations Pig will perform in each stage.

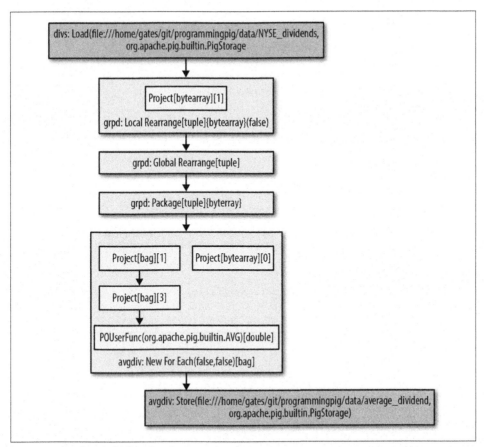

Figure 6-4. Physical plan diagram

Completing our example, the MapReduce plan is shown in Figure 6-5. This looks much the same as the physical plan. The pipeline is now broken into three stages: map, combine, and reduce. The Global Rearrange operator is gone because it was a stand-in for the shuffle. The AVG UDF has been broken up into three stages: Initial in the mapper, Intermediate in the combiner, and Final in the reducer. If there were multiple MapReduce jobs in this example, they would all be shown in this output. The graphical version is shown in Figure 6-6.

```
MapReduce node
Map Plan
grpd: Local Rearrange[tuple]{bytearray}(false)
|   |
|      Project[bytearray][0]
|
|---avgdiv: New For Each(false,false)[bag]
|      |   |
|      |      Project[bytearray][0]
|      |   |
|      |      POUserFunc(org.apache.pig.builtin.AVG$Initial)[tuple]
|      |   |
|      |      |---Project[bag][3]
|      |         |
|      |         |---Project[bag][1]
|      |
|      |---Pre Combiner Local Rearrange[tuple]{Unknown}
|         |
|         |---divs: Load(file:///home/gates/git/programmingpig/data/
|                        NYSE_dividends:org.apache.pig.builtin.PigStorage)


Combine Plan
grpd: Local Rearrange[tuple]{bytearray}(false)
|   |
|      Project[bytearray][0]
|
|---avgdiv: New For Each(false,false)[bag]
|      |   |
|      |      Project[bytearray][0]
|      |   |
|      |      POUserFunc(org.apache.pig.builtin.AVG$Intermediate)[tuple]
|      |   |
|      |      |---Project[bag][1]
|      |
|      |---POCombinerPackage[tuple]{bytearray}


Reduce Plan
avgdiv: Store(file:///home/gates/git/programmingpig/data/average_dividend:
|          org.apache.pig.builtin.PigStorage)
|
|---avgdiv: New For Each(false,false)[bag]
|      |   |
|      |      Project[bytearray][0]
|      |   |
|      |      POUserFunc(org.apache.pig.builtin.AVG$Final)[double]
|      |   |
|      |      |---Project[bag][1]
|      |
|      |---POCombinerPackage[tuple]{bytearray}
Global sort: false
```

Figure 6-5. MapReduce plan

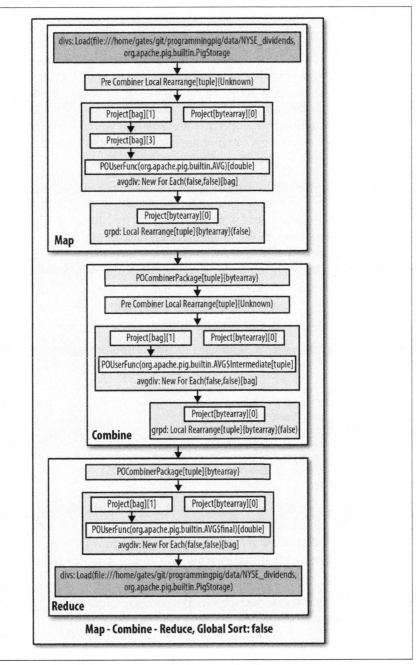

Figure 6-6. MapReduce plan diagram

illustrate

Often one of the best ways to debug your Pig Latin script is to run your data through it. But if you are using Pig, the odds are that you have a large dataset. If it takes several hours to process your data, this makes for a very long debugging cycle. One obvious solution is to run your script on a sample of your data. For simple scripts this works fine. But sampling has another problem: it is not always trivial to pick a sample that will exercise your script properly. For example, if you have a join, you have to be careful to sample records from each input such that at least some have the same key. Otherwise, your join will return no results.

To address this issue, the scientists at Yahoo! Research built `illustrate` into Pig. `illustrate` takes a sample of your data and runs it through your script, but as it encounters operators that remove data (such as `filter`, `join`, etc.), it makes sure that some records pass through the operator and some do not. When necessary, it will manufacture records that look like yours (i.e., that have the same schema) but are not in the sample it took. For example, if your script had `B = filter A by x > 100;` and every record that `illustrate` sampled had a value of less than 100 for x, `illustrate` would keep at least one of these records (to show the filter removing a record), and it would manufacture a record with x greater than 100.

To use `illustrate`, apply it to an alias in your script, just as you would `describe`. Figure 6-7 shows the results of illustrating the following script:

```
--illustrate.pig
divs   = load 'NYSE_dividends' as (e:chararray, s:chararray, d:chararray,
            div:float);
recent = filter divs by d > '2009-01-01';
trimmd = foreach recent generate s, div;
grpd   = group trimmd by s;
avgdiv = foreach grpd generate group, AVG(trimmd.div);
illustrate avgdiv;
```

For each relation here, `illustrate` shows us records as they look coming out of the relation. For the line `recent = filter divs by d > '2009-01-01';`, we intentionally chose a filter that would remove no records in the input to show how `illustrate` manufactures a record that will be removed—in this case, the last record shown in the `divs` output.

Like `explain`, `illustrate` can be given as a command-line option rather than modifying your script—for example:

```
bin/pig -e 'illustrate -script illustrate.pig'
```

Note that `illustrate` is not currently implemented in Tez or Spark mode. You can only use it in MapReduce mode.

Figure 6-7 shows the output of running this command.

```
------------------------------------------------------------------------------------
| divs      | e:chararray     | s:chararray     | d:chararray     | div:float     |
------------------------------------------------------------------------------------
|           | NYSE            | CUB             | 2009-03-06      | 0.09          |
|           | NYSE            | CUB             | 2009-08-19      | 0.09          |
|           | NYSE            | CUB             | 2009-01-0       | 0.09          |
------------------------------------------------------------------------------------

------------------------------------------------------------------------------------
| recent    | e:chararray     | s:chararray     | d:chararray     | div:float     |
------------------------------------------------------------------------------------
|           | NYSE            | CUB             | 2009-03-06      | 0.09          |
|           | NYSE            | CUB             | 2009-08-19      | 0.09          |
------------------------------------------------------------------------------------

--------------------------------------------------------
| trimmd    | s:chararray     | div:float     |
--------------------------------------------------------
|           | CUB             | 0.09          |
|           | CUB             | 0.09          |
--------------------------------------------------------

------------------------------------------------------------------------------------
| grpd      | group:chararray     | trimmd:bag{:tuple(s:chararray,div:float)}     |
------------------------------------------------------------------------------------
|           | CUB                 | {(CUB, 0.09), (CUB, 0.09)}                    |
------------------------------------------------------------------------------------

------------------------------------------------------------------
| avgdiv    | group:chararray     | :double               |
------------------------------------------------------------------
|           | CUB                 | 0.09000000357627869   |
------------------------------------------------------------------
```

Figure 6-7. illustrate output

Pig Statistics

At the end of every run Pig produces a summary set of statistics. For example, suppose you have the following script:[2]

```
--stats.pig
a = load '/user/pig/tests/data/singlefile/studenttab20m' as (name, age, gpa);
b = load '/user/pig/tests/data/singlefile/votertab10k'
    as (name, age, registration, contributions);
c = filter a by age < '50';
d = filter b by age < '50';
e = cogroup c by (name, age), d by (name, age) parallel 20;
f = foreach e generate flatten(c), flatten(d);
```

---

2 The examples in this section assume that MapReduce is the execution engine. We will discuss statistics when Tez is the engine in Chapter 11.

```
g = group f by registration parallel 20;
h = foreach g generate group, SUM(f.d::contributions);
i = order h by $1, $0 parallel 20;
store i into 'student_voter_info';
```

Running *stats.pig* produces the statistics shown in Figure 6-8.

```
HadoopVersion   PigVersion      UserId   StartedAt        FinishedAt       Features
2.6.0   0.15.0   daijy   2015-10-02 00:00:01   2015-10-02 00:03:11   COGROUP,GROUP_BY,ORDER_BY,FILTER

Success!

Job Stats (time in seconds):
JobId   Maps    Reduces MaxMapTime       MinMapTime      AvgMapTime      MedianMapTime  MaxReduceTime   MinReduceTimA
vgReduceTime    MedianReducetime        Alias   Feature Outputs
job_1443760655675_0014  5       20      31      5       22      31      16      7       8       7       a,b,c,d,e  C
OGROUP
job_1443760655675_0015  2       20      12      6       9       9       5       2       3       3       g,h     GROUP
_BY,COMBINER
job_1443760655675_0016  1       1       2       2       2       2       2       2       2       2       i       SAMPL
ER
job_1443760655675_0017  1       20      2       2       2       2       4       3       3       3       i       ORDER
_BY     hdfs://localhost:9000/user/daijy/student_voter_info,

Input(s):
Successfully read 20000000 records from: "/user/pig/tests/data/singlefile/studenttab20m"
Successfully read 10000 records from: "/user/pig/tests/data/singlefile/votertab10k"

Output(s):
Successfully stored 6 records (184 bytes) in: "hdfs://localhost:9000/user/daijy/student_voter_info"

Counters:
Total records written : 6
Total bytes written : 184
Spillable Memory Manager spill count : 0
Total bags proactively spilled: 0
Total records proactively spilled: 0

Job DAG:
job_1443760655675_0014  ->      job_1443760655675_0015,
job_1443760655675_0015  ->      job_1443760655675_0016,
job_1443760655675_0016  ->      job_1443760655675_0017
job_1443760655675_0017
```

Figure 6-8. Statistics output of stats.pig

The first couple of lines give a brief summary of the job. StartedAt is the time Pig submits the job, not the time the first job starts running on the Hadoop cluster. Depending on how busy your cluster is, these two times may vary significantly. Similarly, FinishedAt is the time Pig finishes processing the job, which will be slightly after the time the last MapReduce job finishes.

The section labeled Job Stats gives a breakdown of each MapReduce job that was run. This includes how many map and reduce tasks each job had, statistics on how long these tasks took, a mapping of aliases in your Pig Latin script to the jobs, and Pig features used in the job. The last two pieces of information are especially useful when trying to understand which operations in your script are running in which Map-Reduce job, which can be helpful when determining why a particular job is failing or producing unexpected results.

This is another reason not to reuse aliases in your Pig Latin script. If you do, when you see an alias in the job summary, you will not know what it refers to. But if that happens, you do have a remedy. If you look back at the console message, you will find the name of the alias along with the source location for each job. For example:

```
HadoopJobId: job_1443809933189_0002
Processing aliases g,h
  detailed locations: M: h[11,4],g[10,4] C: h[11,4],g[10,4] R: h[11,4]
```

In addition to the alias, this line shows the location in the script of the job job_1443809933189_0002. M: h[11,4],g[10,4] means the map task is processing alias h at line 11 column 4 and alias g at line 10 column 4. C: h[11,4],g[10,4] means the combiner is also processing alias h at line 11 column 4 and alias g at line 10 column 4. Similarly, R: h[11,4] means the reduce task is processing h at line 11 column 4.

The Input, Output, and Counters sections are self-explanatory. The statistics on spills record how many times Pig spilled records to local disk to avoid running out of memory. Prior to Pig 0.13, in local mode the Counters section will be missing because Hadoop does not report counters in local mode. However, "Total bytes written" is still 0 in local mode.

The Job DAG section at the end describes how data flowed between MapReduce jobs. In this case, the flow was linear.

Job Status

When you are running Pig Latin scripts on your Hadoop cluster, finding the status and logs of your jobs can be challenging. Logs generated by Pig while it plans and manages your queries are stored in the current working directory. You can select a different directory by passing -l *logdir* on the command line. However, Hadoop does not provide a way to fetch back the logs from its tasks. So, the logfile created by Pig contains only log entries generated on your machine. Log entries generated during the execution, including those generated by your UDFs, stay on the task nodes in your Hadoop cluster. All logs written to *stdout* and *stderr* by map and reduce tasks are also kept in the logs on the task nodes.

 This section is specific to MapReduce. When running with other engines, logs for tasks run on the cluster will also be located on the cluster, but you'll need different tools to view them. See Chapter 11 for a discussion of how to locate logs for your Tez jobs.

The first step in locating your logs is to connect to the ResourceManager's web page.[3] This page gives you the status of all jobs currently running on your Hadoop cluster,

---

3 We assume your cluster is Hadoop 2. For Hadoop 1, you will connect to the JobTracker instead. The layout of the Job Tracker's web page (Hadoop 1) is quite different. However, you can find similar information in the page.

plus a list of the last hundred or so finished jobs. Generally, it is located at *http://jt.acme.com:8088*, where *jt.acme.com* is the address of your ResourceManager. Figure 6-9 shows a sample page taken from a cluster running in pseudodistributed mode on a Linux desktop.

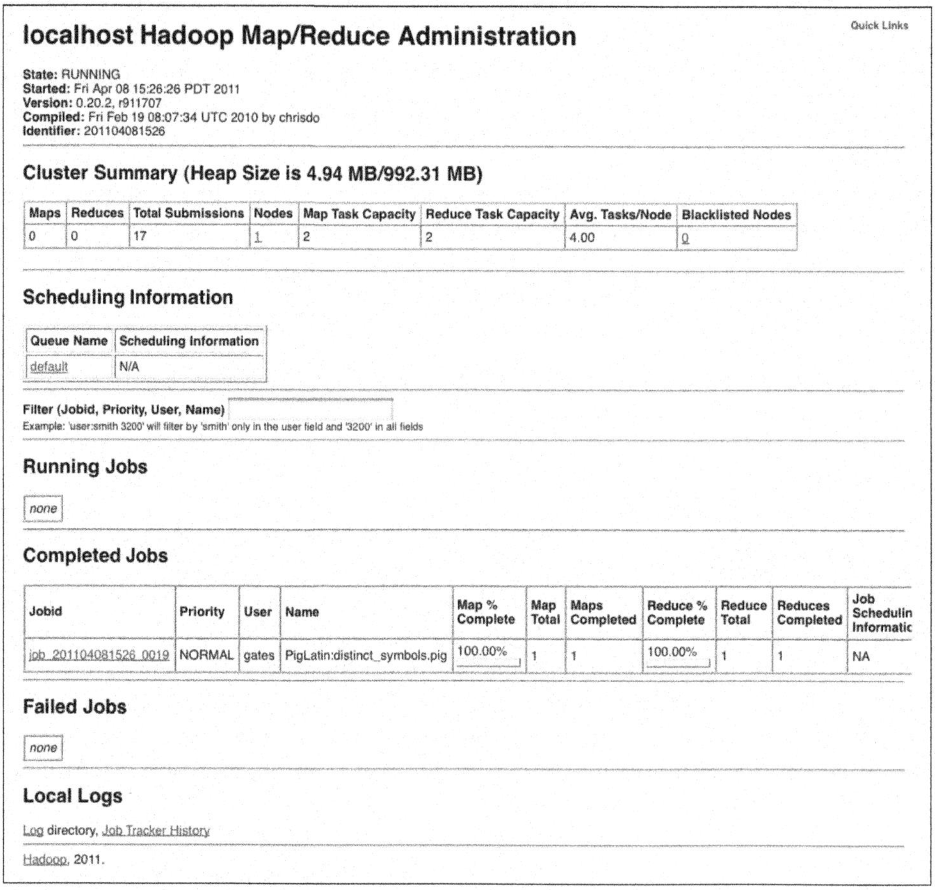

localhost Hadoop Map/Reduce Administration

Quick Links

State: RUNNING
Started: Fri Apr 08 15:26:26 PDT 2011
Version: 0.20.2, r911707
Compiled: Fri Feb 19 08:07:34 UTC 2010 by chrisdo
Identifier: 201104081526

Cluster Summary (Heap Size is 4.94 MB/992.31 MB)

Maps	Reduces	Total Submissions	Nodes	Map Task Capacity	Reduce Task Capacity	Avg. Tasks/Node	Blacklisted Nodes
0	0	17	1	2	2	4.00	0

Scheduling Information

Queue Name	Scheduling Information
default	N/A

Filter (Jobid, Priority, User, Name)
Example: 'user:smith 3200' will filter by 'smith' only in the user field and '3200' in all fields

Running Jobs

Completed Jobs

Jobid	Priority	User	Name	Map % Complete	Map Total	Maps Completed	Reduce % Complete	Reduce Total	Reduces Completed	Job Schedulin Informatic
job_201104081526_0019	NORMAL	gates	PigLatin:distinct_symbols.pig	100.00%	1	1	100.00%	1	1	NA

Failed Jobs

Local Logs

Log directory, Job Tracker History

Hadoop, 2011.

Figure 6-9. ResourceManager web page

In this screenshot you will find four jobs. Job `application_1443809933189_0004` is still running, and the other three are finished. The user who ran each job, the job ID, and the job name are all listed on the page. Jobs are assigned the name of the Pig Latin script that started them, unless you set the `job-name` property to change the job name. All jobs started by a single script will share the same name. As discussed in the previous section, Pig prints a summary at the end of its execution telling you which aliases and operators were run in which jobs. When you have multiple jobs with the same name, this will help you determine which MapReduce job you are interested in.

For the job `application_1443809933189_0001` in the screenshot shown in Figure 6-9, the relevant portions of the summary look like this:

```
Job Stats (time in seconds):
JobId                               Alias       Feature
application_1443809933189_0001      a,b,c,d,e   COGROUP
```

Given this job ID, you now know which job to look at on the ResourceManager page.

Note that jobs are shown on the ResourceManager page only once they start to execute on your Hadoop cluster. It takes Pig a few seconds to parse your script and plan the MapReduce jobs it will run. It then takes Hadoop a few seconds after Pig submits the first job to begin running it. Also, the necessary resources might not be available, in which case your job will not appear until it has been assigned resources.

Clicking the job ID will take you to a screen that summarizes the execution of the job, including when the job started and stopped and how many map and reduce tasks it ran, as shown in Figure 6-10.

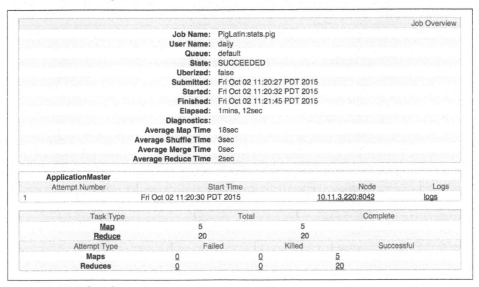

Figure 6-10. Job web page

The web pages for running jobs and finished jobs are also slightly different. The biggest difference is that the page for a running job shows the progress of the job. Here, we're looking at a finished job page. Let's say you want to see the logs for the single map task in this job. In the table toward the bottom of the page that summarizes the results of the map and reduce tasks, clicking the number of successful maps (5, in this example) in the far-right column produces a list of all successful map tasks of this job. For each task it shows the machine it ran on, its status, its start and end times, and a link to its logfile. Clicking that link will (finally) allow you to see the log for that individual task.

In addition to logs, you can click "Counters" in the left menu to find the results of all of the counters, as shown in Figure 6-11.

Counter Group	Counters			
	Name	Map	Reduce	Total
File System Counters	FILE: Number of bytes read	322665693	351323187	673988880
	FILE: Number of bytes written	674733405	355249957	1029983362
	FILE: Number of large read operations	0	0	0
	FILE: Number of read operations	0	0	0
	FILE: Number of write operations	0	0	0
	HDFS: Number of bytes read	438800699	0	438800699
	HDFS: Number of bytes written	0	176375997	176375997
	HDFS: Number of large read operations	0	0	0
	HDFS: Number of read operations	10	60	70
	HDFS: Number of write operations	0	40	40
	Name	Map	Reduce	Total
Job Counters	Data-local map tasks	0	0	5
	Launched map tasks	0	0	5
	Launched reduce tasks	0	0	20
	Total megabyte-seconds taken by all map tasks	0	0	110735360
	Total megabyte-seconds taken by all reduce tasks	0	0	179345408
	Total time spent by all map tasks (ms)	0	0	108140
	Total time spent by all maps in occupied slots (ms)	0	0	1189540
	Total time spent by all reduce tasks (ms)	0	0	175142
	Total time spent by all reduces in occupied slots (ms)	0	0	1926562
	Total vcore-seconds taken by all map tasks	0	0	108140
	Total vcore-seconds taken by all reduce tasks	0	0	175142
	Name	Map	Reduce	Total
Map-Reduce Framework	Combine input records	0	0	0
	Combine output records	0	0	0
	CPU time spent (ms)	0	0	0
	Failed Shuffles	0	0	0
	GC time elapsed (ms)	397	1491	1888
	Input split bytes	1963	0	1963
	Map input records	20010000	0	20010000
	Map output bytes	329984553	0	329984553
	Map output materialized bytes	351323667	0	351323667
	Map output records	10669257	0	10669257
	Merged Map outputs	0	100	100
	Physical memory (bytes) snapshot	0	0	0
	Reduce input groups	0	21632	21632
	Reduce input records	0	10669257	10669257
	Reduce output records	0	2643368	2643368
	Reduce shuffle bytes	0	351323667	351323667
	Shuffled Maps	0	100	100
	Spilled Records	20462748	10669257	31132005
	Total committed heap usage (bytes)	3083337728	9069658112	12152995840
	Virtual memory (bytes) snapshot	0	0	0
	Name	Map	Reduce	Total
MultiInputCounters	Input records from_0_studenttab20m	20000000	0	20000000
	Input records from_1_votertab10k	10000	0	10000
	Name	Map	Reduce	Total
Shuffle Errors	BAD_ID	0	0	0
	CONNECTION	0	0	0
	IO_ERROR	0	0	0
	WRONG_LENGTH	0	0	0
	WRONG_MAP	0	0	0
	WRONG_REDUCE	0	0	0
File Input Format Counters	Name	Map	Reduce	Total
	Bytes Read	0	0	0
File Output Format Counters	Name	Map	Reduce	Total
	Bytes Written	0	0	0

Figure 6-11. Counters web page

You can also find the configuration of the job by clicking the "Configuration" link on the left. You can see the configuration used for the task on this screen (Figure 6-12). For example, `pig.alias.location` shows the aliases and locations the map, combiner, and reducer tasks were processing for this MapReduce job (we saw the same information in the console output, as discussed in the previous section).

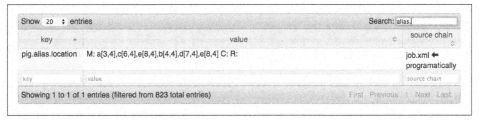

Figure 6-12. Configuration web page

Of course, in this example, finding the map task we wanted was easy because there was only one. But what happens when your job has 10,000 map tasks? How do you know which one to look at? This is a good question that does not always have a concise answer. If your tasks are failing only periodically, you can examine the logs of the failing tasks. If they are all failing, you should be able to pick any of them, since they are all running the same code. If your job is running slower than it seems like it should, you can look for tasks that took much longer than others. It is also often useful to look to see if all maps or all reduces take about the same amount of time. If not, you may have a skew problem.

Debugging Tips

Beyond the tools covered previously, there are a few things we have found useful in debugging Pig Latin scripts. First, if `illustrate` does not do what you need, use local mode to test your script before running it on your Hadoop cluster. In most cases this requires you to work with a sample of your data, which could be difficult, as explained in "illustrate" on page 122. But local mode has several advantages. One, despite its slowness, it provides a faster turnaround than using a Hadoop grid, where you may have to wait to get slots and the minimum job setup time is 30 seconds (versus about 10 seconds in local mode). Two, the logs for your operations appear on your screen, instead of being left on a task node somewhere. Three, local mode runs all in your local process. This means that you can attach a debugger to the process, which is particularly useful when you need to debug your UDFs.

A second tip we have found useful is that sometimes you need to turn off particular features to see whether they are the source of your problem. These can include particular optimizations that Pig attempts or new features that have not had all the bugs worked out yet.[4] Table 6-2 lists features that can be turned off. All of these are options that can be passed to Pig on the command line.

---

4 If you find you are turning off a feature to avoid a bug, please file a JIRA ticket (*https://issues.apache.org/jira/ browse/PIG*) so that the problem can be fixed.

Table 6-2. Turning off optimizations

Command-line option	What it does	When you might want to turn it off
-t ConstantCalculator	Prevents Pig from evaluating a constant expression at compile time. Introduced in Pig 0.14.	Your constant expression in a filter or a foreach is not correctly calculated.
-t SplitFilter	Prevents Pig from splitting filter predicates so portions of them can be pushed higher in the data flow.	Your filter is not removing the rows you expect.
-t MergeFilter	Prevents Pig from merging adjacent filter operators to evaluate them more efficiently.	Your filter is not removing the rows you expect.
-t PushUpFilter	Prevents Pig from pushing filter operators in front of adjacent operators in the data flow.	Your filter is not removing the rows you expect.
-t PushDownForEachFlatten	Prevents Pig from pushing foreach operators with a flatten behind adjacent operators in the data flow.	Your foreach is not producing the rows or fields you expect.
-t ColumnMapKeyPrune	Prevents Pig from determining all fields your script uses and telling the loader to load only those fields.	Your load function is not returning the fields you expect.
-t LimitOptimizer	Prevents Pig from pushing limit operators in front of adjacent operators in the data flow.	Your limit is not returning the number of rows you expect.
-t AddForEach	Prevents Pig from placing foreach operators in your script to trim out unneeded fields.	Your results do not contain the fields you expect.
-t MergeForEach	Prevents Pig from merging adjacent foreach operators to evaluate them more efficiently.	Your foreach is not producing the rows or fields you expect.
-t GroupByConstParallelSetter	Forces parallel 1 for group all statements.	You get one reducer when you should have more.
-t PartitionFilterOptimizer	Pushes down partition filter conditions to the loader implementing LoadMetaData.	Partitions are removed by mistake.
-t PredicatePushdownOptimizer	Pushes down filter predicates to the loader implementing LoadPredicatePushDown.	Records are filtered by mistake in the loader.

Command-line option	What it does	When you might want to turn it off
`-t All`	Turns off all logical optimizations. Physical optimizations (such as use of combiner, multiquery, etc.) will still be done.	Your script is not producing the rows you expect and you want to understand whether the logical optimizer is part of the problem.
`-D pig.exec.nocombiner=true`	Prevents Pig from using Hadoop's combiner.	You want to check if your UDF has a problem in its Alge braic implementation (this is called only when the combiner is used).
`-D opt.multiquery=false (or -M, -no_multiquery)`	Prevents Pig from combining multiple data pipelines into a single MapReduce job.	Your multiquery scripts are running out of memory, underperforming, or otherwise failing.
`-D pig.splitCombination=false`	Prevents Pig from combining input splits to reduce the number of map tasks.	Some input formats, such as HBase, cannot have their splits combined.
`-D pig.exec.nosecondarykey=true`	Prevents Pig from using secondary key sorting on the reducer input.	Secondary sorting takes longer as Pig cannot use the binary comparator and needs to deserialize the data before comparing.
`-D opt.accumulator=false`	Prevents Pig from using the accumulator.	You want to check if your UDF has a problem in its Accumu lator implementation.
`-D pig.exec.mapPartAgg=false`	Prevents Pig from using map-side aggregation.	Your map has many keys and map-side aggregation does not reduce the map output. In this case, you'd better disable the combiner as well.

Testing Your Scripts with PigUnit

As part of your development, you will want to test your Pig Latin scripts. Even once they are finished, regular testing helps ensure that changes to your UDFs, to your scripts, or in the versions of Pig and Hadoop that you are using do not break your code. PigUnit provides a unit-testing framework that plugs into JUnit to help you write unit tests that can be run on a regular basis.

Let's walk through an example of how to test a script with PigUnit. First, you need a script to test:

```
--pigunit.pig
divs    = load 'NYSE_dividends' as (exchange, symbol, date, dividends);
grpd    = group divs all;
```

```
avgdiv = foreach grpd generate AVG(divs.dividends);
store avgdiv into 'average_dividend';
```

Second, you will need the *pigunit.jar* JAR file. This is not distributed as part of the standard Pig distribution, but you can build it from the source code included in your distribution. To do this, go to the directory your distribution is in and type `ant jar -Dhadoopversion=23 pigunit-jar` (assuming you are using Hadoop 2). Once this is finished, there should be two files in the directory: *pig.jar* and *pigunit.jar*. You will need to place these in your classpath when running PigUnit tests.

Third, you need data to run through your script. You can use an existing input file, or you can manufacture some input in your test and run that through your script. We will look at how to do both.

Finally, you need to write a Java class that JUnit can use to run your test. Let's start with a simple example that runs the preceding script:

```java
// java/example/PigUnitExample.java
public class PigUnitExample {
    private PigTest test;
    private static Cluster cluster;

    @Test
    public void testDataInFile() throws ParseException, IOException {
        // Construct an instance of PigTest that will use the script
        // pigunit.pig.
        test = new PigTest("../pigunit.pig");

        // Specify our expected output.  The format is a string for each line.
        // In this particular case we expect only one line of output.
        String[] output = { "(0.27305267014925455)" };

        // Run the test and check that the output matches our expectation.
        // The "avgdiv" tells PigUnit what alias to check the output value
        // against.  It inserts a store for that alias and then checks the
        // contents of the stored file against output.
        test.assertOutput("avgdiv", output);
    }
}
```

You can also specify the input inline in your test rather than relying on an existing datafile:

```java
// java/example/PigUnitExample.java
    @Test
    public void testTextInput() throws ParseException, IOException  {
        test = new PigTest("../pigunit.pig");

        // Rather than read from a file, generate synthetic input.
        // Format is one record per line, tab-separated.
        String[] input = {
            "NYSE\tCPO\t2009-12-30\t0.14",
```

```
        "NYSE\tCPO\t2009-01-06\t0.14",
        "NYSE\tCCS\t2009-10-28\t0.414",
        "NYSE\tCCS\t2009-01-28\t0.414",
        "NYSE\tCIF\t2009-12-09\t0.029",
    };

    String[] output = { "(0.22739999999999996)" };

    // Run the example script using the input we constructed
    // rather than loading whatever the load statement says.
    // "divs" is the alias to override with the input data.
    // As with the previous example, "avgdiv" is the alias
    // to test against the value(s) in output.
    test.assertOutput("divs", input, "avgdiv", output);
}
```

It is also possible to specify the Pig Latin script in your test and to test the output against an existing file that contains the expected results:

```
// java/example/PigUnitExample.java
@Test
public void testFileOutput() throws ParseException, IOException {
    // The script as an array of strings, one line per string.
    String[] script = {
        "divs   = load '../../../data/NYSE_dividends' as",
        "    (exchange, symbol, date, dividends);",
        "grpd   = group divs all;",
        "avgdiv = foreach grpd generate AVG(divs.dividends);",
        "store avgdiv into 'average_dividend';",
    };
    test = new PigTest(script);

    // Test output against an existing file that contains the
    // expected output.
    test.assertOutput(new File("../expected.out"));
}
```

If you don't care about the order of output, you can use assertOutputAnyOrder so the test succeeds if the actual output and expected output differ only in order:

```
// java/example/PigUnitExample.java
@Test
        String[] script = {
        "divs   = load '../../../data/NYSE_dividends' as",
        "    (exchange, symbol, date, dividends);",
        "dates =  foreach divs generate date;",
        "filtereddates = filter dates by date matches '2009-01-.*';",
        "distinctdates = distinct filtereddates;",
        "store distinctdates into 'distinct_dates';",
    };
    test = new PigTest(script);

    String[] output = { "(2009-01-02)","(2009-01-06)","(2009-01-07)",
```

```
                 "(2009-01-08)","(2009-01-12)", "(2009-01-13)","(2009-01-14)",
                 "(2009-01-15)","(2009-01-20)","(2009-01-21)","(2009-01-22)",
                 "(2009-01-26)","(2009-01-28)","(2009-01-29)","(2009-01-30)"};
        test.assertOutputAnyOrder("distinctdates", output);
    }
```

Finally, let's look at how to integrate PigUnit with parameter substitution, and how to specify expected output that will be compared against the stored result (rather than specifying an alias to check):

```
// java/example/PigUnitExample.java
@Test
public void testWithParams() throws ParseException, IOException {
    // Parameters to be substituted in Pig Latin script before the
    // test is run.  Format is one string for each parameter,
    // parameter=value
    String[] params = {
        "input=../../../data/NYSE_dividends",
        "output=average_dividend2"
    };
    test = new PigTest("../pigunitwithparams.pig", params);

    String[] output = { "(0.27305267014925455)" };

    // Test output in stored file against specified result
    test.assertOutput(output);
}
```

These examples can be run by using the *build.xml* file included with the examples from this chapter. These examples are not exhaustive; see the code itself for a complete listing. For more in-depth examples, you can check out the tests for PigUnit located in *test/org/apache/pig/test/pigunit/TestPigTest.java* in your Pig distribution. This file exercises most of the features of PigUnit.

## CHAPTER 7

Making Pig Fly

Who says Pigs can't fly? Knowing how to optimize your Pig Latin scripts can make a significant difference in how they perform. Pig is still a young project and does not have a sophisticated optimizer that can make the right choices. Instead, consistent with Pig's philosophy of user choice, it relies on you to make these decisions. Beyond just optimizing your scripts, Pig and MapReduce can be tuned to perform better based on your workload. And there are ways to optimize your data layout as well. This chapter covers a number of features you can use to help Pig fly.

Before diving into the details of how to optimize your Pig Latin, it is worth understanding what features tend to create bottlenecks in Pig jobs:

Input size

It does not seem that a massively parallel system should be I/O bound. Hadoop's parallelism reduces I/O but does not entirely remove it. You can always add more map tasks. However, the law of diminishing returns comes into effect. Additional maps take more time to start up, and MapReduce has to find more slots in which to run them. If you have twice as many maps as cluster capacity to run them, it will take twice your average map time to run all of your maps. Adding one more map in that case will actually make things worse because the map time will increase to three times the average. Also, every record that is read might need to be decompressed and will need to be deserialized.

Shuffle size

By shuffle size we mean the data that is moved from your map tasks to your reduce tasks. All of this data has to be serialized, sorted, moved over the network, merged, and deserialized. Also, the number of maps and reduces matters. Every reducer has to go to every mapper, find the portion of the map's output that belongs to it, and copy that. So if there are m maps and r reduces, the shuffle will have $m * r$ network connections. And if reducers have too many map inputs to merge in one pass, they will have to do a multipass merge, reading the data from and writing it to disk multiple times.

Output size

Every record written out by a MapReduce job has to be serialized, possibly compressed, and written to the store. When the store is HDFS, it must be written to three separate machines before it is considered written.

Intermediate results size

Pig moves data between MapReduce jobs by storing it in HDFS. Thus, the size of these intermediate results is affected by the input size and output size factors mentioned previously.

Memory

Some calculations require your job to hold a lot of information in memory—for example, joins. If Pig cannot hold all of the values in memory simultaneously, it will need to spill some to disk. This causes a significant slowdown, as records must be written to and read from disk, possibly multiple times.

Writing Your Scripts to Perform Well

There are a number of things you can do when writing Pig Latin scripts to help reduce the bottlenecks we just discussed. It may be helpful to review which operators force new MapReduce jobs in Chapters 4 and 5.

Filter Early and Often

Getting rid of data as quickly as possible will help your script perform better. Pushing filters higher in your script can reduce the amount of data you are shuffling or storing in HDFS between MapReduce jobs. Pig's logical optimizer will push your filters up whenever it can. In cases where a filter statement has multiple predicates joined by and, and one or more of the predicates can be applied before the operator preceding the filter, Pig will split the filter at the and and push the eligible predicate(s). This allows Pig to push parts of the filter when it might not be able to push the filter as a whole. Table 7-1 describes when these filter predicates will and will not be pushed once they have been split.

Table 7-1. When Pig pushes filters

Preceding operator	Filter will be pushed before?	Comments
cogroup	Sometimes	The filter will be pushed if it applies to only one input of the cogroup and does not contain a UDF.
cross	Sometimes	The filter will be pushed if it applies to only one input of the cross.
distinct	Yes	

Preceding operator	Filter will be pushed before?	Comments
filter	No	Pig will seek to merge them with and to avoid passing data through a second operator. This is done only after all filter pushing is complete.
foreach	Sometimes	The filter will be pushed if it references only fields that exist before and after the foreach, and foreach does not transform those fields.
group	Sometimes	The filter will be pushed if it does not contain a UDF.
join	Sometimes	The filter will be pushed if it applies to only one input of the join, and if the join is not outer for that input.
load	No	
mapreduce	No	mapreduce is opaque to Pig, so it cannot know whether pushing will be safe.
sort	Yes	
split	No	
store	No	
stream	No	stream is opaque to Pig, so it cannot know whether pushing will be safe.
union	Yes	
rank	No	
cube	No	
assert	No	An assert is rewritten to a filter, so it behaves the same as a filter.

Also, consider adding filters that are implicit in your script. For example, all of the records with null values in the key will be thrown out by an inner join. If you know that more than a few hundred of your records have null key values, put a filter input by key is not null before the join. This will enhance the performance of your join.

Project Early and Often

Pig's logical optimizer does a fair job of removing fields aggressively when it can tell that they will no longer be used:

```
-- itemid does not need to be loaded, since it is not used in the script
txns        = load 'purchases' as (date, storeid, amount, itemid);
todays      = filter txns by date == '20110513'; -- date not needed after this
bystore     = group todays by storeid;
avgperstore = foreach bystore generate group, AVG(todays.amount);
```

However, you are still smarter than Pig's optimizer, so there will be situations where you can tell that a field is no longer needed but Pig cannot. If AVG(todays.amount) were changed to COUNT(todays) in the preceding example, Pig would not be able to determine that, after the filter, only storeid and amount are required. It cannot see that COUNT does not need all of the fields in the bag it is being passed. Whenever you pass a UDF the entire record (udf(*)) or an entire complex field, Pig cannot determine which fields are required. In this case, you will need to put in the `foreach` your-self to remove unneeded data as early as possible.

Set Up Your Joins Properly

Joins are one of the most common data operations, and also one of the costliest. Choosing the correct join implementation can improve your performance significantly. The flowchart in Figure 7-1 will help you make the correct selection.

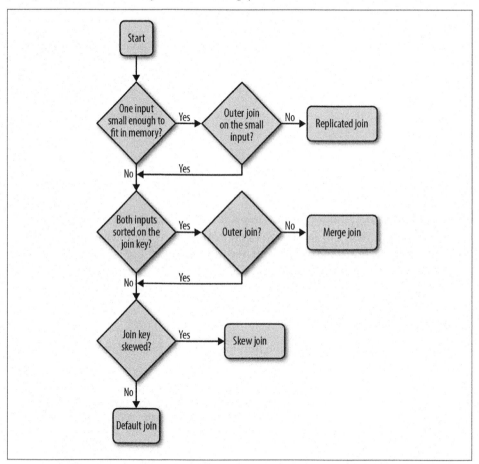

Figure 7-1. Choosing a join implementation

Once you have selected your join implementation, make sure to arrange your inputs in the correct order as well. For replicated joins, the small table must be given as the last input. For skew joins, the first input is the one that is sampled for large keys. For a default join, the rightmost input has its records streamed through, whereas the other input(s) have their records for a given key value materialized in memory. Thus, if you have one join input that you know has more records per key value, you should place it in the rightmost position in the join. For a merge join, the left input is taken as the input for the MapReduce job, and thus the number of maps started is based on this input. If one input is much larger than the other, you should place it on the left in order to get more map tasks dedicated to your jobs. This will also reduce the size of the sampling step that builds the index for the right side. For complete details on each of these join implementations, see the sections "join" on page 62 and "Using Different Join Implementations" on page 83.

Use Multiquery When Possible

Whenever you are doing operations that can be combined by multiquery optimization, such as grouping and filtering, these should be written together in one Pig Latin script so that Pig can combine them. Although adding extra operations does increase the total processing time, it is still much faster than running jobs separately.

Choose the Right Data Type

As discussed elsewhere, Pig can run with or without data type information. In cases where the load function you are using creates data that is already typed, there is little you need to do to optimize the performance. However, if you are using the default PigStorage load function that reads tab-delimited files, then whether you use types will affect your performance.

On the one hand, converting fields from bytearray to the appropriate type has a cost. So, if you do not need type information, you should not declare it. For example, if you are just counting records, you can omit the type declaration without affecting the outcome of your script.

On the other hand, if you are doing integer calculations, types can help your script perform better. When Pig is asked to do a numeric calculation on a bytearray, it treats that bytearray as a double because this is the safest assumption. But floating-point arithmetic is much slower than integer arithmetic on most machines. For example, if you are doing a SUM over integer values, you will get better performance by declaring them to be of type integer.

Select the Right Level of Parallelism

Setting your parallelism properly can be difficult, as there are a number of factors to consider. Before we discuss the factors, a little background will be helpful. It would be natural to think more parallelism is always better; however, that is not the case. Like any other resource, parallelism has a network cost, as discussed at the beginning of this chapter when we looked at the shuffle size performance bottleneck.

Second, increasing parallelism adds latency to your script because there is a limited number of task slots in your cluster, or a limited number that your scheduler will assign to you. If 100 slots are available to you and you specify `parallel 200`, you still will be able to run only 100 reduces at a time. Your reducers will run in two separate waves. Because there is overhead in starting and stopping reduce tasks, and the shuffle gets less efficient as parallelism increases, it is often not efficient to select more reducers than you have slots to run them. In fact, it is best to specify slightly fewer reducers than the number of slots that you can access. This leaves room for MapReduce to restart a few failed reducers and use speculative execution without doubling your reduce time.

Also, it is important to keep in mind the effects of skew on parallelism. MapReduce generally does a good job of partitioning *keys* equally to the reducers, but the number of records per key often varies radically. Thus, a few reducers that get keys with a large number of records will significantly lag the other reducers. Pig cannot start the next MapReduce job until all of the reducers have finished in the previous job, so the slowest reducer defines the length of the job. If you have 10 GB of input to your reducers and you set `parallel` to 10, but one key accounts for 50% of the data (not an uncommon case), nine of your reducers will finish quite quickly while the last lags. Increasing your parallelism will not help; it will just waste more cluster resources. A trick to avoid skew is to use a prime number for `parallel`. This helps if the skew is caused by a crash of the hash function—that is, when several big keys are unfortunately hashed to the same reducer. It will not help if you have a single large key that causes the skew, however. You will need to use Pig's mechanisms to handle skew.

Writing Your UDFs to Perform

Pig has a couple of features intended to enable aggregate functions to run significantly faster. The `Algebraic` interface allows UDFs to use Hadoop's combiner. The `Accumulator` interface allows Pig to break a collection of records into several sets and give each set to the UDF separately. This avoids the need to materialize all of the records simultaneously, and thus spill to disk when there are too many records. For details on how to use these interfaces, see "The Algebraic Interface" on page 186 and "The Accumulator Interface" on page 190. Whenever possible, you should write your aggregate UDFs to make use of these features.

Pig also has optimizations to help loaders minimize the amount of data they load. Pig can tell a loader which fields it needs and which keys in a map it needs. It can also push down certain types of filters. For more, see "Pushing down projections" on page 219, "Loading metadata" on page 216, and "Predicate pushdown" on page 220.

Tuning Pig and Hadoop for Your Job

On your way out of a commercial jet airliner, have you ever peeked around the flight attendant to gaze at all the dials, switches, and levers in the cockpit? In a way, flying a plane is sort of like tuning Hadoop: there are many, many options, some of which make an important difference. But without the proper skills, it can be hard to know which is the right knob to turn. Table 7-2 looks at a few of the important features.

 This table is taken from Tables 7-1 and 7-2 in *Hadoop: The Definitive Guide*, Fourth Edition, by Tom White (O'Reilly), used with permission. See those tables for a more complete list of parameters.

Table 7-2. MapReduce performance-tuning properties

Property name	Type	Default value	Description
mapreduce.task.io.sort.mb	int	100	The size, in megabytes, of the memory buffer to use while sorting map output. Increasing this will decrease the number of spills from the map and make the combiner more efficient, but will leave less memory for your map tasks.
mapreduce.task.io.sort.factor	int	10	The maximum number of streams to merge at once when sorting files. It is fairly common to increase this to 100.
mapreduce.map.combine.minspills	int	3	The minimum number of spill files (from the map) needed for the combiner to run.
mapreduce.reduce.shuffle.input.buffer.percent	float	0.7	The proportion of total heap size to be allocated to the map outputs buffer (reducer buffer for storing map outputs) during the copy phase of the shuffle.
mapreduce.reduce.shuffle.merge.percent	float	0.66	The threshold usage proportion for the map outputs buffer (defined by mapred.job.shuffle.input.buffer.percent) for starting the process of merging the outputs and spilling to disk.

Compared to Hadoop, tuning Pig is much simpler. There are a couple of memory-related parameters that will help ensure Pig uses its memory in the best way possible. These parameters are covered in Table 7-3.

Table 7-3. Pig performance-tuning properties

Property name	Type	Default value	Description
pig.cachedbag.memusage	float	0.2	Percentage of the heap that Pig will allocate for all of the bags in a map or reduce task. Once the bags fill up this amount, the data is spilled to disk. Setting this to a higher value will reduce spills to disk during execution but increase the likelihood of a task running out of heap space.
pig.skewed join.reduce.memusage	float	0.3	Percentage of the heap Pig will use during a skew join when trying to materialize one side in memory. Setting this to a higher value will reduce the number of ways that large keys are split and thus how many times their records must be replicated, but it will increase the likelihood of a reducer running out of memory.

All of these values for Pig and MapReduce can be set using the set option in your Pig Latin script (see "set" on page 106) or by passing them with -D on the command line.

Using Compression in Intermediate Results

As is probably clear by now, some of the costliest tasks in Pig are moving data between map and reduce phases and between MapReduce jobs. Compression can be used to reduce the amount of data to be stored to disk and written over the network. By default, compression is turned off, both between map and reduce tasks and between MapReduce jobs.

To enable compression between map and reduce tasks, two Hadoop parameters are used. To turn on compression, set mapreduce.map.output.compress to true. You will also need to select a compression type to use. The most commonly used types are gzip, Snappy, and LZO. gzip is more CPU-intensive but compresses better. To use gzip, set mapreduce.map.output.compress.codec to org.apache.hadoop.io.com press.GzipCodec. In most cases, Snappy and LZO provide a better performance boost. LZO requires some extra setup; see the sidebar "Setting Up LZO on Your Cluster" on page 143 for details. To use LZO as your codec, set mapred.map.output.com pression.codec to com.hadoop.compression.lzo.LzopCodec. Snappy does not need extra setup. Its combination of better performance and ease of use means it is often the preferred method of compression. However, it is only available in Hadoop 2 and versions 1.0.2 and newer in the Hadoop 1 line. To use the Snappy codec, set mapred.map.output.compression.codec to com.hadoop.compression.SnappyCodec.

Compressing data between MapReduce jobs can also have a significant impact on Pig's performance. This is particularly true of Pig scripts that include joins or other operations that expand your data size. To turn on compression, set pig.tmpfilecom pression to true. Again, you can choose between gzip, Snappy (since Pig 0.12),[1] and LZO by setting pig.tmpfilecompression.codec to gzip, snappy, or lzo, respectively. You may see a slight performance degradation when using gzip compared to Snappy, while performance improvements of up to four times can be observed when using LZO.

Setting Up LZO on Your Cluster

LZO is licensed under the GNU Public License (GPL) and thus cannot be distributed as part of Apache Hadoop or Apache Pig. To use it, you first need to build and install the LZO plug-in for Hadoop and configure your cluster to use it.

To download LZO, go to the project's website (*http://bit.ly/lzodownload*) and click the Downloads tab. Download the *hadoop-gpl-compression* tarball onto your machine and untar it. Then you will need to build the native LZO library on your system. Be sure to do this build on a system that matches your grid machines, as this is C code and not portable. Once you have built the native library, you need to install it on your cluster. Details for both of these tasks are given in the project's FAQs (*http://bit.ly/lzofaq*). A number of fixes for bugs found in this tarball have been committed to Git-Hub (*https://github.com/kevinweil/hadoop-lzo*). You might want to clone and build this version if you have issues with the official tarball.

Data Layout Optimization

How you lay out your data can have a significant impact on how your Pig jobs perform. On the one hand, you want to organize your files such that Pig can scan the minimal set of records. For example, if you have regularly collected data that you usually read on an hourly basis, it likely makes sense to place each hour's data in a separate file. On the other hand, the more files you create, the more pressure you put on your NameNode, and MapReduce operates more efficiently on larger files than it does on files that are less than one HDFS block (64 MB by default). You will need to find a balance between these two competing forces.

When your inputs are files and they are smaller than half an HDFS block, Pig will automatically combine the smaller sections when using the files as input. This allows MapReduce to be more efficient and start fewer map tasks. This is almost always better for your cluster utilization. It is not always better for the performance of your individual queries, however—you will be losing locality of data reads for many of the combined blocks, even though Pig tries to combine splits coming from the same loca-

---

[1] The default temporary file format between map and reduce is tfile, which does not support Snappy compression. To use Snappy, you will need to set it to sequence file: pig.tmpfilecompression.storage=seqfile.

tion, and your map tasks may run for longer. If you need to turn this feature off, pass -Dpig.splitCombination=false on your command line or set the property in your *pig.properties* file.

Map-Side Aggregation

As we have already mentioned, Pig uses the combiner whenever possible to reduce the amount of data it sends to the reducer. However, doing aggregation purely in the combiner is not always the best strategy. The combiner needs to deserialize all the map outputs before processing, which is costly. To decrease the amount of data deserialized in the combiner, Pig can partially aggregate records in the map task. To do this, map output is sent to a local cache first. After accumulating enough records, Pig does an aggregation on the records inside the local cache. The partially aggregated outputs are then sent to the combiner. The combiner is still necessary to produce the final map outputs; it makes sure all the partial results are aggregated together. But since the map has already partially aggregated its output, much less data needs to be deserialized by the combiner.

Aggregation does not always significantly reduce the amount of output data. One such case is a group by with a high number of distinct keys. Pig's map-side aggregation is smart enough to detect this situation and turn itself off automatically. It does this by sampling a certain amount of map output and checking the reduction after aggregation. If the reduction is below a threshold, Pig skips the partial aggregation on the map side and does all the aggregation in the combiner.

Map-side aggregation is off by default. To enable it, you set pig.exec.mapPartAgg to true. You can also tune the threshold to turn off the map-side aggregation by setting the property pig.exec.mapPartAgg.minReduction. The default value is 10, which means map-side aggregation will be turned off if the reduction factor is less than 10 (the number of records after aggregation is at most 1/10 of the original).

Doing an explain will reveal if map-side aggregation is enabled. If it is enabled, you will see a Partial Agg operator in the plan. The inner plan of the Partial Agg operator is the same as the combine plan, except it does not contain a Local Rearrange operator and a Package operator. Here is an example:

```
...
|---c: Partial Agg[bag]scope-38
    |   |
    |   Project[chararray][0] - scope-39
    |   |
    |   POUserFunc(org.apache.pig.builtin.SUM$Intermediate)[tuple] - scope-40
    |   |
    |   |---Project[bag][1] - scope-41
...
Combine Plan
```

```
 b: Local Rearrange[tuple]{chararray}(false) - scope-43
 |   |
 |   Project[chararray][0] - scope-45
 |
 |---c: New For Each(false,false)[bag] - scope-28
     |   |
     |   Project[chararray][0] - scope-29
     |   |
     |   POUserFunc(org.apache.pig.builtin.SUM$Intermediate)[tuple] - scope-30
     |   |
     |   |---Project[bag][1] - scope-31
     |
     |---b: Package(CombinerPackager)[tuple]{chararray} - scope-34-------
 ...
```

We recommend that you turn on map-side aggregation in your *pig.properties* file.

The JAR Cache

When you register a JAR for use with your Pig Latin script, Pig needs to ship it to the Hadoop cluster as part of the job submission so that your JAR is available to the tasks run on the cluster. In the past, Pig would first copy any registered JARs to a temporary directory in HDFS, and then place the JARs in the distributed cache. From there Hadoop assured that all tasks running the job had a copy of your registered JAR. This is not optimal because it requires copying the JAR from your client machine to HDFS on every invocation of the Pig Latin script that uses the JAR. Also, often you will find you register the same JAR in multiple scripts. Thus, Pig was needlessly copying the same JAR to HDFS many times.

Starting in version 0.13, Pig introduced a mechanism to copy registered JARs to an HDFS cache instead of a temporary directory. This includes an important optimization: if the JAR is already in the cache, Pig will reuse it instead of copying it there again. Pig computes an MD5 sum of both files to check if the JAR you registered is the same as the JAR in the cache. To be safe, each user has a separate JAR cache.

Since Pig itself is not installed on a Hadoop cluster but only on gateway machines, Pig also has to ship its own JAR with each job. Previously Pig wrapped all required resources, including *pig.jar*, into a single *job.jar* and copied it to the backend. The resulting *job.jar* was big. Furthermore, it was different for different Pig scripts (due to the inclusion of user JARs) and thus did not benefit from the JAR cache. Since version 0.14, Pig no longer combines all JARs needed in the cluster into one *job.jar*. Instead it it produces two separate JARs, one with all required JARs that do not vary between jobs,[2] and the other containing JARs that change from job to job. In this way

---

2 Required JARs include *pig.jar* and dependent third-party JARs (e.g., *antlr*, *jodatime*, *guava*, etc.).

the required JAR can be cached in the JAR cache, while the variable JAR (which is generally much smaller) is shipped for every job that has extra JARs.

By default the user JAR cache is turned off. To turn it on, set `pig.user.cache.enabled` to `true`. The default location for the user JAR cache directory is */tmp/username*. This can be overridden by setting the property `pig.user.cache.location`.

Processing Small Jobs Locally

The canonical use case for Pig is "big data," where the input is many gigabytes or terabytes in size. When this is the case, the overhead of starting jobs in the Hadoop cluster is minimal compared to the processing time of your Pig job. But of course, not all big data jobs involve scanning large input files. In this case the overhead of launching a job in the Hadoop cluster can add significantly to the overall runtime of the Pig job. In version 0.13 Pig introduced two execution modes for small jobs that avoid launching MapReduce jobs: direct fetch mode and auto local mode.

In direct fetch mode Pig reads and processes input data directly without invoking any MapReduce code. Direct fetch mode is very fast, but it is restricted to queries that contain a `limit` clause.[3] Direct fetch mode also has the following restrictions:

- The script can only contain simple operators: `limit`, `filter`, `union`, `stream`, and `foreach`.
- The script must output data via `dump`; `store` is not allowed.
- Other complex Pig Latin that will result in additional operators being used in execution, such as implicit splits, relations that are used as scalars, etc., are not allowed.

Direct fetch mode is turned on by default. You do not need to do anything to indicate to Pig that it should use direct fetch mode.

In cases where direct fetch mode is not applicable but the input data is small, Pig can automatically choose to use local mode, meaning that the job will be executed directly on your client machine rather than in the cluster. By default, the threshold for automatically converting to local mode is that the combination of all input data to the script is less than 100 MB. This threshold is configurable through the property `pig.auto.local.input.maxbytes`. Other than the input data size, there are no further restrictions. Local mode is slower than direct fetch mode since it still invokes

---

3 This ensures that a limited amount of data will be copied from the cluster to your client machine.

MapReduce code locally, but for small data it is much faster than launching a job on the cluster.

Automatic local mode is disabled by default. You can enable it by setting `pig.auto.local.enabled` to true.

Bloom Filters

Bloom filters are often used in data processing to filter out data before a more expensive operation, such as a join. A Bloom filter has the useful property that, while it sometimes returns a false positive (e.g., it may say a record will pass a filter when it will not), it never returns a false negative (it never filters out a record that would pass the original filter).[4]

Let's look more closely at how a Bloom filter can be used with a join. Suppose you want to join a very large table L with a small table S (but assume that S is still too large to be efficiently held in memory on one node, meaning a fragment-replicate join is not a viable option). You can build a Bloom filter on table S and then apply it to L before the join. Assuming the number of keys in L that match with a key in S is small, you can filter out most records of L before the join. This can save significant time in shuffling data and performing the join.

Pig does not automatically apply Bloom filters before a join. However, Pig does provide two UDFs to help you manually apply one: `BuildBloom` and `Bloom`. `BuildBloom` builds a Bloom filter and stores it on HDFS. `Bloom` retrieves the Bloom filter from HDFS and applies it to its input.

The false positive rate of a Bloom filter is inversely correlated with the number of bits in the filter and the number of hash functions used when mapping elements into the Bloom filter. Obviously, if you set the number of bits and hash functions higher, the Bloom filter requires more storage. Depending on your available space and desired performance, you will need to choose how to build your Bloom filter.

When using `BuildBloom` to create your Bloom filter, you can choose the number of bits and the number of hash functions using the constructor arguments in Table 7-4. Alternatively, you can tell `BuildBloom` your desired false positive rate and it will pick a number of bits and an optimal number of hash functions that will achieve that rate; the constructor arguments to use in this case are listed in Table 7-5.

---

4 For a more complete treatment of Bloom filters and their uses, see Wikipedia (*https://en.wikipedia.org/wiki/Bloom_filter*). This article includes useful information on how to determine the number of bits in your filter based on your desired false positive rate and how to calculate the optimal number of hash functions. Pig uses these algorithms when asked to determine the size of your Bloom filter based on your desired false positive rate.

Table 7-4. Constructor arguments for BuildBloom when choosing the number of bits and hash functions

Argument	Valid values	Comments
hashType	Hash.MURMUR_HASH or Hash.JENKINS_HASH	Hashing algorithm to use—see Hadoop's documentation (*http://bit.ly/hadoophash*) for details
mode		Currently ignored
vectorSize	Integer (as a string)	Number of bits to use in this filter
nbHash	Integer (as a string)	Number of hash function to use in this filter

Table 7-5. Constructor arguments for BuildBloom when choosing a desired false positive rate

Argument	Valid values	Comments
hashType	Hash.MURMUR_HASH or Hash.JENKINS_HASH	Hashing algorithm to use—see Hadoop's documentation (*http://bit.ly/hadoophash*) for details
numElements	Integer (as a string)	Number of distinct elements expected to be placed in this filter
desiredFalsePositive	Floating point (as a string)	Desired false positive rate, with 1.0 as 100% (e.g., 0.01 means a 1% false positive rate).

To use `BuildBloom` you must do a `group all` on the smaller file and give the resulting bag to `BuildBloom`. (It is an algebraic UDF, so this step will be done in parallel.) Once you have built a Bloom filter, you need to store it in HDFS. You can then load it later into the filter function `Bloom` and use it to filter the larger table. `Bloom` takes the name of the file containing the stored Bloom filter as its sole constructor argument. Here is an example that uses a Bloom filter to optimize the join. In this example we tell `BuildBloom` to construct a Bloom filter that expects 2,000 elements with a false positive rate of 0.01%:

```
define bb BuildBloom('Hash.JENKINS_HASH', '2000', '0.0001');
divs       = load 'NYSE_dividends' as (exchange:chararray, symbol:chararray,
                 date:chararray, dividends);
divs_jan
           = filter divs by ToDate(date, 'yyyy-MM-dd') >=
                 ToDate('2009-01-01', 'yyyy-MM-dd')
                 and ToDate(date, 'yyyy-MM-dd')
                 <= ToDate('2009-01-31', 'yyyy-MM-dd');
grpd = group divs_jan all;
divs_fltrd = foreach grpd generate bb(divs_jan.symbol);
store divs_fltrd into 'mybloom';
exec;

define bloom Bloom('mybloom');
daily      = load 'NYSE_daily' as (exchange:chararray, symbol:chararray,
                 date:chararray, open:float, high:float, low:float, close:float,
                 volume:int, adj_close:float);
daily_fltrd = filter daily by bloom(symbol);
```

```
joined      = join daily_fltrd by symbol, divs_jan by symbol;
store joined into 'results';
```

In this example, we want to join *NYSE_daily* with *NYSE_dividends*, which has the dividend distribution for January 2009. Since *NYSE_daily* is big, joining `daily` and `divs_jan` directly would be a large join. With a Bloom filter, we can do a filter of *NYSE_daily* to get rid of the symbols that are guaranteed to have no match in `divs_jan`. Though we still need to do a join, the scale is much smaller. After the Bloom filter, `daily_fltrd` contains only 7,072 records. The original *NYSE_daily*, however, contains 57,391 records. Only about 12% of the records pass the Bloom filter.

Schema Tuple Optimization

In "Using Different Join Implementations" on page 83, we learned that Pig can use a fragment-replicate join algorithm if the right input of the join is small enough to fit in memory. Since a fragment-replicate is executed by a map-only job it runs much faster than the default distributed hash join and does not have issues when there is join key skew. Given these benefits, it makes sense to maximize when users can choose fragment-replicate as their join algorithm. To do this Pig needs to reduce the memory footprint of the right input. By default, for every record, Pig creates a tuple object and puts the column data of the record inside it. The default tuple implementation uses an `ArrayList` as a container for column data, which requires that each column value be stored in a Java object. Primitive data types cannot be used. That is, to store an integer, instead of using an int, Pig needs to create a `java.lang.Integer` object. The schema tuple optimization solves this problem by generating Java code specific to the tuple. This allows it to use primitive types for numeric data.

To see the difference, consider a file with three fields: `name` (chararray), `age` (int), and `gpa` (double). The default tuple will look like this:

```
class DefaultTuple {
    List<Object> mFields;
}
```

A schema tuple will instead be stored in:

```
class SchemaTuple {
    String name;
    int age;
    double gpa;
}
```

How much space can this save? Suppose we have a tuple of 100 integer items: the default tuple will use 2,056 bytes and a schema tuple will use 400 bytes, a memory saving of 80%. This works best when you have a significant number of numeric fields. Tuples with mostly chararray and bytearray data will see less dramatic benefits.

When using schema tuples Pig will generate Java source code specific to the input's schema and compile it on the fly. Thus, you must install a Java Development Kit (JDK) instead of just a Java Runtime Environment (JRE) on your client machine so Pig can compile the Java source code at runtime. Also, Pig must know the schema of the righthand input so that it can construct the appropriate source code.

By default the schema tuple optimization is off. You can turn it on by setting the property `pig.schematuple` to `true`. Please note that the schema tuple optimization is still an experimental feature and only recommended for fragment-replicate joins and input that does not contain complex data types (maps, tuples, or bags). Other algorithms, such as map-side partial aggregation and sorts inside a `foreach`, may also benefit. However, schema tuples are known to be error prone and unstable outside of fragment-replicate joins. More work is required to solidify schema tuples so that they can be used more widely in Pig. You may need to turn this optimization off for other use cases if you hit some bugs:

```
set pig.schematuple.udf false;
set pig.schematuple.foreach false;
set pig.schematuple.merge_join false;
```

Dealing with Failures

When processing gigabytes or terabytes of data, the odds are overwhelming that at least one row will be corrupt or will cause an unexpected result. An example is division by zero, even though no records were supposed to have a zero in the denominator. One bad record causing an entire job to fail is not good.

To avoid these failures, you can capture the exception in your load or store function, insert a null, issue a warning, and continue processing. This way, the job still finishes. Warnings are aggregated and reported as a count at the end. You should check the warnings to be sure that the failure of a few records is acceptable in your job. If you need to know more details about the warnings, you can turn off the aggregation by passing -w on the command line.

If your custom load or store function does not capture the exception-causing bad record, you can let Pig handle it. The way to do that is to implement the `ErrorHandling` interface; see "Handling Bad Records" on page 228 for details.

MapReduce also provides safeguards for failed map tasks and reduce tasks. You can set the `mapreduce.map.failures.maxpercent` and `mapreduce.reduce.failures.maxpercent` properties in your Pig script to configure the percentage of tasks that can fail without causing the job as a whole to fail. Unfortunately, there is currently no counterpart in Tez right now; the issue is tracked in TEZ-3271 (*http://bit.ly/TEZ3271*).

CHAPTER 8

Embedding Pig

In addition to running Pig on the command line, you can also invoke Pig programmatically. In this chapter, we will explore two options: embedding Pig inside a scripting language and using the Pig Java APIs.

Embedding Pig Latin in Scripting Languages

As we've said previously, Pig Latin is a data flow language. Unlike general-purpose programming languages, it does not include control flow constructs such as if and for. For many data-processing applications, the operators Pig provides are sufficient. But there are classes of problems that either require the data flow to be repeated an indefinite number of times or need to branch based on the results of an operator. Iterative processing, where a calculation needs to be repeated until the margin of error is within an acceptable limit, is one example. It is not possible to know beforehand how many times the data flow will need to be run before processing begins.

Blending data flow and control flow in one language is difficult to do in a way that is useful and intuitive. Building a general-purpose language and all the associated tools, such as IDEs and debuggers, is a considerable undertaking; also, there is no lack of control flow languages already, and turning Pig Latin into a general-purpose language would require users to learn a much bigger language to process their data. For these reasons, the decision was made to instead embed Pig in existing scripting languages. This avoids the need to invent a new language while still providing users with the features they need to process their data.[1]

---

[1] In some of the documentation, wiki pages, and issues on JIRA, embedded Pig is referred to as "Turing Complete Pig." This was what the project was called when it first started, even though Pig itself is not Turing complete.

Pig can be embedded into Jython, JavaScript, and Groovy. Since Jython embedding is more mature and popular, we will use Jython to demonstrate Pig embedding in this chapter. If you are interested in JavaScript and Groovy, please check out "k-Means" on page 280; we will cover an example using all scripting languages in that section.

Jython is an implementation of Python on top of the JVM. Jython only supports Python 2, so Python 2 features can be used but not Python 3 features.

This embedding is done in a JDBC-like style, where your Jython script first compiles a Pig Latin script, then binds variables from Jython to it, and finally runs it. It is also possible to do filesystem operations, register JARs, and perform other utility operations through the interface. The top-level class for this interface is `org.apache.pig.scripting.Pig`.

Throughout this chapter we will use an example of calculating page rank from a web crawl to demonstrate different components of Pig embedding. You can find this example under *examples/ch8* in the example code (*https://github.com/alanfgates/ programmingpig/tree/2ed*). This code iterates over a set of URLs and links to produce a page rank for each URL.[2] The input to this example is the *webcrawl* dataset found in the examples. Each record in this input contains a URL, a starting rank of 1, and a bag with a tuple for each link found at that URL:

```
http://pig.apache.org/privacypolicy.html 1 {(http://www.google.com/privacy.html)}
http://www.google.com/privacypolicy.html 1 {(http://www.google.com/faq.html)}
http://desktop.google.com/copyrights.html 1 {}
```

Even though control flow is done via a Jython script, it can still be run using Pig's *bin/pig* script. *bin/pig* looks for the #! line and calls the appropriate interpreter. This allows you to use these scripts with systems that expect to invoke a Pig Latin script. It also allows Pig to include UDFs from this file automatically and to give correct line numbers for error messages.

In order to use the `Pig` class and related objects, the code must first import them into the Jython script:

```
from org.apache.pig.scripting import *
```

Compiling

Calling the static method `Pig.compile` causes Pig to do an initial compilation of the code. Because we have not bound the variables yet, this check cannot completely verify the script. Type checking and other semantic checking is not done at this phase—only the syntax is checked. `compile` returns a `Pig` object that can be bound to a set of variables:

---

2 The example code was graciously provided by Julien Le Dem.

```
# pagerank.py
P = Pig.compile("""
previous_pagerank = load '$docs_in' as (url:chararray, pagerank:float,
                        links:{link:(url:chararray)});
outbound_pagerank = foreach previous_pagerank generate
                        pagerank / COUNT(links) as pagerank,
                        flatten(links) as to_url;
cogrpd            = cogroup outbound_pagerank by to_url,
                        previous_pagerank by url;
new_pagerank      = foreach cogrpd generate group as url,
                        (1 - $d) + $d * SUM (outbound_pagerank.pagerank)
                        as pagerank,
                        flatten(previous_pagerank.links) as links,
                        flatten(previous_pagerank.pagerank) AS previous_pagerank;
store new_pagerank into '$docs_out';
nonulls           = filter new_pagerank by previous_pagerank is not null and
                        pagerank is not null;
pagerank_diff     = foreach nonulls generate ABS (previous_pagerank - pagerank);
grpall            = group pagerank_diff all;
max_diff          = foreach grpall generate MAX (pagerank_diff);
store max_diff into '$max_diff';
""")
```

The only pieces of this Pig Latin script that we have not seen before are the four parameters marked in the script as $d, $docs_in, $docs_out, and $max_diff. The syntax for these parameters is the same as for parameter substitution. However, Pig expects these to be supplied by the control flow script when bind is called.

There are three other compilation methods in addition to the one shown in this example. compile(*String name, String script*) takes a name in addition to the Pig Latin to be compiled. This name can be used in other Pig Latin code blocks to import this block:

```
P1 = Pig.compile("initial", """
A = load 'input';
...
""")
    P2 = Pig.compile("""
import initial;
B = load 'more_input';
...
""")
```

There are also two compilation methods called compileFromFile. These take the same arguments as compile, but they expect the script argument to refer to a file containing the script, rather than the script itself.

Binding

Once your script has been compiled successfully, the next step is to bind variables in the control flow to variables in Pig Latin. In our example script this is done by providing a map to the bind call. The keys are the names of the variables in Pig Latin. The values in the following example are literal string values that are updated as the script progresses. They also could be references to Jython variables:

```
# pagerank.py
params = { 'd': '0.5', 'docs_in': 'data/webcrawl' }

for i in range(10):
    out = "out/pagerank_data_" + str(i + 1)
    max_diff = "out/max_diff_" + str(i + 1)
    params["docs_out"] = out
    params["max_diff"] = max_diff
    Pig.fs("rmr " + out)
    Pig.fs("rmr " + max_diff)
    bound = P.bind(params)
    stats = bound.runSingle()
    if not stats.isSuccessful():
        raise 'failed'
    mdv = float(str(stats.result("max_diff").iterator().next().get(0)))
    print "max_diff_value = " + str(mdv)
    if mdv < 0.01:
        print "done at iteration " + str(i)
        break
    params["docs_in"] = out
```

For the initial run, the Pig Latin $d will take on the value of 0.5, $docs_in the filename webcrawl, $docs_out out/pagerank_data_1, and $max_diff out/max_diff_1.

bind returns a BoundScript object. This object can be run, explained, described, or illustrated. As is shown in this script, a single Pig object can be bound multiple times. A compile is necessary only on the first pass, with different values being bound to it each time.

In our example, bind is given a mapping of the variables to bind. If all of your Jython variables and Pig Latin variables have the same names, you can call bind with no arguments. This will cause bind to look in the Jython context for variables of the same names as the parameters in Pig and use them. If it cannot find appropriate variables, it will throw an error. So, we could change our example script to look like this:

```
# pagerankbindnoarg.py
d = 0.5
docs_in = 'data/webcrawl'

for i in range(10):
    docs_out = "out/pagerank_data_" + str(i + 1)
    max_diff = "out/max_diff_" + str(i + 1)
```

```
Pig.fs("rmr " + docs_out)
Pig.fs("rmr " + max_diff)
bound = P.bind()
stats = bound.runSingle()
if not stats.isSuccessful():
    raise 'failed'
mdv = float(str(stats.result("max_diff").iterator().next().get(0)))
print "max_diff_value = " + str(mdv)
if mdv < 0.01:
    print "done at iteration " + str(i)
    break
docs_in = docs_out
```

Binding multiple sets of variables

Our example page rank script binds its compiled Pig Latin to different variables multiple times in order to iterate over the data. Each of these jobs is run separately, as is required by the iterative nature of calculating page rank. However, sometimes you want to run a set of jobs together. For example, consider calculating census data from countries all over the world. You want to run the same Pig Latin for each country, but you do not want to run the jobs separately. There is no point in having a massively parallel system such as Hadoop if you are going to run jobs one at a time. You want to tell Pig to take your script and run it against input from all the countries at the same time.

There is a form of bind that provides this capability. Instead of taking a map of parameters, it takes a list of maps of parameters. It still returns a single BoundScript object, but when run is called on this object, all of the separate instantiations of the script will be run together:

```
#!/usr/bin/python
from org.apache.pig.scripting import *
pig = Pig.compile("""
    input = load '$country' using CensusLoader();
    ...
    store output into '$country_out';
""")

params = [{'country': 'Afghanistan', 'country_out': 'af.out'},
    ...
            {'country': 'Zimbabwe', 'country_out': 'zw.out'}]

bound = pig.bind(params)
stats = bound.run()
```

Running

Once we have our `BoundScript` object, we can call `runSingle` to run it. This tells Pig to run a single Pig Latin script. This is appropriate when you have bound your script to just one set of variables.

`runSingle` returns a `PigStats` object. This object allows you to get your results and examine what happened in your script, including the status, error codes and messages if there were errors, and statistics about the run itself. Table 8-1 summarizes the more important methods available for `PigStats`.

Table 8-1. PigStats methods

Method	Returns
result(*String alias*)	Given an alias, returns an `OutputStats` object that describes the output stored from that alias. You can get a results iterator from `OutputStats`.
isSuccessful()	Returns `true` if all went well, and `false` otherwise.
getReturnCode()	Gets the return code from running Pig. See Table 2-1 for return code details.
getErrorMessage()	Returns an error message if the run failed. This will try to pick the most relevant error message that was returned, most likely the last.
getAllErrorMessages()	Returns a list of all of the error messages if the run failed.
getOutputLocations()	Returns a list of location strings that were stored in the script. For example, if you wrote output to a file on HDFS, this will return the filename.
getOutputNames()	Returns a list of aliases that were stored in the script.
getRecordWritten()	Returns the total number of records written by the script.
getBytesWritten()	Returns the total number of bytes written by the script.
getNumberRecords(*String location*)	Given an output location, returns the number of records written to that location.
getNumberBytes(*String location*)	Given an output location, returns the number of bytes written to that location.
getDuration()	Returns the wall clock time it took the script to run.
getNumberJobs()	Returns the number of MapReduce jobs run by this script.

As seen in the example, the `OutputStats` object returned by `result()` can be used to get an iterator on the result set. With this you can iterate through the tuples of your data, processing them in your Jython script. Standard `Tuple` methods such as `get` can be used to inspect the contents of each record (see "Interacting with Pig values" on page 168 for a discussion of working with tuples). Based on the results read in the iterator, your Jython script can decide whether to cease iteration and declare success, raise an error, or continue with another iteration.

For this iterator to work, the store function you use to store results from the alias *must* also be a load function. Pig attempts to use the same class to load the results as was used to store it. The default `PigStorage` works well for this.

Running multiple bindings

If you bound your `Pig` object to a list of maps of parameters, rather than `runSingle`, you should call `run`. This will cause Pig to start a thread for each binding and run it. All these jobs will be submitted to Hadoop at the same time, making use of Hadoop's parallelism. `run` returns a list of `PigStats` objects. The `PigStats` objects are guaranteed to be in the same order in the list as in the maps of bound variables passed to `bind`. Thus, the results of the first binding map are in the first position of the `Pig Stats` list, etc.

Utility Methods

In addition to the `compile`, `bind`, and `run` methods presented so far, there are also utility methods provided by `Pig` and `BoundScript`.

Filesystem operations can be done by calling the static method `Pig.fs`. The string passed to it should be a valid string for use in the Grunt shell (see "Grunt" on page 26). The return code from running the shell command will be returned.

You can use `register`, `define`, and `set` in your compiled Pig Latin statements as you do in nonembedded Pig Latin. However, you might wish to register a JAR, define a function alias, or set a value that you want to be effective through all your Pig Latin code blocks. In these cases you can use the static methods of `Pig` described in Table 8-2. The `registers`, `defines`, and `sets` done by these methods will affect all Pig Latin code compiled after they are called:

```
# register etc. will not affect this block.
p1 = Pig.compile("...")

Pig.registerJar("acme.jar")
Pig.registerUDF("acme_python.py", "acme")
Pig.define("d_to_e", "com.acme.financial.CurrencyConverter('dollar', 'euro'")
Pig.set("default_parallel", "100")

# register etc. will affect p2 and p3
p2 = Pig.compile("...")
p3 = Pig.compile("...")
```

Table 8-2. Pig utility methods

Method	Arguments	Pig Latin equivalent
registerJar(*String jar file*)	*jarfile* is the JAR to register.	register *jarfile*;
registerUDF(*String udf file, String namespace*)	*udffile* is the UDF file to register. *namespace* is the namespace to place the UDF in.	register *udffile*; using jython as *namespace*;
define(*String alias, String definition*)	*alias* is the name of the definition. *definition* is the string being aliased.	define *alias* *definition*;
set(*String variable, String value*)	*variable* is the variable to set. *value* is the value to set the variable to.	set *variable value*;

Once a script has been bound and a `BoundScript` returned, in addition to running the script you can also call `describe`, `explain`, or `illustrate`. These do exactly what they would if they were in a nonembedded Pig Latin script. However, they do not return the resulting output to your script; instead, it is dumped to *stdout*. (These operators are intended for use in debugging rather than for returning data directly to your script.)

Using the Pig Java APIs

You can also invoke Pig inside Java. Pig provides Java APIs with which you can launch Pig jobs, get notifications, and collect statistics after a script finishes. Pig exposes two sets of Java APIs: `PigServer` and `PigRunner`. We will look into both APIs in this section. Note that neither Pig Java API is thread-safe, which means you cannot invoke Pig APIs concurrently on different threads inside the same process. On the good side, Pig APIs have been tested over a long period, which means you can keep invoking Pig APIs in your process without worrying about leaking resources (memory, file handles, etc.).

To use the Pig Java APIs, you will need *pig.jar*. If you download the binary distribution of Pig, *pig.jar* is part of it. Alternatively, you can pull it from the Maven repository directly (see "Downloading Pig Artifacts from Maven" on page 15).

PigServer

`PigServer` offers a rich set of methods. They can be divided into several categories: methods for instantiating `PigServer`, setting Pig properties, and launching Pig jobs, and auxiliary methods. Let's explore these one by one.

Instantiating PigServer

Before you can invoke any method of `PigServer`, you will have to instantiate it. Usually you will need to pass the execution type (`local`, `mr`, `tez_local`, or `tez`) to Pig Server:

```
PigServer pigServer = new PigServer("mr");
```

You can also pass a concrete `ExecType` object to `PigServer`:

```
PigServer pigServer = new PigServer(new MRExecType());
```

You can optionally pass a precreated properties object to `PigServer` as well, so you can instantiate `PigServer` with additional properties:

```
Properties properties = new Properties();
properties.put("udf.import.list",
    "org.apache.pig.builtin:org.apache.pig.piggybank.evaluation.string");
PigServer pigServer = new PigServer("mr", properties);
```

Setting Pig properties

You can also set properties of `PigServer` after instantiation. `PigServer` provides methods for setting specific properties:

```
PigServer.setDefaultParallel(int p); // Set default parallelism of PigServer
PigServer.debugOn(); // Turn on debug logging for PigServer
PigServer.debugOff(); // Turn off debug logging for PigServer
PigServer.setJobName(String name); // Set job name
PigServer.setJobPriority(String priority); // Set job priority
```

Most properties don't have a specific `PigServer` method associated with them, however. For those, you can change the underlying `PigContext` directly:

```
PigServer pigServer = new PigServer(new MRExecType());
pigServer.getPigContext().getProperties().setProperty("udf.import.list",
    "org.apache.pig.builtin:org.apache.pig.piggybank.evaluation.string");
```

Launching Pig jobs

Now comes the most important part of the journey. You will need to tell `PigServer` which Pig statements you want to run. The easiest way is to use `registerQuery` for every Pig statement, and then use `openIterator` to iterate through the result:

```
pigServer.registerQuery("daily = load 'NYSE_daily' as (exchange, symbol);");
pigServer.registerQuery("grpd = group daily by exchange;");
pigServer.registerQuery("cnt = foreach grpd generate group, COUNT(daily);");
Iterator<Tuple> iter = pigServer.openIterator("cnt");
while (iter.hasNext()) {
    System.out.println(iter.next());
}
```

You can also `store` an alias in a file (an HDFS file if in `mr` or `tez` mode, or a local file if in `local` or `tez_local` mode) instead of iterating:

```
pigServer.registerQuery("daily = load 'NYSE_daily' as (exchange, symbol);");
pigServer.registerQuery("grpd = group daily by exchange;");
pigServer.registerQuery("cnt = foreach grpd generate group, COUNT(daily);");
pigServer.store("cnt", "output");
```

If there is a `store` statement inside `registerQuery`, `PigServer` will launch Pig jobs immediately. If you want to run Pig statements with multiple `store` statements in a single unit, you can turn on batch mode and use `executeBatch` to run the statements:

```
pigServer.setBatchOn();
pigServer.registerQuery("daily = load 'NYSE_daily' as (exchange, symbol);");
pigServer.registerQuery("store daily into 'output1';");
pigServer.registerQuery("store daily into 'output2';");
pigServer.executeBatch();
```

However, there is one important restriction for `registerQuery`. You can only pass Pig statements, not Grunt commands (see "Grunt" on page 26 and "Controlling Pig from Grunt" on page 28). For example, the following code will throw an exception:

```
pigServer.registerQuery("set mapred.compress.map.output 'true';");
```

If you hate `registerQuery` because of this, you can use `registerScript` instead. `reg isterScript` takes the filename of a Pig script as input, and runs the Pig script file just as if you had run it from the Pig command line:

```
pigServer.registerScript("example.pig");
```

`registerScript` can also take a map of parameters:

```
Map<String, String> params = new HashMap<String, String>();
params.put("input", "NYSE_daily");
pigServer.registerScript("example.pig", params);
```

Auxiliary methods

Besides the methods we have just mentioned, there are other methods that are equally important in `PigServer`. We will cover the leftovers in this section.

Just like in Pig script, you can register JAR files to be used in your Pig statements:

```
pigServer.registerJar("acme.jar");
```

You can also register scripting UDFs:

```
pigServer.registerCode("production.py", "jython", "bballudfs");
```

This is equivalent to the following Pig statement:

```
register 'production.py' using jython as bballudfs;
```

You can do an explain on the Pig statements:

```
pigServer.registerQuery("daily = load 'NYSE_daily' as (exchange, symbol);");
pigServer.registerQuery("grpd = group daily by exchange;");
pigServer.registerQuery("cnt = foreach grpd generate group, COUNT(daily);");
pigServer.explain("cnt", System.out);
```

And do a describe on the Pig statements as well:

```
pigServer.dumpSchema("cnt");
```

Although registerQuery does not allow Grunt commands, PigServer provides some alternatives:

```
pigServer.fileSize("output") // Get the size of a file
pigServer.existsFile("output") // Check the existence of a file
pigServer.deleteFile("output") // Remove a file
pigServer.renameFile("old", "new") // Move a file
pigServer.mkdirs("myoutput"); // Create a directory
pigServer.listPaths("mydir"); // List files under a directory
```

PigRunner

Unlike PigServer, PigRunner only has one static method: run. However, it provides statistics and a Pig progress notification listener (PPNL), which are missing in Pig Server. The definition for PigRunner.run is:

```
PigStats run(String[] args, PigProgressNotificationListener listener)
```

args is an array of the arguments you normally pass on the Pig command line. There are two new data structures in this method: PigProgressNotificationListener and PigStats. You can pass null as the PigProgressNotificationListener if you are not interested in being notified about the progress of the Pig script. Here is an example of using PigRunner without notification:

```
PigStats stats = PigRunner.run(new String[]{"-x", "mr", "test.pig"}, null);
```

This is equivalent to running the following Pig command line:

```
pig -x mr test.pig
```

PigStats collects the statistics of the Pig script after it finishes. Depending on the nature of the Pig script, you will get different subclasses derived from PigStats. If it is a regular Pig script, you will get SimplePigStats; if it is an embedded Pig script, you will get EmbeddedPigStats.

SimplePigStats contains a status report on the Pig script along with the statistics of every input and output. It also contains the statistics of each job the Pig script launches. Here are the most useful methods of SimplePigStats:[3]

```
stats.isSuccessful(); // If all jobs were successful
stats.getNumberJobs(); // Number of jobs
stats.getNumberFailedJobs(); // Number of failed jobs
stats.getAllErrorMessages(); // Error messages
stats.getDuration(); // Execution time in milliseconds
stats.getInputStats().size(); // Number of inputs
stats.getInputStats().get(0)
    .getNumberRecords(); // Number of records of first input
stats.getInputStats().get(0).getBytes(); // Size in bytes of first input
stats.getOutputStats().size(); // Number of outputs
stats.getOutputStats().get(0)
    .getNumberRecords(); // Number of records of first output
stats.getOutputStats().get(0).getBytes(); // Size in bytes of first output
MRJobStats mrStats = (MRJobStats)stats.getJobGraph()
    .getSources().get(0); // Stats of root job
mrStats.getAlias(); // Alias processed in root job
mrStats.getFeature(); // Pig features in root job
mrStats.getHadoopCounters(); // Pig counters in root job
mrStats.getNumberMaps(); // Number of maps in root job
mrStats.getNumberReduces(); // Number of reduces in root job
mrStats.getMaxMapTime(); // Execution time in ms of longest map in root job
mrStats.getMaxReduceTime(); // Execution time of longest reduce in root job
```

EmbeddedPigStats is totally different. Most of the methods just shown will throw an UnsupportedOperationException. The most useful method in the class is getAll Stats, which returns a map of all the Pig scripts the embedded script launches. The key of the map is the unique Pig script ID, and the value of the map is the list of SimplePigStats objects representing the Pig jobs. If the Pig script is bound to multiple sets of variables (see "Binding multiple sets of variables" on page 155), the list contains multiple items. Otherwise, it only contains a single item. Here is an example using EmbeddedPigStats (the actual data type of the stats object):

```
PigStats stats = PigRunner.run(new String[]{"-x", "mr", "kmeans.py"}, null);
stats.getAllStats().size(); // Number of Pig scripts launched
SimplePigStats firstStats = (SimplePigStats)stats.getAllStats()
    .entrySet().iterator().next().getValue()
    .get(0); // Stats of the first Pig script launched
SimplePigStats aStats = (SimplePigStats)stats.getAllStats()
    .get(scriptId).get(0); // Stats of Pig script scriptId
```

---

3 Some statistics are incorrect in local mode (shown as 0 or -1).

Notification

One important reason to use `PigRunner` is to get progress notifications about the Pig script in different stages. To enable this, you will need to implement the `PigProgress NotificationListener` interface and pass an instance of it to `PigRunner.run`. Note that `PigRunner.run` is blocking; it will return only after the Pig script finishes, and the notifications will be sent to your `PigProgressNotificationListener` asynchronously.

The notifications you will get include script-level notifications:

```
/**
 * Invoked before any Hadoop jobs (or a Tez DAG) are run with the plan
 *      that is to be executed.
 *
 * @param scriptId -the unique ID of the script
 * @param plan -the OperatorPlan that is to be executed
 */
public void initialPlanNotification(String scriptId, OperatorPlan<?> plan);

/**
 * Invoked just before launching Hadoop jobs (or Tez DAGs) spawned by the script.
 * @param scriptId -the unique ID of the script
 * @param numJobsToLaunch -the total number of Hadoop jobs (or Tez DAGs)
 *          spawned by the script
 */
public void launchStartedNotification(String scriptId, int numJobsToLaunch);

/**
 * Invoked just before submitting a batch of Hadoop jobs (or Tez DAGs).
 * @param scriptId -the unique ID of the script
 * @param numJobsSubmitted -the number of Hadoop jobs (or Tez DAGs) in the batch
 */
public void jobsSubmittedNotification(String scriptId, int numJobsSubmitted);

/**
 * Invoked just after an output is successfully written.
 * @param scriptId -the unique ID of the script
 * @param outputStats -the {@link OutputStats} object associated with the output
 */
public void outputCompletedNotification(String scriptId, OutputStats outputStats);

/**
 * Invoked to update the execution progress.
 * @param scriptId -the unique ID of the script
 * @param progress -the percentage of the execution progress
 */
public void progressUpdatedNotification(String scriptId, int progress);

/**
 * Invoked just after all Hadoop jobs (Tez DAGs) spawned by the script are
 *      completed.
```

```
 * @param scriptId -the unique ID of the script
 * @param numJobsSucceeded -the total number of Hadoop jobs (Tez DAGs) that
 * succeeded
 */
public void launchCompletedNotification(String scriptId, int numJobsSucceeded);
```

And job-level notifications:

```
/**
 * Invoked after a Hadoop job (or Tez DAG) is started.
 * @param scriptId -the unique ID of the script
 * @param assignedJobId -the Hadoop job ID (or Tez DAG job ID)
 */
public void jobStartedNotification(String scriptId, String assignedJobId);

/**
 * Invoked just after a Hadoop job (or Tez DAG) is completed successfully.
 * @param scriptId -the unique ID of the script
 * @param jobStats -the {@link JobStats} object associated with the Hadoop job
 *               (or Tez DAG)
 */
public void jobFinishedNotification(String scriptId, JobStats jobStats);

/**
 * Invoked when a Hadoop job (or Tez DAG) fails.
 * @param scriptId -the unique ID of the script
 * @param jobStats -the {@link JobStats} object associated with the Hadoop job
 * (or Tez DAG)
 */
public void jobFailedNotification(String scriptId, JobStats jobStats);
```

Some third-party tools rely on the PPNL monitoring the status of Pig jobs. Two great examples are Ambrose (*https://github.com/twitter/ambrose*) from Twitter and Lipstick (*https://github.com/Netflix/Lipstick*) from Netflix. Both tools visualize and monitor the status of each Pig job in an intuitive web UI.

## CHAPTER 9

Writing Evaluation and Filter Functions

It is time to turn our attention to how you can extend Pig. So far we have focused on the operators and functions Pig provides. But Pig also makes it easy for you to add your own processing logic via user-defined functions (UDFs). These are written in Java and scripting languages. This chapter will walk through how you can build evaluation functions, or UDFs that operate on single elements of data or collections of data. It will also cover how to write filter functions, which are UDFs that can be used as part of `filter` statements.

UDFs are powerful tools, and thus the interfaces are somewhat complex. In designing Pig, a central goal was to make easy things easy and hard things possible. So, the simplest UDFs can be implemented in a single method, but you will have to implement a few more methods to take advantage of more advanced features. We will cover both cases in this chapter.

Throughout this chapter we will use several running examples of UDFs. Some of these are built-in Pig UDFs, which can be found in your Pig distribution at *src/org/apache/pig/builtin/*. The others can be found on GitHub (*https://github.com/alanf gates/programmingpig/tree/2ed*) with the other example UDFs, in the directory *udfs*.

Writing an Evaluation Function in Java

Pig and Hadoop are implemented in Java, and so it is natural to implement UDFs in Java. This allows UDFs access to the Hadoop APIs and to many of Pig's facilities.

Before diving into the details, it is worth considering names. Pig locates a UDF by looking for a Java class that exactly matches the UDF name in the script. For details on where it looks, see "Registering Java UDFs" on page 68 and "define and UDFs" on page 71. There is not an accepted standard on whether UDF names should be all uppercase, camelCased (e.g., `MyUdf`), or all lowercase. Even the built-in UDFs provided by Pig vary in this regard. Keep in mind, though, that whatever you choose, you and all of the users of your UDF will have a better user experience if you make the name short, easy to remember, and easy to type.

Where Your UDF Will Run

Writing code that will run in a parallel system presents challenges. A separate instance of your UDF will be constructed and run in each map or reduce task. It is not possible to share state across these instances because they may not all be running at the same time. There will be only one instance of your UDF per map or reduce task, so you can share state within that context.[1]

When writing code for a parallel system, you must remember the power of parallelism. Operations that are acceptable in serial programs may no longer be advisable. Consider a UDF that, when it first starts, connects to a database server to download a translation table. In a serial or low-parallelism environment, this is a reasonable approach. But if you have 10,000 map tasks in your job and they all connect to your database at once, you will most likely hear from your DBA, and the conversation is unlikely to be pleasant.

In addition to an instance in each task, Pig will construct an instance of your UDF on the frontend during the planning stage. It does this for a couple of reasons. One, it wants to test early that it can construct your UDF—it would rather fail during planning than at runtime. Two, as we will cover later in this chapter, it will ask your UDF some questions about schemas and types it accepts as part of the execution planning. It will also give your UDF a chance to store information it wants to make available to the instances of itself that will be run in the backend.

Evaluation Function Basics

All evaluation functions extend the Java class `org.apache.pig.EvalFunc`. This class uses Java generics. It is parameterized by the return type of your UDF. The core method in this class is `exec`. It takes one record and returns one result, which will be invoked for every record that passes through your execution pipeline. As input it takes a tuple, which contains all of the fields the script passes to your UDF. It returns the type by which you parameterized `EvalFunc`. For simple UDFs, this is the only method you need to implement. The following code gives an example of a UDF that raises an integer to an integral power and returns a long result:

```
// java/com/acme/math/Pow.java
/**
```

---

[1] Assuming there is one instance of your UDF in the script. Each reference to a UDF in a script becomes a separate instance on the backend, even if they are placed in the same map or reduce task.

```
 * A simple UDF that takes a value and raises it to the power of a second
 * value.  It can be used in a Pig Latin script as Pow(x, y), where x and y
 * are both expected to be ints.
 */
public class Pow extends EvalFunc<Long> {

    public Long exec(Tuple input) throws IOException {
        try {
            /* Rather than give you explicit arguments, UDFs are always handed
             * a tuple.  The UDF must know the arguments it expects and pull
             * them out of the tuple.  These next two lines get the first and
             * second fields out of the input tuple that was handed in.  Since
             * Tuple.get returns Objects, we must cast them to Integers.  If
             * the case fails, an exception will be thrown.
             */
            int base = (Integer)input.get(0);
            int exponent = (Integer)input.get(1);
            long result = 1;

            // Probably not the most efficient method...
            for (int i = 0; i < exponent; i++) {
                long preresult = result;
                result *= base;
                if (preresult > result) {
                    // We overflowed.  Give a warning, but do not throw an
                    // exception.
                    warn("Overflow!", PigWarning.TOO_LARGE_FOR_INT);
                    // Returning null will indicate to Pig that we failed but
                    // we want to continue execution.
                    return null;
                }
            }
            return result;
        } catch (Exception e) {
            // Throwing an exception will cause the task to fail.
            throw new IOException("Something bad happened!", e);
        }
    }
}
```

EvalFunc is also used to implement aggregation functions. Because the group operator returns a record for each group, with a bag containing all the records in that
group, your eval func still takes one record and returns one record. As an example of
this, let's take a look at the implementation of exec in Pig's COUNT function. Some of
the error-handling code has been removed for ease of reading:

```
// src/org/apache/pig/builtin/COUNT.java
public Long exec(Tuple input) throws IOException {
    try {
        // The data bag is passed to the UDF as the first element of the
        // tuple.
        DataBag bag = (DataBag)input.get(0);
```

```
        Iterator it = bag.iterator();
        long cnt = 0;
        while (it.hasNext()){
            Tuple t = (Tuple)it.next();
            // Don't count nulls or empty tuples.
            if (t != null && t.size() > 0 &&
                t.get(0) != null) {
              cnt++;
            }
        }
        return cnt;
    } catch (Exception e) {
        ...
    }
}
```

Just as UDFs can take complex types as input, they also can return complex types as output. You could, for example, create a `SetIntersection` UDF that took two bags as input and returned a bag as output.

You can also hand a UDF the entire record by passing `*` to it. You might expect that in this case the input `Tuple` argument passed to the UDF would contain all the fields passed into the operator the UDF is in. But it does not. Instead, it contains one field, which is a tuple that contains all those fields. Consider a Pig Latin script like this:

```
data      = load 'input' as (x, y, z);
processed = foreach data generate myudf(*);
```

In this case, `myudf.exec` will get a tuple with one field, which will be a tuple that will have three fields: `x`, `y`, and `z`. To access the `y` field of `data`, you will need to call `t.get(0).get(1)`.

Interacting with Pig values

Evaluation functions and other UDFs are exposed to the internals of how Pig represents data types. This means that when you read a field and expect it to be an integer, you need to know that it will be an instance of `java.lang.Integer`. For a complete list of Pig types and how they are represented in Java, see "Types" on page 31. For most of these types, you construct the appropriate Java objects in the normal way. However, this is not the case for tuples and bags. These are interfaces, and they do not have direct constructors. Instead, you must use factory classes for each of these. This was done so that users and developers could build their own implementations of the tuple and bag types and instruct Pig to use them.

`TupleFactory` is an abstract singleton class that you must use to create tuples. You can also configure which `TupleFactory` is used, since users who provide their own tuples will need to provide their own factory to produce them. To get an instance of `TupleFactory` to construct tuples, call the static method `TupleFactory.getInstance`.

You can now create new tuples with either newTuple or newTuple(*int size*). Whenever possible you should use the second method, which preallocates the tuple with the right number of fields. This avoids the need to dynamically grow the tuple later and is much more efficient. The method creates a tuple with *size* number of fields, all of which are null. You can now set the fields using the Tuple's set(*int fieldNum*, *Object val*) method. As an example, we can look at how the example load function we will build in the next chapter creates tuples:

```
// JsonLoader.java
private TupleFactory tupleFactory = TupleFactory.getInstance();

private Object readField(JsonParser p,
                        ResourceFieldSchema field,
                        int fieldnum) throws IOException {
    ...
        ResourceSchema s = field.getSchema();
        ResourceFieldSchema[] fs = s.getFields();
        Tuple t = tupleFactory.newTuple(fs.length);

        for (int j = 0; j < fs.length; j++) {
            t.set(j, readField(p, fs[j], j));
        }
    ...
}
```

If you do not know the number of fields in the tuple when it is constructed, you can use newTuple. You can then add fields using Tuple's append(*Object val*) method, which will append the field to the end of the tuple.

To read data from tuples, use the get(*int fieldNum*) method. This returns a Java Object because the tuple does not have a schema instance and does not know what type this field is. You must either cast the result to the appropriate type or use the utility methods in org.apache.pig.data.DataType to determine the type.

Similarly, BagFactory must be used to construct bags. You can get an instance using BagFactory.getInstance. To get a new, empty bag, call newDefaultBag. You can then add tuples to it as you construct them using DataBag's add(*Tuple t*) method. You should do this rather than constructing a list of tuples and then passing it using newDefaultBag(*List<Tuple> listOfTuples*), because bags know how to spill to disk when they grow so large that they cannot fit into memory. Again, we can look at JsonLoader to see an example of constructing bags:

```
// JsonLoader.java
private BagFactory bagFactory = BagFactory.getInstance();

private Object readField(JsonParser p,
                        ResourceFieldSchema field,
                        int fieldnum) throws IOException {
    ...
```

```
    DataBag bag = bagFactory.newDefaultBag();

    JsonToken innerTok;
    while ((innerTok = p.nextToken()) != JsonToken.END_ARRAY) {

        t = tupleFactory.newTuple(fs.length);
        for (int j = 0; j < fs.length; j++) {
            t.set(j, readField(p, fs[j], j));
        }

        p.nextToken(); // Read end of object.
        bag.add(t);
    }
    ...
}
```

To read data from a bag, use the iterator provided by the `iterator` method. This also implements Java's `Iterable`, so you can use the construct `for` (*Tuple t : bag*).

 Bags make the assumption that once data is being read from them, no new data will be written to them. Their implementation of how they spill and reread data depends on this assumption. So, once you call `iterator`, you should never call `add` again on the same bag.

Input and Output Schemas

Pig typechecks a script before running it. `EvalFunc` includes a method to allow you to turn on type checking for your UDF as well, both for input and output.

When your UDF returns a simple type, Pig uses Java reflection to determine the return type. However, because `exec` takes a tuple, Pig has no way to determine what input you expect your UDF to take. You can check this at runtime, of course, but your development and testing will go more smoothly if you check it at compile time instead. For example, we could use the `Pow` UDF example from the previous section like this:

```
register 'acme.jar';
A = load 'input' as (x:chararray, y :int);
B = foreach A generate y, com.acme.math.Pow(x, 2);
dump B;
```

Pig will start a job and run your tasks. All the tasks will fail, and you will get an error message `ERROR 2078: Caught error from UDF: com.acme.math.Pow [Something bad happened!]`. Runtime exceptions like this are particularly expensive in Hadoop, both because scheduling can take a while on a busy cluster and because each task is tried three times before the whole job is declared a failure. Let's fix this UDF so it checks up front that it was given reasonable input.

The method to declare the input your UDF expects is outputSchema. The method is called this because it returns the schema that describes the UDF's output. If your UDF does not override this method, Pig will attempt to ascertain your return type from the return type of your implementation of EvalFunc, and pass your UDF whatever input the script indicates. If your UDF does implement this method, Pig will pass it the schema of the input that the script has indicated to pass into the UDF. This is also your UDF's opportunity to throw an error if it receives an input schema that does not match its expectations. An implementation of this method for Pow looks like this:

```
// java/com/acme/math/Pow.java
public Schema outputSchema(Schema input) {
    // Check that we were passed two fields.
    if (input.size() != 2) {
        throw new RuntimeException(
            "Expected (int, int), input does not have 2 fields");
    }

    try {
        // Get the types for both columns and check them.  If they are
        // wrong, figure out what types were passed and give a good error
        // message.
        if (input.getField(0).type != DataType.INTEGER ||
                input.getField(1).type != DataType.INTEGER) {
            String msg = "Expected input (int, int), received schema (";
            msg += DataType.findTypeName(input.getField(0).type);
            msg += ", ";
            msg += DataType.findTypeName(input.getField(1).type);
            msg += ")";
            throw new RuntimeException(msg);
        }
    } catch (Exception e) {
        throw new RuntimeException(e);
    }

    // Construct our output schema, which is one field that is a long.
    return new Schema(new FieldSchema(null, DataType.LONG));
}
```

With this method added to Pow, when we invoke the previous script that mistakenly tries to pass a chararray to Pow, it now fails almost immediately with the message java.lang.RuntimeException: Expected input of (int, int), but received schema (chararray, int).

Pig's Schema is a complicated class, and we will not delve into all its complexities here. The following summary will be enough to help you build your own schemas for outputSchema. At its core, Schema is a list of FieldSchemas and a mapping of aliases to FieldSchemas. Each FieldSchema contains an alias and a type. The types are stored as Java bytes, with constants for each type defined in the class org.apache.pig.data.DataType. Schema is a recursive structure. Each FieldSchema also has a Schema member. This member is nonnull only when the type is complex. In the case of tuples, it defines the schema of the tuple. In the case of bags, it defines the schema of the tuples in the bag. For a map, if a schema is present, it indicates the data type of values in the map:

```
public class Schema implements Serializable, Cloneable {

    // List of all fields in the schema.
    private List<FieldSchema> mFields;

    // Map of alias names to field schemas, so that lookup can be done by alias.
    private Map<String, FieldSchema> mAliases;

    // A FieldSchema represents a schema for one field.
    public static class FieldSchema implements Serializable, Cloneable {

        // Alias for this field.
        public String alias;

        // Data type, using codes from org.apache.pig.data.DataType.
        public byte type;

        // If this is a tuple itself, it can have a schema. Otherwise, this
        // field must be null.
        public Schema schema;

        /**
         * Constructor for any type.
         * @param a Alias, if known. If unknown, leave null.
         * @param t Type, using codes from org.apache.pig.data.DataType.
         */
        public FieldSchema(String a, byte t) { ... }
    }

    /**
     * Create a schema with more than one field.
     * @param fields List of field schemas that describes the fields.
     */
    public Schema(List<FieldSchema> fields) { ... }

    /**
     * Create a schema with only one field.
     * @param fieldSchema Field to put in this schema.
     */
    public Schema(FieldSchema fieldSchema) { ... }

    /**
     * Given an alias name, find the associated FieldSchema.
     * @param alias Alias to look up.
     * @return FieldSchema, or null if no such alias is in this tuple.
```

```
    */
    public FieldSchema getField(String alias) throws FrontendException {
        // Some error checking omitted.
        return mAliases.get(alias);
    }

    /**
     * Given a field number, find the associated FieldSchema.
     *
     * @param fieldNum Field number to look up.
     * @return FieldSchema for this field.
     */
    public FieldSchema getField(int fieldNum) throws FrontendException {
        // Some error checking omitted.
        return mFields.get(fieldNum);
    }
}
```

As mentioned earlier, when your UDF returns a scalar type, Pig can use reflection to figure out that return type. When your UDF returns a bag or a tuple, however, you will need to implement outputSchema if you want Pig to understand the contents of that bag or tuple.

Constructing a Schema object by hand is challenging for complex data types. To make it easier, Pig provides a utility function that takes a schema string and converts it into a schema object: org.apache.pig.impl.util.Utils.getSchemaFromString. The schema string is the same as the schema you write in a load statement. For example:

```
public Schema outputSchema(Schema input) {
    try {
        return Utils.getSchemaFromString("info:{(name:chararray, age:int)}");
    } catch (ParserException e) {
        throw new RuntimeException(e);
    }
}
```

If you want to construct the Schema object by yourself (just to let you feel how tedious it is), here is the code:

```
public Schema outputSchema(Schema input) {
    try {
        FieldSchema nameFieldSchema
            = new FieldSchema("name", DataType.CHARARRAY);
        FieldSchema ageFieldSchema = new FieldSchema("age", DataType.INTEGER);
        List<FieldSchema> tupleInnerSchemaList = new ArrayList<FieldSchema>();
        tupleInnerSchemaList.add(nameFieldSchema);
        tupleInnerSchemaList.add(ageFieldSchema);
        Schema tupleInnerSchema = new Schema(tupleInnerSchemaList);
        FieldSchema tupleFieldSchema
            = new FieldSchema(null, tupleInnerSchema, DataType.TUPLE);
        List<FieldSchema> bagInnerSchemaList = new ArrayList<FieldSchema>();
        bagInnerSchemaList.add(tupleFieldSchema);
```

```
        Schema bagInnerSchema = new Schema(bagInnerSchemaList);
        FieldSchema bagFieldSchema
            = new FieldSchema("info", bagInnerSchema, DataType.BAG);
        List<FieldSchema> outputFieldSchemaList = new ArrayList<FieldSchema>();
        outputFieldSchemaList.add(bagFieldSchema);
        return new Schema(outputFieldSchemaList);
    } catch (FrontendException e) {
        throw new RuntimeException(e);
    }
}
```

Sometimes you may want to access the input schema inside `EvalFunc` at runtime. This can be done by invoking `EvalFunc`'s `getInputSchema` method inside your `exec` method. Here is one UDF using the method:

```
public class GetVolume extends EvalFunc<Integer> {
    @Override
    public Integer exec(Tuple input) throws IOException {
        Schema inputSchema = getInputSchema();
        int pos =
            inputSchema.getFields().indexOf(inputSchema.getField("volume"));
        if (pos == -1) {
            return -1;
        }
        return (Integer)input.get(pos);
    }
}
```

The input for `exec` is a tuple, and we need to retrieve the field by index. Suppose we want to retrieve the field volume, but the UDF writer only knows the name of the field, not the index. By looking up the `inputSchema`, we can find out the index for the particular field and get it from the input. Here is a sample Pig script using the UDF we just wrote:

```
daily       = load 'NYSE_daily' as (exchange:chararray, symbol:chararray,
                date:chararray, open:float, high:float, low:float, close:float,
                volume:int, adj_close:float);
daily_volume = foreach daily generate com.acme.schema.GetVolume(*);
```

Error Handling and Progress Reporting

Our previous examples have given some hints of how to deal with errors. When your UDF encounters an error, you have a couple of choices for how to handle it. The most common case is to issue a warning and return a null. This tells Pig that your UDF failed and its output should be viewed as unknown.[2] We saw an example of this when the `Pow` function detected overflow:

---

2 Recall that in Pig null means that the value is unknown, not that it is 0 or unset.

```
    for (int i = 0; i < exponent; i++) {
        long preresult = result;
        result *= base;
        if (preresult > result) {
            // We overflowed.  Give a warning, but do not throw an
            // exception.
            warn("Overflow!", PigWarning.TOO_LARGE_FOR_INT);
            // Returning null will indicate to Pig that we failed but
            // we want to continue execution.
            return null;
        }
    }
}
```

warn, a method of EvalFunc, takes a message that you provide as well as a warning code. The warning codes are in org.apache.pig.PigWarning, including several user-defined codes that you can use if none of the provided codes matches your situation. These warnings are aggregated by Pig and reported to the user at the end of the job.

Warning and returning null is convenient because it allows your job to continue. When you are processing billions of records, you do not want your job to fail because one record out of all those billions had a chararray where you expected an int. Given enough data, the odds are overwhelming that a few records will be bad, and most calculations will be fine if a few data points are missing.

For errors that are not tolerable, your UDF can throw an exception. If Pig catches an exception, it will assume that you are asking to stop everything, and it will cause the task to fail. Hadoop will then restart your task. If any particular task fails three times, Hadoop will not restart it again. Instead, it will kill all the other tasks and declare the job a failure.

When you have concluded that you do need an exception, you should also issue a log message so that you can read the task logs later and get more context to determine what happened. EvalFunc has a member, log, that is an instance of org.apache.com mons.logging.Log. Hadoop prints any log messages into logfiles on the task machine, which are available from the JobTracker UI. See "Job Status" on page 125 for details. You can also print info messages into the log to help you with debugging.

In addition to error reporting, some UDFs will need to report progress. Hadoop listens to its tasks to make sure they are making progress. If it does not hear from a task for five minutes, it concludes that the task died or went into an infinite loop. It then kills the task if it is still running, cleans up its resources, and restarts the task elsewhere. Pig reports progress to Hadoop on a regular basis. However, if you have a UDF that is very compute-intensive and a single invocation of it might run for more than five minutes, you should also report progress. To do this, EvalFunc provides a member called reporter. By invoking report.progress(String msg) (where msg can say whatever you want) or report.progress at least every five minutes, you can prevent your UDF from being viewed as having timed out.

It is also possible to access the Hadoop's `StatusReporter` and `Progressable` interface directly inside Pig. Simply by invoking `PigStatusReporter.getInstance`, you will get a `PigStatusReporter` object that inherits from `StatusReporter` and implements `Progressable`. You can increment a counter or report progress with it. Here is some sample code:

```
PigStatusReporter reporter = PigStatusReporter.getInstance();
if (reporter != null) {
    reporter.getCounter(key).increment(incr);
    reporter.progress();
}
```

Constructors and Passing Data from Frontend to Backend

Our discussion so far has assumed that your UDF knows everything it needs to know at development time. This is not always the case. Consider a UDF that needs to read a lookup table from HDFS. You would like to be able to declare the filename when you use the UDF. You can do that by defining a nondefault constructor for your UDF.

By default, `EvalFuncs` have a no-argument constructor, but you can provide a constructor that takes one or more string arguments. This alternate constructor is then referenced in Pig Latin by using the `define` statement to define the UDF; see "define and UDFs" on page 71 for details.

As an example, we will look at a new UDF, `MetroResolver`. This UDF takes a city name as input and returns the name of the larger metropolitan area that city is part of. For example, given "Pasadena," it will return "Los Angeles." Based on which country the input cities are in, a different lookup table will be needed. The name of a file in HDFS that contains this lookup table can be provided as a constructor argument. The class declaration, members, and constructor for our UDF look like this:

```java
// java/com/acme/marketing/MetroResolver.java
/**
 * A lookup UDF that maps cities to metropolitan areas.
 */
public class MetroResolver extends EvalFunc<String> {

    String lookupFile;
    HashMap<String, String> lookup = null;

    /*
     * @param file File that contains a lookup table mapping cities to metro
     * areas.  The file must be located on the filesystem where this UDF will
     * run.
     */
    public MetroResolver(String file) {
        // Just store the filename. Don't load the lookup table, since we may
        // be on the frontend or the backend.
        lookupFile = file;
```

```
        }
    }
```

The UDF can now be invoked in a Pig Latin script like this:

```
register 'acme.jar';
define MetroResolver com.acme.marketing.MetroResolver('/user/you/cities/us');
A = load 'input' as (city:chararray);
B = foreach A generate city, MetroResolver(city);
dump B;
```

The filename */user/you/cities/us* will be passed to `MetroResolver` every time Pig constructs it. However, our UDF is not yet complete because we have not constructed the lookup table. In fact, we explicitly set it to `null`. It does not make sense to construct it in the constructor, because the constructor will be invoked on both the frontend and the backend.

 The concepts of *frontend* and *backend* are important in the Hadoop world. The frontend is the client code running on the gateway. The backend is the actual task running on the Task-Tracker (Hadoop 1) or NodeManager (Hadoop 2). The execution path of Pig code is very different on the frontend and the backend. The Pig frontend will compile a Pig script, optimize it, and convert it into MapReduce or Tez jobs. The Pig backend will execute the actual data pipeline assigned to a task.

In your `EvalFunc`, you can use `UDFContext.isFrontend` to distinguish the execution context and fork the code accordingly. However, it is much simpler to put the initialization code in the `exec` method rather than the constructor, as we know the `exec` method will be called only in the backend.

`EvalFunc` does not provide an initialize method that it calls on the backend before it begins processing. You can work around this by keeping a flag to determine whether you have initialized your UDF in a given task. The `exec` function for `MetroResolver` does this by tracking whether `lookup` is `null`:

```
public String exec(Tuple input) throws IOException {
    if (lookup == null) {
        // We have not been initialized yet, so do it now.

        lookup = new HashMap<String, String>();
        // Get an instance of the HDFS FileSystem class so
        // we can read a file from HDFS.  We need a copy of
        // our configuration to do that.
        // Read the configuration from the UDFContext.
        FileSystem fs = FileSystem.get(UDFContext.getUDFContext().getJobConf());
        DataInputStream in = fs.open(new Path(lookupFile));
        String line;
        while ((line = in.readLine()) != null) {
```

```
                    String[] toks = new String[2];
                    toks = line.split(":", 2);
                    lookup.put(toks[0], toks[1]);
            }
            in.close();
        }
        return lookup.get((String)input.get(0));
    }
```

This initialization section handles opening the file and reading it. In order to open the file, it must first connect to HDFS. This is accomplished by `FileSystem.get`. This method in turn needs a `JobConf` object, which is where Hadoop stores all its job information. The `JobConf` object can be obtained using `UDFContext`, which we will cover in more detail later. Note that obtaining `JobConf` in this way works only on the backend, as no job configuration exists on the frontend.

Once we are connected to HDFS, we open the file and read it as we would any other file. It is parsed into two fields and put into the hash table. All subsequent calls to `exec` will just be lookups in the hash table.

Loading the distributed cache

Our `MetroResolver` UDF opens and reads its lookup file from HDFS, which is what you will often want. However, having hundreds or thousands of map tasks open the same file on HDFS at the same time puts significant load on the NameNode and the DataNodes that host the file's blocks. To avoid this situation, Hadoop provides the distributed cache, which allows users to preload HDFS files locally onto the nodes their tasks will run on.

Let's write a second version of `MetroResolver` that uses the distributed cache. `Eval Func` provides a method called `getCacheFiles` that is called on the frontend. Your UDF returns a list of HDFS files from this method that it wants in the distributed cache. The format of each filename is *hdfs_path#task_file*, where *hdfs_path* is the path to the file on HDFS and *task_file* is the name the file will be given on your task node. The second part is called a `symlink` and is optional. If it is omitted, the filename part of the HDFS path will be used as the filename on the task node. *task_file* is relative to your UDF's working directory on the backend. You should place any files in your working directory rather than using an absolute path. *task_file* will be a local file on the task node and should be read using standard Java file utilities. It should not be read using HDFS's `FileSystem`. Here's our version of `MetroResolver` that uses the distributed cache:

```
// java/com/acme/marketing/MetroResolverV2.java
/**
 * A lookup UDF that maps cities to metropolitan areas, this time using the
 * distributed cache.
 */
```

```java
public class MetroResolverV2 extends EvalFunc<String> {

    String lookupFile;
    HashMap<String, String> lookup = null;

    /*
     * @param file File that contains a lookup table mapping cities to metro
     * areas.  The file must be located on the filesystem where this UDF will
     * run.
     */
    public MetroResolverV2(String file) {
        // Just store the filename. Don't load the lookup table, since we may
        // be on the frontend or the backend.
        lookupFile = file;
    }

    public String exec(Tuple input) throws IOException {
        if (lookup == null) {
            // We have not been initialized yet, so do it now.
            lookup = new HashMap<String, String>();

            // Open the file as a local file.
            FileReader fr = new FileReader("./mrv2_lookup");
            BufferedReader d = new BufferedReader(fr);
            String line;
            while ((line = d.readLine()) != null) {
                String[] toks = new String[2];
                toks = line.split(":", 2);
                lookup.put(toks[0], toks[1]);
            }
            fr.close();
        }
        return lookup.get((String)input.get(0));
    }

    public List<String> getCacheFiles() {
        List<String> list = new ArrayList<String>(1);
        // We were passed the name of the file on HDFS.  Append a
        // name for the file on the task node.
        list.add(lookupFile + "#mrv2_lookup");
        return list;
    }
}
```

Since Pig 0.14, there is also a similar method in EvalFunc called getShipFiles, which deals with files on your local filesystem instead of HDFS. You can override this method and return a list of local files you would like put in the distributed cache. Note, however, that unlike with getCacheFiles, you cannot specify a filename to be used on the task nodes. (That is, you need to omit the #task_file part in the filename.) The name of each file will be the same on the task nodes as on your local filesystem.

UDFContext

Constructor arguments work as a way to pass information into your UDF, if you know the data at the time the script is written. You can extend this using parameter substitution (see "Parameter Substitution" on page 108) so that data can be passed when the script is run. But some information you want to pass from frontend to backend cannot be known when the script is run, or it might not be accessible in string form on the command line. An example is collecting properties from the environment and passing them.

To allow UDFs to pass data from the frontend to the backend, Pig provides a singleton class, UDFContext. Your UDF obtains a reference to it by calling getUDFContext. We have already seen that UDFs can use UDFContext to obtain a copy of the JobConf. UDFContext also captures the System properties on the client and carries them to the backend. Your UDF can then obtain them by calling getClientSystemProperties.

UDFContext also provides mechanisms for you to pass a properties object explicitly for your UDF. You can either pass a properties object for all UDFs of the same class or pass a specific object for each instance of your UDF. To use the same one for all instances of your UDF, call getUDFProperties(this.getClass()). This will return a properties object that is a reference to a properties object kept by UDFContext. UDFContext will capture and transmit to the backend any changes made in this object. You can call this in outputSchema, which is guaranteed to be called in the frontend. When you want to read the data, call the same method again in your exec method. When using the object in the exec method, keep in mind that any changes made to the returned properties object will not be transmitted to other instances of the UDF on the backend, unless you happen to have another instance of the same UDF in the same task. This is a mechanism for sending information from the frontend to the backend, not between instances in the backend.

Sometimes you will want to transmit different data to different instances of the same UDF (by "different instances," we mean different invocations in your Pig Latin script, not different instantiations in various map and reduce tasks). To support this, UDFContext provides getUDFProperties(Class, String[]). The constructor arguments to your UDF are a good candidate to be passed as the array of String. This allows each instance of the UDF to differentiate itself. If your UDF does not take constructor arguments, or all arguments have the same value, you can add one unused argument that is solely to distinguish separate instances of the UDF.

Consider a UDF that has its own properties file, which might be useful if you want to pass different properties to different UDFs, or if you have many UDF-specific properties that you want to change without changing your Pig properties file. Let's write a second version of the stock analyzer UDF that we used in Chapter 5:

```java
// java/com/acme/financial/AnalyzeStockV2.java
/**
 * This UDF takes a bag of information about a stock and
 * produces a floating-point score between 1 and 100,
 * 1 being sell, 100 being buy.
 */
public class AnalyzeStockV2 extends EvalFunc<Float> {

    Properties myProperties = null;

    @Override
    public Float exec(Tuple input) throws IOException {
        if (myProperties == null) {
            // Retrieve our class-specific properties from UDFContext.
            myProperties =
                UDFContext.getUDFContext().getUDFProperties(this.getClass());
        }

        // Make sure the input isn't null and is of the right size.
        if (input == null || input.size() != 1) return null;

        DataBag b = (DataBag)input.get(0);
        for (Tuple t : b) {
            // Do some magic analysis, using properties from myProperties to
            // decide how ...
        }
        return 0f;
    }
    @Override
    public Schema outputSchema(Schema input) {
        try {
            // Read our properties file.
            Properties prop = new Properties();
            prop.load(new FileInputStream("/tmp/stock.properties"));
            // Get a properties object specific to this UDF class.
            UDFContext context = UDFContext.getUDFContext();
            Properties udfProp = context.getUDFProperties(this.getClass());
            // Copy our properties into it.  There is no need to pass it
            // back to UDFContext.
            for (Map.Entry<Object, Object> e : prop.entrySet()) {
                udfProp.setProperty((String)e.getKey(), (String)e.getValue());
            }
        } catch (Exception e) {
            throw new RuntimeException(e);
        }

        return new Schema(new Schema.FieldSchema(null, DataType.FLOAT));
    }

}
```

Overloading UDFs

Sometimes you want different UDF implementations depending on the data type the UDF is processing. For example, MIN(*long*) should return a long, whereas MIN(*int*) should return an int. To enable this, EvalFunc provides the getArgToFuncMapping method. If this method returns null, Pig will use the current UDF. To provide a list of alternate UDFs based on the input types, this function returns a list of FuncSpecs (FuncSpec is a Pig class that describes a UDF). Each of these FuncSpecs describes a set of expected input arguments and the UDF, as a Java class, that should be used to handle them. Pig's typechecker will use this list to determine which Java class to place in the execution pipeline (more on this later). The getArgToFuncMapping of Pig's built-in MIN function looks like this:

```
// src/org/apache/pig/builtin/MIN.java
public List<FuncSpec> getArgToFuncMapping()
throws FrontendException {
  List<FuncSpec> funcList = new ArrayList<FuncSpec>();

  // The first element in the list is this class itself, which is built to
  // handle the case where the input is a bytearray.  So we return our own
  // classname and a schema that indicates this function expects a BAG with
  // tuples that have one field, which is a bytearray.  generateNestedSchema is
  // a helper method that generates schemas of bags that have tuples with one
  // field.
  funcList.add(new FuncSpec(this.getClass().getName(),
      Schema.generateNestedSchema(DataType.BAG, DataType.BYTEARRAY)));

  // If our input schema is a bag with tuples with one field that is a double,
  // then we use the class DoubleMin instead of MIN to implement min.
  funcList.add(new FuncSpec(DoubleMin.class.getName(),
      Schema.generateNestedSchema(DataType.BAG, DataType.DOUBLE)));

  // And so on...
  funcList.add(new FuncSpec(FloatMin.class.getName(),
      Schema.generateNestedSchema(DataType.BAG, DataType.FLOAT)));

  funcList.add(new FuncSpec(IntMin.class.getName(),
      Schema.generateNestedSchema(DataType.BAG, DataType.INTEGER)));

  funcList.add(new FuncSpec(LongMin.class.getName(),
      Schema.generateNestedSchema(DataType.BAG, DataType.LONG)));

  funcList.add(new FuncSpec(StringMin.class.getName(),
      Schema.generateNestedSchema(DataType.BAG, DataType.CHARARRAY)));

  return funcList;
}
```

Pig's typechecker goes through a set of steps to determine which FuncSpec is the closest match, and thus which Java class it should place in this job's execution pipeline.

At each step, if it finds a match, it uses that match. If it finds more than one match at a given step, it will return an error that gives all the matching possibilities. If it finds no match in the whole list, it will also give an error. As an example of this, let's consider another version of the Pow UDF we built earlier. We will call this one PowV2. It takes either two longs or two doubles as input. Its getArgToFuncMapping looks like the following:

```
// java/com/acme/math/PowV2.java
public List<FuncSpec> getArgToFuncMapping() throws FrontendException {
    List<FuncSpec> funcList = new ArrayList<FuncSpec>();
    Schema s = new Schema();
    s.add(new Schema.FieldSchema(null, DataType.DOUBLE));
    s.add(new Schema.FieldSchema(null, DataType.DOUBLE));
    funcList.add(new FuncSpec(this.getClass().getName(), s));
    s = new Schema();
    s.add(new Schema.FieldSchema(null, DataType.LONG));
    s.add(new Schema.FieldSchema(null, DataType.LONG));
    funcList.add(new FuncSpec(LongPow.class.getName(), s));
    return funcList;
}
```

In the typechecker's search for the best UDF to use, step one is to look for an exact match, where all of the expected input declared by the UDF is matched by the actual input passed in Pig Latin. Pow(2.0, 3.1415) passes two doubles, so Pig Latin will choose PowV2. Pow(2L, 3L) passes two longs, so LongPow will be used.

Step two is to look for bytearrays that are passed into the UDF and see whether a match can be made by inserting casts for those bytearrays. For example, Pig will rewrite Pow(x, 2L), where x is a bytearray, as Pow((long)x, 2L) and use LongPow. This rule can confuse Pig when all arguments are bytearrays, because bytearrays can be cast to any type. Pow(x, y), where both x and y are bytearrays, results in an error message:

```
Multiple matching functions for com.acme.math.PowV2 with input schema:
    ({double,double}, {long,long}). Please use an explicit cast.
```

Step three is to look for an implicit cast that will match one of the provided schemas. The implicit cast that is "closest" will be used. Implicit casting of numeric types goes from int to long to float to double, and by closest we mean the cast that requires the least steps in that list. So, Pow(2, 2) will use LongPow, whereas Pow(2.0, 2) will use PowV2.

Step four is to look for a working combination of steps two and three, bytearray casts plus implicit casts. Pow(x, 3.14f), where x is a bytearray, will use PowV2 by promoting 3.14f to a double and casting x to a double.

If after all these steps Pig still has not found a suitable method, it will fail and say it cannot determine which method to use. Pow('hello', 2) gives an error message:

```
Could not infer the matching function for com.acme.math.PowV2 as multiple or
none of them fit. Please use an explicit cast.
```

Variable-Length Input Schema

From 0.13, Pig supports variable-length inputs for evaluation functions. To make
your UDF accept a variable number of arguments you need to override the method
getSchemaType. If getSchemaType returns SchemaType.VARARG, the last field of the
input is repeatable. Note that all the additional fields must share the same data type as
the last field. In this case your UDF is expected to handle variable-length input arguments in the outputSchema and exec methods. Now when Pig searches for the appropriate UDF implementation based on input schema it will take into account the fact
that your UDF can accept a variable number of arguments. For example, the Pig buil-
tin EvalFunc StringConcat is able to process two or more chararray inputs. In the
getArgToFuncMapping method of CONCAT, you will see the following code snippet:

```
public List<FuncSpec> getArgToFuncMapping() throws FrontendException {
    ...
    s = new Schema();
    s.add(new Schema.FieldSchema(null, DataType.CHARARRAY));
    s.add(new Schema.FieldSchema(null, DataType.CHARARRAY));
    funcList.add(new FuncSpec(StringConcat.class.getName(), s));
    ...
}
```

Though there are only two chararray fields declared in getArgToFuncMapping,
StringConcat.getSchemaType still matches the input data of three (or more) chararray fields since StringConcat.getSchemaType returns VARARG:

```
public class StringConcat extends EvalFunc<String> {
    @Override
    public SchemaType getSchemaType() {
        return SchemaType.VARARG;
    }
    ...
}
```

Memory Issues in Eval Funcs

Some operations you will perform in your UDFs will require more memory than is
available. As an example, you might want to build a UDF that calculates the cumula-
tive sum of a set of inputs. This will return a bag of values because, for each input, it
needs to return the intermediate sum at that input.

Pig's bags handle spilling data to disk automatically when they pass a certain size
threshold or when only a certain amount of heap space remains. Spilling to disk is
expensive and should be avoided whenever possible. But if you must store large
amounts of data in a bag, Pig will manage it.

Bags are the only Pig data type that know how to spill. Tuples and maps must fit into memory. Bags that are too large to fit in memory can still be referenced in a tuple or a map; this will not be counted as those tuples or maps not fitting into memory.

Compile-Time Evaluation

If all the inputs of an EvalFunc are constants Pig can evaluate it at compile time. The obvious benefit is Pig does not need to repeat the calculation for every input record. But further, replacing a UDF with a constant enables some optimizations that would not be used otherwise. For example, some loaders can accept filter conditions from Pig. However, loaders do not know how to execute EvalFuncs, so Pig does not push a filter that includes a UDF into a loader. Converting the UDF to a constant enables Pig's optimizer to push that filter:

```
logs = load 'web_server_logs' using HCatLoader();
cleaned = filter logs by date = ToDate('20110614', 'yyyyMMdd');
```

Note the data type for the field date is datetime.

In some rare cases you do not want to evaluate the EvalFunc at compile time. An example is RANDOM; in this case you want Pig to generate a different random number for every record. To be safe, Pig disables the compile-time evaluation by default. If your function is eligible to be evaluated at compile time when all its inputs are constants, which will usually be the case, you should override the method EvalFunc.allowCompileTimeCalculation so that it returns true:

```
@Override
public boolean allowCompileTimeCalculation() {
    return true;
}
```

Shipping JARs Automatically

As noted in "Registering Java UDFs" on page 68, if the JAR for your UDF is in your classpath then there is no need to register the JAR explicitly in your Pig Latin script. Pig will search your classpath, locate the JAR with your class, and ship that to the Hadoop cluster automatically.

If your UDF has all of its dependencies in that JAR, or it only depends on classes already included in Pig, then nothing more is required. But if it requires additional JARs, Pig has no way to determine what those JARs are. To avoid forcing users of your UDF to register all of its dependencies, Pig provides a way for your UDF to declare the JARs it requires. Pig will then ship these JARs to the cluster as part of the job. You can override the getCacheFiles or getShipFiles method of EvalFunc as discussed in "Loading the distributed cache" on page 178. If a file returned by one of those methods is a JAR it will automatically be added to your task's classpath on the backend.

Of course, your UDF will not know the location of the JARs it needs on every client machine it is run on. Pig also provides utilities to help locate your JAR files. The class `FuncUtils` has a method `getShipFiles` that can take either an array or a list of `java.lang.Class` objects. From there, Pig uses the class loader to locate the JAR files. To use this you need to provide the class objects for classes from the libraries you need. Here's an example:

```
@Override
    public List<String> getShipFiles() {
        List<String> cacheFiles = new ArrayList<String>();
        Class[] classList = new Class[] {JsonFactory.class};
        return FuncUtils.getShipFiles(classList);
    }
```

In this case, we need to declare *jackson-core-asl.jar* as a dependency for our UDF. Since `JsonFactory` is the class our UDF requires, that is what we pass to `FuncU tils.getShipFiles`.

Note that this mechanism to automatically ship containing and dependent JAR files applies to load and store functions as well.

The Algebraic Interface

We have already mentioned in a number of other places that there are significant advantages to using Hadoop's combiner whenever possible. It lowers skew in your reduce tasks, as well as the amount of data sent over the network between map and reduce tasks.

Use of the combiner is interesting when you are working with sets of data, usually sets you intend to aggregate and then compute a single value or a small set of values for. There are two classes of functions that fit nicely into the combiner: distributive and algebraic. A function is *distributive* if the same result is obtained by 1) dividing its input set into subsets, applying the function to those subsets, and then applying the function to those results; or 2) applying the function to the original set. SUM is an example of this. A function is said to be *algebraic* if it can be divided into initial, intermediate, and final functions (possibly different from the initial function), where the initial function is applied to subsets of the input set, the intermediate function is applied to results of the initial function, and the final function is applied to all of the results of the intermediate function. COUNT is an example of an algebraic function, with count being used as the initial function and sum as the intermediate and final functions. A distributive function is a special case of an algebraic function, where the initial, intermediate, and final functions are all identical to the original function.

An `EvalFunc` can declare itself to be algebraic by implementing the Java interface `Algebraic`. `Algebraic` provides three methods that allow your UDF to declare Java classes that implement its initial, intermediate, and final functionality. These classes must extend `EvalFunc`:

```
// src/org/apache/pig/Algebraic.java
public interface Algebraic {

    /**
     * Get the initial function.
     * @return A function name of f_init. f_init should be an eval func.
     */
    public String getInitial();

    /**
     * Get the intermediate function.
     * @return A function name of f_intermed. f_intermed should be an eval func.
     */
    public String getIntermed();

    /**
     * Get the final function.
     * @return A function name of f_final. f_final should be an eval func
     * parameterized by the same datum as the eval func implementing this
     * interface.
     */
    public String getFinal();
}
```

Each of these methods returns the name of a Java class, which should itself implement `EvalFunc`. Pig will use these UDFs to rewrite the execution of your script. Consider the following Pig Latin script:

```
input = load 'data' as (x, y);
grpd  = group input by x;
cnt   = foreach grpd generate group, COUNT(input);
store cnt into 'result';
```

The execution pipeline for this script would initially look like:

Map
    load

Reduce
    foreach(group, COUNT), store

After being rewritten to use the combiner, it would look like:

Map
    load

    foreach(group, COUNT.Initial)

Combine
```
foreach(group, COUNT.Intermediate)
```

Reduce
```
foreach(group, COUNT.Final), store
```

As an example, we will walk through the implementation for COUNT. Its algebraic functions look like this:

```
// src/org/apache/pig/builtin/COUNT.java
public String getInitial() {
    return Initial.class.getName();
}

public String getIntermed() {
    return Intermediate.class.getName();
}

public String getFinal() {
    return Final.class.getName();
}
```

Each of these referenced classes is a static internal class in COUNT. The implementation of Initial is:

```
// src/org/apache/pig/builtin/COUNT.java
static public class Initial extends EvalFunc<Tuple> {

    public Tuple exec(Tuple input) throws IOException {
        // Since Initial is guaranteed to be called
        // only in the map, it will be called with an
        // input of a bag with a single tuple - the
        // count should always be 1 if bag is nonempty.
        DataBag bag = (DataBag)input.get(0);
        Iterator it = bag.iterator();
        if (it.hasNext()){
            Tuple t = (Tuple)it.next();
            if (t != null && t.size() > 0 && t.get(0) != null)
                return mTupleFactory.newTuple(Long.valueOf(1));
        }
        return mTupleFactory.newTuple(Long.valueOf(0));
    }
}
```

Even though the initial function is guaranteed to receive only one record in its input, that record will match the schema of the original function. So, in the case of COUNT, it will be a bag. Thus, this initial method determines whether there is a nonnull record in that bag. If so, it returns 1; otherwise, it returns 0. The return type of the initial function is a tuple. The contents of that tuple are entirely up to you as the UDF implementer. In this case, the initial function returns a tuple with one long field.

COUNT's `Intermediate` class sums the counts seen so far:

```
// src/org/apache/pig/builtin/COUNT.java
static public class Intermediate extends EvalFunc<Tuple> {

    public Tuple exec(Tuple input) throws IOException {
        try {
            return mTupleFactory.newTuple(sum(input));
        } catch (ExecException ee) {
            ...
        }
    }
}

static protected Long sum(Tuple input)
throws ExecException, NumberFormatException {
    DataBag values = (DataBag)input.get(0);
    long sum = 0;
    for (Iterator<Tuple> it = values.iterator(); it.hasNext();) {
        Tuple t = it.next();
        sum += (Long)t.get(0);
    }
    return sum;
}
```

The input to the intermediate function is a bag of tuples that were returned by the initial function. The intermediate function may be called zero, one, or many times on both map and reduce. So, it needs to output tuples that match the input tuples it expects. The framework will handle placing those tuples in bags. COUNT's intermediate function returns a tuple with a long. As we now want to sum the previous counts, this function implements SUM rather than COUNT.

The final function is called in the reducer and is guaranteed to be called only once. Its input type is a bag of tuples that both the initial and intermediate implementations return. Its return type needs to be the return type of the original UDF, which in this case is long. In COUNT's case, this is the same operation as the intermediate function because it sums the intermediate sums:

```
// src/org/apache/pig/builtin/COUNT.java
static public class Final extends EvalFunc<Long> {
    public Long exec(Tuple input) throws IOException {
        try {
            return sum(input);
        } catch (Exception ee) {
            ...
        }
    }
}
```

Implementing `Algebraic` does not guarantee that the algebraic implementation will always be used. Pig chooses the algebraic implementation only if all UDFs in the

---

same `foreach` statement are algebraic. This is because testing has shown that using the combiner with data that cannot be combined significantly slows down the job. And there is no way in Hadoop to route some data to the combiner (for algebraic functions) and some straight to the reducer (for nonalgebraic functions). This means that your UDFs must always implement the `exec` method, even if you hope they will always be used in algebraic mode.

The Accumulator Interface

Some calculations cannot be done in an algebraic manner. In particular, any function that requires its records to be sorted before beginning is not algebraic. But many of these methods still do not need to see their entire input at once; they can work on subsets of the data as long as they are guaranteed all of the data is available. This means Pig does not have to read all of the records into memory at once. Instead, it can read a subset of the records and pass them to the UDF. To handle these cases, Pig provides the `Accumulator` interface. Rather than calling a UDF once with the entire input set in one bag, Pig will call it multiple times with a subset of the records. When it has passed in all the records, it will then ask for a result. Finally, it will give the UDF a chance to reset its state before passing it records for the next group:

```
// src/org/apache/pig/Accumulator.java
public interface Accumulator <T> {
    /**
     * Pass tuples to the UDF.
     * @param b A tuple containing a single field, which is a bag.  The bag will
     * contain the set of tuples being passed to the UDF in this iteration.
     */
    public void accumulate(Tuple b) throws IOException;

    /**
     * Called when all tuples from current key have been passed to accumulate.
     * @return The value for the UDF for this key.
     */
    public T getValue();

    /**
     * Called after getValue() to prepare processing for next key.
     */
    public void cleanup();
}
```

As an example, let's look at COUNT's implementation of the accumulator:

```
// src/org/apache/pig/builtin/COUNT.java
private long intermediateCount = 0L;

public void accumulate(Tuple b) throws IOException {
    try {
        DataBag bag = (DataBag)b.get(0);
```

```
        Iterator it = bag.iterator();
        while (it.hasNext()){
            Tuple t = (Tuple)it.next();
            if (t != null && t.size() > 0 && t.get(0) != null) {
                intermediateCount += 1;
            }
        }
    } catch (Exception e) {
        ...
    }
}

public void cleanup() {
    intermediateCount = 0L;
}

public Long getValue() {
    return intermediateCount;
}
```

By default, Pig passes `accumulate` 20,000 records at once. You can modify this value by setting the property `pig.accumulative.batchsize` either on the command line or using `set` in your script.

As mentioned earlier, one major class of methods that can use the accumulator are those that require sorted input, such as for session analysis. Usually such a UDF will want records within the group sorted by timestamp. As an example, let's say you have log data from your web servers that includes the user ID, the timestamp, and the URL the user viewed, and you want to do session analysis on this data:

```
logs    = load 'serverlogs' as (id:chararray, ts: long, url: chararray);
byuser  = group logs by id;
results = foreach byuser {
            sorted = order logs by ts;
            generate group, SessionAnalysis(sorted);
};
```

Pig can move the sort done by the `order` statement to Hadoop, to be done as part of the shuffle phase. Thus, Pig is still able to read a subset of records at a time from Hadoop and pass those directly to `SessionAnalysis`. This important optimization allows accumulator UDFs to work with sorted data.

Whenever possible, Pig will choose to use the algebraic implementation of a UDF over the accumulator. This is because the accumulator helps avoid spilling records to disk, but it does not reduce network cost or help balance the reducers. If all UDFs in a `foreach` implement `Accumulator` and at least one does not implement `Algebraic`, Pig will use the accumulator. If at least one does not implement `Accumulator`, Pig will not use the accumulator. This is because Pig already has to read the entire bag into memory to pass to the UDF that does not implement that interface, so there is no longer any value in the accumulator.

Writing Filter Functions

Filter functions are evaluation functions that return a Boolean value. Pig does not support Boolean as a full-fledged type, so filter functions cannot appear in statements such as foreach where the results are output to another operator. However, filter functions can be used in filter statements. Consider a "nearness" function that, given two zip codes, returns true or false depending on whether those two zip codes are within a certain distance of each other:

```
/**
 * A filter UDF that determines whether two zip codes are within a given
 * distance.
 */
public class CloseEnough extends FilterFunc {

    int distance;

    /*
     * @param miles Distance in miles that two zip codes can be apart and
     * still be considered close enough.
     */
    public CloseEnough(String miles) {
        // UDFs can only take strings; convert to int here.
        distance = Integer.valueOf(miles);
    }

    public Boolean exec(Tuple input) throws IOException {
        // Expect two strings
        String zip1 = (String)input.get(0);
        String zip2 = (String)input.get(1);
        if (getDistance(zip1, zip2) <= distance) return true;
        return false;
    }

    private int getDistance(String zip1, String zip2) {
        // Do some lookup on zip code tables.
        // Use a fake distance here for simplicity here.
        if (zip1.equals(zip2)) {
            return 0;
        }
        return 100;
    }
}
```

Writing Evaluation Functions in Scripting Languages

Pig and Hadoop are implemented in Java, so Java is a natural choice for UDFs as well. But not being forced into Java would be nice. For simple UDFs of only a few lines, the cycle of write, compile, package into a JAR, and deploy is an especially heavyweight process. And different developers have different language preferences. So, in addition to Java, Pig allows users to write UDFs in scripting languages. Currently Pig supports Jython, JavaScript, Groovy, and JRuby. Supporting any scripting language that compiles down to the JVM requires only a few hundred lines of code. Pig also supports non-JVM scripting languages, but currently Python is the only language in this category. We will start with Jython UDFs, and also walk through UDFs in other scripting languages in the following sections.

Jython UDFs

Jython UDFs consist of a single function that is used in place of the exec method of a Java function. They can be annotated to indicate their schema. The more advanced features of evaluation functions—such as overloading, constructor arguments, and the Algebraic and Accumulator interfaces—are not available yet.

Jython UDFs are executed using the Jython framework. Pig uses Jython because it can be compiled to Java bytecode and run with relatively little performance penalty. A downside is that Jython is only compatible with version 2 of Python, so Python 3 features are not available to UDF writers. Another downside is that Python libraries that depend on the CPython implementation (such as SciPy) cannot be used.

For details on how to register and define your Jython UDFs in Pig Latin, see "Registering UDFs in Scripting Languages" on page 70. In this section we will focus on writing the UDFs themselves. Let's take a look at the production UDF we used in that earlier section:

```
# production.py
@outputSchema("production:float")
def production(slugging_pct, onbase_pct):
    return slugging_pct + onbase_pct
```

The code is self-explanatory. The annotation of @outputSchema tells Pig that this UDF will return a float and that the name of the field is production. The output schema annotation can specify any Pig type. The syntax for tuples and bags matches the syntax for declaring a field to be a tuple or a bag in load; see "Schemas" on page 36 for details.

Here is one example with complex data types for the input and output:

```
@outputSchema("m:[chararray]")
def constructMapFromBag(bag, value):
    output = {};
```

```
    for t in bag:
        output[t[0]] = value;
    return output;

@outputSchema("keys:{(key:chararray)}")
def getAllMapKeys(m):
    output = [];
    for key in m.iterkeys():
        output.append(key);
    return output;
```

Invoking this UDF in a script looks like this:

```
register 'complextest.py' using jython as complexudf;

player = load 'baseball' as (name:chararray, team:chararray,
                    pos:bag{t:(p:chararray)}, bat:map[double]);
transformed = foreach player generate complexudf.constructMapFromBag(pos, name),
    complexudf.getAllMapKeys(bat);
```

Sometimes schemas are variable and not statically expressible. For these cases you can provide a schema function that will define your schema. Let's write a Jython UDF that squares a number, always returning a number of the same type:

```
# square.py
@outputSchemaFunction("schema")
def square(num):
    return num * num

@schemaFunction("schema")
def schema(input):
    # Return whatever type we were handed
    return input
```

The input to the schema function is an org.apache.pig.impl.logical Layer.schema.Schema object. You can invoke any method of that class inside the function. Alternatively, you can use toString to convert it into a string (which follows the Pig standard schema syntax). The return type can be a Schema object, a Schema.FieldSchema object, or a schema string (again using the standard schema syntax). Here are some examples:

```
# The output schema is the same as the first input field
@outputSchemaFunction("schemaFunc1")
def schemaFunction1(input):
    return input.getField(0)
# The output schema is a bag of tuples,
# the tuple schema is the first and third input fields
@outputSchemaFunction("schemaFunc2")
def schemaFunc2(input):
    fields = input.toString()[1:-1].split(',')
    return '{(' + fields[0] + ',' + fields[2] + ')}'
```

If neither @outputSchema nor @outputSchemaFunction is provided for a Jython function, it will be assumed to return a single bytearray value. Because there will be no load function for the value, Pig will not be able to cast it to any other type, so it will be worthless for anything but store or dump.

In order to pass data between Java and Jython, Pig must define a mapping of types. Table 9-1 describes the mapping from Pig to Jython types, and Table 9-2 describes the mapping from Jython to Pig.

Table 9-1. Pig to Jython type translations

Pig type	Jython type
Int	Int
Long	Long
Float	Float
Double	Float
Chararray	String
Bytearray	Array of bytes
Boolean	Bool
Datetime	`org.joda.time.DateTime`
Biginteger	`java.math.BigInteger`
Bigdecimal	`java.math.BigDecimal`
Map	Dictionary
Tuple	Tuple
Bag	List of tuples
Any null value	None

Table 9-2. Jython to Pig type translations

Jython type	Pig type
Int	Int
Long	Long
Float	Double
String	Chararray
Array of bytes	Bytearray
Bool	Boolean
Dictionary	Map
Tuple	Tuple
List of tuples	Bag
None	A null of the expected type

It is not possible to produce datetime, bigdecimal, or biginteger values in Jython UDFs.

It is your UDF's responsibility to return the proper data type. Pig will not convert the output to match the output schema.

Pig will ship the file *jython-standalone.jar* to the backend when a Jython UDF is used in a job. This JAR bundles standard Jython libraries so you can use them in your Jython UDF. If you are using Jython libraries that are not included in *jython-standalone.jar*, you will need to install these modules in Jython on your client. Once installed, Pig is able to figure out the dependent Jython libraries and ship them to the backend automatically.

One last issue to consider is performance. What is the cost of using Jython instead of Java? Of course, it depends on your script, the computation you are doing, and your data. And because Jython UDFs do not yet support advanced features such as algebraic mode, it can be harder to optimize them. Given all those caveats, tests have shown that Jython functions have a higher instantiation overhead. Once that is paid, they take about 1.2 times longer than the equivalent Java functions. Due to the instantiation overhead, tests with few input lines (10,000 or so) took twice as long as their Java equivalents. These tests were run on simple functions that did almost no processing, so it is not a measure of Jython versus Java, but rather of Pig's overhead in working with Jython.

JavaScript UDFs

Pig's JavaScript UDF implementation is based on Rhino (*http://www.mozilla.org/ rhino*). Rhino is a JVM-based JavaScript implementation from Mozilla. Currently it only supports JavaScript 1.7, while the most recent JavaScript version at the time of writing is 1.8.5.

Every Pig scripting UDF is defined as a JavaScript function. You can assign an output schema to the function. Here is a simple JavaScript UDF:

```
// production.js
production.outputSchema = "production:float";
function production(slugging_pct, onbase_pct) {
    return slugging_pct + onbase_pct;
}
```

To learn how to register JavaScript UDFs in Pig Latin, see "Registering UDFs in Scripting Languages" on page 70.

It is also possible to use complex data types for the input and output of a JavaScript UDF. Here is the example we used in the previous section, rewritten in JavaScript:

```
// complextest.js
constructMapFromBag.outputSchema = "m:[chararray]";
function constructMapFromBag(bag, value) {
    output = new Array();
    for (var i = 0; i < bag.length; i++) {
```

```
            var t = bag[i];
            output[t.p] = value;
        }
        return output;
    }

    getAllMapKeys.outputSchema = "keys:{(key:chararray)}";
    function getAllMapKeys(m){
        var output = [];
        var tuple;
        for (var mapkey in m) {
            var tuple = {key:mapkey}
            output.push(tuple);
        }
        return output;
    }
```

Table 9-3 shows the mapping from Pig to JavaScript types, and Table 9-4 gives the mapping from JavaScript to Pig.

Table 9-3. Pig to JavaScript type translations

Pig type	JavaScript type
Int	Number
Long	Number
Float	Number
Double	Number
Chararray	String
Bytearray	`org.apache.pig.data.DataByteArray`
Boolean	Boolean
Datetime	`org.joda.time.DateTime`
Biginteger	`java.math.BigInteger`
Bigdecimal	`java.math.BigDecimal`
Map	Array
Tuple	JavaScript object
Bag	Array
null	null

Table 9-4. JavaScript to Pig type translations

JavaScript type	Pig type
Number	Int or Double, depending on best fit
String	Chararray
Boolean	Boolean
Array	Map or bag depending on the output schema
Object	Tuple
Null	Null

JavaScript UDFs do not support dynamically declaring the output schema based on the input schema. There is no automatic shipping of dependent modules to the back-end for JavaScript UDFs.

JRuby UDFs

Pig also supports Ruby UDFs via Ruby's JVM-based implementation called JRuby (*http://jruby.org/*).

UDFs in JRuby are somewhat different from what we have seen before, in that you will need to wrap all your UDFs inside a class. The class name is not important; it is a structural requirement only. You will also need to put the statement `require 'pigudf'` at the beginning of your JRuby source code since your UDFs will need functionality provided by the `pigudf` module. Here is a simple JRuby UDF:

```
# production.rb
require 'pigudf'
class ProductionUdfs < PigUdf
    outputSchema "production:float"
    def production(slugging_pct, onbase_pct)
        return slugging_pct + onbase_pct;
    end
end
```

To learn how to register JRuby UDFs in Pig Latin, see "Registering UDFs in Scripting Languages" on page 70.

Continuing with the same complex data type example we have been using in previous sections, here it is in JRuby:

```
# complextest.rb
require 'pigudf'

class TestUDFs < PigUdf
    outputSchema "m:[chararray]"
    def constructMapFromBag(bag, name)
        output = {}
        bag.each do |x|
            output[x[0]] = name
        end
        return output
    end

    outputSchema "keys:{(key:chararray)}"
    def getAllMapKeys(m)
        output = DataBag.new
        m.keys.each do |key|
            t = Array.new(1)
            t[0] = key
            output.add(t)
        end
```

```
        return output
    end
end
```

Pig needs to convert Pig objects into JRuby objects before invoking a JRuby UDF. Table 9-5 shows the mapping from Pig types to JRuby types, and Table 9-6 gives the JRuby to Pig mappings.

Table 9-5. Pig to JRuby type translations

Pig type	JRuby type
Int	Fixnum
long	Fixnum
Float	Float
Double	Float
Chararray	String
Bytearray	`DataByteArray` (Pig custom class, defined in *RubyDataByteArray.java*)
Boolean	Boolean
Datetime	Not supported
Biginteger	Not supported
Bigdecimal	Not supported
Map	Hash
Tuple	Array
Bag	`DataBag` (Pig custom class, defined in *RubyDataBag.java*)
Null	Nil

Table 9-6. JRuby to Pig type translations

JRuby type	Pig type
Integer	Int
Float	Double
Fixnum	Long
Bignum	Long
String	Chararray
Boolean	Boolean
Custom `DataByteArray`	Bytearray
Hash	Map
Array	Tuple
Custom DataBag	Bag
Nil	Null

Pig will throw an exception if your JRuby UDF produces a return value with a data type not listed in the table.

JRuby allows you to specify an output schema function. To do that, declare output SchemaFunction in your class:

```
outputSchemaFunction :productSchema
def productSchema input
    input
end
```

You can also return a field of the input schema as the output schema:

```
outputSchemaFunction :productSchema
def productSchema input
    return input[1]
end
```

The parameter input is a Schema; it provides a several useful methods, such as b, which creates a bag, and t and m, which create tuples and maps. The next example creates a bag of tuples. The tuples consist of two fields from the input schema:

```
outputSchemaFunction :genBagSchema
    def genBag(a, b, c)
        ...
    end
    def genBagSchema input
        return Schema.b("b", [input[0], input[2]])
    end
```

In addition to EvalFunc, JRuby supports the Algebraic and Accumulator interfaces. As with a Java algebraic UDF, you will need to write a JRuby class and put initial, intermed, and final functions in the class. However, the input data for these functions is different from in a Java algebraic UDF. The input is made simpler by skipping unnecessary wrapping. In initial, it is simply the input field itself. In intermed, it is a bag of input fields. In final it is a bag of partially aggregated results (each partial aggregate is the product of an invocation of intermed).

You can define an output schema for the final output. However, you can only define a static output schema, not an output schema function:

```
require 'pigudf'

class Max < AlgebraicPigUdf
    max = -1;
    output_schema "double"
    def initial d
      d
    end
    def intermed bag
        bag.flatten.max
    end
    def final bag
        bag.flatten.max
    end
```

```
    def maxSchema input
        input
    end
end
```

Similarly, to implement an accumulator UDF, you will need to write a class and define the methods `exec` and `get`. You can define an output schema by defining a function `output_schema`. Here is an example:

```
require 'pigudf'

class Max < AccumulatorPigUdf
    output_schema { |i| i.get.get[0] }
    def exec items
        @sum = items.flatten.max
    end
    def get
        @sum
    end
end
```

Currently JRuby UDFs do not auto-ship dependent modules or gems to the backend. You will need to manually register them in your Pig script or install them on all machines if you want to use them in your UDFs.

Groovy UDFs

Pig also supports Groovy UDFs. Here is the simple UDF example we have used throughout this chapter written in Groovy:

```
// production.groovy
import org.apache.pig.builtin.OutputSchema;

class GroovyUDFs {
  @OutputSchema('production:float')
  float production(float slugging_pct, float onbase_pct) {
    return slugging_pct + onbase_pct;
  }
}
```

To learn how to register a Groovy UDF in Pig Latin, see "Registering UDFs in Scripting Languages" on page 70.

Here is the complex data type example rewritten in Groovy:

```
// complextest.groovy
import org.apache.pig.builtin.OutputSchema;
import org.apache.pig.data.DataBag;
import org.apache.pig.data.DefaultBagFactory;
import org.apache.pig.data.DefaultTupleFactory;
import org.apache.pig.data.Tuple;
```

```
import java.util.HashMap;
import java.util.Map;
import java.util.Iterator;

class GroovyUDF {
    @OutputSchema("m:[chararray]")
    static Map<String, String> constructMapFromBag
            (groovy.lang.Tuple bag, String value) {
        Map<String, String> output = new HashMap<String, String>();
        Iterator<groovy.lang.Tuple> iter = bag.get(1);
        while (iter.hasNext()) {
            output.put(iter.next().get(0), value);
        }
        return output;
    }

    @OutputSchema("keys:{(key:chararray)}")
    static DataBag getAllMapKeys(Map<String, String> m) {
        DataBag output = DefaultBagFactory.getInstance().newDefaultBag();
        for (String key : m.keySet()) {
            Tuple t = DefaultTupleFactory.getInstance().newTuple(1);
            t.set(0, key);
            output.add(t);
        }
        return output;
    }
}
```

Since the Groovy type system is very close to Java's, most type mapping is straightforward. There are several exceptions, though:

- A Pig bag will be converted into a Groovy tuple of two items. The first item is the size of the bag (the number of tuples inside the bag) and the second item is the iterator.

- A Groovy array will be converted into a Pig tuple.

- A Groovy list will be converted into a Pig bag. If it is not a list of org.apache.pig.data.Tuple objects, Pig will wrap each list element inside a tuple automatically.

- If you want your Groovy UDF to return a Pig bag, you will need to create an org.apache.pig.data.DataBag object inside Groovy.

Groovy UDFs support the ability to specify an output schema via a function so that your UDF can dynamically declare its output schema based on its input schema. To do that, use the tag OutputSchemaFunction:

```
import org.apache.pig.scripting.groovy.OutputSchemaFunction;
class GroovyUDFs {
    @OutputSchemaFunction('squareSchema')
    square(x) {
```

```
            return x * x
        }
        public static squareSchema(input) {
            return input;
        }
    }
```

You can return a field of your input schema as the output schema:

```
import org.apache.pig.scripting.groovy.OutputSchemaFunction;
class GroovyUDFs {
    @OutputSchemaFunction('productSchema')
    production(slugging_pct, onbase_pct) {
        return slugging_pct + onbase_pct;
    }
    public static productSchema(input) {
        return input[0];
    }
}
```

Alternatively, you can convert the input schema into a string and return a schema string after processing inside Groovy. The strings follow the standard Pig schema syntax:

```
import org.apache.pig.scripting.groovy.OutputSchemaFunction;
class GroovyUDFs {
    @OutputSchemaFunction('genBagSchema')
    genBag(a, b, c) {
        ...
    }
    public static genBagSchema(input) {
        def fields = input.toString().split(",")
        return "{(" + fields[0] + "," + fields[2] + ")}";
    }
}
```

You can also write algebraic and accumulator UDFs in Groovy.

To write an algebraic UDF you will need to implement `initial`, `intermed`, and `final` functions. The input data and output structure for the three functions are similar to those of their Java counterparts. For `initial`, the real input data is wrapped into a bag of a single tuple. As noted previously, a Pig bag is translated to a Groovy tuple with two items: the first is the size and second item is an iterator. To access the input row, use `t[1].next()[0]`. The output data for `initial` is a Groovy tuple wrapping the output record. For `intermed`, the input data is a Groovy tuple. The first field of the tuple is the number of records and the second field is an iterator. Using the iterator, you will get `initial`'s output. You need to aggregate the data and wrap the result into a tuple as the output of `intermed`. `final` is similar to `intermed`, except that you don't need to wrap the result into a tuple. The return type of the `final` function declares the data type of the UDF.[3] Other than the return type, you have no other way to specify the output schema for the UDF; you do not have the option to declare a schema function. Here is an example:

```
import org.apache.pig.scripting.groovy.AlgebraicInitial;
import org.apache.pig.scripting.groovy.AlgebraicIntermed;
import org.apache.pig.scripting.groovy.AlgebraicFinal;

class GroovyUDFs {
  @AlgebraicInitial('max')
  public static Tuple initial(Tuple t) {
    return t[1].next();
  }
  @AlgebraicIntermed('max')
  public static Tuple intermed(Tuple t) {
    long max = -1;
    for (Tuple inner: t[1]) {
      max = Math.max(max, inner[0]);
    }
    return [max];
  }
  @AlgebraicFinal('max')
  public static long algFinal(Tuple t) {
    long max = -1;
    for (Tuple inner: t[1]) {
      max = Math.max(max, inner[0]);
    }
    return max;
  }
}
```

To write an accumulator UDF, you will need to implement `accumulate`, `getValue`, and `cleanup` functions. The three functions can have arbitrary names, but you need to tag them properly using `@AccumulatorAccumulate`, `@AccumulatorGetValue`, and `@AccumulatorCleanup`. The input data structure for `accumulate` is a tuple representing a bag (as before, the first item is the size and the second item is the iterator). Iterating through the records in the bag will get you tuples containing the original input data. You will need to use `@OutputSchema` to tag the output schema of your `getValue` function. However, you cannot write a function to dynamically determine the schema for Groovy accumulator UDFs. Here is an example:

```
import org.apache.pig.builtin.OutputSchema;
import org.apache.pig.scripting.groovy.AccumulatorAccumulate;
import org.apache.pig.scripting.groovy.AccumulatorGetValue;
import org.apache.pig.scripting.groovy.AccumulatorCleanup;
```

---

3 Currently algebraic Groovy UDFs only work when the return type is long, due to bug PIG-4756 (*https://issues.apache.org/jira/browse/PIG-4756*).

```
class GroovyUDFs {
  private double max = -1;
  @AccumulatorAccumulate('max')
  public void accuAccumulate(Tuple t) {
    for (Object o: t[1]) {
      max = Math.max(max, o[0]);
    }
  }
  @AccumulatorGetValue('max')
  @OutputSchema('max: double')
  public accuGetValue() {
    return this.max;
  }
  @AccumulatorCleanup('max')
  public void accuCleanup() {
    this.max = -1;
  }
}
```

Streaming Python UDFs

With Jython UDFs, you are able to write UDFs in Python. However, Jython only supports Python 2, not Python 3. Further, Jython does not support Python libraries that have CPython dependencies (e.g., SciPy). To allow you to use CPython when necessary, Pig also provides streaming Python UDFs. These support CPython UDFs directly. By default, Pig will use the *python* binary in your PATH. If you have multiple versions of Python installed, you can choose which one you want to use by setting the Pig property pig.streaming.udf.python.command to the path of the *python* binary you want to use.

From the user's point of view, writing a streaming Python UDF is very similar to writing a Jython UDF. The only difference is that you need to include the following statement in your Python UDF source code:

```
from pig_util import outputSchema
```

Streaming Python UDFs are implemented very differently from the other scripting UDFs we have seen so far. That is because CPython is not JVM-based. Pig uses a mechanism similar to that described in "stream" on page 99 to implement streaming Python UDFs (which is why they have that name). As in a stream operator, Pig serializes the parameters to the *stdin* of the external program and then deserializes the program output from *stdout* back into Pig types. This process is tedious and error prone, especially for complex data types. It is also less performant, as it has to move data between processes and serialize and deserialize every row twice (once for input, once for output). Streaming Python UDFs do the heavy lifting and let you focus on your UDF's logic, by providing Python code to handle the serialization and deserialization of data via a predefined encoding.

Streaming Python UDFs do not support automatic dependency shipping. You will need to install the dependencies on all the backend machines, or use the distributed cache to ship those JARs to the backend (see the relevant discussion in "stream" on page 99).

Comparing Scripting Language UDF Features

Scripting UDFs share a lot of characteristics in common. You can write a scripting UDF to process both simple and complex data types. You can declare output schemas for your UDF. You need to register your UDF in your Pig Latin script in the same way. However, there are slight feature differences among the various scripting UDFs available today. In most cases the differences are not due to inherent limitations in Pig or the scripting languages; the equivalent features have just not been implemented yet. Hopefully in future releases these differences will be addressed. Table 9-7 summarizes the feature differences for both UDFs and embedding your Pig Latin in the scripting languages (see "Embedding Pig Latin in Scripting Languages" on page 151) at the time of writing.

Table 9-7. Scripting language UDF and embedding feature differences

	Jython	JavaScript	JRuby	Groovy	Streaming Python
Algebraic and Accumulator interfaces available	No	No	Yes	Yes	No
Output schema definable by a function	Yes	No	Yes	Yes	No
Automatic shipping of required modules	Yes	No	No	No	No
Pig Latin can be embedded	Yes	Yes	No	Yes	No

CHAPTER 10

Writing Load and Store Functions

We will now consider some of the more complex and most critical parts of Pig: data input and output. Operating on huge datasets is inherently I/O-intensive. Hadoop's massive parallelism and movement of processing to the data mitigates but does not remove this. Having efficient methods to load and store data is therefore critical. Pig provides default load and store functions for text data and for HBase, but many users find they need to write their own load and store functions to handle the data formats and storage mechanisms they use.

As with evaluation functions, the design goal for load and store functions in Pig was to make easy things easy and hard things possible. Another aim was to make load and store functions a thin wrapper over Hadoop's `InputFormat` and `OutputFormat`. The intention is that once you have an input format and output format for your data, the additional work of creating and storing Pig tuples is minimal. In the same way evaluation functions are implemented, more complex features such as schema management and projection pushdown are done via separate interfaces to avoid cluttering the base interface.

One other important design goal for load and store functions was to not assume that the input sources and output sinks are HDFS. In the examples throughout this book, `A = load 'foo';` has implied that `foo` is a file, but there is no need for that to be the case. `foo` is a resource locator that makes sense to your load function. It could be an HDFS file, an HBase table, a database JDBC connection string, or a web service URL. Because reading from HDFS is the most common case, though, many defaults and helper functions are provided for this case.

In this chapter we will walk through writing a load function and a store function for JSON data on HDFS called `JsonLoader` and `JsonStorage`, respectively. These are located in the example code in *udfs/java/com/acme/io* (*https://github.com/alanfgates/programmingpig/tree/2ed/udfs/java/com/acme/io*). They use the Jackson JSON library, which is included in your Pig distribution. However, the Jackson JAR is not shipped to the backend by Pig, so when using these UDFs in your script, you will need to register the Jackson JAR in addition to the Acme examples JAR:

```
register 'acme.jar';
register 'src/pig/trunk/build/ivy/lib/Pig/jackson-core-asl*.jar';
```

 As discussed in "Shipping JARs Automatically" on page 228, if you are using Pig 0.14 or later, you don't need to register both JARs explicitly. Pig will register dependent JARs automatically as long as they are in the classpath.

These UDFs will serve as helpful examples, but they will not cover all of the functionality of load and store functions. For those elements not touched on by these examples, we will look at other existing load and store functions.

Load Functions

Pig's load function is built on top of a Hadoop `InputFormat`. `InputFormat` is the class that Hadoop uses to read data. It serves two purposes: it determines how input will be split between map tasks, and it provides a `RecordReader` that produces key/value pairs as input to those map tasks. The load function takes these key/value pairs and returns a Pig tuple.

The base class for the load function is `LoadFunc`. This is an abstract class, which allows it to provide helper functions and default implementations. Many load functions will only need to extend `LoadFunc`.

Load functions' operations are split between Pig's frontend and backend. On the frontend, Pig does job planning and optimization, and load functions participate in this in several ways that we will discuss later. On the backend, load functions get each record in turn from the `RecordReader`, convert it to a tuple, and pass it on to Pig's map task. Load functions also need to be able to pass data between the frontend and backend invocations so they can maintain state.

Frontend Planning Functions

For frontend planning, Pig requires three things of its load functions:

1. It needs to know the input format it should use to read the data.

2. It needs to be sure that the load function understands where its data is located.

3. It needs to know how to cast bytearrays returned from the load function.

Determining the InputFormat

Pig needs to know which `InputFormat` to use for reading your input. It calls the `getInputFormat` method to get an instance of the input format. It gets an instance rather than the class itself so that your load function can control the instantiation: any generic parameters, constructor arguments, etc. For our example load function, this method is very simple. It uses `TextInputFormat`, an input format that reads text data from HDFS files:

```
// JsonLoader.java
public InputFormat getInputFormat() throws IOException {
    return new TextInputFormat();
}
```

Determining the location

Pig communicates the location string provided by the user to the load function via `setLocation`. So, if the load operator in Pig Latin is `A = load 'input';`, "input" is the location string. This method is called on both the frontend and the backend, possibly multiple times. Thus, you need to take care that it does not do anything that will cause problems if done more than one time. Your load function should communicate the location to its input format. For example, `JsonLoader` passes the filename via a helper method on `FileInputFormat` (a superclass of `TextInputFormat`):

```
// JsonLoader.java
public void setLocation(String location, Job job) throws IOException {
    FileInputFormat.setInputPaths(job, location);
}
```

The Hadoop `Job` is passed along with the location because that is where input formats usually store their configuration information.

`setLocation` is called on both the frontend and the backend because input formats store their location in the `Job` object, as shown in the preceding example. For Map-Reduce jobs, which always have only one input, only setting the input path in the frontend works fine. For Pig jobs, where the same input format might be used to load multiple different inputs (such as in the `join` or `union` case), one instance of the input path will overwrite another in the `Job` object. To work around this, Pig remembers the location in an input-specific parameter and calls `setLocation` again on the backend so that the input format can get itself set up properly before reading.

For files on HDFS, the locations provided by the user might be relative rather than absolute. Pig needs to resolve these to absolute locations based on the current working directory at the time of the load. Consider the following Pig Latin:

```
cd /user/joe;
input1 = load 'input';
```

```
cd /user/fred;
input2 = load 'input';
```

These two load statements should load different files. But Pig cannot assume it understands how to turn a relative path into an absolute path, because it does not know what the input is. It could be an HDFS path, a database table name, etc. So, it leaves this to the load function. Before calling setLocation, Pig passes the location string to relativeToAbsolutePath to do any necessary conversion. Because most loaders are reading from HDFS, the default implementation in LoadFunc handles the HDFS case. If your loader will never need to do this conversion, it should override this method and return the location string passed to it.

Getting the casting functions

Some Pig functions, such as PigStorage and HBaseStorage, load data by default without understanding its type information, and place the data unchanged in DataBy teArray objects. At a later time, when Pig needs to cast that data to another type, it does not know how to because it does not understand how the data is represented in the bytearray. Therefore, it relies on the load function to provide a method to cast from bytearray to the appropriate type.

Pig determines which set of casting functions to use by calling getLoadCaster on the load function. This should return either null, which indicates that your load function does not expect to do any bytearray casts, or an implementation of the LoadCaster interface, which will be used to do the casts. We will look at the methods of LoadCas ter in "Casting bytearrays" on page 218.

Our example loader returns null because it provides typed data based on the stored schema and, therefore, does not expect to be casting data. Any bytearrays in its data are binary data that should not be cast.

Passing Information from the Frontend to the Backend

As with evaluation functions, load functions can make use of UDFContext to pass information from frontend invocations to backend invocations (for details on this class, see "UDFContext" on page 180). One significant difference between using UDF Context in evaluation and load functions is determining the instance-specific signature of the function. In evaluation functions, constructor arguments were suggested as a way to do this. For load functions, the input location usually will be the differentiating factor. However, LoadFunc does not guarantee that it will call setLocation before other methods where you might want to use UDFContext. To work around this, setUDFContextSignature is provided. It provides an instance-unique signature that you can use when calling getUDFProperties. This method is guaranteed to be called before any other methods on LoadFunc in both the frontend and the backend. Your UDF can then store this signature and use it when getting its property object:

```
// JsonLoader.java
private String udfcSignature = null;

public void setUDFContextSignature(String signature) {
    udfcSignature = signature;
}
```

setLocation is the only method in the load function that is guaranteed to be called on the frontend. It is therefore the best candidate for storing needed information into the UDFContext. You might need to check that the data you are writing is available and nonnull to avoid overwriting your values when setLocation is called on the backend.

Backend Data Reading

On the backend, your load function takes the key/value pairs produced by its input format and produces Pig tuples.

Getting ready to read

Before reading any data, Pig gives your load function a chance to set itself up by calling prepareToRead. This is called in each map task and passes a copy of the Record Reader, which your load function will need later to read records from the input. RecordReader is a class that InputFormat uses to read records from an input split. Pig obtains the record reader it passes to prepareToRead by calling getRecordReader on the input format that your store function returned from getInputFormat. Pig also passes an instance of the PigSplit that contains the Hadoop InputSplit corresponding to the partition of input this instance of your load function will read. If you need split-specific information, you can get it from here.

Our example loader, beyond storing the record reader, also reads the schema file that was stored into UDFContext in the frontend so that it knows how to parse the input file. Notice how it uses the signature passed in setUDFContextSignature to access the appropriate properties object. Finally, it creates a JsonFactory object that is used to generate a parser for each line:

```
// JsonLoader.java
public void prepareToRead(RecordReader reader, PigSplit split)
throws IOException {
    this.reader = reader;

    // Get the schema string from the UDFContext object.
    UDFContext udfc = UDFContext.getUDFContext();
    Properties p =
        udfc.getUDFProperties(this.getClass(), new String[]{udfcSignature});
```

```
String strSchema = p.getProperty("pig.jsonloader.schema");
if (strSchema == null) {
    throw new IOException("Could not find schema in UDF context");
}

// Parse the schema from the string stored in the properties object.
ResourceSchema schema =
    new ResourceSchema(Utils.getSchemaFromString(strSchema));
fields = schema.getFields();

jsonFactory = new JsonFactory();
}
```

Reading records

Now we have reached the meat of the load function: reading records from the record reader and returning tuples to Pig. Pig will call getNext and place the resulting tuple into its processing pipeline. It will keep doing this until getNext returns a null, which indicates that the input for this split has been fully read.

Pig does not copy the tuple that results from this method, but instead feeds it directly to its pipeline to avoid the copy overhead. This means this method cannot reuse objects, and instead must create a new tuple and contents for each record it reads. On the other hand, record readers may choose to reuse their key and value objects from record to record; most standard implementations do. So, before writing a loader that tries to be efficient and wraps the keys and values from the record reader directly into the tuple to avoid a copy, you must make sure you understand how the record reader is managing its data.

 For information on creating the appropriate Java objects when constructing tuples for Pig, see "Interacting with Pig values" on page 168.

Our sample load function's implementation of getNext reads the value from the Hadoop record (the key is ignored), constructs a JsonParser to parse it, parses the fields, and returns the resulting tuple. If there are parse errors, it does not throw an exception. Instead, it returns a tuple with null fields where the data could not be parsed. This prevents bad lines from causing the whole job to fail. Warnings are issued so that users can see which records were ignored:

```
// JsonLoader.java
public Tuple getNext() throws IOException {
    Text val = null;
    try {
        // Read the next key/value pair from the record reader.  If it's
        // finished, return null.
```

```
            if (!reader.nextKeyValue()) return null;

            // Get the current value.  We don't use the key.
            val = (Text)reader.getCurrentValue();
        } catch (InterruptedException ie) {
            throw new IOException(ie);
        }
        // Create a parser specific for this input line.  This might not be the
        // most efficient approach.
        ByteArrayInputStream bais = new ByteArrayInputStream(val.getBytes());
        JsonParser p = jsonFactory.createJsonParser(bais);

        // Create the tuple we will be returning.  We create it with the right
        // number of fields, as the Tuple object is optimized for this case.
        Tuple t = tupleFactory.newTuple(fields.length);

        // Read the start object marker.  Throughout this file if the parsing
        // isn't what we expect, we return a tuple with null fields rather than
        // throwing an exception.  That way a few mangled lines don't fail the job.
        if (p.nextToken() != JsonToken.START_OBJECT) {
            log.warn("Bad record, could not find start of record " +
                val.toString());
            return t;
        }

        // Read each field in the record.
        for (int i = 0; i < fields.length; i++) {
            t.set(i, readField(p, fields[i], i));
        }

        if (p.nextToken() != JsonToken.END_OBJECT) {
            log.warn("Bad record, could not find end of record " +
                val.toString());
            return t;
        }
        p.close();
        return t;
    }

    private Object readField(JsonParser p,
                        ResourceFieldSchema field,
                        int fieldnum) throws IOException {
        // Read the next token.
        JsonToken tok = p.nextToken();
        if (tok == null) {
            log.warn("Early termination of record, expected " + fields.length
                + " fields bug found " + fieldnum);
            return null;
        }

        // Check to see if this value was null.
        if (tok == JsonToken.VALUE_NULL) return null;
```

```
// Read based on our expected type.
switch (field.getType()) {
case DataType.INTEGER:
    // Read the field name.
    p.nextToken();
    return p.getValueAsInt();

case DataType.LONG:
    p.nextToken();
    return p.getValueAsLong();

case DataType.FLOAT:
    p.nextToken();
    return (float)p.getValueAsDouble();

case DataType.DOUBLE:
    p.nextToken();
    return p.getValueAsDouble();

case DataType.BYTEARRAY:
    p.nextToken();
    byte[] b = p.getBinaryValue();
    // Use the DBA constructor that copies the bytes so that we own
    // the memory.
    return new DataByteArray(b, 0, b.length);

case DataType.CHARARRAY:
    p.nextToken();
    return p.getText();

case DataType.MAP:
    // Should be the start of the map object.
    if (p.nextToken() != JsonToken.START_OBJECT) {
        log.warn("Bad map field, could not find start of object, field "
            + fieldnum);
        return null;
    }
    Map<String, String> m = new HashMap<String, String>();
    while (p.nextToken() != JsonToken.END_OBJECT) {
        String k = p.getCurrentName();
        String v = p.getText();
        m.put(k, v);
    }
    return m;

case DataType.TUPLE:
    if (p.nextToken() != JsonToken.START_OBJECT) {
        log.warn("Bad tuple field, could not find start of object, "
            + "field " + fieldnum);
        return null;
    }
```

```
        ResourceSchema s = field.getSchema();
        ResourceFieldSchema[] fs = s.getFields();
        Tuple t = tupleFactory.newTuple(fs.length);

        for (int j = 0; j < fs.length; j++) {
            t.set(j, readField(p, fs[j], j));
        }

        if (p.nextToken() != JsonToken.END_OBJECT) {
            log.warn("Bad tuple field, could not find end of object, "
                + "field " + fieldnum);
            return null;
        }
        return t;

case DataType.BAG:
        if (p.nextToken() != JsonToken.START_ARRAY) {
            log.warn("Bad bag field, could not find start of array, "
                + "field " + fieldnum);
            return null;
        }

        s = field.getSchema();
        fs = s.getFields();
        // Drill down the next level to the tuple's schema.
        s = fs[0].getSchema();
        fs = s.getFields();

        DataBag bag = bagFactory.newDefaultBag();

        JsonToken innerTok;
        while ((innerTok = p.nextToken()) != JsonToken.END_ARRAY) {
            if (innerTok != JsonToken.START_OBJECT) {
                log.warn("Bad bag tuple field, could not find start of "
                    + "object, field " + fieldnum);
                return null;
            }

            t = tupleFactory.newTuple(fs.length);
            for (int j = 0; j < fs.length; j++) {
                t.set(j, readField(p, fs[j], j));
            }

            if (p.nextToken() != JsonToken.END_OBJECT) {
                log.warn("Bad bag tuple field, could not find end of "
                    + "object, field " + fieldnum);
                return null;
            }
            bag.add(t);
        }
        return bag;
```

```
        default:
            throw new IOException("Unknown type in input schema: " +
                field.getType());
        }

    }
```

Additional Load Function Interfaces

Your load function can provide more complex features by implementing additional interfaces. (Implementation of these interfaces is optional.)

Loading metadata

Many data storage mechanisms can record the schema along with the data. Pig does not assume the ability to store schemas, but if your storage can hold the schema, it can be very useful. This frees script writers from needing to specify the field names and types as part of the load operator in Pig Latin. This is user-friendly and less error prone, and avoids the need to rewrite scripts when the schema of your data changes.

Some types of data storage also partition the data. If Pig understands this partitioning, it can load only those partitions that are needed for a particular script. Both of these functions are enabled by implementing the LoadMetadata interface.

getSchema in the LoadMetadata interface gives your load function a chance to provide a schema. It is passed the location string the user provides as well as the Hadoop Job object, in case it needs information in this object to open the schema. It is expected to return a ResourceSchema, which represents the data that will be returned. ResourceSchema is very similar to the Schema class used by evaluation functions. (See "Input and Output Schemas" on page 170 for details.) There is one important difference, however. In ResourceFieldSchema, the schema object associated with a bag always has one field, which is a tuple. The schema for the tuples in the bag is described by that tuple's ResourceFieldSchema.

Our example load and store functions keep the schema in a side file[1] named _schema_ in HDFS. Our implementation of getSchema reads this file and also serializes the schema into UDFContext so that it is available on the backend:

```
// JsonLoader.java
public ResourceSchema getSchema(String location, Job job)
throws IOException {
    // Open the schema file and read the schema.
```

---

1 A file in the same directory that is not a part file. The names of side files start with an underscore character. MapReduce's FileInputFormat knows to ignore them when reading input for a job.

```
    // Get an HDFS handle.
    FileSystem fs = FileSystem.get(job.getConfiguration());
    DataInputStream in = fs.open(new Path(location + "/_schema"));
    String line = in.readLine();
    in.close();

    // Parse the schema.
    ResourceSchema s = new ResourceSchema(Utils.getSchemaFromString(line));
    if (s == null) {
        throw new IOException("Unable to parse schema found in file " +
            location + "/_schema");
    }

    // Now that we have determined the schema, store it in our
    // UDFContext properties object so we have it when we need it on the
    // backend.
    UDFContext udfc = UDFContext.getUDFContext();
    Properties p =
        udfc.getUDFProperties(this.getClass(), new String[]{udfcSignature});
    p.setProperty("pig.jsonloader.schema", line);

    return s;
}
```

If your loader implements getSchema, load statements that use your loader do not need to declare their schemas in order for the field names to be used in the script. For example, if we had data with a schema of (user:chararray, age:int, gpa:dou ble), the following Pig Latin would compile and run:

```
register 'acme.jar';
register 'src/pig/trunk/build/ivy/lib/Pig/jackson-core-asl-1.6.0.jar';

A = load 'input' using com.acme.io.JsonLoader();
B = foreach A generate user;
dump B;
```

LoadMetadata also includes a getStatistics method. Pig does not yet make use of statistics in job planning; this method is for future use.

Using partitions

Some types of storage partition their data, allowing you to read only the relevant sections for a given job. The LoadMetadata interface also provides methods for working with partitions in your data. In order for Pig to request the relevant partitions, it must know how the data is partitioned. Pig determines this by calling getPartitionKeys. If this returns a null or the LoadMetadata interface is not implemented by your loader, Pig will assume it needs to read the entire input.

Pig expects getPartitionKeys to return an array of strings, where each string represents one field name. Those fields are the keys used to partition the data. Pig will look for a `filter` statement immediately following the `load` statement that includes one or more of these fields. If such a statement is found, it will be passed to `setPartition` `Filter`. If the `filter` includes both partition and nonpartition keys and it can be split,[2] Pig will split it and will pass just the partition key–related expression to `setPar` `titionFilter`. As an example, consider an HCatalog[3] table `web_server_logs` that is partitioned by two fields, `date` and `colo`:

```
logs    = load 'web_server_logs' using HCatLoader();
cleaned = filter logs by date = '20110614' and NotABot(user_id);
...
```

Pig will call `getPartitionKeys`, and `HCatLoader` will return two key names, `date` and `colo`. Pig will find the `date` field in the `filter` statement and rewrite the filter as shown in the following example, pushing down the `date = '20110614'` predicate to `HCatLoader` via `setPartitionFilter`:

```
logs    = load 'web_server_logs' using HCatLoader();
cleaned = filter logs by NotABot(user_id);
...
```

It is now up to the HCatalog loader to ensure that it only returns data from `web_server_logs` where `date` is `20110614`.

The one exception to this is fields used in eval funcs or filter funcs. Pig assumes that loaders do not understand how to invoke UDFs, so Pig will not push these expressions. However, if the inputs of the eval funcs or filter funcs are constants, Pig will evaluate the functions at compile time and push the resulting filter to the loader; see "Compile-Time Evaluation" on page 185.

Our example loader works on file data, so it does not implement `getPartitionKeys` or `setPartitionFilter`. For an example implementation of these methods, see the HCatalog code on GitHub (*http://bit.ly/hcatloaderjava*).

Casting bytearrays

If you need to control how binary data that your loader loads is cast to other data types, you can implement the `LoadCaster` interface. Because this interface contains a lot of methods, implementers often implement it as a separate class. This also allows load functions to share implementations of `LoadCaster`, since Java does not support multiple inheritance.

---

2 Meaning that the filter can be broken into two filters—one that contains the partition keys and one that does not—and produce the same end result. This is possible when the expressions are connected by and but not when they are connected by or.

3 HCatalog is a table-management service for Hadoop. It includes Pig load and store functions. See "HCatalog" on page 264 for more information on HCatalog.

The interface consists of a series of methods: bytesToInteger, bytesToLong, etc. These will be called to convert a bytearray to the appropriate type. From Pig 0.9, there are two bytesToMap methods. You should implement the one that takes a Resource FieldSchema; the other one is for backward-compatibility. The bytesToBag, bytesTo Tuple, and bytesToMap methods take a ResourceFieldSchema that describes the field being converted. Calling getSchema on this object will return a schema that describes this bag, tuple, or map, if one exists. If Pig does not know the intended structure of the object, getSchema will return null. Keep in mind that the schema of the bag will be one field, a tuple, which in turn will have a schema describing the contents of that tuple.

A default load caster, Utf8StorageConverter, is provided. It handles converting UTF8-encoded text to Pig types. Scalar conversions are done in a straightforward way. Maps are expected to be surrounded by [ ] (square brackets), with keys separated from values with a # (hash) and key/value pairs separated by a , (comma). Tuples are surrounded by ( ) (parentheses) and have fields separated by , (commas). Bags are surrounded by { } (braces) and have tuples separated by , (commas). There is no ability to escape these special characters.

Pushing down projections

Often a Pig Latin script will need to read only a few fields in the input. Some types of storage formats store their data by fields instead of by records (for example, Hive's RCFile). For these types of formats, there is a significant performance gain to be had by loading only those fields that will be used in the script. Even for record-oriented storage formats, it can be useful to skip deserializing fields that will not be used.

As part of its optimizations, Pig analyzes Pig Latin scripts and determines what fields in an input it needs at each step in the script. It uses this information to aggressively drop fields it no longer needs. If the loader implements the LoadPushDown interface, Pig can go a step further and provide this information to the loader.

Once Pig knows the fields it needs, it assembles them in a RequiredFieldList and passes that to pushProjection. In the load function's reply, it indicates whether it can meet the request. It responds with a RequiredFieldResponse, which is a fancy wrapper around a Boolean. If the Boolean is true, Pig will assume that only the required fields are being returned from getNext. If it is false, Pig will assume that all fields are being returned by getNext, and it will handle dropping the extra ones itself.

The RequiredField class used to describe which fields are required is slightly complex. Beyond allowing a user to specify whether a given field is required, it provides the ability to specify which subfields of that field are required. For example, for maps, certain keys can be listed as required. For tuples and bags, certain fields can be listed as required.

Load functions that implement `LoadPushDown` should not modify the schema object returned by `getSchema`. This should always be the schema of the full input. Pig will manage the translation between the schema having all of the fields and the results of `getNext` having only some.

Our example loader does not implement `LoadPushDown`. For an example of a loader that does, see `HCatLoader` (*http://bit.ly/hcatloaderjava*).

Predicate pushdown

In "Using partitions" on page 217 we saw that Pig is able to push filter conditions that the loader is guaranteed to honor (that is, the loader will not return any records that would pass the pushed filter). This is useful for pushing a Hive table's partition keys into the loader. However, there are times when it is useful to be able to push a filter that the loader cannot guarantee it will execute for every record. An example is `Orc Storage`. Every ORC file consists of stripes, and every stripe consists of row groups. Each ORC file, stripe, and row group includes metadata that contains statistics, indices, and Bloom filters for the data inside it. By evaluating the predicate against the metadata ORC is sometimes able to avoid reading the file or stripe or row group. Consider, for example, if your data has a `user_age` field. If the statistics for a row group indicate that the minimum `user_age` value in that row group is 25, and your Pig Latin includes `filter users by user_age < 21;`, then ORC can skip over that row group. However, ORC cannot guarantee that it will not return any records that would fail the filter. For the data in files, stripes, and row groups with at least one record that passes the predicate, ORC will return all the records. That is, it will not apply the filter to the data. It just uses the filter to do input pruning. Thus, Pig will need to evaluate the filter condition against the returned records.

To support predicate pushdown, Pig introduced the `LoadPredicatePushdown` interface in version 0.14. If your loader supports predicate pushdown, you need to implement this interface. However, even if a loader is able to take predicate filters, it may have limitations on the types of predicates it supports. Conditions apply to:

- The data types of the fields supported in the predicates. For example, ORC does not support predicate pushdown of complex data types. So, if a predicate contains a complex field, it cannot be pushed into `OrcStorage`. This is conveyed by the `getPredicateFields` method of the `LoadPredicatePushdown` interface.
- The operators supported in the predicates. Some operators supported by Pig may not be supported by the loader. For example, ORC does not support regular expressions, so if the predicate contains a `matches` operator, it cannot be pushed into `OrcStorage`. This is conveyed by the `getSupportedExpressionTypes` method of the `LoadPredicatePushdown` interface.

If a predicate satisfies both conditions, Pig will push the expression to the loader via the `setPushdownPredicate` method. You can view this as an optimization hint to the loader. Even if the loader does not filter any records, Pig will do the filtering and generate the right result. However, if the loader aggressively filters the records based on the predicate, Pig will load much less data; thus, your performance will be improved.

For an example of how this can be implemented, see `OrcStorage` (*http://bit.ly/orcstorage*).

Store Functions

Pig's store function is, in many ways, a mirror image of the load function. It is built on top of Hadoop's `OutputFormat`. The store function takes Pig tuples as input and creates key/value pairs that its associated output format writes to storage.

`StoreFunc` is an abstract class, which allows it to provide default implementations for some methods. However, some functions implement both load and store functionality; `PigStorage` is one example. Because Java does not support multiple inheritance, the interface `StoreFuncInterface` is provided. These dual load/store functions can implement this interface rather than extending `StoreFunc`.

Store function operations are split between the frontend and backend of Pig. Pig does planning and optimization on the frontend. Store functions have an opportunity at this time to check that a valid schema is being used and set up the storage location. On the backend, store functions take a tuple from Pig, convert it to a key/value pair, and pass it to a Hadoop `RecordWriter`. Store functions can pass information from frontend invocations to backend invocations via `UDFContext`.

Store Function Frontend Planning

Store functions have three tasks to fulfill on the frontend:

1. Instantiate the `OutputFormat` they will use to store data.
2. Check the schema of the data being stored.
3. Record the location where the data will be stored.

Determining the OutputFormat

Pig calls `getOutputFormat` to get an instance of the output format that your store function will use to store records. This method returns an instance rather than the class name or the class itself. This allows your store function to control how the class is instantiated. The example store function `JsonStorage` uses `TextOutputFormat`. This is an output format that stores text data in HDFS. We have to instantiate this with a key of `LongWritable` and a value of `Text` to match the expectations of `TextIn putFormat`:

```
// JsonStorage.java
public OutputFormat getOutputFormat() throws IOException {
    return new TextOutputFormat<LongWritable, Text>();
}
```

Setting the output location

Pig calls `setStoreLocation` to communicate the location string the user provides to your store function. Given the Pig Latin `store Z into 'output';`, "output" is the location string. This method, called on both the frontend and the backend, may be called multiple times; consequently, it should not have any side effects that will cause a problem if this happens. Your store function will need to communicate the location to its output format. Our example store function uses the `FileOutputFormat` utility function `setOutputPath` to do this:

```
// JsonStorage.java
public void setStoreLocation(String location, Job job) throws IOException {
    FileOutputFormat.setOutputPath(job, new Path(location));
}
```

The Hadoop `Job` is passed to this function as well. Most output formats store the location information in this object.

Pig calls `setStoreLocation` on both the frontend and the backend because output formats usually store their location in the `Job` object, as we can see in our example store function. For MapReduce jobs, where a single output format is guaranteed, only setting the output path in the frontend works fine. But due to the `split` operator, Pig can have more than one instance of the same store function in a job. If multiple instances of a store function call `FileOutputFormat.setOutputPath`, whichever instance calls it last will overwrite the others. Pig avoids this by keeping output-specific information and calling `setStoreLocation` again on the backend so that it can properly configure the output format.

For HDFS files, the user might provide relative paths. Pig needs to resolve these to absolute paths using the current working directory at the time the store is called. To accomplish this, Pig calls `relToAbsPathForStoreLocation` with the user-provided location string before calling `setStoreLocation`. This method translates between relative and absolute paths. For store functions writing to HDFS, the default implementation in `StoreFunc` handles the conversion. If you are writing a store function that does not use file paths (e.g., for HBase), you should override this method to return the string it is passed.

Checking the schema

As part of frontend planning, Pig gives your store function a chance to check the schema of the data to be stored. If you are storing data to a system that expects a certain schema for the output (such as an RDBMS) or you cannot store certain data types, checkSchema is the place to perform those checks. Oddly enough, this method returns a void rather than a Boolean, so if you detect an issue with the schema, you must throw an IOException.

Our example store function does not have limitations on the schemas it can store. However, it uses this function as a place to serialize the schema into UDFContext so that it can be used on the backend when writing data:

```
// JsonStorage.java
public void checkSchema(ResourceSchema s) throws IOException {
    UDFContext udfc = UDFContext.getUDFContext();
    Properties p =
        udfc.getUDFProperties(this.getClass(), new String[]{udfcSignature});
    p.setProperty("pig.jsonstorage.schema", s.toString());
}
```

Store Functions and UDFContext

Store functions work with UDFContext exactly as load functions do with one exception: the signature is passed to the store function via setStoreFuncUDFContextSignature. See "Passing Information from the Frontend to the Backend" on page 210 for a discussion of how load functions work with UDFContext. Our example store function stores the signature in a member variable for later use:

```
// JsonStorage.java
public void setStoreFuncUDFContextSignature(String signature) {
    udfcSignature = signature;
}
```

Writing Data

During backend processing, the store function is first initialized and then takes Pig tuples and converts them to key/value pairs to be written to storage.

Preparing to write

Pig calls your store function's prepareToWrite method in each map or reduce task before writing any data. This call passes a RecordWriter instance to use when writing data. RecordWriter is a class that OutputFormat uses to write individual records. Pig will get the record writer it passes to your store function by calling getRecordWriter on the output format your store function returned from getOutputFormat. Your store function will need to keep this reference so that it can be used in putNext.

The example store function JsonStorage also uses this method to read the schema out of the UDFContext. It will use this schema when storing data. Finally, it creates a JsonFactory for use in putNext:

```
// JsonStorage.java
public void prepareToWrite(RecordWriter writer) throws IOException {
    // Store the record writer reference so we can use it when it's time
    // to write tuples.
    this.writer = writer;

    // Get the schema string from the UDFContext object.
    UDFContext udfc = UDFContext.getUDFContext();
    Properties p =
        udfc.getUDFProperties(this.getClass(), new String[]{udfcSignature});
    String strSchema = p.getProperty("pig.jsonstorage.schema");
    if (strSchema == null) {
        throw new IOException("Could not find schema in UDF context");
    }

    // Parse the schema from the string stored in the properties object.
    ResourceSchema schema =
        new ResourceSchema(Utils.getSchemaFromString(strSchema));
    fields = schema.getFields();

    // Build a Json factory.
    jsonFactory = new JsonFactory();
    jsonFactory.configure(
        JsonGenerator.Feature.WRITE_NUMBERS_AS_STRINGS, false);
}
```

Writing records

putNext is the core method in the store function class. Pig calls this method for every tuple it needs to store. Your store function needs to take these tuples and produce the key/value pairs that its output format expects. For information on the Java objects in which the data will be stored and how to extract them, see "Interacting with Pig values" on page 168.

JsonStorage encodes the contents of the tuple in JSON format and writes the resulting string into the value field of TextOutputFormat. The key field is left null:

```
// JsonStorage.java
public void putNext(Tuple t) throws IOException {
    // Build a ByteArrayOutputStream to write the JSON into.
    ByteArrayOutputStream baos = new ByteArrayOutputStream(BUF_SIZE);
    // Build the generator.
    JsonGenerator json =
        jsonFactory.createJsonGenerator(baos, JsonEncoding.UTF8);

    // Write the beginning of the top-level tuple object.
    json.writeStartObject();
```

```
        for (int i = 0; i < fields.length; i++) {
            writeField(json, fields[i], t.get(i));
        }
        json.writeEndObject();
        json.close();

        // Hand a null key and our string to Hadoop.
        try {
            writer.write(null, new Text(baos.toByteArray()));
        } catch (InterruptedException ie) {
            throw new IOException(ie);
        }
    }

    private void writeField(JsonGenerator json,
                            ResourceFieldSchema field,
                            Object d) throws IOException {

        // If the field is missing or the value is null, write a null.
        if (d == null) {
            json.writeNullField(field.getName());
            return;
        }

        // Based on the field's type, write it out.
        switch (field.getType()) {
        case DataType.INTEGER:
            json.writeNumberField(field.getName(), (Integer)d);
            return;

        case DataType.LONG:
            json.writeNumberField(field.getName(), (Long)d);
            return;

        case DataType.FLOAT:
            json.writeNumberField(field.getName(), (Float)d);
            return;

        case DataType.DOUBLE:
            json.writeNumberField(field.getName(), (Double)d);
            return;

        case DataType.BYTEARRAY:
            json.writeBinaryField(field.getName(), ((DataByteArray)d).get());
            return;

        case DataType.CHARARRAY:
            json.writeStringField(field.getName(), (String)d);
            return;

        case DataType.MAP:
            json.writeFieldName(field.getName());
```

```
        json.writeStartObject();
        for (Map.Entry<String, Object> e : ((Map<String, Object>)d).entrySet()) {
            json.writeStringField(e.getKey(), e.getValue().toString());
        }
        json.writeEndObject();
        return;

    case DataType.TUPLE:
        json.writeFieldName(field.getName());
        json.writeStartObject();

        ResourceSchema s = field.getSchema();
        if (s == null) {
            throw new IOException("Schemas must be fully specified to use "
                + "this storage function.  No schema found for field " +
                field.getName());
        }
        ResourceFieldSchema[] fs = s.getFields();

        for (int j = 0; j < fs.length; j++) {
            writeField(json, fs[j], ((Tuple)d).get(j));
        }
        json.writeEndObject();
        return;

    case DataType.BAG:
        json.writeFieldName(field.getName());
        json.writeStartArray();
        s = field.getSchema();
        if (s == null) {
            throw new IOException("Schemas must be fully specified to use "
                + "this storage function.  No schema found for field " +
                field.getName());
        }
        fs = s.getFields();
        if (fs.length != 1 || fs[0].getType() != DataType.TUPLE) {
            throw new IOException("Found a bag without a tuple "
                + "inside!");
        }
        // Drill down the next level to the tuple's schema.
        s = fs[0].getSchema();
        if (s == null) {
            throw new IOException("Schemas must be fully specified to use "
                + "this storage function.  No schema found for field " +
                field.getName());
        }
        fs = s.getFields();
        for (Tuple t : (DataBag)d) {
            json.writeStartObject();
            for (int j = 0; j < fs.length; j++) {
                writeField(json, fs[j], t.get(j));
            }
```

```
            json.writeEndObject();
        }
        json.writeEndArray();
        return;
    }
}
```

Failure Cleanup

When jobs fail after execution has started, your store function may need to clean up partially stored results. Pig will call `cleanupOnFailure` to give your store function an opportunity to do this. It passes the location string and the `Job` object so that your store function knows what it should clean up.

In the HDFS case, the default implementation handles removing any output files created by the store function. You need to implement this method only if you are storing data somewhere other than HDFS.

Storing Metadata

If your storage format can store schemas in addition to data, your store function can implement the interface `StoreMetadata`. This provides a `storeSchema` method that is called by Pig as part of its frontend operations. Pig passes `storeSchema` a `Resource Schema`, the location string, and the `Job` object so that it can connect to its storage. `ResourceSchema` is very similar to the `Schema` class described in "Input and Output Schemas" on page 170. There is one important difference, however. In `Resource FieldSchema`, the schema object associated with a bag always has one field, which is a tuple. The schema for the tuples in the bag is described by that tuple's `ResourceField Schema`.

The example store function `JsonStorage` stores the schema in a side file named *_schema* in the same directory as the data. The schema is stored as a string, using the `toString` method provided by the class:

```
// JsonStorage.java
public void storeSchema(ResourceSchema schema, String location, Job job)
throws IOException {
    // Store the schema in a side file in the same directory.  MapReduce
    // does not include files starting with "_" when reading data for a job.
    FileSystem fs = FileSystem.get(job.getConfiguration());
    DataOutputStream out = fs.create(new Path(location + "/_schema"));
    out.writeBytes(schema.toString());
    out.writeByte('\n');
    out.close();
}
```

`StoreMetadata` also has a `storeStatistics` function, but Pig does not use this yet.

Shipping JARs Automatically

Since version 0.14, Pig supports automatic shipping of JARs for `LoadFunc` and `Store Func` just as it does for `EvalFunc`. The two methods `getCacheFiles` and `getShip Files` are also in `LoadFunc` and `StoreFunc`. Again, Pig will automatically ship JARs containing the loader and storer itself; this capacity is for shipping additional dependencies. For more details concerning automatically shipping JARs, see "Shipping JARs Automatically" on page 185.

Handling Bad Records

If you hit a bad record in your `LoadFunc` or `StoreFunc`, you'll probably want to ignore the record and keep the Pig job running. However, if the number of bad records exceeds a certain threshold, something must be wrong in your Pig script or your data. It is not meaningful to continue the job any more; you need to figure out the problem and then rerun it. You can implement this error handling logic by yourself in your `LoadFunc` or `StoreFunc`. You can capture the exception, keep a count of it, and then compare the count with the threshold. Or you can save your time and leave the counting business to Pig. Starting from version 0.16, Pig provides the `ErrorHandling` interface for this purpose. Note, however, that at the time of writing `ErrorHandling` only works on the `StoreFunc`. The loader side is likely to work the same way in a future version.

To leverage this functionality, you will need to implement `ErrorHandling` for your `StoreFunc`. There is only one method in `ErrorHandling`: `getErrorHandler`. Most of time, the provided `CounterBasedErrorHandler` should be enough:

```
public ErrorHandler getErrorHandler() {
    return new CounterBasedErrorHandler();
}
```

The threshold can be defined in *pig.properties* or your Pig script. You'll need to set the following properties:

`pig.error-handling.enabled`
   Whether Pig error handling is on (default `false`)

`pig.error-handling.min.error.records`
   The minimum number of errors to trigger error handling (default `0`)

`pig.error-handling.error.threshold`
   The percentage of the number of records as a fraction exceeding which an error is thrown (default `0.0`)

For example, if `pig.error-handling.min.error.records` is `100` and `pig.error-handling.error.threshold` is `0.1`, the first 99 bad records will not cause the Pig task to fail. If we hit 100 bad records, Pig will calculate the error rate. Suppose we have processed 2,000 records. The error rate is 100/2,000=0.05, which is below 0.1, so the Pig task will not fail. Note that both `pig.error-handling.min.error.records` and `pig.error-handling.error.threshold` are particular to a task, not the whole Pig job.

## CHAPTER 11

Pig on Tez

Pig 0.14 introduced a new execution engine called Tez. You can view Tez as a faster and better MapReduce. Whenever possible, you should use Tez to run Pig instead of MapReduce.

What Is Tez?

As we have learned in previous chapters, Pig traditionally uses MapReduce as the execution engine. That is, a Pig Latin script will be translated into a series of Map-Reduce jobs for execution. For a long time, MapReduce was the only option to run a workload on a Hadoop cluster. However, with the introduction of YARN in Hadoop 2.0, this situation changed. With YARN, you can have different types of workloads on a single cluster; MapReduce is merely one of them.

MapReduce is not an optimal engine for Pig. MapReduce is very rigid; it requires Pig to decompose its workload into one or more MapReduce jobs. This prevents Pig from mixing map and reduce tasks in other ways or using other types of tasks. Also, MapReduce requires that data be stored in HDFS between jobs, preventing optimizations in data movement. Finally, MapReduce's job scheduler thinks about each job in isolation; it does not understand that the series of jobs Pig is submitting are related. This limits its ability to schedule efficiently.

One of the important features of MapReduce is that it has a simple API—it is easy for a programmer to understand and write MapReduce code. However, for Pig, Map-Reduce is just an internal engine and the MapReduce API is not exposed to the user. The simplicity of the MapReduce API does not benefit Pig users. Instead, Pig users suffer from the performance penalty due to the inflexibility of MapReduce.

Apache Tez (*https://tez.apache.org/*) has emerged as an alternative execution engine that offers the flexibility and performance that MapReduce lacks. It is a general directed acyclic graph (DAG) execution engine. The vertex of the DAG is a processing unit that runs the tasks, and the edges between vertices represent data movement and can have different semantics. DAG engines are common in parallel data processing.

Tez is a low-level execution engine. The API is much more complex than MapReduce's, so it is not end user–facing. However, for Pig, this is not a problem. Pig hides the complexity from the user.

In short, Tez provides the following benefits to Pig:

- Performance improvements
- Scalability
- Low latency
- Closer to Pig semantics

We will go through these benefits in detail in the rest of this section.

With Tez, since Pig is no longer forced to adhere to the strict MapReduce paradigm, it can freely construct a DAG that is optimal for the targeted workload. In particular, map tasks in noninitial MapReduce jobs can often be omitted in Tez. For example, consider the following Pig Latin script:

```
daily    = load 'NYSE_daily' as (exchange:chararray, symbol:chararray,
               date:chararray, open:float, high:float, low:float,
               close:float, volume:int, adj_close:float);
grpd1    = group daily by symbol;
avg1     = foreach grpd1 generate group as symbol, AVG(daily.close) as avg_close;
divs     = load 'NYSE_dividends' as (exchange:chararray, symbol:chararray,
               date:chararray, dividends:float);
grpd2    = group divs by symbol;
avg2     = foreach grpd2 generate group as symbol, AVG(divs.dividends) as
           avg_dividents;
joined   = join avg1 by symbol, avg2 by symbol;
```

In MapReduce, this script is compiled into three MapReduce jobs as shown on the left side of Figure 11-1. We can see that the map phase of the third MapReduce job (the join job) is not doing anything meaningful. It simply loads the temporary file produced by the first two MapReduce jobs and sends them to the reducer. In Tez, the no-op node is skipped in the DAG plan, as shown on the right side of the same figure. Instead of three MapReduce jobs consisting of a total of six processing nodes in the MapReduce plan, the Tez plan only contains five processing nodes. Further, there are no temporary files written to HDFS. The results of the group operators are sent to the join operator directly through the network (and cached on the local disk for durability). This saves the overhead of writing temporary output to HDFS and reading it back. Also, in the Tez plan Pig only interacts with HDFS when loading initial inputs and writing final outputs, which reduces the workload for HDFS's NameNode and thus makes the cluster more scalable. If the data-processing pipeline is longer, there will be more no-op nodes and intermediate HDFS files to skip in the Tez plan, and thus the savings will be even larger. Also, the Tez Application Master (AM) can now schedule the Pig job all at once, rather than requiring three separate job submissions as in the MapReduce case.

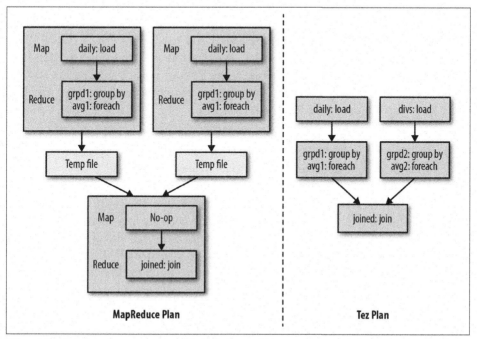

Figure 11-1. Join after group in MapReduce and Tez

In MapReduce data has to be shuffled and sorted between map and reduce tasks. This is overly restrictive for Pig's data processing. Tez, in contrast, provides more choices. These include a conventional scatter-gather edge, similar to that of MapReduce (it performs a shuffle and a sort), a broadcast edge (which sends data from one task to a collection of other tasks), and a one-to-one edge (which sends data from one task to one task). These options enable Pig to be efficient when transferring data. Consider the following Pig Latin script, introduced in "Casting a Relation to a Scalar" on page 82:

```
daily = load 'NYSE_daily' as (exchange:chararray, symbol:chararray,
        date:chararray, open:float, high:float, low:float,
        close:float, volume:int, adj_close:float);
grouped = group daily all;
scalar_relation = foreach grouped generate MAX(daily.volume) as max_volume;
volumn_percent = foreach daily generate symbol,
        (double)volume/scalar_relation.max_volume;
```

The execution plans for both MapReduce and Tez are illustrated side by side in Figure 11-2. Pig needs to broadcast the scalar value to the downstream node that executes the volumn_percent foreach. In MapReduce, a simple workaround is to put the file containing the scalar value in HDFS; then every task of the downstream node reads the file from HDFS. This is problematic since, with potentially thousands of tasks reading from HDFS simultaneously, we can slow down the NameNode significantly. Pig on MapReduce handles this by putting the scalar file in the distributed cache. This is better than the former approach, but it still requires multiple HDFS reads since every node needs to localize the distributed cache once. In Tez, it is natural to use a broadcast edge between the scalar_relation foreach and the volumn_percent foreach. Thus, Tez gives Pig a way to broadcast the scalar result to every task instance without burdening HDFS.

Also notice there is a one-to-one edge in the Tez plan. After loading the input file, Pig needs the scalar calculated by the group all node to process the foreach statement. Since it requires a new dependency, Pig needs to create a separate Tez vertex for the foreach. However, shuffle and sort are not required between load and foreach; the loaded data can be transmitted as is to the foreach. To achieve this, Pig chooses a one-to-one Tez edge. In most cases, both tasks are colocated, so there is no network traffic between adjacent nodes connected by the one-to-one edge. For MapReduce, the choices are limited, so Pig has to write to an intermediate HDFS file and load it back to process the foreach, which is very inefficient compared to the Tez plan.

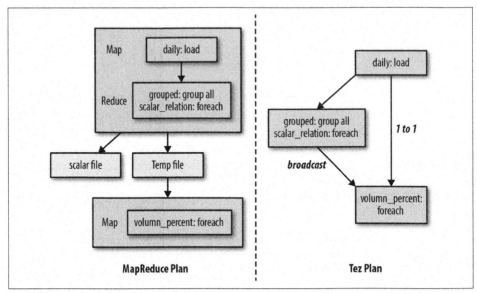

Figure 11-2. Scalar in MapReduce and Tez

In addition to throughput improvement, the latency for Tez is much less than that of MapReduce, thanks to session reuse and container reuse. The Tez AM and Tez container are long-running JVM processes. In MapReduce, once the job finishes, all of the associated tasks (map, reduce, and MapReduce's AM) are killed. The cost of restarting the JVM may be negligible for large jobs, but for small and repeated jobs such as iterative machine learning, it can be significant. In Tez, both the AM[1] and containers are reusable. AMs can be reused across jobs. For a new task in a job, Tez will try to run the task on an existing container whenever possible. This saves the initial cost of starting a JVM. Further, some vertices have resources that require initialization. For example, in a fragment-replicate join, the replicated table must be loaded into memory. With container reuse, we can store the replicated table in an `ObjectReg istry` that is preserved across tasks so that the next task that runs in the container can reuse the memory structure without reloading it. Another benefit of container reuse is congestion avoidance. In a congested cluster, requesting a new container means waiting in line and competing for resources with other jobs. This significantly delays processing.

Compared to MapReduce, a Tez DAG is closer to the actual data pipeline described by a Pig Latin script. As an example, look at Figure 11-3, which is a diagram of a regular join in Pig. MapReduce's map task can only take one input. But to do a join properly the reduce task must have two (or more) inputs. Pig solves this problem by annotating each record with its input source in the map task, as we discussed in "join" on page 62. Though this works, the implementation is not intuitive for Pig users. If things go wrong, it is harder for them to debug. In Tez a vertex can take multiple inputs, which allows Pig to define a vertex for each input, both of which are then shuffled and sorted to the join vertex. There is no need to annotate the input records since Tez can tell which vertex each record came from.

Last but not least, Tez is not a completely new engine. Tez's developers did not want to lose the years of learning and development that went into MapReduce. Thus, rather than beginning again from scratch, they sought to make Tez a generalization and improvement of MapReduce. This is helpful to you, the user, as much of your MapReduce knowledge still applies. If you are familiar with MapReduce, you will find a lot of the same pieces are still there in Tez. The shuffle code in MapReduce is used in Tez. The parameters to tune the sort and shuffle in MapReduce are also applicable in Tez. Your skills for debugging and diagnosing a MapReduce job continue to be relevant. Further, Tez automatically translates many of the configuration parameters of MapReduce, which means often you do not need to change a single line of your Pig Latin script to make it work with Tez.

---

1 In Tez terminology, AM reuse is referred to as session reuse.

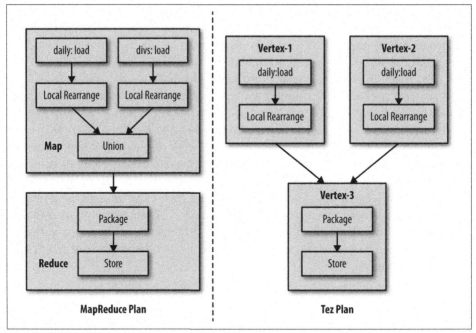

Figure 11-3. Join in MapReduce and Tez

Running Pig on Tez

If you are using a Hadoop distribution that does not come with Tez, you need to install it first. Tez is a client-side library, so you do not need to deploy it on your cluster nodes. All you need to do is:

1. Get the Tez tarball. This might be the trickiest part of installing Tez. Since Tez does not publish a binary tarball, you will have to compile and generate it yourself. Go to *https://tez.apache.org/releases/* and download the Tez source tarball compatible with your version of Pig. For Pig 0.14, you should download Tez 0.5.2. For Pig 0.15, download Tez 0.7.0. The complete instructions on how to generate *tez.tar.gz* can be found at *https://tez.apache.org/install.html*. In short, you will need to run the following Maven command line to generate it:

   ```
   mvn clean package -DskipTests=true
   ```

   You will find *tez.tar.gz* in the *tez-dist/target* directory.

2. Upload *tez.tar.gz* to HDFS.

3. On your gateway, untar *tez.tar.gz*, make a *conf* directory, and create a *tez-site.xml* file in that directory. Then put the following entry in it:

```
<configuration>
  <property>
    <name>tez.lib.uris</name>
    <value>${fs.default.name}/path_to_tez_tarball/tez.tar.gz
  </property>
</configuration>
```

There are more config entries you can put into *tez-site.xml*, but `tez.lib.uris` is the only required entry. For a complete list of Tez configurations, please refer to the documentation (*http://bit.ly/configuretez*).

Once you have finished installing Tez, you will also need to add the Tez libraries and the directory containing *tez-site.xml* to Pig's classpath. Usually you can do this by setting the environment variable `PIG_CLASSPATH`:

```
export TEZ_HOME=/location_to_your_tez
export PIG_CLASSPATH=$PIG_CLASSPATH:$TEZ_HOME/*:$TEZ_HOME/lib/*:$TEZ_HOME/conf
```

Now you can run Pig on Tez simply by adding the `-x tez` parameter on the Pig command line:

```
pig_path/bin/pig -x tez script.pig
```

You may also run Tez in local mode to debug your Pig scripts using the Tez execution engine:

```
pig_path/bin/pig -x tez_local script.pig
```

Alternatively, you can put the following entry in your *conf/pig.properties* file so that Pig will run on Tez by default:

```
exectype=tez
```

However, it will not work if you put the statement `set exectype 'tez'` inside a Pig Latin script. This is because Pig decides the execution engine before parsing the script.

In most cases, you do not need to make any changes to your Pig Latin scripts. This is even true for the `set` statement for MapReduce properties. If a Tez property is defined, Pig will use the Tez property. If not, the corresponding MapReduce property will be used if defined. Table 11-1 lists some of the most useful Tez properties and their MapReduce counterparts.

Table 11-1. MapReduce properties translated to Tez

Tez property	MapReduce property	Description
`tez.queue.name`	`mapreduce.job.queuename`	The queue to use for Tez jobs.
`tez.task.launch.cmd-opts`	`mapreduce.map.java.opts`, `mapreduce.reduce.java.opts`	JVM command-line options. This can be used to set the heap size. If `tez.task.launch.cmd-opts` is not set, `mapreduce.map.java.opts` will be used for source vertices and `mapreduce.reduce.java.opts` for intermediate and nonsource final vertices.
`tez.task.resource.memory.mb`	`mapreduce.map.memory.mb` settings, `mapreduce.reduce.memory.mb` settings	The amount of memory, in megabytes, to be used by tasks.
`tez.am.launch.cmd-opts`	`yarn.app.mapreduce.am.command-opts`	Java options for the AM processes.
`tez.am.resource.memory.mb`	`yarn.app.mapreduce.am.resource.mb`	The amount of memory the AM needs, in megabytes.
`tez.runtime.io.sort.mb`	`mapreduce.task.io.sort.mb`	The size, in megabytes, of the memory buffer to use while sorting map output.
`tez.runtime.io.sort.factor`	`mapreduce.task.io.sort.factor`	The maximum number of streams to merge at once when sorting files.
`tez.runtime.combine.min.spills`	`mapreduce.map.combine.min.spills`	The minimum number of spill files (from the map) needed for the combiner to run.
`tez.runtime.shuffle.fetch.buffer.percent`	`mapreduce.reduce.shuffle.input.buffer.percent`	The proportion of total heap size to be allocated to the map outputs buffer during the copy phase of the shuffle.
`tez.runtime.shuffle.merge.percent`	`mapreduce.reduce.shuffle.input.buffer.percent`	The threshold usage percentage at which the map outputs buffer starts merging the outputs and spilling to disk.

Potential Differences When Running on Tez

Though Pig hides a lot of the differences in the underlying execution engine, you still need to be aware of some unique aspects of running Pig on Tez.

UDFs

In most cases your Pig UDFs can remain the same when moving from MapReduce to Tez. However, you need to be aware of one issue. With container reuse a static variable may have already been initialized by another container of the DAG, or even by a container of a different DAG. If your UDF uses static variables you need to use the new annotation `StaticDataCleanup` and the new class `JVMReuseManager` to reset them for each task. Here we show an example of the side effect a static variable can have and how to use the new annotation and class to clean it up:

```
public class Lookup extends EvalFunc<Integer> {
    String filename = null;
    static Set<String> mKeys = null;

    // Register cleanup hook
    static {
        JVMReuseManager.getInstance()
            .registerForStaticDataCleanup(Lookup.class);
    }

    // Clean up static variable
    @StaticDataCleanup
    public static void staticDataCleanup() {
        mKeys = null;
    }
    public Lookup(String filename) {
        this.filename = filename;
    }

    public void init() throws IOException {
        mKeys = new HashSet<String>();
        Properties props = ConfigurationUtil.toProperties(
                UDFContext.getUDFContext().getJobConf());
        BufferedReader reader = null;
        InputStream is = null;
        try {
            is = FileLocalizer.openDFSFile(filename, props);
        } catch (IOException e) {
            String msg = "Lookup : Cannot open file " + filename;
            throw new IOException(msg, e);
        }
        try {
            reader = new BufferedReader(new InputStreamReader(is));
            String line;
            while ((line = reader.readLine()) != null) {
                mKeys.add(line);
            }
            is.close();
        } catch (IOException e) {
            String msg = "Lookup : Cannot read file " + filename;
            throw new IOException(msg, e);
```

```
        }
    }

    @Override
    public Integer exec(Tuple input) throws IOException {
        if (mKeys == null) {
            init();
        }
        if (mKeys.contains(input.get(0).toString()))
            return 1;
        return 0;
    }
}
```

This EvalFunc uses a static variable mKeys. If it is already defined, Pig will not load it again from HDFS. This works fine in MapReduce. In Tez, however, this EvalFunc may have been initiated already with a different parameter, and the contents in mKeys may not be correct for the current invocation. To register the static variable cleanup hook you need to invoke the registerForStaticDataCleanup method of JVMReuse Manager within the static constructor. This registers the class in the JVMReuseMan ager. Put the logic to clean up static variables in the method tagged with @StaticDataCleanup. This method will be invoked before any code in your EvalFunc each time the UDF is loaded in a new container.

The same mechanism is applicable to LoadFunc and StoreFunc as well.

Using PigRunner

PigRunner (see "PigRunner" on page 161) is a Java API for Pig. The only method it contains is run. While the method signature does not change for Tez, the type of the returned object and the PigProgressNotificationListener object you will need to pass are changed to reflect the Tez-specific characteristics.

As with MapReduce, the actual return type depends on whether the Pig Latin script is regular or embedded Pig Latin. If it is a regular Pig Latin script, you will get an instance of TezPigScriptStats. If it is an embedded Pig script, you will get Embedded PigStats.

TezPigScriptStats captures the statistics of the Pig script at three levels: script, Tez DAG, and vertex. Here are examples of how to dive into the TezPigScriptStats object and find the DAG and vertex statistics:

```
PigStats stats = PigRunner.run(new String[]{"-x", "tez", "test.pig"}, null);
TezDAGStats dagStats = (TezDAGStats)stats.getJobGraph()
    .getSources().get(0); // Get root DAG statistics
dagStats.getHadoopCounters(); // Get DAG counters
TezVertexStats vertexStats = (TezVertexStats)dagStats.getPlan()
```

```
        .getSources().get(0); // Get statistics of the first vertex in DAG
    vertexStats.getAlias(); // Alias processed in the vertex
```

For an embedded Pig Latin script, behavior is similar to that of MapReduce. The only difference is that the map value in the result of getAllStats is of type TezPigScript Stats instead of SimplePigStats.

If you want to get progress notifications, you will need to extend PigTezProgressNo tificationListener. There are four DAG notification methods added to this new abstract class:

```
/**
 * Invoked just before launching a Tez DAG spawned by the script.
 *
 * @param scriptId - the unique ID of the script
 * @param dagId - the unique name of the Tez DAG
 * @param dagPlan - the OperatorPlan that is to be executed
 * @param numVerticesToLaunch - the total number of vertices spawned by
 * the Tez DAG
 */
public abstract void dagLaunchNotification(String scriptId, String dagId,
        OperatorPlan<?> dagPlan, int numVerticesToLaunch);


/**
 * Invoked after a Tez DAG is started.
 *
 * @param scriptId - the unique ID of the script
 * @param dagId - the unique name of the Tez DAG
 * @param assignedApplicationId  - the YARN application ID for the Tez DAG.
 *          More than one Tez DAG can share the same application ID if session
 *          reuse is turned on. Session reuse is turned on by default.
 */
public abstract void dagStartedNotification(String scriptId, String dagId,
    String assignedApplicationId);


/**
 * Invoked to update the execution progress.
 *
 * @param scriptId - the unique ID of the script
 * @param dagId - the unique name of the Tez DAG
 * @param numVerticesCompleted - the number of vertices completed so far
 * @param progress - the percentage of the execution progress based on total
 *          number of tasks of all vertices
 */
public abstract void dagProgressNotification(String scriptId, String dagId,
    int numVerticesCompleted, int progress);


/**
 * Invoked just after the Tez DAG is completed (successful or failed).
 *
 * @param scriptId - the unique ID of the script
 * @param dagId - the unique name of the Tez DAG
```

```
 * @param success - true if the Tez DAG was successful, false otherwise
 * @param tezDAGStats - the stats information for the DAG
 */
public abstract void dagCompletedNotification(String scriptId, String dagId,
    boolean success, TezDAGStats tezDAGStats);
```

The job-level notifications in MapReduce correspond to DAG level in Tez. There is
no vertex-level notification currently implemented.

Testing and Debugging

Pig tries to keep the testing and debugging process the same for both Tez and Map-
Reduce. However, since the execution engine is different, there will be some differences, especially in the execution plan and the job status web page.

Tez execution plan

As with MapReduce, you can do an explain in Pig in tez mode to see how Pig is
going to execute the script in Tez. In this section, we will use the following example
to illustrate the Tez execution plan:

```
--explain.pig
divs   = load 'NYSE_dividends' as (exchange, symbol, date, dividends);
grpd   = group divs by symbol;
avgdiv = foreach grpd generate group, AVG(divs.dividends);
final  = order avgdiv by avg desc;
store final into 'average_dividend_sorted';
```

We can use the following command line to do an explain in Tez mode:

```
pig_path/bin/pig -x tez -e 'explain -script explain.pig'
```

The explain command will show the logical plan, the physical plan, and the Tez
plan. The logical plan and physical plan the command produces are the same as when
using MapReduce. However, instead of a MapReduce execution plan, we will see a
Tez plan, as shown here:

```
#-------------------------------------------------
# There are 1 DAGs in the session
#-------------------------------------------------
#-------------------------------------------------
# TEZ DAG plan: pig-0_scope-0
#-------------------------------------------------
Tez vertex scope-15 ->  Tez vertex scope-16,
Tez vertex scope-16 ->  Tez vertex scope-25,Tez vertex scope-35,
Tez vertex scope-25 ->  Tez vertex scope-35,
Tez vertex scope-35 ->  Tez vertex scope-37,
Tez vertex scope-37

Tez vertex scope-15
# Plan on vertex
```

```
grpd: Local Rearrange[tuple]{bytearray}(false) - scope-53 ->     scope-16
|   |
|   Project[bytearray][0] - scope-55
|
|---avgdiv: New For Each(false,false)[bag] - scope-41
    |   |
    |   Project[bytearray][0] - scope-42
    |   |
    |   POUserFunc(org.apache.pig.builtin.AVG$Initial)[tuple] - scope-43
    |   |
    |   |---Project[bag][3] - scope-44
    |       |
    |       |---Project[bag][1] - scope-45
    |
    |---Pre Combiner Local Rearrange[tuple]{Unknown} - scope-56
        |
        |---divs: Load(hdfs://localhost:9000/user/daijy/NYSE_dividends:org.apach
e.pig.builtin.PigStorage) - scope-0
Tez vertex scope-16
# Combine plan on edge <scope-15>
grpd: Local Rearrange[tuple]{bytearray}(false) - scope-57 ->     scope-16
|   |
|   Project[bytearray][0] - scope-59
|
|---avgdiv: New For Each(false,false)[bag] - scope-46
    |   |
    |   Project[bytearray][0] - scope-47
    |   |
    |   POUserFunc(org.apache.pig.builtin.AVG$Intermediate)[tuple] - scope-48
    |   |
    |   |---Project[bag][1] - scope-49
    |
    |---grpd: Package(CombinerPackager)[tuple]{bytearray} - scope-52
# Plan on vertex
Local Rearrange[tuple]{tuple}(false) - scope-19 ->       scope-25
|   |
|   Constant(DummyVal) - scope-18
|
|---New For Each(false,true)[tuple] - scope-24
    |   |
    |   Project[double][1] - scope-12
    |   |
    |   POUserFunc(org.apache.pig.impl.builtin.GetMemNumRows)[tuple] - scope-23
    |   |
    |   |---Project[tuple][*] - scope-22
    |
    |---ReservoirSample - scope-21
        |
        |---final: Local Rearrange[tuple]{double}(false) - scope-17 ->    scope-35
            |   |
            |   Project[double][1] - scope-12
            |
```

```
                    |---avgdiv: New For Each(false,false)[bag] - scope-11
                          |     |
                          |   Project[bytearray][0] - scope-5
                          |     |
                          |   POUserFunc(org.apache.pig.builtin.AVG$Final)[double] - scope-
9
                          |     |
                          |   |---Project[bag][1] - scope-50
                          |
                          |---grpd: Package(CombinerPackager)[tuple]{bytearray} - scope-2
Tez vertex scope-25
# Plan on vertex
POValueOutputTez - scope-34 ->    [scope-35]
|
|---New For Each(false)[tuple] - scope-33
    |     |
    |   POUserFunc(org.apache.pig.backend.hadoop.executionengine.tez.plan.udf.Fin
dQuantilesTez)[tuple] - scope-32
    |     |
    |   |---Project[tuple][*] - scope-31
    |
    |---New For Each(false,false)[tuple] - scope-30
        |     |
        |   Constant(-1) - scope-29
        |     |
        |   Project[bag][1] - scope-27
        |
        |---Package(Packager)[tuple]{bytearray} - scope-26
Tez vertex scope-35
# Plan on vertex
POIdentityInOutTez - scope-36 <-          scope-16 ->       scope-37
|   |
|   Project[double][1] - scope-12
Tez vertex scope-37
# Plan on vertex
final: Store(hdfs://localhost:9000/user/daijy/average_dividend_sorted:org.apache.
pig.builtin.PigStorage) - scope-14
|
|---New For Each(true)[tuple] - scope-40
    |     |
    |   Project[bag][1] - scope-39
    |
    |---Package(LitePackager)[tuple]{double} - scope-38
```

The graphical version of the plan is shown in Figures 11-4 and 11-5.

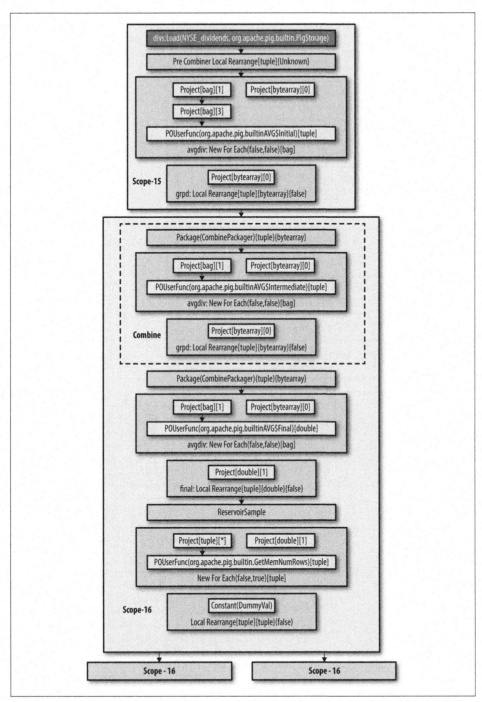

Figure 11-4. Tez plan diagram

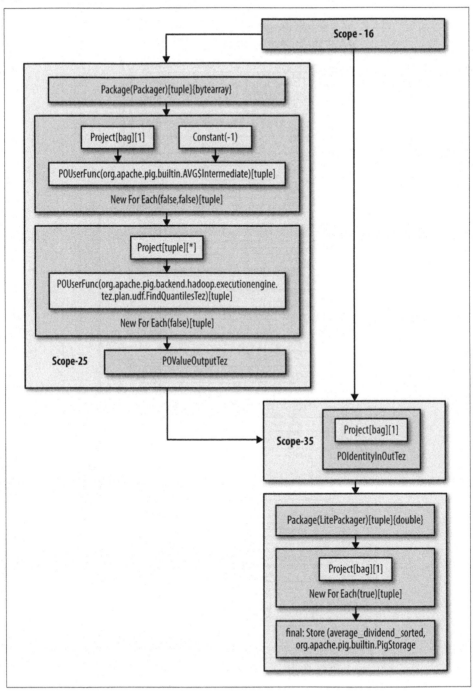

Figure 11-5. Tez plan diagram (continued)

The header of the Tez execution plan shows the number of Tez DAGs in the plan. Pig tries to construct only one DAG for each Pig Latin script. However, if your script contains an `exec` command, which breaks the Pig script into several execution units, it will be compiled into multiple Tez DAGs. In addition, there is currently a limitation in the merge join implementation, so if you are using a merge join, you will see two DAGs instead of one.

After the header comes the execution plan of each DAG. The top section of a Tez DAG shows the edges between vertices. From that we can construct the topology of the Tez DAG. After that, each vertex is listed. For each vertex the data pipeline is given, as in a MapReduce plan. The only exception is that the combine plan will be included inside the downstream vertex shown as the edge property. Note that in reality, the combine plan will be executed in both the upstream vertex and the downstream vertex.

Tez UI

The MapReduce job status web page shown in "Job Status" on page 125 has proven to be one of the most effective tools for debugging a Pig Latin script. In Tez the corresponding tool is the Tez UI. Some setup is required in Tez and YARN to use the Tez UI. Please refer to the Tez website (*https://tez.apache.org/tez-ui.html*) for details. Once you have deployed *tez-ui.war* to Tomcat (or another Java container server), you can open the Tez UI home page in your browser. Depending on the settings of Tomcat, the URL for the Tez UI home page may be different. A typical location will be *http://jt.acme.com:8080/tez-ui-version*. Figure 11-6 shows a sample Tez UI home page.[2] The Tez UI is hierarchical: you can start with coarse-level aggregated information and navigate to fine-grained details. The hierarchy from high to low is: DAG, vertex, task, and task attempt.

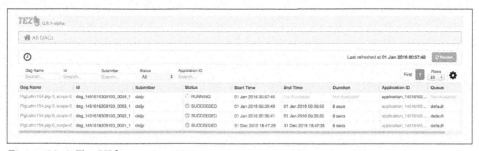

Figure 11-6. Tez UI home page

In the Tez UI screenshot shown here there are four Tez DAGs. DAG `dag_1451616309193_0004` is still running. Click the DAG's name and you will see the

---

2 Depending on the version of the Tez UI, what you see might be slightly different.

DAG summary, as shown in Figure 11-7. You can also view DAG-level counters or see a graphical view of the DAG (as shown in Figure 11-8) by clicking the "DAG Counters" link or the "Graphical View" links.

Figure 11-7. Tez DAG summary

By clicking "All Vertices," you can find details for each individual vertex. Usually every vertex has bunch of tasks associated with it. Clicking a specific task will show you the task attempts (that is, each time Tez attempted to run the task). On this page you will find several very helpful pieces of information for diagnosing your Pig job: task counters and task logs, as shown in Figure 11-9.

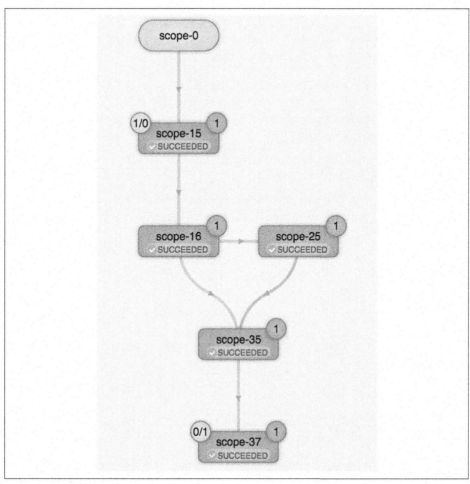

Figure 11-8. Tez DAG graphical view

Figure 11-9. Tez task attempt

Other changes

Besides `explain` plans and the job status web page, there are some other changes in testing and debugging Pig Latin scripts on Tez:

- The statistics Pig produces (see "Pig Statistics" on page 123) will be slightly different in Tez to adapt to the new execution engine. Instead of statistics per Map-Reduce job, Pig will show statistics per vertex. An example of the Tez statistics output is shown in Figure 11-10.

- `illustrate` is not supported in Tez yet. If you want to run the `illustrate` command, run Pig in MapReduce mode.

- PigUnit supports `tez` and `tez_local` modes. To select a mode, simply set the Java property `pigunit.exectype` to `tez` or `tez_local` in your Java code.

```
        HadoopVersion: 2.6.0
           PigVersion: 0.16.0-SNAPSHOT
           TezVersion: 0.7.0
               UserId: daijy
             FileName: teztest.pig
            StartedAt: 2016-04-03 20:42:47
           FinishedAt: 2016-04-03 20:43:08
             Features: GROUP_BY,ORDER_BY

Success!


DAG 0:

                                Name: PigLatin:teztest.pig-0_scope-0
                       ApplicationId: job_1459741040982_0001
                    TotalLaunchedTasks: 5
                        FileBytesRead: 12651
                     FileBytesWritten: 12555
                        HdfsBytesRead: 17027
                     HdfsBytesWritten: 1863
        SpillableMemoryManager spill count: 0
               Bags proactively spilled: 0
            Records proactively spilled: 0

DAG Plan:
Tez vertex scope-24     ->      Tez vertex scope-25,
Tez vertex scope-25     ->      Tez vertex scope-34,Tez vertex scope-44,
Tez vertex scope-34     ->      Tez vertex scope-44,
Tez vertex scope-44     ->      Tez vertex scope-46,
Tez vertex scope-46

Vertex Stats:
VertexId Parallelism TotalTasks    InputRecords  ReduceInputRecords OutputRecords FileBytesRead FileBytesWritten HdfsBytesRead HdfsBytesWritten
Alias          Feature Outputs
scope-24         1         1          670              0            670            32            3720          17027           0
avgdiv,divs,grpd
scope-25         1         1            0            148            248          3752            5951             0            0
avgdiv,final GROUP_BY,SAMPLER
scope-34         1         1            0            100              1          2958             136             0            0

scope-44         1         1          149              0            148          3161            2748             0            0
final
scope-46        -1         1            0            148            148          2748               0             0         1863
     ORDER_BY    hdfs://localhost:9000/user/daijy/average_dividend_sorted,

Input(s):
Successfully read 670 records (17027 bytes) from: "hdfs://localhost:9000/user/daijy/NYSE_dividends"

Output(s):
Successfully stored 148 records (1863 bytes) in: "hdfs://localhost:9000/user/daijy/average_dividend_sorted"
```

Figure 11-10. Tez statistics output

Pig on Tez Internals

In this section, we'll take a look at what's under the hood that makes Pig run on Tez.

Multiple Backends in Pig

In version 0.14 Pig was redesigned to support multiple backend execution engines. Figure 11-11 shows a diagram of how multiple backends work in Pig. After the user submits a Pig Latin script, it is compiled into a logical plan and then converted into a physical plan. Depending on the execution engine, Pig will then transform the physical plan into a MapReduce plan or a Tez plan.

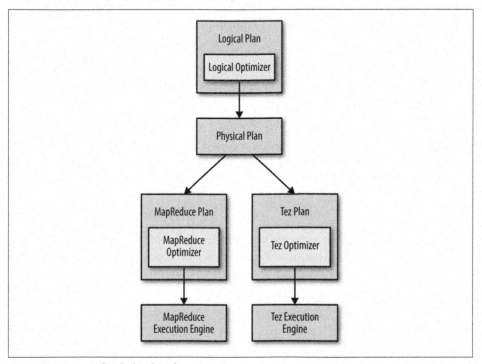

Figure 11-11. Multiple backends

The Tez plan is completely independent from the MapReduce plan, as can be seen in the diagram. However, there are also many similarities between the Tez engine and the MapReduce engine. The topology of the Tez plan is very different from that of the MapReduce plan, but the building blocks underneath are very similar. For example:

- The data-processing pipeline inside a Tez vertex is mostly the same as that of MapReduce.
- The process of transforming the physical plan into a Tez plan is very similar to MapReduce.
- The Tez optimizer's rules are similar to those of the MapReduce optimizer.

To be able to share code between Tez and MapReduce, Pig refactored a significant amount of code in the MapReduce engine, putting it in a shared library that is now used by both the MapReduce and Tez engines.

The Tez Optimizer

As we discussed in the last section, Tez optimization rules are similar to those of MapReduce. Here we list several important Tez optimization rules and discuss the similarities and differences relative to MapReduce rules of the same names:

CombinerOptimizer

> This rule decides when to make use of the combiner in a Tez edge. It is similar to the MapReduce rule, except that the combiner is not a property of a MapReduce job; it is a property of an edge.

SecondaryKeyOptimizer

> This rule decides when to optimize a nested sort by making use of a secondary sort key, similar to in MapReduce (see "Nested foreach" on page 79). However, in Tez the secondary sort key is a property on a particular edge instead of the whole job.

MultiQueryOptimizer

> This rule decides when to merge multiple groupings of the same input into a single vertex. Here's an example Pig Latin script that does a multidimensional group:

```
f = LOAD 'foo' AS (x, y, z);
g1 = GROUP f BY y;
g2 = GROUP f BY z;
store g1 into 'ooo1';
store g2 into 'ooo2';
```

> A diagram of how this optimized in Tez is shown in Figure 11-12. The Multi QueryOptimizer merges the upper three vertices into a single vertex, making the pipeline shorter. Note that there is a difference between the MultiQueryOptim izer in Tez and MapReduce. In MapReduce, the MultiQueryOptimizer also merges the bottom two vertices into a single reduce. This is important in Map-Reduce since it means the entire operation can be executed in one MapReduce job. However, in Tez, this horizontal merge is not useful. A Tez vertex can have multiple output edges and still process efficiently. This simplifies the processing inside the vertex.

UnionOptimizer

> This rule is unique to Tez. It uses the VertexGroup functionality provided by Tez to optimize the union operator (see "union" on page 89). Figure 11-13 shows a diagram of a union followed by two groups. Before optimization, Pig needs to

use a separate vertex to collect results from each input to the union and write to the final output. The data is not being altered; this is just a concatenation. Rather than reading and writing the data again, it would be more efficient to have each of the preceding vertices write to a temporary location and then each move their output to the final location. That is what Tez's VertexGroup does, allowing Pig to save one read and write of the output data.

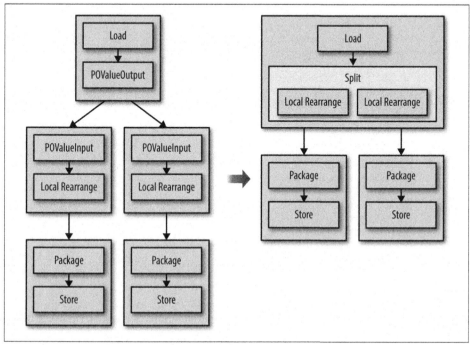

Figure 11-12. MultiQueryOptimizer for Tez

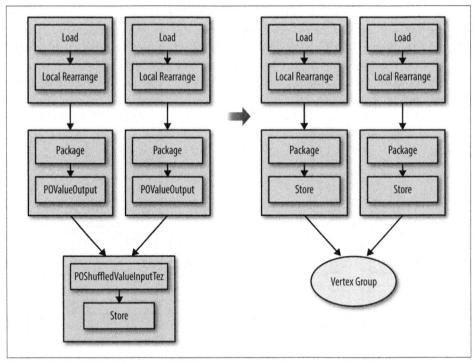

Figure 11-13. UnionOptimizer for Tez

Operators and Implementation

On the backend Pig executes via a set of operators, such as `filter`, `foreach`, `load`, `store`, etc. These do the work of processing the user's data. When considering how these operators interact with MapReduce, they can be divided into three categories:

- Operators that can be merged into an existing map or reduce task: `assert`, `filter`, `foreach`, fragment-replicate joins, `limit`, `load`, `sample`, `store`, `stream`, and `union`.[3]

- Operators that require an exchange of data: `cogroup`, `cross`, `cube`, `distinct`, `group`, and default joins. Since MapReduce only does data exchange in a shuffle between the map and reduce phases, these operators end up creating a new Map-Reduce job.

---

3 `split` is not included since it will be translated into a vertex with multiple output edges in the data flow and is not a standalone operator in Pig. See "split and Nonlinear Data Flows" on page 102.

- Operators that require multiple passes over the input data and thus result in multiple MapReduce jobs: merge joins, skew joins, `order by`, and `rank`.

As we mentioned in "Multiple Backends in Pig" on page 251, the Pig data pipeline inside a task does not change in Tez. Whatever was previously in a map or reduce task can be put in a Tez vertex, so the implementation of the operators in the first category does not change.

For the operators in the second category, there are two possible changes:

- If the operator has more than one exchange of data, in Tez Pig uses the map-reduce-reduce paradigm. The map phase of the second MapReduce job will be merged into the reduce operator of the first MapReduce job.

- For an operator that takes multiple inputs, such as a default join, Pig will not read both inputs in one map task and annotate the records with their input source. Instead, it will create a vertex for each input and make use of Tez's ability to have multiple inputs to a vertex.

Both of these changes are demonstrated in Figure 11-1.

The biggest changes are for the operators in the third category. The algorithm of the operator implementation remains the same, but the topology of the tasks changes quite a bit. In the rest of this section, we will take a look at the new execution plans for those operators.

order by

Figure 11-14 shows how `order by` (see "order by" on page 60) is implemented in Tez. Pig uses four vertices to implement `order by`. First, the sampler vertex collects samples from the input using reservoir sampling and sends them to the sample aggregation vertex. The sample aggregation vertex uses all the samples collected to determine how to range partition the input. The partition boundaries are broadcast to the partition vertex. The partition vertex uses these range boundaries to partition each record in the input into the correct instance of the sort vertex. Finally, the sort vertex sorts the input locally. (Since the data was already range partitioned no final global sort is required.) The one-to-one edge in the diagram passes the input from the sampler vertex to the partition vertex, so Pig does not need to read it again from HDFS.

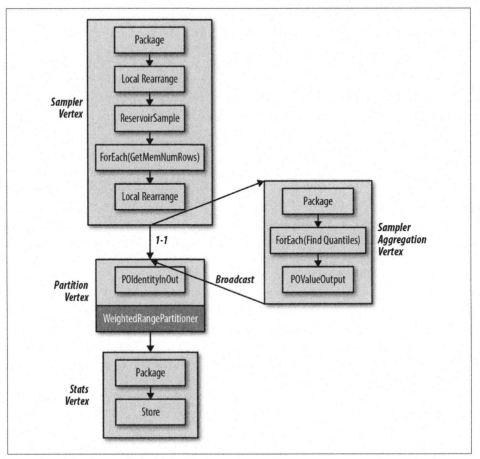

Figure 11-14. order by in Tez

Skew join

Like an order by, a skew join requires sampling the input data. Figure 11-15 shows how skew joins are implemented in Tez. The algorithm is the same as it is for Map-Reduce; a detailed description can be found in "Joining skewed data" on page 85. In the diagram, the left input sampler vertex and the left input sample aggregation vertex sample the left input of the join and decide which keys occur enough times to be considered skewed and how many tasks will be required to process them. The skewed keys are broadcast to both input vertices. The left input vertex uses the information to distribute the skewed keys to the correct tasks in the join vertex. The right input vertex use the skewed key information to duplicate the right join input to the appropriate tasks in the join vertex. As before, the one-to-one edge passes the input from the sampler vertex to the left input vertex, avoiding the need to read it again from HDFS.

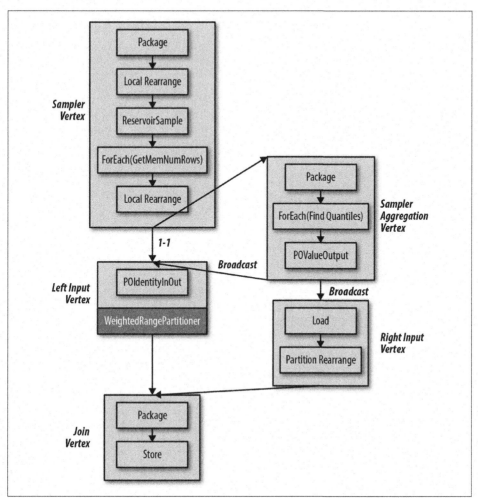

Figure 11-15. Skew join in Tez

rank

We already discussed the implementation of the rank operator, in "rank" on page 93. Figure 11-16 shows a regular rank in Tez. As with MapReduce, Pig first does an order by on the rank field. We can easily identify the order by components in the diagram: sampler vertex, sample aggregation vertex, partition vertex, and sort vertex. The only difference from the order by operator is that we have a POCounter operation inside the sort vertex. It is used to count the number of records that share the same rank key. This information is then sent to the stats vertex to calculate a global count, and the global count is broadcast to the rank vertex to do the final ranking.

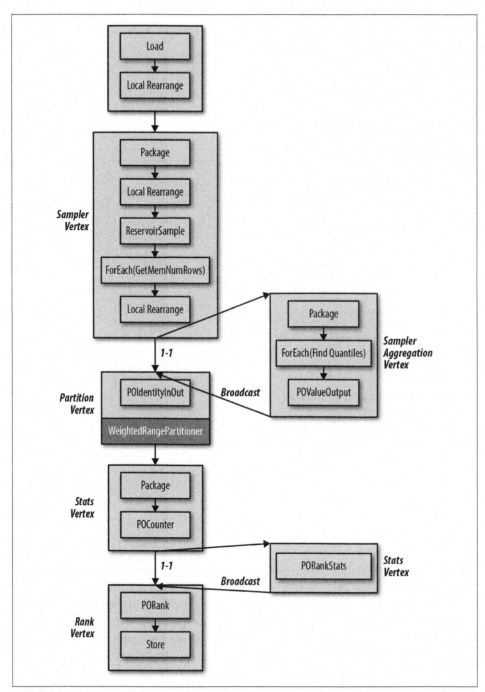

Figure 11-16. rank in Tez

Merge join

The merge join is the only operation that still requires two Tez DAGs, due to a limitation in the current implementation. This makes the Tez plan very similar to the MapReduce plan (see "Joining sorted data" on page 87). The first Tez DAG is equivalent to the first MapReduce job in the MapReduce plan; it produces the index file of the right join input. The second Tez DAG does the same thing as the second map-only MapReduce job in the MapReduce plan. The merge join operation uses the index to do a quick lookup in the right join input and merge the records that share the same join key in the left join input. Note that this is temporary, and in future releases the merge join will be changed to use a single DAG as well (Figure 11-17).

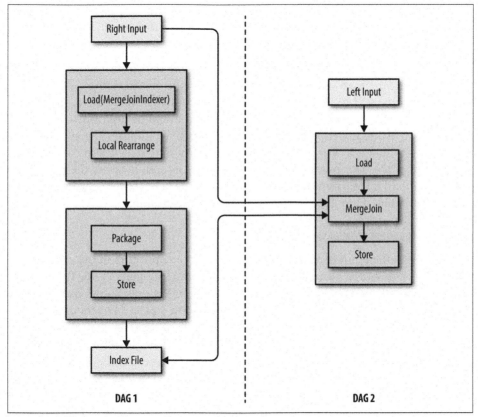

Figure 11-17. Merge join in Tez

Automatic Parallelism

In Pig, you can set the parallelism of a task by using the `parallel` phrase in a statement (see "parallel" on page 65), or you can define a global `default_parallel` level in your Pig Latin script. Both approaches work for Pig on Tez. However, estimating parallelism manually is hard. In MapReduce, if the optimal parallelism is not specified in the Pig Latin script, Pig is able to estimate the parallelism based on the size of the input data, regardless of what kind of operation the MapReduce job is performing. In Tez, the mechanism for automatic parallelism is quite different. On the one hand, estimating parallelism in Tez is much harder: in MapReduce we only need to estimate the parallelism for one MapReduce job, whereas in Tez we need to estimate the parallelism for every vertex in a Tez DAG. On the other hand, Tez uses a more sophisticated algorithm to estimate the parallelism.

In MapReduce, Pig uses the input data size to estimate the optimal reducer parallelism. However, the map task may significantly explode or shrink the data size. The real data volume sent to the reducer might be very different from the original input size. In Tez, the container chain is longer; the issue would be even worse if we used input size to estimate the parallelism of the vertices. To improve the situation, Pig adopts two techniques: first, in addition to the input data size, it also considers the complexity of the data pipeline inside each vertex; second, it defers the parallelism estimation until it has a better idea of the data volume being sent to a vertex. We will explore the details of both techniques in the rest of this section.

Operator-dependent parallelism estimation

In addition to the input data size, Pig also looks at the operators in the vertex's data pipeline to estimate the vertex's output data volume. In Figure 11-18, Pig needs to estimate the input data volume of vertex C. However, Pig only knows that the input data volume of vertex B is 10 GB. When looking at a pipeline's operators, Pig uses several heuristics to do the estimation. For example, it assumes that a `filter` will reduce the data volume by 30%, that a `foreach` with `flatten` will increase the data volume by a factor of 10, and that a `foreach` without `flatten` will produce the same amount of output as input. In the diagram, since the data pipeline contains a filter and a non-`flatten` foreach, the output data volume is estimated to be 3 GB. Obviously these heuristics result in very rough estimations, but it is better than simply assuming input size equals output size.

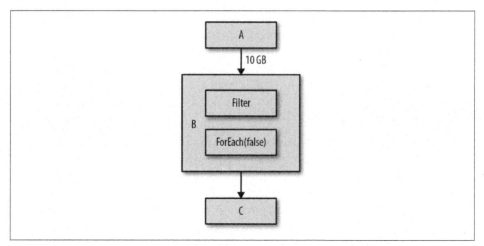

Figure 11-18. Tez automatic parallelism

Deferred parallelism estimation

Using the algorithm just described, we can estimate the data volume for every vertex inside the DAG based on the original input data size. However, the estimations will be far from accurate. The errors in each estimate compound, so that once you reach a vertex several hops down the graph, the estimation is almost useless. Fortunately, when a Tez vertex finishes, Tez tells Pig the actual output size of that vertex. Pig can use this information to do parallelism estimation based on the actual data volume closer to the target vertex. However, this does not mean that Pig can always know the exact input size for each vertex. An upstream vertex cannot begin executing until it knows the parallelism of the next vertex.[4] So, we can use the actual output size of the upstream vertex along with an estimate of the output size of the downstream vertex to estimate the input size of the vertex after the downstream vertex. Using Figure 11-18 as an example, we have to decide the parallelism of vertex C before we can start vertex B. Vertex B needs this information to partition the output properly. Pig will estimate the parallelism of vertex C when vertex A finishes and vertex B is about to start. Using the fact that the output volume for vertex A is 10 GB, it estimates the output data volume for vertex B to be 3 GB, and sets the parallelism of vertex C to 3 (assuming that we want 1 GB of input data for each task).

order by and skew joins

In the last section, when we said an upstream vertex cannot start if the parallelism of the downstream vertex is unknown, this is not applicable for the partition vertex of order by or the left/right input vertex of a skew join. In both cases, the incoming

---

4 This is because Tez has to know how to partition data between instances of the downstream vertex.

edges are not scatter-gather edges and the upstream vertices do not need to partition their output. In fact, the sample aggregation vertex is able to estimate the input data volume very accurately. In both cases, Pig will defer the parallelism estimation of the vertex until the sample aggregation vertex finishes and tells Pig the estimated size of the input data.

Dynamic parallelism

Once we have decided the parallelism of a vertex, Tez might be able to change that value in certain conditions. This capability is provided by Tez's `ShuffleVertexMan ager`. The prerequisite is that all input edges of the vertex are scatter-gather edges. Suppose that is true for vertex C in Figure 11-18. By default, after seeing 75% of the tasks of vertex B finish, Tez can accurately estimate what the input data volume of vertex C will be. If it is less than the original estimate, it can decrease the parallelism. `ShuffleVertexManager` achieves this by assigning multiple output partitions of vertex B to a single task of vertex C. While this is very helpful, it also has limitations:

- `ShuffleVertexManager` can only decrease the parallelism; it is not able to increase it.
- If the upstream vertex is skewed, the data volume of the 75% finished tasks might not represent the total data volume accurately.

Note in all three mechanisms of automatic parallelism estimation, Pig will use the parameter `pig.exec.reducers.bytes.per.reducer` to control the parallelism with regard to the estimated input data size. The default value is to allocate one task for every 1 GB of input data. This can be changed by using a `set` statement in your Pig script, or by changing the config file *pig.properties*.

## CHAPTER 12

Pig and Other Members of the Hadoop Community

The community of applications that run on Hadoop has grown significantly as the adoption of Hadoop has increased. Many (but not all) of these applications are Apache projects. Some are quite similar in functionality. It can be confusing, especially for those new to Hadoop, to understand how these different applications interwork and overlap. In this chapter we will look at the different projects from a Pig perspective, focusing on how they complement, integrate with, or compete with Pig.

Pig and Hive

Apache Hive (*http://hive.apache.org*) provides a SQL layer on top of Hadoop. It takes SQL queries and translates them to MapReduce jobs, much in the same way that Pig translates Pig Latin. It stores data in tables and keeps metadata concerning those tables, such as partitions and schemas. Many view Pig and Hive as competitors. Since both provide a way for users to operate on data stored in Hadoop without writing Java code, this is a natural conclusion. However, as was discussed in "Comparing Query and Data Flow Languages" on page 2, SQL and Pig Latin have different strengths and weaknesses. Because Hive provides SQL, it is a better tool for doing traditional data analytics. Most data analysts are already familiar with SQL, and business intelligence tools expect to speak to data sources in SQL. Pig Latin is a better choice when building a data pipeline or doing research on raw data.

HCatalog

Now part of Apache Hive,[1] HCatalog (*http://bit.ly/HCatalogHive*) provides a meta-data and table management layer for Hadoop. It allows Hadoop users—whether they use MapReduce, Pig, Hive, or other tools—to view their data in HDFS as if it were in tables. These tables are partitioned and have consistent schemas. As a consequence of this abstraction, Pig users do not need to be concerned with where a file is located, which load and store functions should be used, and whether the file is compressed. It also makes it much easier for Pig, MapReduce, and Hive users to share data because HCatalog provides a single schema and data type model for all of these tools. That data type model, taken from Hive, varies slightly from Pig's, but the load and store functions take care of mapping between the models. HCatalog uses Hive's metastore to store metadata.

HCatalog includes the load function HCatLoader. The location string for HCatLoader is the name of the table. It implements LoadMetadata, so you do not need to specify the schema as part of your load statement; Pig will get it from HCatLoader. Also, because it implements this interface, Pig can work with HCatalog's partitioning. If you place the filter statement that describes which partitions you want to read immediately after the load, Pig will push that into the load so that HCatalog returns only the relevant partitions.

HCatStorer is the store function for HCatalog. As with the load function, the location string indicates the table to store records to. The store function also requires a constructor argument to indicate the partition key values for this store. It can write into one partition or multiple partitions using dynamic partitioning. HCatStorer expects the schema of the alias being stored to match the schema of the table that records are being stored into.

As an example, let's consider a very simple data pipeline that reads in raw web logs from a table web_server_logs, does some processing, and stores them back into HCatalog in a table named processed_logs. web_server_logs's schema is (userid:chararray, date:chararray, time:chararray, url:chararray), and processed_logs's schema is (userid:chararray, user_ref:int, date:charar ray, time:chararray, pageid:int, url:chararray). A Pig Latin script to do this processing would look like the following:

```
logs   = load 'web_server_logs' using HCatLoader();
-- use parameter substitution so script doesn't have to be rewritten every day
-- filter will be split and date portion pushed to the loader
today = filter logs by date = '$DATE' and NotABot(user_id);
...
```

---

1 HCatalog was an Apache Incubator project on its own before it was merged into Hive.

```
-- schema of output must exactly match HCatalog schema
-- of processed_logs, including field names
output = foreach rslvd generate userid, user_ref, date, time, pageid, url;
store output into 'processed_logs' using HCatStorer('date=$DATE');
```

WebHCat

WebHCat (*http://bit.ly/WebHCatHive*) is a REST server for Pig, Hive, and Hadoop. It is a component in Hive that provides a common interface to submit Pig, Hive, and Hadoop jobs. For example, if you want to submit a Pig job to WebHCat, use the curl command:

```
curl -d file=daily.pig -d arg=-param -d arg="DATE=2009-12-17" -d statusdir=output
'http://localhost:50111/templeton/v1/pig?user.name=tester'
```

This REST request will run the Pig script *daily.pig* using WebHCat. Additional arguments tell WebHCat to replace the parameter $DATE with an actual value and to store the *stdout* and *stderr* output of the Pig job in the directory *output*. Before submitting the job, you first need to upload *daily.pig* to HDFS.

You can also run the Pig job in Tez mode—just put -x tez in the curl command line:

```
curl -d file=daily.pig -d arg=-param -d arg="DATE=2009-12-17"
-d arg=-x -d arg=tez -d statusdir=output
'http://localhost:50111/templeton/v1/pig?user.name=tester'
```

WebHCat runs as a REST server. Once it receives a Pig REST request, it will launch a map-only job called TempletonControllerJob, which will invoke the Pig command line.

If you want to register some JARs in your Pig script, you need to tell WebHCat to ship the local JAR files to TempletonControllerJob using the comma-separated argument files:

```
curl -d file=register.pig -d files=piggybank.jar,myudf.jar -d statusdir=output
'http://localhost:50111/templeton/v1/pig?user.name=tester'
```

Cascading

Another data-processing framework available for Hadoop is Cascading (*http://www.cascading.org*). The goal of Cascading is similar to Pig in that it enables users to build data flows on Hadoop. However, its approach differs significantly. Rather than presenting a new language, Cascading data flows are written in Java. A library of operators is provided so that users can string together data operators as well as implementing their own. This allows users more control but requires more low-level coding.

Spark

Apache Spark (*http://spark.apache.org/*) is a data-processing framework with an emphasis on in-memory computing. This makes the latency of Spark significantly lower compared to traditional MapReduce. The Pig on Spark effort, which uses Spark as the underlying executing engine for Pig, takes advantage of that fact. Pig on Spark also features DAG processing and container reuse, both of which contribute to lower latencies. In real-world use cases, we see most people using Pig for extract–transform–load (ETL) processes, as it was designed for the heavy-lifting ETL workload. Pig is more stable and robust than Spark when processing large volumes of data that do not fit in memory. Spark is often used for machine learning and graph processing, with its support of GraphX and MLLib libraries, and is seeing increasing adoption in ETL and analytics.

The data-processing pipeline is similar in Pig and Spark. They share most operators in common, such as `filter`, `sample`, `foreach` (`map` in Spark), `stream` (`pipe` in Spark), `union`, `distinct`, `group`, `join`, `cogroup`, `cross` (`cartesian` in Spark), and `order by` (`sortByKey` in Spark).

The programming model for Spark is similar to that of Cascading, but with support for multiple languages. You write your data flow, then compile (or interpret) and run your program in Scala, Java, or Python with the respective Spark libraries. This approach allows developers to easily integrate their code with Spark's operators.

NoSQL Databases

Over the last few years a number of NoSQL databases have arisen. These databases break one or more of the traditional rules of relational database systems. They do not expect data to be normalized. Instead, the data accessed by a single application lives in one large table, so that few or no joins are necessary. Many of these databases do not implement full ACID semantics.[2]

Like MapReduce, these systems are built to manage terabytes of data. Unlike MapReduce, they are focused on random reads and writes of data. Where as MapReduce and the technologies built on top of it (such as Pig) are optimized for reading vast quantities of data very quickly, these NoSQL systems are optimized for finding a few records very quickly. This different focus does not mean that Pig does not work with these systems—users often want to analyze the data stored in these databases. Also, because NoSQL databases offer good random lookup, certain types of joins could benefit from having the data stored in these systems.

---

2 Atomicity, consistency, isolation, and durability. See Wikipedia (*http://en.wikipedia.org/wiki/ACID*) for a discussion of these properties in relational databases.

NoSQL databases that have been integrated with Pig include HBase, Accumulo, and Cassandra.

HBase

Apache HBase (*https://hbase.apache.org/*) is a NoSQL database that uses HDFS to store its data. HBase presents its data to users in tables. Every row inside the table consists of a key and multiple columns organized into column families. There is no constraint that each row have the same columns as any other row in a given column family. Thus, an HBase table T might have one column family F, which every row in that table would share, but a row with key x could have columns a, b, c in F, while another row with key y has columns a, b, d in F. Column values also have a version number. HBase keeps a configurable number of versions, so users can access the most recent version or previous versions of a column value. All keys and column values in HBase are arrays of bytes. Reads in HBase are done by a key, a range of keys, or a bulk scan. Users can also update or insert individual rows by keys.

Pig provides HBaseStorage to read data from and write data to HBase tables. All these reads and writes are bulk operations. Bulk reads from HBase are slower than scans in HDFS. However, if the data is already in HBase, it is faster to read it directly than it is to extract it, place it in HDFS, and then read it.

When loading from HBase, you must tell Pig what table to read from and what column families and columns to read. You can read individual columns or the whole column families. Because column families contain a variable set of columns and their values, they must be cast to Pig's map type. As an example, let's say we have an HBase table users that stores information on users and their links to other users. It has two column families: user_info and links. The key for the table is the user ID. The user_info column family has columns such as name, email, etc. The links column family has a column for each user that the user is linked to. The column name is the linked user's ID, and the value of the columns is the type of the link—friend, relation, colleague, etc.:

```
user_links = load 'hbase://users'
            using org.apache.pig.backend.hadoop.hbase.HBaseStorage(
            'user_info:name, links:*', '-loadKey true -gt 10000')
            as (id, name:chararray, links:map[]);
```

The load location string is the HBase table name. The appropriate HBase client configuration must be present on your machine to allow the HBase client to determine how to connect to the HBase server. Two arguments are passed as constructor arguments to HBaseStorage. The first tells it which column families and columns to read, and the second passes a set of options.

In HBase, columns are referenced as *column_family:column*. In the preceding example, user_info:name indicates the column name in the column family user_info.

When you want to extract a whole column family, you give the column family and an asterisk: for example, `links:*`. You can also get a subset of the columns in a column family. For example, `links:100*` would result in a map having all columns whose names start with "100". The map that contains a column family has the HBase column names as keys and the column values as values.

The options string allows you to configure `HBaseStorage`. This can be used to control whether the key is loaded, which rows are loaded, and other features. All of these options are placed in one string, separated by spaces. Table 12-1 describes each of these options.

Table 12-1. HBaseStorage options

Option	Valid values	Default	Description
loadKey	Boolean	`false`	If `true`, the key will be loaded as the first column in the input.
gt	Row key	None	Only load rows with a key greater than the provided value.
gte	Row key	None	Only load rows with a key greater than or equal to the provided value.
lt	Row key	None	Only load rows with a key less than the provided value.
lte	Row key	None	Only load rows with a key less than or equal to the provided value.
regex	String	None	Only load rows with a key matching this regular expression.
cacheBlocks	Boolean	`false`	Whether blocks should be cached for the scan.
caching	Integer	100	The number of rows the scanners should cache.
limit	Integer	None	The maximum number of rows to read from each HBase region.
maxResultsPerColumn Family	Integer	None	The maximum number of values to return per row per column family.
delim	String	Whitespace	The column delimiter.
ignoreWhitespace	Boolean	`true`	Whether to ignore spaces when parsing the column list when `delim` is set to something other than whitespace.
caster	Java classname	Utf8Stora ge Converter	The Java class to use to do casting between Pig types and the bytes that HBase stores. This class must implement Pig's `LoadCaster` and `StoreCaster` interfaces. The default `Utf8StorageConverter` can be used when the data stored in HBase is in UTF8 format and the numbers are stored as strings (rather than in binary). `HBaseBinaryConverter` uses Java's methods `Byte.toInt`, `Byte.toString`, etc. It is not possible to cast to maps using this converter, so you cannot read entire column families.
noWal	Boolean	`false`	Whether to bypass the write-ahead log (WAL) when writing.

Option	Valid values	Default	Description
minTimestamp	Long	None	Only return cell values that have a creation timestamp greater than or equal to this value.
maxTimestamp	Long	None	Only return cell values that have a creation timestamp less than this value.
timestamp	Long	None	Only return cell values that have a creation timestamp equal to this value.
includeTimestamp	Boolean	false	Include the timestamp after the row key when writing.
includeTombstone	Boolean	false	Include the tombstone marker after the row key when writing.

HBaseStorage stores data into HBase as well. When storing data, you specify the table name as the location string, just as in load. The constructor arguments are also similar to the load case. The first describes the mapping of Pig fields to the HBase table, using the same *column_family:column* syntax as load. Any Pig value can be mapped to a column. A Pig map can be mapped to a column family with *column_family:**. The row key is not referenced in this argument, but it is assumed to be the first field in the Pig tuple. The optional second argument is the options string, described in Table 12-1.

Assume at the end of processing that our Pig data has a schema of (id: long, name:chararray, email:chararray, links:map). Storing into the example HBase table we used earlier looks like this:

```
// Schema of user_links is (id, name, email, links).
// Notice how the id (key) field is omitted in the argument.
store user_links into 'hbase://users'
    using org.apache.pig.backend.hadoop.hbase.HBaseStorage(
    'user_info:name user_info:email links:*');
```

Accumulo

The design of Apache Accumulo (*https://accumulo.apache.org/*) is similar to HBase. It is also accessed by row key and it also provides column families with variable columns. However, Accumulo was designed from the start to provide cell-level security, which was originally missing in HBase. Though HBase added cell-level security, later in version 0.98, Accumulo still has a more mature security implementation.

Similar to HBaseStorage, Pig provides AccumuloStorage to read data from and write data to Accumulo tables.

When loading from or writing to Accumulo, the first parameter of AccumuloStorage specifies the columns or column families you want to read or write. The syntax for columns/column families is exactly the same as for HBaseStorage (for details, refer to the previous section). The second parameter is an option string passed to the operation; it is optional. Table 12-2 lists the meanings of the supported options.

Table 12-2. AccumuloStorage options

Option	Valid values	Default	Description
start	String	None	The row to begin reading from, inclusive
end	String	None	The row to read until, inclusive
mutation-buffer-size	Long	50MB	The number of bytes to buffer when writing data
write-threads	Integer	3	The number of threads to use when writing data
max-latency	Integer	MAX_VALUE	The maximum latency in milliseconds before mutations are flushed
separator	String	,	The separator string to use when parsing columns
ignore-whitespace	Boolean	true	Whether or not whitespace should be stripped from the column list

Cassandra

Apache Cassandra (*http://cassandra.apache.org/*) is another scalable database used for high-volume random reading and writing of data. It differs from HBase in its approach to distribution. Whereas HBase guarantees consistency between its servers, Cassandra has an eventual consistency model, meaning that servers might have different values for the same data for some period of time. For more information about Cassandra, see *Cassandra: The Definitive Guide*, by Eben Hewitt (O'Reilly).

Cassandra comes with support for Pig, which means that you can load data from and store data to Cassandra column families. This works just as it does with any other storage mechanism that is used with Pig, such as HDFS, including data locality for input splits.

Pig and Cassandra can be used together in a number of ways. Pig can be used to do traditional analytics while Cassandra performs real-time operations. Because Pig and MapReduce can be run on top of Cassandra, this can be done without moving data between Cassandra and HDFS. HDFS is still required for storing intermediate results; however, Pig can be used to do data exploration, research, testing, validation, and correction over Cassandra data as well. It can be used to populate the data store with new data as new tables or column families are added.

The Pygmalion project (*https://github.com/jeromatron/pygmalion*) was written to ease development when using Pig with data stored in Cassandra. It includes helpful UDFs to extract column values from the results, marshal the data back to a form that Cassandra accepts, and more.

In order to properly integrate Pig workloads with data stored in Cassandra, the Cassandra cluster needs to colocate the data with Hadoop task trackers. This allows the Hadoop job tracker to move the data processing to the nodes where the data resides. Traditionally, Cassandra is used for heavy writes and real-time, random-access queries. Heavy Hadoop analytic workloads can be performed on Cassandra without degrading the performance of real-time queries by splitting the cluster by workload type: a set of nodes is dedicated to handling analytic batch processing and another set is dedicated to handling real-time queries. Cassandra's cross-datacenter replication copies data transparently between these sections of the cluster so that manual copying of data is never required, and the analytic section always has updated data.

DataFu

Apache DataFu (*https://datafu.apache.org/*) contains a large collection of Pig UDFs. They can be divided into the following categories:

Bags
UDFs to do basic bag manipulation operations, such as append, concatenate, split, group, join, distinct, and counting

Geo
UDF to compute distance between two latitude–longitude pairs

Hashing
UDFs for computing MD5, SHA, and LSH hashes

Link analysis
UDF for running the PageRank algorithm

Randomization
UDFs for generating random UUIDs and random integers within a range

Sampling
UDFs for producing random samples, weighted samples, and reservoir samples

Sessions
UDF for sessionizing a stream of events

Sets
UDFs to perform set operations (intersection, union, difference) between two bags

Stats
UDFs to compute quantile, variance, median, Wilson binary confidence, Markov pairs, HyperLogLog++, and entropy

Natural language processing (NLP)
UDFs for tokenization and part-of-speech (POS) tagging

URLs
UDFs for decomposition and agent classification

Oozie

Apache Oozie (*https://oozie.apache.org/*) is a workflow scheduler for Hadoop jobs. In a real-world application, it is common that a task consists of multiple stages, with each stage using a different tool. We need to have a way to weave these stages together. Oozie is such a tool, which has a rich feature set. An Oozie workflow is a DAG, and each node of the DAG is called an action. An Oozie action node can be a Hadoop job, such as Pig, Hive, MapReduce, Sqoop, or DistCp, or a simple job such as a shell, *ssh*, Java, or email. Because the Oozie workflow is a DAG, it supports branches but not loops. You can run an Oozie workflow immediately, or you can schedule the workflow to run at a specific time or periodically. The latter is done with an Oozie `coordinator`. You can also ask Oozie to run the workflow once the input datasets are available. This is quite useful if your input datasets are generated by an external system asynchronously. Oozie provides a WebUI to monitor the status of the workflow as well.

When you submit a workflow to Oozie, you will need to create a *workflow.xml* file to describe the workflow and the action nodes inside it. Here is a sample Oozie workflow containing one Pig job (taken from the Oozie codebase):

```xml
<workflow-app xmlns="uri:oozie:workflow:0.2" name="pig-wf">
    <start to="pig-node"/>
    <action name="pig-node">
        <pig>
            <job-tracker>${jobTracker}</job-tracker>
            <name-node>${nameNode}</name-node>
            <prepare>
                <delete path="${nameNode}/user/${wf:user()}/${examplesRoot}
                    /output-data/pig"/>
            </prepare>
            <configuration>
                <property>
                    <name>mapred.job.queue.name</name>
                    <value>${queueName}</value>
                </property>
                <property>
                    <name>mapred.compress.map.output</name>
                    <value>true</value>
                </property>
            </configuration>
            <script>id.pig</script>
            <param>INPUT=/user/${wf:user()}/${examplesRoot}/input-data/text
                </param>
            <param>OUTPUT=/user/${wf:user()}/${examplesRoot}/output-data/pig
                </param>
        </pig>
        <ok to="end"/>
        <error to="fail"/>
    </action>
```

```
    <kill name="fail">
        <message>Pig failed, error message[${wf:errorMessage
            (wf:lastErrorNode())}]</message>
    </kill>
    <end name="end"/>
</workflow-app>
```

The workflow contains a single action node: pig-node. job-tracker specifies the location of the JobTracker (Hadoop 1) or ResourceManager (Hadoop 2). name-node specifies the location of the NameNode. prepare instructs Oozie to remove the output directory of the Pig script before launching it. The configuration, script, and param elements are used to construct Pig command-line arguments:

```
pig -Dmapred.job.queue.name=${queueName} -Dmapred.compress.map.output=true
-param INPUT=/user/${wf:user()}/${examplesRoot}/input-data/text
-param OUTPUT=/user/${wf:user()}/${examplesRoot}/output-data/pig
id.pig
```

The ${jobTracker}, ${nameNode}, ${examplesRoot}, and ${queueName} that appear in *workflow.xml* are Oozie properties specified in a separate file: *job.properties*. You will also need to specify oozie.wf.application.path, which is the workflow root directory. The content of *job.properties* is:

```
nameNode=hdfs://sandbox.hortonworks.com:8020
jobTracker=sandbox.hortonworks.com:8050
queueName=default
examplesRoot=examples

oozie.use.system.libpath=true
oozie.wf.application.path=${nameNode}/user/${user.name}/${examplesRoot}/apps/pig
```

You need to copy *workflow.xml* and *id.pig* to the ${oozie.wf.application.path} directory. If you are using custom UDFs in your Pig script, you also need to put your JAR in ${oozie.wf.application.path}/lib. It will be added to Pig's classpath, and Pig should find the containing JAR and ship it automatically. However, if your UDFs have external dependencies, you will also need to register the external JARs in your Pig script unless your UDFs implement auto-shipping (see "Shipping JARs Automatically" on page 185 and "Shipping JARs Automatically" on page 228). *job.properties* must be a local file.

Now you can submit your workflow to the Oozie server using the following command line:

```
oozie job --oozie http://localhost:11000/oozie -run -config job.properties
```

The Oozie server will launch a map-only job and invoke *PigRunner.run* (see "PigRunner" on page 161) in the map task. This allows Oozie to launch a large number of Pig jobs without using too many of the server's resources.

## CHAPTER 13

Use Cases and Programming Examples

In this chapter we will take a look at several comprehensive Pig examples and real-world Pig use cases.

Sparse Tuples

In "Schema Tuple Optimization" on page 149 we introduced a more compact tuple implementation called the schema tuple. However, if your input data is sparse, a schema tuple is not the most efficient way to represent your data. You only need to store the position and value of *nonempty* fields of the tuple—which you can do with a *sparse tuple*. Since the vast majority of fields in the tuple will be empty, you can save a lot of space with this data structure. Sparse tuples are not natively supported by Pig. However, Pig allows users to define custom tuple implementations, so you can implement them by yourself. In this section, we will show you how to implement the sparse tuple and use it in Pig.

First, we will need to write a SparseTuple class that implements the Tuple interface. However, implementing all methods of the Tuple interface is tedious. To make it easier we derive SparseTuple from AbstractTuple, which already implements most common methods. Inside SparseTuple, we create a TreeMap that stores the index and value of each nonempty field. We also keep track of the size of the tuple. With both fields, we have the complete state of the sparse tuple. Here is the data structure along with the getter and setter methods of SparseTuple:

```
public class SparseTuple extends AbstractTuple {

    Map<Integer, Object> matrix = new TreeMap<Integer, Object>();
    int size;

    public SparseTuple(int size) {
```

```
        this.size = size;
    }

    @Override
    public int size() {
        return size;
    }

    @Override
    public Object get(int fieldNum) throws ExecException {
        return matrix.get(fieldNum);
    }

    // Flatten size/matrix into a List
    @Override
    public List<Object> getAll() {
        List<Object> result = new ArrayList<Object>(size);
        for (int i=0;i<=size;i++) {
            result.add(null);
        }
        for (Map.Entry<Integer, Object> entry : matrix.entrySet()) {
            result.set(entry.getKey(), entry.getValue());
        }
        return result;
    }

    @Override
    public void set(int fieldNum, Object val) throws ExecException {
        if (val == null) {
            return;
        }
        if (fieldNum >= size) {
            throw new ExecException("Index out of boundary."
                    + "Try to access field " + fieldNum +
                    ", but the size of the tuple is " + size);
        }
        matrix.put(fieldNum, val);
    }

    @Override
    public void append(Object val) {
        if (val != null) {
            matrix.put(size, val);
        }
        size++;
    }
}
```

The implementation of the getter and setter methods is quite natural in the new data
structure, but the serialization and deserialization methods of SparseTuple are not as
straightforward. SparseTuple uses BinInterSedes to serialize and deserialize. The
reason is that after serialization Pig currently assumes the binary tuple encoding is

BinSedesTuple. So, SparseTuple needs to serialize using BinInterSedes to make sure it can be read back properly.[1] Here are the serialization and deserialization methods of SparseTuple:

```
@Override
public void write(DataOutput out) throws IOException {
    bis.writeDatum(out, this);
}

@Override
public void readFields(DataInput in) throws IOException {
    Tuple t = (Tuple)bis.readDatum(in);
    size = t.size();
    for (int i=0;i<size;i++) {
        set(i, t.get(i));
    }
}
```

We also need to write a method to estimate the memory size of the tuple:

```
@Override
public long getMemorySize() {
    long memorySize = 40 * matrix.size() + 4;
    for (Map.Entry<Integer, Object> entry : matrix.entrySet()) {
        memorySize += 16;
        memorySize += SizeUtil.getPigObjMemSize(entry.getValue());
    }
    return memorySize;
}
```

Every entry in the TreeMap occupies 40 bytes, plus we use 4 bytes for the size of the sparse tuple. Every map entry contains an integer index, which is 4 bytes, plus the size of the value object.

The remaining methods are for comparisons with other tuples. When comparing a SparseTuple to another tuple the hash code will be checked first. Then, if that yields the same for both values, the objects themselves will be compared. We therefore need to make two SparseTuples that contain the same fields generate the same hash code. We use the same algorithm as for DefaultTuple to calculate the hash code of Sparse Tuple. In compareTo we do object comparisons for each field in the tuple. We take into account the fact that TreeMap is sorted by key. We first compare the index of the matrix of both SparseTuples and then compare the values, entry by entry. Here is the code for both methods:

```
@Override
public int hashCode() {
```

---

[1] This might change in a future release since ideally Pig should use the serialization and deserialization methods of the custom tuple implementation.

```
        int hash = 17;
        for (Map.Entry<Integer, Object> entry : matrix.entrySet()) {
            if (entry.getValue() != null) {
                hash = 31 * hash + entry.getValue().hashCode();
            }
        }
        return hash;
    }

    @Override
    public int compareTo(Object other) {
        if (other instanceof SparseTuple) {
            SparseTuple t = (SparseTuple) other;
            int mySz = size();
            int tSz = t.size();
            if (tSz < mySz) {
                return 1;
            } else if (tSz > mySz) {
                return -1;
            } else {
                Iterator<Map.Entry<Integer, Object>> otherEntryIter
                    = t.matrix.entrySet().iterator();
                for (Map.Entry<Integer, Object> entry : matrix.entrySet()) {
                    Map.Entry<Integer, Object> otherEntry =
                        otherEntryIter.next();
                    int c = entry.getKey() - otherEntry.getKey();
                    if (c != 0) {
                        return c;
                    }
                    c = DataType.compare(entry.getValue(),
                        otherEntry.getValue());
                    if (c != 0) {
                        return c;
                    }
                }
                return 0;
            }
        } else {
            return DataType.compare(this, other);
        }
    }
```

We also need to implement a `TupleFactory` to generate `SparseTuples`. The code for this is as follows:

```
public class SparseTupleFactory extends TupleFactory {
    @Override
    public Tuple newTuple() {
        return new SparseTuple();
    }

    @Override
    public Tuple newTuple(int size) {
```

```
            return new SparseTuple(size);
        }

        @Override
        public Tuple newTuple(List c) {
            Tuple t = new SparseTuple(c.size());
            try {
                for (int i=0;i<c.size();i++) {
                    if (c.get(i) != null) {
                        t.set(i, c.get(i));
                    }
                }
            } catch (ExecException e) {
                throw new RuntimeException(e);
            }
            return t;
        }

        @Override
        public Tuple newTupleNoCopy(List list) {
            return newTuple(list);
        }

        @Override
        public Tuple newTuple(Object datum) {
            Tuple t = new SparseTuple(1);
            t.append(datum);
            return t;
        }

        @Override
        public Class<? extends Tuple> tupleClass() {
            return SparseTuple.class;
        }

        @Override
        public Class<? extends TupleRawComparator> tupleRawComparatorClass() {
            return BinSedesTuple.getComparatorClass();
        }

        @Override
        public boolean isFixedSize() {
            return false;
        }
    }
```

In the preceding code, newTupleNoCopy and tupleRawComparatorClass might cause
some confusion:

- `newTupleNoCopy` is an optimized version of `newTuple` that makes the tuple share the reference to the `List` object without copying it. However this makes no difference in `SparseTupleFactory` because it does not have a reference to a `List`.

- `tupleRawComparatorClass` returns the comparator class for the serialized tuple. Since `SparseTuple` is serialized into `BinSedesTuple`, we use the comparator of `BinSedesTuple`.

Now we have created `SparseTuple` and `SparseTupleFactory`. To use them in Pig we first need to compile and package them into a JAR and then put the JAR in Pig's classpath by defining the `PIG_CLASSPATH` environment variable. We also need to set the Java property `pig.data.tuple.factory.name` to our `TupleFactory`:

```
export PIG_CLASSPATH=/path_to/acme.jar
export PIG_OPTS=-Dpig.data.tuple.factory.name=com.acme.tuple.SparseTupleFactory
```

Pig will not automatically ship *acme.jar* to the backend; you will need to register it in your Pig Latin script. You must set the Java property `pig.data.tuple.factory.name` to `SparseTupleFactory` in the backend as well, by defining `mapred.map.child.java.opts` and `mapred.reduce.child.java.opts` in your Pig Latin script:

```
register /path_to/acme.jar
set mapred.map.child.java.opts
    '-Dpig.data.tuple.factory.name=com.acme.tuple.SparseTupleFactory'
set mapred.reduce.child.java.opts
    '-Dpig.data.tuple.factory.name=com.acme.tuple.SparseTupleFactory'
```

With all of this done, you can now use `SparesTuple` for some sparse datasets and see how much it improves performance.

k-Means

In "Embedding Pig Latin in Scripting Languages" on page 151, we saw how to embed Pig in Jython and walked through a page rank example. In this section, we will show a more comprehensive example that implements a *k*-means algorithm using Pig. You can find the example code on GitHub (*https://github.com/alanfgates/programming pig/tree/2ed*), in *examples/ch13/kmeans*. In this example, we will show how to embed Pig in three scripting languages: Jython, JavaScript, and Groovy. We will also cover how to use an inline scripting UDF in our code. Further, in the latter part of the section we will show how to implement the algorithm in Java with the Pig Java API.

The goal of the k-means algorithm (*http://en.wikipedia.org/wiki/K-means_clustering*) is to group data into *k* clusters, with each observation belonging to the cluster with the nearest mean. It is an iterative process and converges only when the cluster centroids do not move any further. To simplify the example, we only calculate the *k*-

means of one-dimensional data. We will make use of Pig embedding to implement the iterative algorithm and leave the centroid assignation to an inline scripting UDF.

As discussed in "Embedding Pig Latin in Scripting Languages" on page 151, we first need to compile the Pig script.

Here's how we do this in Jython:

```
P = Pig.compile("""register 'kmeans.py' using jython as util;
raw = load 'student.txt' as (name:chararray, age:int, gpa:double);
centroided = foreach raw generate gpa,
    util.findCentroid('$centroids', gpa) as centroid;
grouped = group centroided by centroid;
result = foreach grouped generate group, AVG(centroided.gpa);
store result into 'output';
""")
```

In JavaScript:

```
var P = pig.compile("register 'kmeans.js' using javascript as util;" +
"raw = load 'student.txt' as (name:chararray, age:int, gpa:double);" +
"centroided = foreach raw generate gpa," +
"    util.findCentroid('$centroids', gpa) as centroid;" +
"grouped = group centroided by centroid;" +
"result = foreach grouped generate group, AVG(centroided.gpa);" +
"store result into 'output';");
```

And in Groovy:

```
def P = Pig.compile("register './kmeans.groovy' using groovy as util;" +
"raw = load 'student.txt' as (name:chararray, age:int, gpa:double);" +
"centroided = foreach raw generate gpa," +
"    util.findCentroid('\$centroids', gpa) as centroid;" +
"grouped = group centroided by centroid;" +
"result = foreach grouped generate group, AVG(centroided.gpa);" +
"store result into 'output';");
```

The embedded Pig Latin is quite simple. First, it registers the scripting UDF. Since the scripting UDF is in the same file as the main program, we simply register the script file itself. Second, the Pig Latin loads the input data and applies the UDF to every record. The UDF, as we will see later, outputs the nearest centroid among the k centroids for the record. The centroids of the current iteration are passed to the UDF as a colon-delimited string. Then the Pig Latin groups the outputs by the centroids and calculates the average for the records belonging to each centroid. These averages will be used as the centroids in the next iteration. The `compile` statement must be invoked outside the loop since it only needs to happen once.

Here are versions in each scripting language of the UDF referenced in the Pig Latin.

For Jython:

```
@outputSchemaFunction("findCentroidSchema")
def findCentroid(initialCentroid, value):
```

```
        centroids = initialCentroid.split(":")

        min_distance = float("inf")
        closest_centroid = 0
        for centroid in centroids:
            distance = fabs(float(centroid) - value)
            if distance < min_distance:
                min_distance = distance
                closest_centroid = centroid
        return float(closest_centroid)

    @schemaFunction("findCentroidSchema")
    def findCentroidSchema(input):
        return input.getField(1)
```

For JavaScript:

```
    findCentroid.outputSchema = "value:double";
    function findCentroid(initialCentroid, value) {
        var centroids = initialCentroid.split(":");

        var min_distance = Infinity;
        var closest_centroid = 0;
        centroids.forEach(function(centroid) {
            distance = Math.abs(Number(centroid) - value);
            if (distance < min_distance) {
                min_distance = distance;
                closest_centroid = centroid;
            }
        });
        return Number(closest_centroid);
    }
```

And for Groovy:

```
    @OutputSchemaFunction('findCentroidSchema')
    public static findCentroid(initialCentroid, value) {
        def centroids = initialCentroid.split(":");

        def min_distance = Double.MAX_VALUE;
        def closest_centroid = 0;
        centroids.each { centroid ->
            def distance = Math.abs(Double.parseDouble(centroid) - value);
            if (distance < min_distance) {
                min_distance = distance;
                closest_centroid = centroid;
            }
        }
        return Double.parseDouble(closest_centroid);
    }

    public static findCentroidSchema(input) {
        return input[1];
    }
```

The first thing to notice in the UDFs is the return type. In Jython and Groovy, we use a schema function to derive the return type from the input. In JavaScript schema functions are not supported, so we have to statically declare the return type. The UDF takes two input parameters. The first parameter is a colon-delimited string that represents the centroids of the current iteration. This parameter is a constant for each iteration. In a Java UDF we can declare it as a constructor parameter. However, constructor parameters are not supported in scripting UDFs, so we have to pass the constant on every record as a regular parameter. The second parameter is the field for which we are calculating the k-means. In our example this is the field gpa. The distance is calculated as the absolute value between the input data and each centroid. The centroid with the smallest distance is designated as the nearest centroid and is returned as the output for the record.

Inside the loop, we bind the parameter of the Pig script with the current centroids and run it.

In Jython:

```
Q = P.bind({'centroids':initial_centroids})
results = Q.runSingle()
```

In JavaScript:

```
var Q = P.bind({'centroids':initial_centroids});
var results = Q.runSingle();
```

And in Groovy:

```
def Q = P.bind(['centroids':initial_centroids]);
def results = Q.runSingle();
```

This iteration continues until convergence; that is, when the centroids stop moving.

Now let's see how to implement this algorithm in Java with Pig's Java API. The structure of the program is quite similar. However, the Java API does not provide a method to bind variables, so we need to register slightly different Pig Latin statements in every iteration of the loop:

```
pig.registerQuery("DEFINE find_centroid "
    + FindCentroid.class.getName() + "('" + initial_centroids + "');");
pig.registerQuery("raw = load 'student.txt' as "
    + "(name:chararray, age:int, gpa:double);");
pig.registerQuery("centroided = foreach raw generate "
    + "gpa, find_centroid(gpa) as centroid;");
pig.registerQuery("grouped = group centroided by centroid;");
pig.registerQuery("result = foreach grouped generate group,
    AVG(centroided.gpa);");
```

The UDF used in the script will be defined as a static class:

```
static public class FindCentroid extends EvalFunc<Double> {
    double[] centroids;
```

```
public FindCentroid(String initialCentroid) {
    String[] centroidStrings = initialCentroid.split(":");
    centroids = new double[centroidStrings.length];
    for (int i=0;i<centroidStrings.length;i++)
        centroids[i] = Double.parseDouble(centroidStrings[i]);
}
@Override
public Double exec(Tuple input) throws IOException {
    double min_distance = Double.MAX_VALUE;
    double closest_centroid = 0;
    for (double centroid : centroids) {
        double distance = Math.abs(centroid - (Double)input.get(0));
        if (distance < min_distance) {
            min_distance = distance;
            closest_centroid = centroid;
        }
    }
    return closest_centroid;
}
}
```

Unlike the scripting UDFs, the Java UDF defines a constructor that takes a string representation of the centroids as a parameter. This way we do not to have to pass it for every record.

Now we invoke `openIterator` to kick off the Pig job, and we can then iterate through the result:

```
Iterator<Tuple> iter = pig.openIterator("result");
for (int i=0;i<k;i++) {
    Tuple tuple = iter.next();
    ...
}
```

The other big difference between Pig embedded in a scripting language and the Java API is that for embedded Pig you can simply pass the scripting file to the Pig command line and it will interpret the script and manage the dependencies for you, while in Java you will have to compile and run the program by yourself. That means you need to add all the necessary JARs in the classpath.

In our sample code, *build.xml* will pull all the dependent JARs from Maven repositories before compiling. You simply invoke *ant* to compile the program. The final output is a single JAR file: *kmeans.jar*. This file includes the UDF and the main program. To run the program with the JAR, you will need to run the following command line:

```
java -cp kmeans.jar:`hadoop classpath`:lib/* KMeans
```

As you can see here, you need to add *kmeans.jar*, all of the Hadoop dependencies (which are generated by `hadoop classpath`), and Pig's dependencies (which *ant* has already pulled into the *lib* directory) into the classpath.

intersect and except

intersect and except are two commonly used set operations. Currently, Pig has implemented neither operators. However, they can be implemented by combining existing operators in Pig. In this section, we will show you how to implement inter sect and except as a macro in Pig.

First, let's take a look at what the intersect and except operations are using an example. Suppose we have two relations, A and B. Here is relation A:

```
Blue
Blue
Orange
Orange
Orange
Green
```

And here is relation B:

```
Orange
Orange
Green
Red
```

intersect returns only the common elements among relations. The result of A intersect B is:

```
Orange
Green
```

Only the common elements Orange and Green appear in the result. Notice the duplicates in the result are removed.

A variation of intersect is intersect all, which takes the smallest number of occurrence of each elements in the result. The result of A intersect all B is:

```
Orange
Orange
Green
```

except is used to find the elements in A but not in B. The result of A except B is:

```
Blue
```

Duplicates are removed from the result. A variation of except is except all, which takes the number of occurrences in the first input minus the number of occurrences of the rest of inputs in the result. The result of A except all B is:

```
Blue
Blue
Orange
```

Note that "Blue" occur twice in the except all result, and "Orange", which does not exist in the except result, exists in the result of except all.

intersect, except, and their variations can be implemented with a Pig script of the same pattern:

```
1 a = load 'input1';
2 b = load 'input2';
3 a1 = group $a by $0..;
4 a2 = foreach a1 generate group, COUNT(a);
5 b1 = group $b by $0..;
6 b2 = foreach b1 generate group, COUNT(b);
7 c = cogroup a2 by group, b2 by group;
8 d = foreach c generate replicateRows(a2, b2), flatten(group);
9 outputs = foreach d generate flatten($0), $1..;
```

The Pig script can be divided into three steps:

- Aggregate each input, generating the number of copies for every record of each input (line 3 to line 6)
- Cogroup by record, using a UDF replicateRows to decide the number of copies of each record in the result (line 7, 8)
- Flatten bags produced by UDF to generate the actual result (line 9)

The UDF replicateRows generates a bag of size N. Bag elements are empty tuples, so after flatten, Pig will not generate additional columns. The record will repeat N times in the flattened result.

The size of bag can be determined according to the type of operator:

intersect
    If any input does not contain the record, 0; otherwise, 1

intersect all
    Take the minimum count among all inputs

except
    If the first input contains the record but all other inputs do not contain it, 1; otherwise, 0

except all
    The count of first input minus sum of counts of all other inputs

The UDF takes a construct argument that specifies the type of the operator. You will need to define the UDF with the desired operator type:

```
DEFINE replicateRows com.acme.intersectexcept.ReplicateRows('$mode');
-- define UDF ReplicateRows to implement operator intersect
```

Here is the simplified version of the implementation of `ReplicateRows`:

```java
public class ReplicateRows extends EvalFunc<DataBag> {
    enum Mode {INTERSECT, INTERSECT_ALL, EXCEPT, EXCEPT_ALL};
    Mode mode;
    public ReplicateRows(String mode) {
        this.mode = Mode.valueOf(mode);
    }
    @Override
    public DataBag exec(Tuple input) throws IOException {
        switch (mode) {
        case INTERSECT:
            // outputCount = 0 if any input does not contain the record,
            // otherwise, outputCount = 1
            break;
        case INTERSECT_ALL:
            // outputCount = min(count(input(*)))
            break;
        case EXCEPT:
            // outputCount = 1 if the first input contains the record
            // but all other inputs do not contain it,
            // otherwise, outputCount = 0
            break;
        case EXCEPT_ALL:
            // outputCount = count(input(0)) - sum(count(input(1..)))
            break;
        default:
            throw new IOException("Unknown execution mode");
        }
        DataBag outputBag = bagFactory.newDefaultBag();
        for (int i=0;i<outputCount;i++) {
            Tuple t = tupleFactory.newTuple();
            outputBag.add(t);
        }
        return outputBag;
    }
}
```

Now we get the idea how to implement `intersect` and `except` in Pig. Next, we will further wrap the code into macros. To reduce the code duplication, we can write a macro for shared workflow:

```
DEFINE INTERSECT_EXCEPT_BASE2(a, b, mode) returns outputs {
    DEFINE replicateRows com.acme.intersectexcept.ReplicateRows('$mode');
    a1 = group $a by $0..;
    a2 = foreach a1 generate group, COUNT(a);
    b1 = group $b by $0..;
    b2 = foreach b1 generate group, COUNT(b);
    c = cogroup a2 by group, b2 by group;
    d = foreach c generate replicateRows(a2, b2), flatten(group);
    $outputs = foreach d generate flatten($0), $1..;
};
```

Then, the macros INTERSECT2, INTERSECT_ALL2, EXCEPT2, and EXCEPT_ALL2 will invoke the shared macro with different mode parameter. For example, the following is the macro implementing intersect:

```
DEFINE INTERSECT2(a, b) returns outputs {
    $outputs = INTERSECT_EXCEPT_BASE2($a, $b, 'INTERSECT');
}
```

Now we have implemented all operators taking 2 input relations. If you have more than 2 inputs, you have to implement a separate set of macros, since the macro does not take a variable number of inputs. For example, we also implemented macros for 3 input relations in the sample code. Here is the base macro for 3 inputs:

```
DEFINE INTERSECT_EXCEPT_BASE3(a, b, c, mode) returns outputs {
    DEFINE replicateRows com.acme.intersectexcept.ReplicateRows('$mode');
    a1 = group $a by $0..;
    a2 = foreach a1 generate group, COUNT(a);
    b1 = group $b by $0..;
    b2 = foreach b1 generate group, COUNT(b);
    c1 = group $c by $0..;
    c2 = foreach c1 generate group, COUNT(c);
    d = cogroup a2 by group, b2 by group, c2 by group;
    e = foreach d generate replicateRows(a2, b2, c2), flatten(group);
    $outputs = foreach e generate flatten($0), $1..;
};
```

And the corresponding macro for intersect:

```
DEFINE INTERSECT3(a, b, c) returns outputs {
    $outputs = INTERSECT_EXCEPT_BASE3($a, $b, $c, 'INTERSECT');
};
```

For simplicity, we don't implement macros of 4 or more inputs, but if you do want to implement them, you can follow the same pattern.

We put all these macros into a single macro file *intersect_except.pig*, and import the file in the Pig script invoking them:

```
register intersectexcept.jar
import 'intersect_except.pig';
a = load 'A' as (color:chararray);
b = load 'B' as (colorname:chararray);
c = INTERSECT2(a, b);
dump c;
```

Note that due to a limitation in the Pig macro, you cannot register a UDF JAR inside the macro. You will need to register it in the Pig script invoking the macro.

The complete UDF and macros can be found in example code in *examples/ch13/intersectexcept*.

There are other implementations for `intersect` and `except`. The implementation we illustrate here is similar to Hive's implementation (see HIVE-12764 (*https:// issues.apache.org/jira/browse/HIVE-12764*)). The good thing about this approach is that we can unify the operators into a single pattern. And by aggregating each individual input relation first, we can reduce the volume of data, since duplicate records are aggregated first, and Pig only needs to deal with one copy of the duplicates in the follow up processing.

Pig at Yahoo!

—By Rohini Palaniswamy and Sumeet Singh

At Yahoo!, where it was developed and open sourced, Apache Pig is the de facto platform for performing ETL on big data, accounting for well over 14 million Hadoop jobs per month as of January 2016.

Pig accounts for more than 42% of all Hadoop jobs on average at Yahoo! (Figure 13-1)—or 52% if Oozie launcher jobs are discounted on the Hadoop clusters —with 70% of all tasks (Figure 13-2) launched on the clusters coming from Pig.

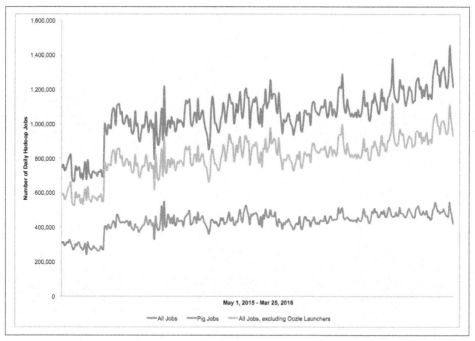

Figure 13-1. Hadoop and Pig jobs at Yahoo! (May 2015–Mar 2016)

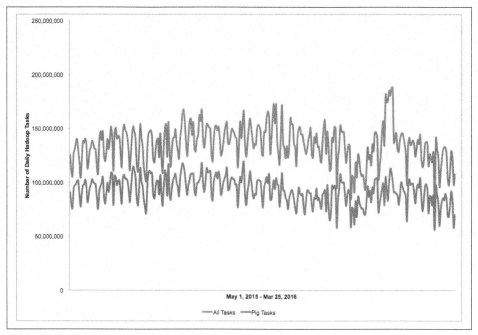

Figure 13-2. Hadoop and Pig tasks at Yahoo! (May 2015–Mar 2016)

Apache Pig Use Cases at Yahoo!

Some of the notable use cases where Apache Pig is used at Yahoo! include:

- *Content personalization* for increasing engagement by presenting personalized content to users based on their profile and current activity, along with faster access to their behavioral profile records

- *Ad targeting and optimization* for serving the right ad to the right customer by targeting billions of impressions every day based on recent user activities

- *New revenue streams* from native ads and mobile search monetization through better serving, budgeting, reporting, and analytics

- *Data-processing pipelines* for aggregating various dimensions of event-level traffic data (page, ad, link views, link clicks, etc.) across billions of audience, search, and advertising events every day

- *Mail anti-spam and membership anti-abuse* for blocking billions of spam emails and hundreds of thousands of abusive accounts per day through machine learning

- *Search Assist and Analytics* for improving the search experience on Yahoo! by processing billions of web pages

Large-Scale ETL with Apache Pig

One of the primary reasons for Pig's success at Yahoo! has been its ability to express complex data-processing needs well through feature-rich constructs and operators ideal for large-scale ETL pipelines—something that is not easy to accomplish in SQL. Pig is not only easier to write but easier to maintain. Researchers and engineers working on data systems at Yahoo! have found working with Pig an order of magnitude better than working with Hadoop directly.

Large-scale data-processing pipelines support many of our key businesses and products. Data pipelines help to transform, organize, and aggregate key datasets for our audience, advertising and search businesses, internal analytics, and many science use cases. These pipelines process billions of events and many terabytes a day. The data pipelines at Yahoo! in general have the following stages, and Pig Latin has been the main language for each of them:

- Transformation of events that are collected from datacenters around the globe
- Decoration of data with dimension data coming from user and business systems
- Joining of events with secondary events (e.g., joining a user's click with the user's original page view)
- Validation of data to determine if the activity is human or spam and also to determine if data contains all the proper information to be classified as a storable transaction for analytics and revenue counting
- Aggregation of datasets for specific internal and external data consumers
- Accessing datasets internal to the pipeline with a data warehouse system for data consumers

Features That Make Pig Attractive

Here are some of the commonly used features of Pig at Yahoo! that have provided great value to our users in terms of ease of use, features, and performance.

Multiquery optimization

The MultiQueryOptimizer is one of Pig's greatest advantages. Doing group by operations and aggregations on multiple different dimensions on the same data is a very common occurrence in Pig Latin scripts at Yahoo!. The input data is only read once in the mapper, which makes it efficient. MapReduce plans perform the multiple group bys in a single MapReduce job, by tagging the different operations in the mapper and running them through different plans in the reducer. As multiple outputs are possible with the DAG construct, the Tez plans have separate outputs from the mapper vertex for each group by and different reducer vertices to process them. This also makes it possible for the different group bys to have different parallelism. The Tez DAG in Figure 13-3 belongs to a Pig Latin script that does group bys and aggregations on 28 dimensions and does some calculations against the total aggregates from group all.

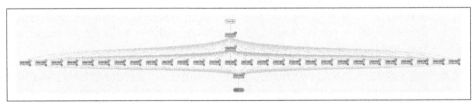

Figure 13-3. Structure of Pig's multiquery optimization on Apache Tez

Macros

Macros can simplify complex Pig Latin scripts and help keep scripts short and easily readable. For example, a group by and aggregation on multiple dimensions can be accomplished in just a few lines using macros:

```
DEFINE calculateAggregate(dataSet, column) {
dimGroup = GROUP $dataSet BY $column;
dimAggregate = FOREACH dimGroup GENERATE
        group as $column,
        SUM ($dataSet.timespent) as timespent,
        SUM ($dataSet.page_views) AS page_views,
        SUM ($dataSet.ad_clicks) AS ad_clicks,

STORE dimAggregate into '$outputLocation/$column';
}

data = LOAD 'events.clickview' using org.apache.hive.hcatalog.pig.HCatLoader();
filteredData = filter data by dt == '20151220';
gender_Result = calculateMetrics(filteredData, gender);
browser_Result = calculateMetrics(filteredData, browser);
user_country_Result = calculateMetrics(filteredData, user_country);
user_state_Result = calculateMetrics(filteredData, user_state);
```

Skew joins and distributed order by

When dealing with large volumes of data, it is very common to have skewed data. Pig's implementation that uses sampling to automatically partition skewed data evenly for join and order by operations makes those operations quite easy for our users, even with heavily skewed data.

Nested foreach

This is one of the features of Pig that provides great flexibility to do more complex processing with the output of a `group by`. Using `order by`, `limit`, and `distinct` inside a nested `foreach` statement is very common.

Jython UDFs

Many of our users like to write Python scripts and make use of the public Python libraries available for data processing. Jython support in Pig makes it really easy for them to use the Python libraries as UDFs instead of using Pig streaming.

Public availability of UDFs

Our users use a wide variety of UDFs from the PiggyBank, DataFu, and Elephant Bird libraries (see "User-Defined Functions" on page 68) and the recently open sourced Sketches library (*http://datasketches.github.io*) from Yahoo!.

Data formats

With Pig's support for unstructured data and the availability of different `LoadFuncs` and `StoreFuncs` (either built in or publicly available in libraries like Elephant Bird), our users use a lot of different data formats for processing, including Avro, ORCFile, JSON, protobuf, and bzip- or gzip-compressed delimited text. Though any format can be used, the formats we generally recommend for use for their efficiency and better schema evolution support are Avro (row format) for raw source data and ORCFile (columnar format) for processed data that is queried often.

HCatalog integration

`HCatLoader` and `HCatStorer` are extensively used, as most of the data is stored as tables using the Apache Hive Metastore to facilitate querying by both Pig and Hive. Lots of data has been migrated to tables with ORCFile as the format, as it provides excellent compression and also supports predicate pushdowns, which makes querying faster.

Scale and stability

Pig has been very stable and scales well. Our users run scripts with execution times varying from under a minute to more than three days, launching anywhere from 1 to 100 Hadoop jobs and 1 to 600,000 tasks, with some scripts even exceeding 3,000 lines. We have not had a case where something could not be processed by Pig due to high volume of data or complex processing logic.

Pig on Tez

Over the past two years, we have put in a lot of effort in the Apache Pig community to scale, stabilize, and make Pig on Tez more performant. Our primary goals have been to increase performance by orders of magnitude and to lower memory and CPU utilization at the same time. Resource utilization, especially memory, is extremely important in a multitenant environment like ours where processing is done on tens of petabytes of web-scale data. Many of our users have faced slowness due to hitting limits on their YARN queues. Yahoo! uses Hadoop's capacity scheduler (*http://bit.ly/ HBaseCapacitySched*) for resource allocation. The maximum capacity configuration over the allotted limit generally allows users to use any extra idle cluster resources. But users still encounter resource crunches, especially during reprocessing or catch-up scenarios or while doing test runs. Slowness happens when:

- Tasks of a job get launched in multiple waves, causing them to take more time. For example, if the queue capacity is 1,000 GB of memory and there are 1,000 tasks each requiring 4 GB of memory, it will take four waves for the tasks to be completed. If the tasks were to each use 1 GB of memory or only 250 tasks were required, then they could be completed in one wave.

- Multiple jobs running at the same time slow each other down due to scheduling delays with the contention for resources. Sometimes performance can get worse than if the jobs were to be run sequentially one after another.

- Limits are hit on the maximum number of Application Masters (AMs) within a given queue, which is there to avoid deadlocks.

Tez helped us tackle resource utilization problems as follows:

- When running a Pig Latin script that used to create multiple MapReduce jobs, Pig on Tez produces a map-reduce-reduce pattern in the DAG. This eliminates unnecessary map phases, resulting in fewer tasks and reduced disk usage.

- Pig on Tez performs better when there is contention from other jobs, as it reuses the containers it has been allocated by YARN instead of waiting for more containers.

- Since most of the time a single Pig script maps to a single Tez DAG that is run using one AM, more Pig scripts can be run in the queue at the same time compared to with MapReduce without hitting queue limits on AMs.

- With auto-parallelism, Tez can use fewer tasks for processing than the estimated number by dynamically adjusting the number of tasks to be equal to the uncompressed output size of source vertex divided by `pig.exec.reduc ers.bytes.per.reducer`. It also eliminates the need for the user to manually tune the `parallel` clause to a low value to prevent the higher number of automatically estimated reducers producing smaller output files and filling up the HDFS namespace.

Figure 13-4 shows Pig's memory utilization as compared to total memory utilization on all our clusters from May 2015 to March 2016. As you can see if you look back at Figures 13-1 and 13-2, the number of Pig jobs and tasks as a percentage of all jobs and tasks held steady during this period, but in the later part of Figure 13-4, Pig's memory utilization as a percentage of the total has started to go down, with the Pig on Tez rollout demonstrating the effectiveness of Apache Tez over MapReduce when it comes to improving Hadoop clusters' utilization. We expect the numbers to fall a lot further when the migration is completed.

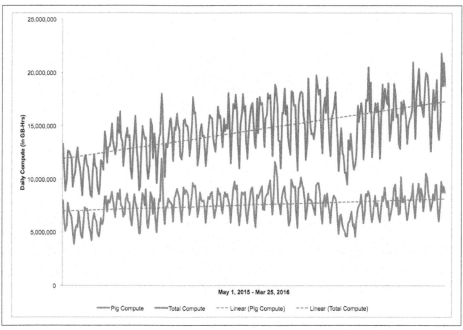

Figure 13-4. Improving Pig's memory utilization with Pig on Tez rollout (May 2015– Mar 2016)

The Tez DAG in Figure 13-5 is from a Pig script that has lots of `join`, `group by`, and `distinct` operations. In MapReduce mode it used to launch 46 MapReduce jobs, taking more than an hour to run with 45,758 2 GB containers for tasks and 46 1 GB containers for the AMs. With Tez, the same Pig script runs in under 40 minutes using 22,879 2 GB containers for tasks and 1 3 GB container for the AM—it completes in two-thirds of the time, using only half as many resources.

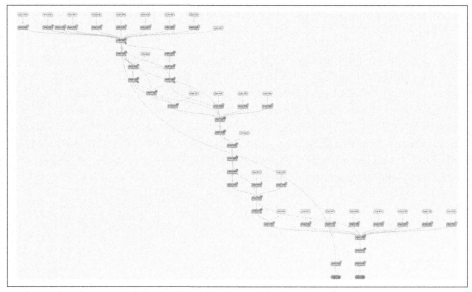

Figure 13-5. Structure of a Pig on Tez DAG

Moving Forward

Yahoo! has consistently invested in Apache Pig since its inception and will continue to do so going forward, with performance and resource utilization as the focus areas. There are some long-standing issues in Pig that we look forward to addressing, which have the potential to greatly lower the overall memory utilization:

- Using order by followed by limit in a nested foreach is one of the common operations done by our users, but currently it uses a lot of memory. Introducing combiners for that scenario and also applying the limit while doing the sort will greatly reduce the memory needed.

- Pig's column pruning optimizer makes users' lives easier, as they don't have to bother about pruning columns in the script for efficiency. But Pig currently only prunes columns for primitive types, so users are forced to include a foreach statement before the group by operation if they want to improve the performance of group by. Support for nested column pruning will greatly reduce the memory utilization of group by and other bag operations.

- The following configuration values mapreduce.reduce.memory.mb, mapreduce.reduce.java.opts, as well as mapreduce.map.memory.mb, and mapreduce.map.java.opts apply to the whole Pig Latin script and all operations performed by it. Pig should support using different configurations for different stages of a script. This would allow users to allocate more memory only for operations that require them. For example, a replication join could be configured to run with 2 GB of heap, but other operations could be run with 1 GB of heap. `pig.maxCombinedSplitSize`, which controls the parallelism of map tasks, is another candidate that would benefit from this optimization. Higher parallelism could also be used for a bzip-compressed file or ORCFile `load` statement, which can blow up to a lot of data when uncompressed.

- We are also actively looking into further performance improvements with Tez DAG processing and planning, incorporating concepts like shared edges and adding additional types of joins.

Pig at Particle News

—By Zongjun Qi and Yiping Han

Particle News (*http://www.particlenews.com*) is a startup company that produces a mobile app that delivers personalized news to smartphone users. It aggregates news from sources around the globe and classifies it into channels. Users can subscribe to channels according to their personal interests. Every day thousands of users use the app to catch up with the latest news, reading evergreen articles that are gathered according to their personal interests. In addition, the mobile app make predictions based on the user's behavior and pushes articles it determines the user might be interested in. It also sends breaking news notifications and editor-picked personalized articles to the users.

Particle News uses Pig extensively in its data pipeline. All logs generated by the backend system and frontend apps are stored into Hive tables, which later are consumed by analytics tools like Pig to compute various metrics to get business insights.

Here we illustrate a few use cases dealing with push notification in Particle News. Push notification is an important means used by mobile app providers to communicate with users directly. It helps to keep users updated with developments in topics they are subscribed to, and in turn also helps the business refine logic based on user feedback. Analytics we are interested in include:

- What is the push arrival rate? This is defined as the percentage of the users it was sent to who actually got the push.

- What is the click conversion rate? This is defined as the percentage of the users who got the push and clicked on the article. It helps us determine the quality of the article picked.

- How many sessions are triggered by a push? This counts the number of user sessions directly initiated as the result of a push.

A session is defined as a series of consecutive user activities that occur within a short period of time. The starting activity within a session tells us the reason the session started. For example, if the starting activity is the user reading an article directly, then this session is considered a session started proactively by the user. On the other hand, if the starting activity is the user getting a push notification message, then this session is considered to have been started by a push notification. Analysis of this helps the business better understand user behavior and make adjustments accordingly to maximize the user experience.

The two related Hive tables for push notifications are push_log, which contains the information from the backend push server, and app_log, which contains the logs collected from each client app. The definitions of these two tables are given in Tables 13-1 and 13-2.

Table 13-1. push_log

Field name	Field type
user_id	string
push_doc_id	string
push_time	biginteger

Table 13-2. app_log

Field name	Field type
user_id	string
user_event	string
event_time	biginteger
doc_id	string

Now let's take a deeper look at Pig use cases in Particle News.

Compute Arrival Rate and Conversion Rate

Particle News uses the following Pig Latin script to compute the arrival rate and click conversion rate for a push. We first load the push log generated by our backend, which has information on the article pushed, when the push was sent, and target users the push was sent to. We then load the user event log reported by the client app, which has a list of events including when the push was received and whether the user clicked on it. We perform a join of these two fields to calculate the push arrival rate and click conversion rate. Here is the script, where recv_push_article is the event when the app receives the pushed article, and click_push_article is the event the app generates when the user clicks on the pushed article. Notice the nested foreach used at the end to compute both statistics in one loop:

```
-- First, load push_log from Hive table generated by backend
push_log = load 'push_log' using org.apache.hive.hcatalog.pig.HCatLoader();

-- Second, compute number of users each pushed article is sent to. This info
-- we can only get from the original log from the backend.
sent_to = foreach (group push_log by push_doc_id) {
    generate group as push_doc_id, COUNT(push_log) as num_sent;
};

-- Add number of users sent to back to the push log
decorated_push_log = join push_log by push_doc_id, sent_to by push_doc_id;
decorated_push_log = foreach decorated_push_log generate
    push_log::push_doc_id as push_doc_id, user_id as user_id, push_time as
    push_time, sent_to::num_sent as num_sent;

-- Load logs collected from frontend apps
app_log = load 'app_log' using org.apache.hive.hcatalog.pig.HCatLoader();
app_push_log = filter app_log by (user_event=='click_push_article' or
    user_event=='recv_push_article');

-- Join data from backend with frontend using doc_id
j_ = join decorated_push_log by push_doc_id, app_push_log by doc_id;
j = foreach j_ generate app_push_log::doc_id as doc_id,
    app_push_log::user_id as user_id, app_push_log::user_event as user_event,
    decorated_push_log::num_sent as num_sent;

-- Group by doc_id to compute the stats
stat = foreach (group j by doc_id) {
    received = filter j by user_event=='recv_push_article';
    received_users = distinct received.user_id;
    read = filter j by user_event=='click_push_article';
    read_users = distinct read.user_id;
    generate group as doc_id,
    COUNT(received_users) as num_received_users,
    COUNT(read_users) as num_read_users,
    (float)COUNT(received_users)/MAX(j.num_sent) as arrival_rate,
    (float)COUNT(read_users)/COUNT(received_users) as ctr;
};
```

Compute Sessions Triggered by a Push

Computing the number of new sessions triggered by a push is much more involved. For a session to be considered triggered purely by push, the first event in that session should be the push event the user received—i.e., recv_push_article in the Particle News app.

Therefore, we need to first collect all events for each user, sort these events by time-stamp, then iterate over the list of events and mark a session as triggered by push if a session start event (`start_new_session`) is found right after a push event (`recv_push_article`).

The session computation is done by a Python UDF. Here is the main Pig Latin script:

```
REGISTER 'sessionize.py' using jython as sessionize;

%default day `date +%F`

ood = load 'app_log' using org.apache.hive.hcatalog.pig.HCatLoader();
ood = filter ood by (p_day == '$day');
ood = foreach ood generate user_id, timestamp, event_type;

events_sessionized = foreach (group ood by (user_id)) {
    ordered = order ood by date, event_type;
    generate group as user_id, flatten(sessionize.get_num_sessions(ordered))
        as (session_count);
}

session_sum = foreach (group events_sessionized all) {
    generate '$day' as day, SUM(events_sessionized.session_count)
        as total_session;
}

rmf /push_stats/$day
store events_sessionized into '/push_stats/$day'
    using PigStorage('\t','-schema');
```

Here is the code of the Pig Python UDF:

```
RECV_PUSH = 'recv_push_article'
START_NEW_SESSION = 'start_new_session'

'''
Given list of sorted events, return number of sessions triggered by push
'''
@outputSchema("num_push_sessions:int")
def get_num_sessions(event_list):
    num_push_sessions = 0
    for i in range(len(event_list)):
        if event_list[i] == RECV_PUSH and event_list[i+1] == START_NEW_SESSION:
            num_push_sessions += 1
            i += 1
    return num_push_sessions
```

Built-in User Defined Functions and PiggyBank

This appendix covers UDFs that come as part of the Pig distribution, including built-in UDFs and user-contributed UDFs in PiggyBank.

Built-in UDFs

Pig comes prepackaged with many UDFs that can be used directly in Pig without using `register` or `define`. These include load, store, evaluation, and filter functions.

Built-in Load and Store Functions

Pig's built-in load functions are listed in Table A-1; Table A-2 lists the store functions.

Table A-1. Load functions

Function	Location string indicates	Constructor arguments	Description
AccumuloStorage	Accumulo table	The first argument is a string describing the column family and column to Pig field mapping. The second is an option string (optional).	Load data from Accumulo.
AvroStorage	HDFS file (Avro files)	The first argument is the input schema or record name (optional). The second is an option string (optional).	Load data from Avro files on HDFS.
HBaseStorage	HBase table	The first argument is a string describing the column family and column to Pig field mapping. The second is an option string (optional).	Load data from HBase (see "HBase" on page 267).

Function	Location string indicates	Constructor arguments	Description
JsonLoader	HDFS file (JSON files)	The first argument is the input schema (optional).	Load data from JSON files on HDFS.
OrcStorage	HDFS file (ORC files)	None.	Load data from ORC files on HDFS.
ParquetLoader	HDFS file (Parquet files)	The first argument is a subset schema to load (optional).	Load data from Parquet files on HDFS.
PigStorage	HDFS file	The first argument is a field separator (optional; defaults to tab).	Load text data from HDFS (see "load" on page 46).
TextLoader	HDFS file	None.	Read lines of text, each line as a tuple with one chararray field.
TrevniStorage	HDFS file (Trevni files)	The first argument is the input schema or record name (optional). The second is an option string (optional).	Load data from Trevni files on HDFS.

Table A-2. Store functions

Function	Location string indicates	Constructor arguments	Description
AccumuloStorage	Accumulo table	The first argument is a string describing the Pig field to HBase column family and column mapping. The second is an option string (optional).	Store data to Accumulo.
AvroStorage	HDFS file (Avro files)	The first argument is the output schema or record name (optional). The second is an option string (optional).	Store data to Avro files on HDFS.
HBaseStorage	HBase table	The first argument is a string describing the Pig field to HBase column family and column mapping. The second is an option string (optional).	Store data to HBase (see "HBase" on page 267).
JsonStorage	HDFS file (JSON files)	None.	Store data to JSON files on HDFS.
OrcStorage	HDFS file (ORC files)	The first argument is an option string (optional).	Store data to ORC files on HDFS.
ParquetStorer	HDFS file (Parquet files)	None.	Store data to Parquet files on HDFS.
PigStorage	HDFS file	The first argument is a field separator (optional; defaults to tab).	Store text to HDFS in text format (see "store" on page 48).
TrevniStorage	HDFS file (Trevni files)	The first argument is the output schema or record name (optional). The second is an option string (optional).	Store data to Trevni files on HDFS.

Built-in Evaluation and Filter Functions

The evaluation functions can be divided into math functions that mimic many of the Java math functions; aggregate functions that take a bag of values and produce a single result; functions that operate on or produce complex types; chararray and bytearray functions; filter functions; and miscellaneous functions.

Each of the built-in evaluation and filter functions is discussed in the following lists. In these lists, for brevity, a bag of tuples with a given type is specified by braces surrounding parentheses and a list of the tuples' fields. For example, a bag of tuples with one integer field is denoted as {(int)}. For the return types, surrounding parentheses indicates a tuple.

Built-in math UDFs

double ABS(double *input*)

> *Parameter:*
> input
>
> *Returns:*
> Absolute value
>
> *Since version:*
> 0.8

double ACOS(double *input*)

> *Parameter:*
> input
>
> *Returns:*
> Arc cosine
>
> *Since version:*
> 0.8

double ASIN(double *input*)

> *Parameter:*
> input
>
> *Returns:*
> Arc sine
>
> *Since version:*
> 0.8

double ATAN(double *input*)

> *Parameter:*
>> *input*

> *Returns:*
>> Arc tangent

> *Since version:*
>> 0.8

double CBRT(double *input*)

> *Parameter:*
>> *input*

> *Returns:*
>> Cube root

> *Since version:*
>> 0.8

double CEIL(double *input*)

> *Parameter:*
>> *input*

> *Returns:*
>> Next-highest double value that is a mathematical integer

> *Since version:*
>> 0.8

double COS(double *input*)

> *Parameter:*
>> *input*

> *Returns:*
>> Cosine

> *Since version:*
>> 0.8

double COSH(double *input*)

> *Parameter:*
>> *input*

Returns:
   Hyperbolic cosine

Since version:
   0.8

`double EXP(double `*`input`*`)`

Parameter:
   input

Returns:
   Euler's number (*e*) raised to the power of *input*

Since version:
   0.8

`double FLOOR(double `*`input`*`)`

Parameter:
   input

Returns:
   Next-lowest double value that is a mathematical integer

Since version:
   0.8

`double LOG(double `*`input`*`)`

Parameter:
   input

Returns:
   Natural logarithm of *input*

Since version:
   0.8

`double LOG10(double `*`input`*`)`

Parameter:
   input

Returns:
   Logarithm base 10 of *input*

Since version:
   0.8

long ROUND(double *input*)

> *Parameter:*
>> *input*

> *Returns:*
>> Long nearest to the value of *input*

> *Since version:*
>> 0.8

double ROUND_TO(double *input*, int *digits*)

> *Parameters:*
>> *input*

>> *digits*

> *Returns:*
>> Double rounded to the given precision

> *Since version:*
>> 0.13

double SIN(double *input*)

> *Parameter:*
>> *input*

> *Returns:*
>> Sine

> *Since version:*
>> 0.8

double SINH(double *input*)

> *Parameter:*
>> *input*

> *Returns:*
>> Hyperbolic sine

> *Since version:*
>> 0.8

double SQRT(double *input*)

> *Parameter:*
>> *input*

Returns:
    Square root

Since version:
    0.8

```
double TAN(double input)
```

Parameter:
    input

Returns:
    Tangent

Since version:
    0.8

```
double TANH(double input)
```

Parameter:
    input

Returns:
    Hyperbolic tangent

Since version:
    0.8

Built-in aggregate UDFs

```
int AVG({(int)} input)
```

Parameter:
    input

Returns:
    Average of all values in *input*; nulls are ignored

Since version:
    0.2

```
long AVG({(long)} input)
```

Parameter:
    input

Returns:
    Average of all values in *input*; nulls are ignored

Since version:
0.2

`float AVG({(float)}` *input*`)`

Parameter:
input

Returns:
Average of all values in *input*; nulls are ignored

Since version:
0.2

`double AVG({(double)}` *input*`)`

Parameter:
input

Returns:
Average of all values in *input*; nulls are ignored

Since version:
0.2

`double AVG({(bytearray)}` *input*`)`

Parameter:
input

Returns:
Average of all bytearrays, cast to doubles, in *input*; nulls are ignored

Since version:
0.1

`biginteger AVG({(biginteger)}`*input*`)`

Parameter:
input

Returns:
Average of all values in *input*; nulls are ignored

Since version:
0.12

```
bigdecimal AVG({(decimal)}input)
```

Parameter:
  input

Returns:
  Average of all values in input; nulls are ignored

Since version:
  0.12

```
long COUNT
```
A version of COUNT that matches SQL semantics for COUNT(col)

Parameter:
  input

Returns:
  Number of records in input, excluding null values

Since version:
  0.1

```
long COUNT_STAR
```
A version of COUNT that matches SQL semantics for COUNT(*)

Parameter:
  input

Returns:
  Number of records in input, including null values

Since version:
  0.4

```
int MAX({(int)} input)
```

Parameter:
  input

Returns:
  Maximum value in input; nulls are ignored

Since version:
  0.2

long MAX({(long)} *input*)

> *Parameter:*
>> input

> *Returns:*
>> Maximum value in *input*; nulls are ignored

> *Since version:*
>> 0.2

float MAX({(float)} *input*)

> *Parameter:*
>> input

> *Returns:*
>> Maximum value in *input*; nulls are ignored

> *Since version:*
>> 0.2

double MAX({(double)} *input*)

> *Parameter:*
>> input

> *Returns:*
>> Maximum value in *input*; nulls are ignored

> *Since version:*
>> 0.2

chararray MAX({(chararray)} *input*)

> *Parameter:*
>> input

> *Returns:*
>> Maximum value in *input*; nulls are ignored

> *Since version:*
>> 0.2

double MAX({(bytearray)} *input*)

> *Parameter:*
>> input

Returns:
Maximum of all bytearrays, cast to doubles, in *input*; nulls are ignored

Since version:
0.1

`datetime MAX({(datetime)}` *input*`)`

Parameter:
input

Returns:
Maximum value in *input*; nulls are ignored

Since version:
0.12

`biginteger MAX({(biginteger)}` *input*`)`

Parameter:
input

Returns:
Maximum value in *input*; nulls are ignored

Since version:
0.12

`bigdecimal MAX({(bigdecimal)}` *input*`)`

Parameter:
input

Returns:
Maximum value in *input*; nulls are ignored

Since version:
0.12

`int MIN({(int)}` *input*`)`

Parameter:
input

Returns:
Minimum value in *input*; nulls are ignored

Since version:
0.2

long MIN({(long)} *input*)

> *Parameter:*
> > input
>
> *Returns:*
> > Minimum value in *input*; nulls are ignored
>
> *Since version:*
> > 0.2

float MIN({(float)} *input*)

> *Parameter:*
> > input
>
> *Returns:*
> > Minimum value in *input*; nulls are ignored
>
> *Since version:*
> > 0.2

double MIN({(double)} *input*)

> *Parameter:*
> > input
>
> *Returns:*
> > Minimum value in *input*; nulls are ignored
>
> *Since version:*
> > 0.2

chararray MIN({(chararray)} *input*)

> *Parameter:*
> > input
>
> *Returns:*
> > Minimum value in *input*; nulls are ignored
>
> *Since version:*
> > 0.2

double MIN({(bytearray)} *input*)

> *Parameter:*
> > input

Returns:

Minimum of all bytearrays, cast to doubles, in *input*; nulls are ignored

Since version:

0.1

`datetime MIN({(datetime)} input)`

Parameter:

input

Returns:

Minimum value in *input*; nulls are ignored

Since version:

0.12

`biginteger MIN({(biginteger)} input)`

Parameter:

input

Returns:

Minimum value in *input*; nulls are ignored

Since version:

0.12

`bigdecimal MIN({(bigdecimal)} input)`

Parameter:

input

Returns:

Minimum value in *input*; nulls are ignored

Since version:

0.12

`long SUM({(int)} input)`

Parameter:

input

Returns:

Sum of all values in the bag; nulls are ignored

Since version:

0.2

```
long SUM({(long)} input)
```

Parameter:
input

Returns:
Sum of all values in the bag; nulls are ignored

Since version:
0.2

```
double SUM({(float)} input)
```

Parameter:
input

Returns:
Sum of all values in the bag; nulls are ignored

Since version:
0.2

```
double SUM({(double)} input)
```

Parameter:
input

Returns:
Sum of all values in the bag; nulls are ignored

Since version:
0.2

```
double SUM({(bytearray)} input)
```

Parameter:
input

Returns:
Sum of all bytearrays, cast to doubles, in *input*; nulls are ignored

Since version:
0.1

```
biginteger SUM({(biginteger)} input)
```

Parameter:
input

Returns:
    Sum of all values in the bag; nulls are ignored

Since version:
    0.12

```
bigdecimal SUM({(bigdecimal)} input)
```

Parameter:
    input

Returns:
    Sum of all values in the bag; nulls are ignored

Since version:
    0.12

Built-in chararray and bytearray UDFs

```
chararray BagToString(databag input)
```

Parameter:
    input

Returns:
    Chararray representation for *input*

Since version:
    0.11

```
chararray CONCAT(chararray c1, chararray c2, ...)
```

Parameters:
    c1

    c2

    ...

Returns:
    Concatenation of *c1*, *c2*, etc.

Since version:
    Two-argument version is supported since 0.1, more than two arguments
    since 0.13

```
bytearray CONCAT(bytearray b1, bytearray b2, ...)
```

Parameters:
    b1

b2

. . .

Returns:
    Concatenation of *b1*, *b2*, etc.

Since version:
    0.1

boolean ENDSWITH(chararray *input*, chararray *suffix*)

Parameters:
    input: The chararray to search in

    suffix: The suffix to check

Returns:
    Whether *input* contains *suffix*

Since version:
    0.11

boolean EqualsIgnoreCase(chararray *input1*, chararray *input2*)

Parameters:
    input1: The first chararray

    input2: The second chararray

Returns:
    Whether *input1* and *input2* are equal without regard to case

Since version:
    0.8

int INDEXOF(chararray *source*, chararray *search*)

Parameters:
    source: The chararray to search in

    search: The chararray to search for

Returns:
    Index of the first instance of *search* in *source*; -1 if *search* is not in *source*

Since version:
    0.8

int LAST_INDEX_OF(chararray *source*, chararray *search*)

Parameters:
   source: The chararray to search in

   search: The chararray to search for

Returns:
   Index of the last instance of *search* in *source*; -1 if *search* is not in *source*

Since version:
   0.8

chararray LCFIRST(chararray *input*)

Parameter:
   input

Returns:
   input with the first character converted to lowercase

Since version:
   0.8

chararray LOWER(chararray *input*)

Parameter:
   input

Returns:
   input with all characters converted to lowercase

Since version:
   0.8

boolean LTRIM(chararray *input*)

Parameter:
   input

Returns:
   input with leading whitespace omitted

Since version:
   0.12

chararray REGEX_EXTRACT(chararray *source*, chararray *regex*, int *n*)

Parameters:
   source: The chararray to search in

regex: The regular expression to search for

n: The index of the match if there are multiple matches, counting from 0

Returns:
   *n*th subset of *source* matching *regex*; `null` if there are no matches

Since version:
   0.8

`(chararray) REGEX_EXTRACT_ALL(chararray source, chararray regex)`

Parameters:
   source: The chararray to search in

   regex: The regular expression to search for

Returns:
   Tuple containing all subsets of *source* matching *regex*; `null` if there are no matches

Since version:
   0.8

`chararray REPLACE(chararray source, chararray toReplace, chararray new Value)`

Parameters:
   source: The chararray to search in

   toReplace: The chararray to be replaced

   newValue: The new chararray to replace it with

Returns:
   source with all instances of *toReplace* changed to *newValue*

Since version:
   0.8

`boolean RTRIM(chararray input)`

Parameter:
   input

Returns:
   input with trailing whitespace omitted

Since version:
   0.12

`long SIZE(chararray `*`input`*`)`

> *Parameter:*
> > *input*
>
> *Returns:*
> > Number of characters in *input*
>
> *Since version:*
> > 0.2

`long SIZE(bytearray `*`input`*`)`

> *Parameter:*
> > *input*
>
> *Returns:*
> > Number of bytes in *input*
>
> *Since version:*
> > 0.2

`chararray SPRINTF(chararray `*`template`*`, Object `*`params`*` ...)`

> *Parameters:*
> > *template*: Format string
> >
> > *params*: Objects to be formatted
>
> *Returns:*
> > *params* formatted according to *template*
>
> *Since version:*
> > 0.14

`boolean STARTSWITH(chararray `*`input`*`, chararray `*`prefix`*`)`

> *Parameters:*
> > *input*: The chararray to search in
> >
> > *prefix*: The prefix to check
>
> *Returns:*
> > Whether *input* contains *prefix*
>
> *Since version:*
> > 0.11

`(chararray) STRSPLIT(chararray `*`source`*`)`
> Split a chararray by whitespace

Parameter:

> *source*: The chararray to split

Returns:

> Tuple with one field for each section of *source*

Since version:

> 0.8

`(chararray) STRSPLIT(chararray `*`source`*`, chararray `*`regex`*`)`
Split a chararray by a regular expression

Parameters:

> *source*: The chararray to split
>
> *regex*: The regular expression to use as the delimiter

Returns:

> Tuple with one field for each section of *source*

Since version:

> 0.8

`(chararray) STRSPLIT(chararray `*`source`*`, chararray `*`regex`*`, int `*`maxsplits`*`)`
Split a chararray by a regular expression

Parameters:

> *source*: The chararray to split
>
> *regex*: The regular expression to use as the delimiter
>
> *max*: The maximum number of splits

Returns:

> Tuple with one field for each section of *source*; if there is more than one *maxsplits* section, only the first *maxsplits* section will be in the tuple

Since version:

> 0.8

`chararray SUBSTRING(chararray `*`source`*`, int `*`start`*`, int `*`end`*`)`

Parameters:

> *source*: The chararray to split
>
> *start*: The start position (inclusive), counting from 0
>
> *end*: The end position (exclusive), counting from 0

Returns:
> Subchararray; error if any input value has a length shorter than *start*

Since version:
> 0.8

`{(chararray)}` `TOKENIZE(chararray` *source*`)`

Parameter:
> *source*: The chararray to split

Returns:
> *source* split on whitespace, with each resulting value being placed in its own tuple and all tuples placed in the bag

Since version:
> 0.1

`chararray TRIM(chararray` *input*`)`

Parameter:
> *input*

Returns:
> *input* with all leading and trailing whitespace removed

Since version:
> 0.8

`chararray UCFIRST(chararray` *input*`)`

Parameter:
> *input*

Returns:
> *input* with the first character converted to uppercase

Since version:
> 0.8

`chararray UPPER(chararray` *input*`)`

Parameter:
> *input*

Returns:
> *input* with all characters converted to uppercase

Since version:
0.8

Built-in datetime UDFs

datetime AddDuration(datetime *input*, chararray *duration*)

Parameters:
input

duration: The duration as a chararray

Returns:
Result of a datetime object plus a duration object

Since version:
0.11

datetime CurrentTime()

Returns:
Current time as a datetime object

Since version:
0.11

long DaysBetween(datetime *datetime1*, datetime *datetime2*)

Parameters:
datetime1

datetime2

Returns:
Number of days between two datetimes

Since version:
0.11

int GetDay(datetime *input*)

Parameter:
input

Returns:
The day of a month extracted from a datetime

Since version:
0.11

```
int GetHour(datetime input)
```

Parameter:
   input

Returns:
   The hour of a day extracted from a datetime

Since version:
   0.11

```
int GetMilliSecond(datetime input)
```

Parameter:
   input

Returns:
   The millisecond of a second extracted from a datetime

Since version:
   0.11

```
int GetMinute(datetime input)
```

Parameter:
   input

Returns:
   The minute of an hour extracted from a datetime

Since version:
   0.11

```
int GetMonth(datetime input)
```

Parameter:
   input

Returns:
   The month of a year extracted from a datetime

Since version:
   0.11

```
int GetSecond(datetime input)
```

Parameter:
   input

Returns:
   The second of a minute extracted from a datetime

Since version:
   0.11

int GetWeek(datetime *input*)

Parameter:
   input

Returns:
   The week of a year extracted from a datetime

Since version:
   0.11

int GetWeekYear(datetime *input*)

Parameter:
   input

Returns:
   The week year extracted from a datetime

Since version:
   0.11

int GetYear(datetime *input*)

Parameter:
   input

Returns:
   The year extracted from a datetime

Since version:
   0.11

long HoursBetween(datetime *datetime1*, datetime *datetime2*)

Parameters:
   datetime1

   datetime2

Returns:
   Number of hours between two datetimes

Since version:
    0.11

long MilliSecondsBetween(datetime *datetime1*, datetime *datetime2*)

Parameters:
    datetime1

    datetime2

Returns:
    Number of milliseconds between two datetimes

Since version:
    0.11

long MinutesBetween(datetime *datetime1*, datetime *datetime2*)

Parameters:
    datetime1

    datetime2

Returns:
    Number of minutes between two datetimes

Since version:
    0.11

long MonthsBetween(datetime *datetime1*, datetime *datetime2*)

Parameters:
    datetime1

    datetime2

Returns:
    Number of months between two datetimes

Since version:
    0.11

long SecondsBetween(datetime *datetime1*, datetime *datetime2*)

Parameters:
    datetime1

    datetime2

Returns:
> Number of seconds between two datetimes

Since version:
> 0.11

`datetime SubtractDuration(datetime `*`input`*`, chararray `*`duration`*`)`

Parameters:
> *input*

> *duration*: The duration as a chararray

Returns:
> Result of a datetime object minus a duration object

Since version:
> 0.11

`datetime ToDate(long `*`milliseconds`*`)`

Parameter:
> *milliseconds*

Returns:
> Unix timestamp converted to a datetime

Since version:
> 0.11

`datetime ToDate(chararray `*`string`*`)`

Parameter:
> *string*: ISO format datetime string

Returns:
> ISO-format datetime string converted to a datetime

Since version:
> 0.11

`datetime ToDate(chararray `*`string`*`, chararray `*`format`*`)`

Parameters:
> *string*: The ISO-format datetime string

> *format*: The format string

Returns:
> *string* converted to a datetime according to the format string

`datetime ToDate(chararray string, chararray format, chararray timezone)`

Parameters:
    string: The ISO-format datetime string

    format: The format string

    time zone: The timezone string

Returns:
    string converted to the datetime of *timezone* according to the format string

Since version:
    0.11

`long ToMilliSeconds(datetime input)`

Parameter:
    input

Returns:
    Number of milliseconds since January 1, 1970 00:00:00.000 GMT

Since version:
    0.11

`chararray ToString(datetime input)`

Parameter:
    input

Returns:
    ISO-format datetime string

Since version:
    0.11

`chararray ToString(datetime input, chararray format)`

Parameters:
    input format: The format string

Returns:
    input converted to a string according to the format string

Since version:
    0.11

```
long ToUnixTime(datetime input)
```

Parameter:
   input

Returns:
   input converted to Unix time

Since version:
   0.11

```
long WeeksBetween(datetime datetime1, datetime datetime2)
```

Parameters:
   datetime1

   datetime2

Returns:
   Number of weeks between two datetimes

Since version:
   0.11

```
long YearsBetween(datetime datetime1, datetime datetime2)
```

Parameters:
   datetime1

   datetime2

Returns:
   Number of years between two datetimes

Since version:
   0.11

Built-in complex type UDFs

```
{(chararray, chararray, double)} COR({(double)} b1, {(double)} b2)
```
   Calculate the correlation between two bags of doubles

Parameters:
   b1

   b2

Returns:
   First chararray is the name of *b1*, second chararray is the name of *b2*, double
   is the correlation between *b1* and *b2*

`{(chararray, chararray, double)} COV({(double)} b1, {(double)} b2)`

Calculate the covariance of two bags of doubles

Parameters:

b1

b2

Returns:

First chararray is the name of *b1*, second chararray is the name of *b2*, double is the covariance of *b1* and *b2*

Since version:
0.8

`bag DIFF(bag b1, bag b2)`

Parameters:

b1

b2

Returns:

All records from *b1* that are not in *b2*, and all records from *b2* that are not in *b1*

Since version:
0.1

`tuple PluckTuple(tuple input, chararray prefix)`

Parameters:

input

prefix: Prefix of the field name wanted

Returns:

A tuple that contains only items with *prefix* in their name

Since version:
0.12

`long SIZE(map input)`

Parameter:

input

Returns:
Number of key/value pairs in *input*

Since version:
0.2

`long SIZE(tuple `*`input`*`)`

Parameter:
input

Returns:
Number of fields in *input*

Since version:
0.2

`long SIZE(bag `*`input`*`)`

Parameter:
input

Returns:
Number of tuples in *input*

Since version:
0.2

`bag TOBAG(...)`

Parameter:
Variable

Returns:
If all inputs have the same schema the resulting bag will have that schema, and otherwise it will have a null schema; if the parameters are tuples, all schemas must have the same field names in addition to types

Since version:
0.8

`map TOMAP(...)`

Parameter:
Variable

Returns:
> Input parameters are paired up and placed in a map as key/value, key/value; all keys must be chararrays; an odd number of arguments will result in an error

Since version:
> 0.9

`bag TOP(int` *numRecords*`, int` *field*`, bag` *source*`)`

Parameters:
> *numRecords*: The number of records to return

> *field*: The field to sort on

> *source*: The bag to return records from

Returns:
> A bag with *numRecords* records

Since version:
> 0.8

`tuple TOTUPLE(...)`

Parameter:
> Variable

Returns:
> A tuple with all of the fields passed in as arguments

Since version:
> 0.8

Built-in filter functions

`boolean IsEmpty(bag)`

Parameter:
> *input*

Returns:
> Boolean

Since version:
> 0.1

```
boolean IsEmpty(tuple)
```

Parameter:
   input

Returns:
   Boolean

Since version:
   0.1

Miscellaneous built-in UDFs

```
double RANDOM()
```

Returns:
   A random double between 0 and 1

Since version:
   0.4

```
chararray UniqueID()
```

Returns:
   A unique ID for each record

Since version:
   0.14

PiggyBank

PiggyBank is Pig's repository of user-contributed functions. PiggyBank functions are distributed as part of the Pig distribution, but they are not built in. You may need to register the PiggyBank JAR to use them, which you can do in your distribution at *contrib/piggybank/java/piggybank.jar*.

At the time of writing, there is no central website or set of documentation for Piggy-Bank. To find out what is in there, you will need to browse through the code. You can see all of the included functions by looking in your distribution under *contrib/piggy-bank/*. PiggyBank does not yet include any Python functions, but it is set up to allow users to contribute functions in languages other than Java, so hopefully this will change in time.

Index

Symbols

!= inequality operator, 55
\# pound sign, 50
$ dollar sign, 49
() parentheses, 35, 49, 50
* multiplication operator, 50
\+ addition operator, 50
, comma, 52
\- subtraction operator, 50
\-\- single line comment operator, 2, 46
. dot operator, 51
/ division operator, 50
/* */ multiline comment operator, 46
: colon, 69
:: prepend character, 62
< inequality operator, 55
<= inequality operator, 55
== equality operator, 55
> inequality operator, 55
>= inequality operator, 55
[] square brackets, 34, 49, 72
\ backslash codes, 33
{} braces, 35, 49, 109

A

ABS function, 303
AbstractGenericUDAFResolver class (Hive), 73
Accumulator interface (Pig)
    about, 190-192
    invokers and, 73
    UDFs and, 81, 140
Accumulo database, 269
AccumuloStorage function, 269, 301, 302
ACID acronym, 266

ACOS function, 303
AddDuration function, 322
addition operator (+), 50
aggregate UDFs, 307-315
aggregation, map-side, 144
algebraic calculations, 59, 186
Algebraic interface (Pig)
    about, 186-190
    combiners and, 59
    invokers and, 73
    UDFs and, 140
aliases (relation names), 45, 71, 115
Amazon Elastic MapReduce (EMR), 11, 21
Ambrose tool, 164
and Boolean operator, 56
Apache Accumulo database, 269
Apache Cassandra database, 270
Apache Hive, 73-75, 219, 263-265
Apache Ooozie workflow scheduler, 272-273
Apache open source project, 1, 13
Apache Tez (see Tez engine)
arithmetic operators, 50, 53
ArrayList class (Java), 149
as clause
    foreach operator, 54
    load function, 47
    stream operator, 99
ASIN function, 303
assert operator, 98, 254
ATAN function, 304
auto local mode, 146
AVG functions, 307-309
AvroStorage function, 301, 302
AWS Command Line Interface, 21

AWS console, 21

B

backend
 passing data to, 176-180, 210
 reading data on, 211-216
 Tez engine and, 251, 254
 writing data, 223-227
backslash (\) codes, 33
bag data type
 about, 35
 constructing bags, 169
 counting tuples in bags, 57
 projection and, 51
 schema syntax, 37
 special characters surrounding, 35, 49
 spilling data, 184
BagFactory class (Pig), 169
BagToString function, 315
bdutil command-line tool, 23
behavior prediction models, 8
BigDecimal class (Java), 32
bigdecimal data type, 37, 40
BigInteger class (Java), 31
biginteger data type, 37, 40
bincond (binary condition) operator, 50
bind call, 154-155
Bloom filters, 147-149
Bloom UDF, 147
Boolean class (Java), 33
boolean data type, 33, 37, 40
Boolean operators, 56
BoundScript object, 154, 156
braces {}, 35, 49, 109
brackets [], 34, 49, 72
BuildBloom UDF, 147
bytearray data type
 about, 33
 casting, 218
 schema syntax, 37
 sorting, 60
 supported casts, 41
bytearray UDFs, 315-321

C

-c command-line option, 114
cache clause (define statement), 101
capacity scheduler (Hadoop), 294
Cascading framework, 265

case sensitivity (Pig Latin), 46
CASE statement, 55
Cassandra database, 270
Cassandra: The Definitive Guide (Hewitt), 270
casts
 about, 39-42
 bytearrays, 218
 load functions and, 210
 relations to scalars, 82
cat command, 27
CBRT function, 304
CEIL function, 304
chararray data type
 about, 33
 schema syntax, 37
 sorting, 60
 supported casts, 40
chararray UDFs, 315-321
-check command-line option, 114
chgrp command, 27
chmod command, 27
chown command, 27
clear command, 29
cloud computing, 21-23
Cloudera CDH, downloading Pig from, 16
Codd, E. F., 78
cogroup operator
 about, 88
 filter operator and, 136
 keys and, 88
 nested foreach operator and, 92
 parallel clause and, 65
 partition clause and, 107
 Tez engine and, 254
colon (:), 69
combiner (Hadoop), 59, 105
CombinerOptimizer rule (Tez), 252
comma (,), 52
command-line options, 23
comment operators (Pig Latin), 46
compile method, 152
complex data types, 34-35, 52
complex type UDFs, 328-331
compression, using in intermediate results, 142
CONCAT functions, 184, 315
Configurable interface (Hadoop), 107
constructors, 176-180
copyFromLocal command, 27
copyToLocal command, 27

parallelism
    map, 67
    Tez engine and, 260-262
parameter substitution, 108-109, 110
-param_file command-line option, 108
parentheses (), 35, 49, 50
ParquetLoader function, 302
ParquetStorer function, 302
Particle News (company), 297-300
partition clause, 107
Partitioner class (Hadoop), 107
partitions, LoadMetadata interface and, 217
PATH environment variable, 205
performance considerations (see optimizing
    scripts)
performance counters, 128
PERLLIB environment variable, 100
Pig
    about, 1
    command-line and configuration options,
        23-25
    controlling from Grunt shell, 28-29
    differences from MapReduce, 6-8
    downloading artifacts from Maven, 15
    downloading from Apache, 13-14
    downloading from distributions, 15-16
    downloading source code, 15
    embedded, 151-164
    history of, 10
    installation and setup, 14
    Java APIs, 158-164
    name origins, 11
    performance tuning for jobs, 141
    project philosophy, 10
    running in Hadoop cluster, 19-21
    running in local mode, 17-18
    running in the cloud, 21-23
    strength of typing, 42
    version control page, 15
Pig class
    bind call, 154-155
    compile method, 152-153
    define method, 158
    fs method, 157
    importing, 152
    registerJar method, 158
    registerUDF method, 158
    set method, 158
Pig Latin

PPNL (Pig progress notification listener), 161, 240
"Practical Skew Handling in Parallel Joins" (DeWitt et al.), 86
predicate pushdown, 220
preprocessor (Pig Latin)
    about, 108
    including scripts in other scripts, 111
    macros and, 109-111
    parameter substitution, 108-109
programming examples and use cases
    intersect and except operators, 285-289
    k-means algorithm, 280-284
    Pig at Particle News, 297-300
    Pig at Yahoo!, 289-297
    sparse tuples, 275-280
progress reporting, evaluation functions and, 174-176
Progressable interface (Hadoop), 176
projection operators, 50
projections, pushing down, 219
-propertyfile command-line option, 24
pwd command, 27
Pygmalion project, 270
Python scripting language
    Jython and, 68
    registering UDFs, 71
    scripting language comparison table, 206
    writing streaming UDFs, 205

Q

Qi, Zongjun, 297-300
query languages, 2-3
quit command (Grunt), 26
quotation marks, 33

R

RANDOM function, 185, 332
rank operator, 93-95, 255, 257
raw data, 9
RCFile format (Hive), 219
RDBMS versus Hadoop environments, 3
ReadScalars return type, 83
RecordReader class (Hadoop), 208, 211
RecordWriter class (Hadoop), 221, 223
reduce phase (MapReduce), 4, 5-6, 59
Reed, Ben, 26
REGEX_EXTRACT function, 317
REGEX_EXTRACT_ALL function, 54, 318

register statement, 69-71
registerJar method, 158
registerUDF method, 158
regular expression format, 56
regular mode (rank operator), 93
relation names (aliases), 45, 71, 115
relational operations
    about, 49
    assert operator, 98, 254
    casting relations to scalars, 82
    cogroup operator, 65, 88, 92, 107, 136, 254
    cross operator, 65, 90-93, 107, 136, 254
    cube operator, 95-98, 254
    distinct operator, 61, 65, 80, 107, 136, 254
    filter operator, 55-57, 146, 254
    foreach operator, 49-55, 77-82, 92, 137, 146, 254, 293
    group operator, 57-60, 65, 107, 137, 254
    join operator, 7, 62-64, 65, 83-88, 107, 137
    limit operator, 64, 65, 146, 254
    order by operator, 6, 60-61, 65, 255, 261, 292
    parallel clause, 65-67, 139
    partition clause and, 107
    pushing filters, 136
    rank operator, 93-95, 255, 257
    sample operator, 65, 254
    schemas and, 39
    split operator, 103
    stream operator, 10, 99-101, 146, 254
    union operator, 65, 89-90, 137, 146, 252, 254
relations
    about, 45
    applying relational operators, 80
    casting to scalars, 82
REPLACE function, 318
RequiredField class (Pig), 219
research on raw data, 9
ResourceManager, 3, 19, 125-127
ResourceSchema class (Pig), 216, 227
REST server, 265
result method, 156
return codes, 25
returns clause (define statement), 109
Reverse UDF, 68
Rhino language, 196
rm command, 27
rmf command, 27

About the Authors

Alan Gates was a member of the original engineering team that took Pig from a Yahoo! Labs research project to a successful Apache open source project. In that role, he oversaw the implementation of the language, including programming interfaces and the overall design. He has presented Pig at numerous conferences and user groups, universities, and companies. Alan is a member of the Apache Software Foundation and a cofounder of Hortonworks. He has a BS in Mathematics from Oregon State University and an MA in Theology from Fuller Theological Seminary.

Daniel Dai joined the Apache Pig development team back in 2008. He has actively participated in Pig development from version 0.1 to 0.16, and is a Pig committer and PMC member. Daniel has a BS in Computer Science from Shanghai Jiaotong University and a PhD in Computer Science from University of Central Florida, specializing in distributed computing, data mining, and computer security.

Colophon

The animal on the cover of *Programming Pig* is a domestic pig (*Sus scrofa domesticus* or *Sus domesticus*). While the larger pig family is naturally distributed in Africa, Asia, and Europe, domesticated pigs can now be found in nearly every part of the world that people inhabit. In fact, some pigs have been specifically bred to best equip them for various climates; for example, heavily coated varieties have been bred in colder climates. People have brought pigs with them almost wherever they go, for good reason: in addition to their primary use as a source of food, humans have been using the skin, bones, and hair of pigs to make various tools and implements for millennia.

Domestic pigs are directly descended from wild boars, and evidence suggests that there have been three distinct domestication events; the first took place in the Tigris River Basin as early as 13,000 BC, the second in China, and the third in Europe, though the last likely occurred after Europeans were introduced to domestic pigs from the Middle East. Despite the long history, however, taxonomists do not agree as to the proper classification for the domestic pig. Some believe that domestic pigs remain simply a subspecies of the larger pig group including the wild boar (*Sus scrofa*), while others insist that they belong to a species all their own. In either case, there are several hundred breeds of domestic pig, each with its own particular characteristics.

Perhaps because of their long history and prominent role in human society, and their tendency toward social behavior, domestic pigs have appeared in film, literature, and other cultural media with regularity. Examples include "The Three Little Pigs," Miss Piggy, and Porky the Pig. Additionally, domestic pigs have recently been recognized for their intelligence and their ability to be trained (similar to dogs), and have consequently begun to be treated as pets.

The cover image is from the Dover Pictorial Archive. The cover fonts are URW Typewriter and Guardian Sans. The text font is Adobe Minion Pro; the heading font is Adobe Myriad Condensed; and the code font is Dalton Maag's Ubuntu Mono.

Learn from experts.
Find the answers you need.

Sign up for a **10-day free trial** to get **unlimited access** to all of the content on Safari, including Learning Paths, interactive tutorials, and curated playlists that draw from thousands of ebooks and training videos on a wide range of topics, including data, design, DevOps, management, business—and much more.

Start your free trial at:
oreilly.com/safari

(No credit card required.)

CPSIA information can be obtained
at www.ICGtesting.com
Printed in the USA
BVOW04s0817121116
467615BV00004B/4/P